FEAR AND INSECURITY

JONATHAN G. LESLIE

Fear and Insecurity

Israel and the Iran Threat Narrative

OXFORD
UNIVERSITY PRESS

OXFORD
UNIVERSITY PRESS

Oxford University Press is a department of the
University of Oxford. It furthers the University's objective
of excellence in research, scholarship, and education
by publishing worldwide.

Oxford New York

Auckland   Cape Town   Dar es Salaam   Hong Kong   Karachi
Kuala Lumpur   Madrid   Melbourne   Mexico City   Nairobi
New Delhi   Shanghai   Taipei   Toronto

With offices in

Argentina   Austria   Brazil   Chile   Czech Republic   France   Greece
Guatemala   Hungary   Italy   Japan   Poland   Portugal   Singapore
South Korea   Switzerland   Thailand   Turkey   Ukraine   Vietnam

Oxford is a registered trade mark of Oxford University Press
in the UK and certain other countries.

Published in the United States of America by
Oxford University Press
198 Madison Avenue, New York, NY 10016

Library of Congress Cataloging-in-Publication Data is available

ISBN: 9780197685556

Printed in the United Kingdom
by Bell and Bain Ltd, Glasgow

For Noah

CONTENTS

LIST OF FIGURES

ACKNOWLEDGEMENTS

No project of this magnitude is ever achieved without help, and there are not enough pages in this book to express the gratitude owed to those who assisted me in this endeavor. I am indebted to many people on three continents who aided me in my efforts to conceive and develop an original idea, conduct field research, and synthesize and refine source material into the final product. I am more grateful than I can possibly express here, but I shall try.

The community at the School of Oriental and African Studies in London provided the setting and support for the start of this project during my doctoral studies. I want to thank my doctoral advisor, Dr. Arshin Adib-Moghaddam, for all his guidance over the long course of this project. His wisdom and experience not only contributed to the academic product, but also boosted me emotionally. Whenever I walked into Arshin's office burdened by worry and uncertainties, I reemerged assured and freshly confident that I was on the right path. Our discussions helped me refine my thinking and added dimensions of scholarship to my work that I could not have achieved on my own. I am especially appreciative of his encouragement and assistance in bringing this and other writings to publication.

I am also grateful to Dr. Felix Berenskoetter for his help and advice over the years of this undertaking. Before I penned my application for admission to SOAS, Felix enlightened me on the details of doctoral life and research projects. He later helped me navigate the murky waters of international relations theory, encouraging me to embrace the field, and has remained a constant source of advice and wisdom.

Several scholars contributed to the intellectual development of this project. Tugba Basaran of the University of Cambridge generously offered advice and help in refining the theoretical foundation of my thesis. Kevan Harris of the University of California at Los Angeles gave me useful guidance both before embarking on a doctoral program and in the early stages of my research. David Menashri of Tel Aviv University and Meir Javedanfar of Reichman University were both extremely generous with their time and willingness to assist me in arranging interviews during my fieldwork in Israel. Yael Berda of Hebrew University and Harvard University gave me valuable research suggestions. Nina Wacholder, of Rutgers University, introduced me to the software and techniques of corpus analysis. Trita Parsi of the Quincy Institute for Responsible Statecraft has, since before I even embarked on my doctoral program, been willing to assist me in my research and academic endeavors. From my days as a Princeton undergraduate, Former Ambassador Daniel Kurtzer, among the most knowledgeable scholars of Middle Eastern politics, has provided advice and insights. Professor Stan Katz of Princeton University has always been willing to share thoughts and suggestions whenever I dropped by his office unannounced. I am, of course, grateful to all the people who are identified in this manuscript as providing on-the-record observations and information in interviews. A few others wished to remain anonymous, but I appreciate their assistance.

I was particularly inspired by three individuals. Jan-Werner Müller of Princeton University, who spoke with me about his impressive insights on populism that enabled me to develop my theory of populist securitization. David Roxburgh of Harvard University, who, as my on-the-ground guide to Iran, instilled in me a greater appreciation for its ancient history and culture (although he was unable to get me to abandon my study of modern politics). Most importantly, I cannot sufficiently express my thanks to Mohamad Esmaili-Sardari of the Johns Hopkins School of Advanced International Studies for first piquing my interest in Iran so many years ago. Without his endless enthusiasm and friendship, I may have never embarked on this journey.

ACKNOWLEDGEMENTS

I owe a debt of gratitude to the team at Hurst Publishers: Michael Dwyer for his willingness to take a chance on a first-time author; Alice Clarke for shepherding me through the publication process with firm, yet reasonable, deadlines; and Anna Benn for her diligent copy editing. I am also grateful to the Hurst marketing department for their efforts to promote the book.

On a personal level, I could not have achieved this without my parents, Leslie Gerwin and Bruce Leslie. This book represents so much more than several years of hard work; it is the culmination of a lifetime of their support and love. Even this public acknowledgement, I believe, is insufficient to express my gratitude for everything they have done and continue to do for me (including, among other things, my countless requests for proofreading along the way). I am hopeful that they are as proud of me as a son as I am of them as parents. I love you both so very much.

A doctoral program can be an all-consuming force, but my friends, old and new, kept me tethered to reality and, more importantly, to my sanity. I especially wish to acknowledge Stephan H. Miller, who, in addition to being my lifelong friend and serving as the best man at my wedding, was an invaluable source of guidance during my fieldwork in Israel. Ollie Rosenblatt and his family could not have been more generous or hospitable during my time in London. Finally, a special thank you to Abir Ray, who, in addition to being a very understanding employer and colleague, has also been a great friend and squash partner.

The most important contributors to my life are my beautiful wife, Anne, and my son, Noah. This milestone is as much theirs as it is mine. This book has grown up alongside Noah, whose birth in 2020 coincided with the beginning of my work toward its publication. Anne's love and encouragement kept me going and drove me to achieve things I never thought I could. Even amidst all the turmoil of life with an infant and later toddler, she never stopped cheering me on and pushing me toward the finishing line. Coincidentally, this book is due to arrive with our second child, who will be born without the added stress of a looming publication deadline. Yet while this project is coming to an end, I know that our family's journey together is only beginning. I cannot wait to see what the future has in store.

INTRODUCTION

In 1961, a young Israeli diplomat arrived in Tehran on his first overseas posting. Unlike his colleagues at the diplomatic mission in Tehran, Zvi Rafiah's portfolio did not include collaboration with military officers or high government officials in the Shah's court. Instead, Rafiah aimed to engage with Iran's vibrant cultural scene. Among his responsibilities was arranging intellectual and cultural exchanges with prominent Iranians across academia, politics, art, and culture. These 'hasbara'—or public promotion—missions provided select Iranians with all-expenses-paid trips to Israel to showcase the glory and innovation of the still relatively new Israeli state. Participants would be expected to return home to sing Israel's praises in elite circles, planting important psychological seeds that would bolster Israel's image and improve its foreign standing.

Two years later, in February 1963, a famous Iranian writer and scholar named Jalal Al-e Ahmad embarked on one of those trips. His presence on such an obviously promotional endeavor was odd considering that he was among the most vocal intellectual opponents of Shah Mohammad Reza Pahlavi's regime. At the time of the trip, Iran and Israel were partners in the Periphery Alliance, which included intelligence sharing, military cooperation, and other strategic exchanges between member states within the 'Periphery,' or non-Arab, nations of the Middle East. The previous year, Al-e Ahmad had published *Gharbzadegi* (Westoxification), a harsh critique of the Shah's regime that decried the monarch's—and by extension,

Iran's—efforts to initiate Western-style reforms. This had earned him favor with some of Iran's most prominent anti-Shah critics, including two clerics named Ruhollah Khomeini and Ali Khamenei, both of whom were also vocal opponents of the Shah and the Jewish State.[1]

While not devoutly religious himself, Al-e Ahmad appreciated the role religion played in Iranian national identity, and he frequently used the language and philosophy of Shiite Islam in his writing to describe Iranian culture.[2] Thus, while on his trip to the 'Holy Land,' Al-e Ahmad analyzed his surroundings through a uniquely religious lens, publishing his thoughts in a brief travelogue following his return. He began his account in *Journey to the Land of Israel*[3] by describing Israel as a '*velayat*,' a term typically associated with Shiite jurisprudence involving the concept of guardianship. In the political context, the term refers to the idea that the authority of government comes from more than the people within its borders. To be considered a legitimate *velayat*, the leadership must have its legitimacy bestowed by a higher power.[4] In hindsight, Al-e Ahmad's association of this concept with Israel is ironic, since Ayatollah Ruhollah Khomeini would later incorporate it into his political vision for the Iranian state. Khomeini espoused a form of government based on the idea of *Velayat e-Faqih*, or 'Guardianship of the Jurist,' describing it in a book of the same name published in 1970.[5] Just shy of a decade later, Khomeini would establish the new political system of the Islamic Republic of Iran on the same principle, setting himself atop the republic's hierarchy as its first 'Supreme Leader.'[6]

For Al-e Ahmad, Israel was not just a country of two million inhabitants in a small strip of desert land, but also a symbol of global Jewry's newfound strength and a representative of its people. Much like Israel's founders, he called the establishment of the state 'a true miracle,' and he saw in it the perfect hybrid of religio-civic institutionalism that he desired for his homeland. He described the country's leaders as modern-day prophets, writing that 'Ben-Gurian [sic] is no less than Enoch, and Moshe Dayan no less than Joab.' Invoking *velayat*, he continued, 'These guardians, each one with his own prophecies or—at least—clear-vision, built a guardianship state in the land of Palestine and called to it all the Children of Israel.'[7] Thus, Al-e Ahmad concluded, 'Like it or not, [the State of

Israel] now governs and acts in the name of all twelve million Jews scattered around the world.'[8] This respected Iranian intellectual, whose writings would play a significant role in inspiring the Islamic Revolution sixteen years after his visit to Israel, conveyed to his readers an appreciation of Israel's purpose not just as a nation-state but also as a homeland for the Jewish people.

At the same time, Al-e Ahmad identified two important criticisms of its leaders' policies. The first concerned the frequent invocation of the Holocaust as justification for its treatment of Muslims. The second questioned the promotion of fear among its Jewish citizens for political ends. Al-e Ahmad critiqued the use of the Holocaust both as a justification for the founding of the state and for its being embraced as a rhetorical tool to generate political fear. Identifying himself as a representative of the global East, he condemned the role that the West had played in forcing the creation of the state of Israel upon the Palestinian people, who had nothing to do with the crimes that had necessitated the creation of a Jewish homeland. If the Holocaust was a sin of the West, he asked, why then was the Muslim world being forced to surrender its territory to pay for the crime? Al-e Ahmad's phrasing suggested he understood the relative unpopularity of this view, at least in powerful Western circles. It also indicated that he knew that, while many of Israel's regional opponents in the Muslim world were upset by the contradiction of Palestinian disinheritance as recompense for Western atrocities, Western leaders would be unwilling even to acknowledge the logical fallacy. The need for Israel to exist as a safe haven for the Jewish people apparently dwarfed all other concerns about its moral legitimacy.

Al-e Ahmad also found it problematic that Israelis still possessed such a high degree of insecurity about their place in the region. This feeling was evident in their frequent displays of insecurity and belligerence. Since its founding, Israel had participated in numerous conflicts. Israel's founders had made a point of establishing the country in the image of a new, muscular Judaism that would fight to defend its territory and secure its survival.[9] In this regard, they had been highly successful. Israel dominated in its military engagements with the Arabs, yet still there remained an overlying buzz of historical victimhood within Israeli society.

Al-e Ahmad wrote about a visit to a kibbutz, a type of socialist farming collective, in northern Israel near the Syrian and Lebanese borders.[10] During the visit, an Israeli military commander lectured the visiting group on various types of weaponry, took them on a tour of the kibbutz's extensive underground bunker network, and walked them through their preparation for inevitable upcoming wars with the Arabs. In a conversation with a local teacher following the presentation, Al-e Ahmad questioned the wisdom of the seemingly pervasive use of fear in Israel as a motivational tool. In response, the teacher explained that displays of power and war preparations were necessary for a small country like Israel and would remain so 'as long as we are under siege by the Arabs.' While Al-e Ahmad reported encountering this common refrain throughout the country, he remained skeptical. He noted that he warned the teacher, 'You yourselves are constantly playing with fire. When you frighten their side, you yourselves have to become frightened as well. And in place of eliminating your class differences, you spend your resources building shelters.'[11]

Al-e Ahmad's account of his trip captured the tension between his admiration of the Israeli state as a concept and his distaste for elements of its behavior. Although he was clearly troubled by some of the things he saw during his brief visit, overall he concluded that the good that Israel offered the world far outweighed the bad, or even the potential for bad that could come from some of its more troubling aspects. Ironically, this was one of the few points on which Al-e Ahmad found himself in agreement with the Shah. From Al-e Ahmad's perspective, Israel provided a model for emulation by a future, better iteration of the Iranian state.

One suspects that, as he recorded his observations, Al-e Ahmad considered what lessons Israel's experience held for a future Islamic state. Could Iran so seamlessly blend religious principles with socialist policies? Could Iran build a society that was tolerant of secularism and embraced allies in a way that transcended the fraught and complicated history of the Middle East? Could they, too, make the desert bloom? That an intellectual of his stature and ideological bent could think so highly of the Israeli experiment certainly raises questions about the nature of their relationship, even—or perhaps especially—in light of what was to come. His work thus provides us with a fleeting glimpse of a narrative that might have been, one that challenges the idea that Iran and Israel were destined to become mortal enemies, locked in a zero-sum struggle for survival. That this Iranian intellectual was able to come to Israel, observe its politics and culture, and come away so impressed with what he saw testifies not only to how remarkable the Iran-Israel alliance was, but also the potential for a constructive relationship between a Muslim nation and the Jewish State. In short, Al-e Ahmad's travelogue questions whether the present was inevitable.

Al-e Ahmad died in 1969, a decade before the Islamic Revolution that his writings would help inspire. Thus, we can only speculate what Al-e Ahmad would have thought had he had the opportunity to return to Israel in the twenty-first century. He likely would have been disillusioned and perhaps surprised at what he found. The *velayat* he had once so admired, with its unique blend of religiously inspired principles and socialist politics, had transformed during the intervening half-century into a fractured and hyper-capitalist society with an intensively right-wing political culture heavily influenced by powerful religious and nationalist factions. The founders he had once praised as being modern prophets had been replaced by a demagogue who was on his way to becoming the longest-serving prime minister in the nation's history.

But, above all, it was Israel's view of Iran which would have most saddened Al-e Ahmad. Israeli leaders were not only still engaging in the promotion of fear as a political tactic, but they had redirected their attention from their Arab neighbors to Iran, identifying and promoting it as Israel's most pressing and terrifying security threat. To say that Iran dominated Israel's foreign policy and security agenda would have been a severe understatement. No political leader's speech was complete without a reference to the Iranian menace and its connections to Israel's myriad other security concerns, while nearly every utterance by Iranian officials regarding Israel turned into breaking news. Rumors of low-level military operations to preemptively destroy Iran's nuclear facilities bubbled beneath the surface, with the occasional clandestine operation occasionally exploding into the fore, threatening to spark a wider conflagration.

From a purely rhetorical standpoint, the Israelis' description of Al-e Ahmad's homeland would have felt distinctly foreign to him. Instead of a complicated and complex society beset by competing political factions, each of them pursuing a wide range of interests, 'Iran,' as it existed in Israel, was a monolithic totalitarian state, a nation of bloodthirsty zealots, dominated by a regime so extreme that its threat to Israel and its people was comparable only to that of the Third Reich.

Had Al-e Ahmad the opportunity to see the course of events leading up to the present, he might have thought critically about the nature of change, and about how the relationship between these two countries had declined in the intervening decades. As a writer, he may have thought about the diverse and divergent narratives that Israeli leaders had offered to define their relationship with Iran over the course of their nation's relatively short national history. These ranged from a mutually supportive, yet somewhat secretive, friendship; to an unspoken and uneasy cooperation amidst postrevolutionary hostility; to, at last, outright enmity. The recent twist in the plot saw Israel's longest serving leader effectively attempting to rewrite the nation's history to include a chapter in which Iran and its ancient ancestors have long been a threat to the existence of the Jewish people. Al-e Ahmad would have been saddened, no doubt, to arrive at this moment only to learn that Israelis now consider Iran to be a mortal enemy, an existential threat to which the only viable solution is the destruction of its government by force and its replacement with something more obsequious to Western interests. Given this, he would surely have asked himself: What happened?

* * *

This book offers an answer to this question by analyzing the narrative that Israeli leaders have constructed about the Islamic Republic over the course of the first two decades of the twenty-first century. Echoing Al-e Ahmad's observations, I deconstruct the narrative, the policies it promoted, and the actions it supported to show that the hostile relationship that developed did not stem inevitably from results in Iran, the Middle East region, or even the United States.

In fact, during its construction and dissemination, narrative content diverged in material respects from both history and the reality on the ground, with most of the driving force behind that change coming from a single geographical place: Israel.

To introduce the discussion that follows, I offer two paradigmatic narrative versions that illustrate the divergence between a factual reporting and an interpretative recounting of the foundational events for the narrative examined in this study. I call these versions the historical narrative and the threat narrative. Although the latter bases its content on the former, it delivers different messages that evoke different reactions.

The historical narrative is essentially observational and analytical. It could be considered academic, as it offers to educate the listener, either by advancing knowledge or by informing public discourse about issues on the public's agenda. By contrast, the threat narrative is tendentious. It seeks to crystalize in the listener a sense of insecurity and fear of harm in order to build support for the narrator's agenda. In the threat narrative outlined here, truth is less important than believability; reason less important than emotion; and reality less important than perception. The historical narrative informs and instructs the exercise of power, but the threat narrative provides the basis for securing and exercising that power.

The historical account of the relationship exists in many iterations that share a narrative arc spanning millennia of assorted interactions between Persians and Jews. The long history of interaction between these two ancient peoples preceding the establishment of the modern State of Israel in 1948 included varying periods of coexistence, antagonism, and isolation. Post-1948, the modern historical narrative is fraught with ambiguity occasioned by the complexities of the region, Cold War politics, and uncertainty concerning the meaning and impact of major geopolitical and regional events. The establishment of a Jewish homeland built through mass immigration of European Jewry into a strip of land surrounded by Muslim-majority Arab nations presented a major disruption in the international order. Iran, as a non-Arab outlier state in the region, offered Israel the opportunity for covert collaboration, if not overt cooperation, for their mutual security interests. At the same time, there were instances of public antagonism and rhetorical warfare between the two nations.

The 1979 Islamic Revolution opened a new chapter in the historical narrative. For Iran, the break with over two millennia of monarchial rule also meant denouncing the Zionist State that had forged a relationship with the deposed and despised Shah. Iran's new leader, Ayatollah Ruhollah Khomeini, embraced anti-Zionism with rhetorical attacks and symbolic gestures, such as handing the keys to Israel's embassy in Tehran over to Palestinian leader Yasser Arafat. At the same time, the establishment of a Shia theocracy also antagonized and worried Arab states ruled by Sunni Muslims. One of those countries, Iraq, seized on the postrevolutionary chaos confronting the government of the new Islamic Republic and attacked its neighbor, engaging Iran in a long, bitter, and costly war.

Historical analysis reveals that Iranian antipathy to the 'Zionist regime,' as they called it, paled in comparison to the bloody internecine conflict waged between the neighboring rivals. Hence, despite the public posturing, Iran and Israel continued to find occasion for cooperation, each in its own self-interest. In a secret deal brokered by the United States, Israel supplied arms to Iran for its war effort against Iraq and Iran sold oil to Israel, revealing that neither history nor the Islamic Revolution dictated the end of their clandestine dealings.

History, as opposed to speculation, provides no reason why Iran's subsequent decision to restart its nuclear development program, which had been initiated by the Shah with assistance from the United States, needed to fundamentally change the already-hostile public posturing between the two nations. Reportedly, Iran's Supreme Leader reluctantly agreed to the restart, influenced in large measure by the suffering inflicted on Iranian civilians by Iraq's use of chemical weapons against Iranian targets. Iran also had a population of 80 million people with growing energy demands, which at the very least provided a façade of legitimacy to the claim that nuclear energy would be of some nonmilitary use to the country. To be sure, the building of nuclear capability let the genie out of the bottle, allowing Iran to begin acquiring the knowledge and capacity that could, one day, lead it to develop a nuclear weapon. But it also repeatedly insisted that its program had no military component and indicated that it intended to honor its signing of the Nuclear Non-Proliferation Treaty (NPT), which forbade signatories without nuclear weapons from developing them and committed them to implementing safeguards to promote peaceful use and prevent proliferation of nuclear weaponry. By contrast, Israel, widely known to possess nuclear weapons despite its lack of public disclosure, refused to sign the NPT and remains one of five countries in the world not to do so.[12]

The historical narrative notes that Iran's resumption of its nuclear program was premised on a revision in its approach to the nation's security and regional strategy. It was reasonable, therefore, to assume that in pursuing nuclear knowledge, Iran might significantly change its behavior toward Israel, the Middle East's only nuclear-armed state. History offers analogies for evaluating the potential impact of enemy nations when each possesses a nuclear weapon.[13] It suggests that the potential for mutually assured destruction is more likely to lead to a standoff than a nuclear war. By contrast, we can only speculate on the importance Israel's leaders attached to maintaining its monopoly over nuclear weapons possession in the Middle East.

More significant than speculating on Iran's future intentions, the historical narrative details the complexity of Iran's politics during those fraught years. Iran, having just come out of a brutal eight-year war with Iraq that had claimed hundreds of thousands of lives, was physically and emotionally spent. With enemies still in power in Baghdad and on the Arabian Peninsula, not to mention ongoing tensions with the West, the Islamic Republic still saw itself as immensely vulnerable to another attack. These concerns would situate Israel at the margins of Iran's security considerations. Internally, the unity of opposition first to the Shah, and later to a foreign invader, gave way to a period of differing expectations and demands upon government leaders. Religious hardliners still maintained control over most of the levers of Iranian power, but revolutionary fervor was beginning to wane in favor of more pragmatic considerations of survival.

Against this backdrop, the historical narrative contextualizes Iran's actions against Israel. It highlights the sponsorship by Iran's hardline military elements, such as the Iran Revolutionary Guard

Corps (IRGC), of non-state militants that targeted Israel. Despite the IRGC's limited capability for assistance, it still had the potential to inflict devastating injury to Israeli civilians that evoked strong emotions and caused lingering insecurity. Having endured terrorist attacks since their nation's founding, however, most Israelis were unlikely to consider Iran's contribution to these groups as a unique threat. Thus, the historical narrative alone cannot explain Israel's singular focus on Iran as its principal enemy toward which its leaders should direct the brunt of both their political focus and the state's foreign policy agenda.

A threat narrative can be constructed by according meaning to the uncertainties inherent in the historical account. In analyzing the danger that Iran poses to Israel's security, Israeli leaders cannot be faulted for wanting answers to the many questions regarding issues of concern. Can the Islamic regime be trusted? Should their disavowal of a nuclear weapons program be believed? Why are the ruling clerics unwilling or unable to prevent the IRGC's support for terror attacks against Israel? Do these attacks portend a larger and more ambitious, perhaps even reckless, objective?

These questions spawned more questions still. Even if most Israelis saw nothing new in Iran's adding its voice to the ongoing verbal attacks on Zionism, did not the nuclear program add a new dimension to the threat calculus? Even if Iran did not intend to target Israel, should Israel tolerate a challenge to its nuclear monopoly? In articulating the threat, is there any reason Israeli leaders should disabuse their Jewish constituents, both domestic and foreign, of their anti-Islamic bias and stereotypical images of Muslims? Was there value in calling out Iran's government leaders as extremists, immoral, and corrupt, with which the world should not peacefully coexist?

The wealth of uncertainty and the lack of satisfactory answers to these questions made it easy for Israeli leaders—many of whom were quick to express preexisting biases against Iran—to conjure up a believable worst-case scenario. Having addressed their questions to the interstices in the historical narrative, Israeli leaders could provide answers that filled the gaps with opinions, predictions, and exaggerations disguised as factual clarifications. To position Iran's intention to acquire a nuclear weapon as its leaders' principal objective, the narrative would also need to omit facts that might undermine the resonance of the threat with listeners. By claiming to have access to secret information, manipulating uncertainty, and offering expert insight, Israeli leaders constructed a counterfactual threat narrative that represented Iran's nuclear program as the proverbial 'tipping point,' from which, according to one Israeli author, there could be 'no return.'[14]

Inherent in such a narrative is the imperative for an Israeli response. Thus, the narrative's purpose is more than simply to convey important information to the public. Rather, in promoting Iran as an 'existential' threat, one that could threaten the life of every single person living in the Israeli state, Israeli leaders intended for the public to internalize their message so that the resulting insecurity would compel them to support the claimed necessary response, even if such action would dramatically change the status quo. However, the Israeli experience has revealed that even if a threat narrative effectively articulates a believable existential danger, it requires something more to achieve its objective. To exert its full power, it needs a unique narrator.

* * *

This monograph examines the process of constructing the Iran threat narrative, contextualizing its content using both history and contemporaneous events. It analyzes the narrative's power and the power of the narrator, exploring the role of Benjamin Netanyahu, Israel's longest-serving prime minister, in deploying it to affect the course of history.

The study focuses on the words of the politicians and public officials involved in construction of the narrative, and it uses contemporaneously generated materials as sources of meaning and enhanced public understanding of the narrative.[15] From multiple sources, both original and derivative, I piece together the multiple iterations and situate them within the context of unfolding events. These include texts of speeches, newspaper accounts, and minutes of legislative and cabinet debates. Interviews with willing journalists, academics, and authors who contributed to or analyzed the political discourse also inform this effort.[16] I examine popular portrayals of

Iranians in Israel's narrative accounts of political developments and culture, and I review contemporary Iranian sources to see how their words and actions corresponded to the image presented by their Israeli rivals.

Focusing primarily on the Israeli perspective of Iran was initially a decision necessitated by limited access to materials in Iran.[17] My research soon revealed, however, that the two nations' threat perceptions of the other were asymmetrical. Israeli leaders viewed Iran as a far greater danger to their state's security than Iranian leaders perceived Israel to be.[18] Moreover, in the end, it was the Israeli narrative and the actions of narrator Benjamin Netanyahu that defined the enmity between the two nations and affected international decisions.

I present my study in six chapters. Chapter 1 explores the power of narrative. It contextualizes the threat as a species of the political narrative, which constructs a policy agenda based upon citizens' fears and insecurity. It discusses how the recently developed theory of securitization modifies conventional international relations theory, and how a further modification, which I call 'populist securitization,' provides a framework for understanding Netanyahu's success in constructing and disseminating a persistent threat narrative with the power to change the course of history, challenging both democratic governance and global stability in the process.

Chapter 2 presents the history of the relationship of Persians and Jews and, later, Iranians and Israelis. This chapter provides the basis for analyzing the divergence between the Israeli threat narrative and the actual events as they transpired. It also enables examination of how Israeli leaders misused history as a messaging technique. That the disconnect between the facts and the account offered to support Israeli policy and message did not elicit significant objections from listeners who should have known better is a testament to the power of the threat narrative in political discourse.

Chapters 3 and 4 examine the events and conditions that facilitated the construction of a political narrative in which Iran assumed an outsized role in Israel's security concerns, eventually morphing from a peripheral issue into an existential threat. Chapter 3 explores how events rendered Israelis susceptible to the messages that would lead to the internalization of their insecurity. Chapter 4 focuses on two specific incidents that enabled Benjamin Netanyahu to perfect his version of the threat and deploy it in support of his agenda, namely the 2005 election of Mahmoud Ahmadinejad as president of Iran and the 2006 Lebanon War. Netanyahu's sharp opposition to a diplomatic initiative to engage Iran, which would have altered the threat calculus by improving Israel's relationship with the source of the existential threat, offers another example of narrative power.

Chapter 5 analyzes Netanyahu's strategic use of populism to promote the threat narrative and, by extension, his leadership. As the original conclusion of the story, the chapter looks at how Netanyahu's narrative succeeded domestically but met rejection internationally, primarily due to the fact that other more powerful actors were unwilling to accept Netanyahu's preferred construction of the conflict. The election of Donald Trump as president of the United States drastically changed that calculus, thus necessitating a sixth chapter. As a fellow populist who embraced Netanyahu as both a strategic and a political ally, Trump revived Netanyahu's political fortunes at a crucial moment in time.

As this study ends, both Trump and Netanyahu were forced from office in 2021. Yet, at the time of this writing, both men remain relevant and disruptive forces in the politics of their respective nations. This book thus offers only the potential for stasis in the current phase of the conflict between Israel and Iran. It illuminates the past but cannot predict the future. While successor governments in the United States and Israel profess a desire to overcome the instability occasioned by the actions of their predecessors, one obstacle to their efforts remains the enduring power of the Iran threat narrative.

1

THE POWER OF NARRATIVE

The modern conflict between the State of Israel and the Islamic Republic of Iran is rooted in the political narratives that each nation's leaders have crafted about the other. As Israel and Iran are two sovereign states with few overlapping vital strategic interests, each narrative focuses less on policy justifications for action against one another than on shaping perceptions. These narratives were designed principally to serve the interests of the narrator and his nation, both at home and on the global stage.

The Islamic Republic and the Jewish State are located thousands of miles apart and seemingly exist on opposite ends of the political spectrum. Yet, they are more alike than they seem. Each nation faces domestic governing challenges stemming from the tension inherent in its societal divides between religious, national, and secular components. In both Iran and Israel, powerful conservative factions seek to institutionalize national religious identity, using it to staunch the flow of modernization. Both states also exist in their own hostile neighborhood. Israel's population, which has lived under a state of emergency since the founding of the modern state in 1948, has endured a series of armed conflicts and countless terrorist attacks. Iran's postrevolutionary government, ruling over a non-Arab population comprised almost entirely of Shia Muslims, fought a brutal eight-year war with neighboring Iraq immediately after its founding. Today the state provokes wariness and suspicion from regional powers that are predominantly Arab and Sunni Muslim. Historically speaking, the tension between the Shia and Sunni sects has been more contentious than that between Persians and Jews. There were, of course, many reasons and causes for Israeli and Iranian leaders to publicly disparage one another, but the myriad of other concerns facing the leaders of these two outlier nations should have cautioned against the prioritization of direct hostilities.

This monograph examines how and why political narratives defined the dynamics of the relationship between Israel and Iran. It focuses primarily on the construction by Israeli leaders of a threat narrative in which fear of the Islamic Republic and its rulers provided the foundation of Israel's foreign policy and justified actions that impacted both regional and global politics. This Israeli narrative, built on claims disconnected from facts both historical and present and designed to appeal to emotion over reason, succeeded in convincing Israelis that Iran is an existential threat to be feared. It also ran in direct contrast to the advice of senior military and intelligence officials, who advised against the policies being pursued by Israel's national leaders, including what former Prime Minister and Chief of the IDF General Staff Ehud Barak called the 'delusional' decision to push the United States to abandon the 2015 Joint Comprehensive Plan of Action. In the end, however, the decision to embrace Iran as an all-encompassing existential enemy was a political one. It was also a decision that many former Netanyahu advisors and military officials, with the benefit of hindsight, would later characterize as a failure.[1]

Contrary to how Israel portrayed the two nations' relationship, Israel's position among the policy priorities of Iranian leaders and public perceptions of an Israeli threat to Iranian sovereignty were more nuanced. This asymmetry between how each of the nations perceived the other was especially ironic given the significant power disparity between them. Not only was Israel a more technologically advanced belligerent, capable of inflicting significant damage and projecting its power abroad via firepower and alliances with global superpowers, but it was also the only nation in the region in possession of the weapon it so vehemently opposed, a nuclear bomb.

To understand how the early twenty-first-century conflict between Iran and Israel was not the inevitable consequence of either history or events on the ground, it is first necessary to examine the power of the Iran threat narrative that was strategically generated and disseminated by an ambitious political leader untroubled by truth or democratic values. In this chapter, I begin by contextualizing the threat narrative as a species of political discourse, which constructs a policy agenda based upon citizens' fears and insecurity. I review how Israeli leader Benjamin Netanyahu constructed a counterfactual narrative about Iran as an existential danger to Israel, which he used as a strategy to attain and maintain power and to justify Israel's foreign policy actions. In advance of later chapters that will deconstruct the narrative, in this chapter I explore how the theory of securitization modifies conventional international relations theory to account for the power of narrative. I conclude by offering a framework, which I call 'populist securitization,' for understanding how Netanyahu constructed and disseminated the Iran threat narrative so as to maximize his power and achieve personal and policy objectives. I suggest that the impact on subsequent global events of Netanyahu's use of populist strategy for securitizing Iran as an existential threat to Israel provides a cautionary tale of a modern challenge to democratic governance and global stability.

I. Constructing a Threat Narrative

According to comparative literature scholar Peter Brooks, a narrative 'is one of the large categories or systems we use in our negotiations with reality.'[2] While Brooks is referring to the literary narrative, the political narrative is a subcategory of that genre, in which a leader attempts to craft a version of reality for their followers. Politicians craft stories, which are both descriptive and normative, in order to shore up public support. The strategy employed to choose messages that resonate with listeners is, in effect, a negotiation.[3] The narrator seeks to be believed, or at least be believable, in the description of events. At the same time, the narrative is part of a larger political strategy in which the politician seeks to build a base of active supporters willing to take some action on behalf of a particular cause. In a democracy, this can range from the simple act of casting a vote or contributing money, to more aggressive actions of repeating the politician's message or raising funds, to a willingness to accept sacrifice or behavioral change in their daily life.

Politicians frequently prevaricate, exaggerate, and mythologize in the narratives they use to secure and maintain power. Hannah Arendt famously observed that 'No one has ever doubted that truth and politics are on rather bad terms with each other, and no one, as far as I know, has ever counted truthfulness among the political virtues.'[4] For a narrator seeking to build a political base to make common cause with his supporters, a goal is to make truth irrelevant or at least unproblematic.[5] As a preliminary matter, the narrator confects an identity that supports and justifies his claim of leadership. Often, he mythologizes the origin story that affirms the identity of the collective, into which he can situate himself as its savior and protector.

Origin stories that serve the interest of a political narrator are designed to promote the familiar and positive feelings about one's group or nation, engendering patriotic solidarity. The listener who invests in group membership can be exhorted to disregard the truth of the myth.[6] Not all origin stories are benign, especially when they are used to effect societal divisiveness by excluding and vilifying those who do not share the group's characteristics or ideology. A politician seeking to mobilize a group to support his quest for power may manipulate their perception of his personal characteristics to create a compatible identity. Experience, ambitions, biases, ideology, motivations, hopes, and desires are all malleable concepts in his negotiation for public acceptance. He may then repeat this creative process in formulating and advocating his policy agenda. It is when the narrator invents the facts that serve as the foundation and justification for his policy actions, in direct contradiction with reality, that the untruths can result in dangerous consequences.

A successful political narrative creates a 'communication bond' between power and public.[7] The bond can enable the shared enterprise of democratic governance or secure adherence to the selfish objectives of the powerful. In general, it is far easier to sustain a mobilized constituency against a problem or enemy than it is to implement a policy solution. Potentially the most powerful political narrative is one that rallies listeners to save their group or nation from an exogenous threat to the nation's security. This species of political narrative can be a particularly unifying and compelling force. It promotes active citizen engagement and coalesces the public against a shared enemy. It also provides the narrator with an opportunity to set the agenda and position himself to lead the response.

For listeners to perceive a threat as real, immediate, and dangerous, the narrative must identify the characteristics of the threat and weave them into a comprehensive vision that, at the very least, resembles the felt reality of the narrator's constituents. The power of the security narrative rests in listeners realizing their insecurity and wanting to take action to address their feelings. While each threat narrative involves a calculus that evaluates the obviousness, imminence, and nature of the potential harm, the skill of the narrator contributes to its capacity for inducing fear. The elements of the calculus are qualitative but not quantifiable, which makes them malleable for political purposes. If they are unverifiable, the narrator's power to define the threat increases. Narratives achieve salience as the basis for active public support if listeners believe the proffered facts or trust the narrator. The less listeners know about the subject matter, the greater the need for this trust. The strength of the communication bond helps secure public acceptance of both narrative and narrator.

When a threat is not obvious—that is, it cannot readily be seen by citizens in their daily lives—the narrator becomes the interpreter of reality.[8] This increases the opportunity not just to manipulate but to manufacture facts. An enemy in possession of a nuclear weapon presents a danger, but a narrator must explain that, beyond merely possessing the weapon, the enemy has both the capability and the intention to use it. The narrator might then explain how, if left unchecked, the enemy will probably do so in the foreseeable future.[9] This line of thinking is easily reversed, making the intent itself a threat, even for enemies not currently in possession of a weapon. Even if the likelihood of a confluence of destructive intent and capability is extremely remote, the mere possibility coupled with the destructive potential makes the threat too difficult to ignore. Such a narrative can build public support for preemptive action.[10]

A narrative can also deny the existence of an obvious threat. This can have tragic consequences for those convinced that a prophylactic vaccine is more dangerous than catching the deadly disease it prevents.[11] Threat narratives may also be employed to disguise extraordinary actions that might generate significant public opposition. For example, a narrator might justify a humanitarian intervention consistent with American values as also being in America's strategic interest.

One danger inherent in inventing a threat to a nation's security is that it may be difficult to control the consequences if the deception is discovered. This can then have undesirable political consequences for the narrator. By contrast, an autocrat can use a manufactured threat to promote his leadership. By controlling the public's access to information and suppressing public opposition, he can nullify the political risk inherent to a counterfactual threat narrative. By generating fear of an enemy attack, a dictator can mandate a correct display of public behavior and quash expressions of resentment. This also serves an authoritarian regime that deems it useful to maintain popular appeal, perhaps to strengthen its grip on power or to bolster the nation's participation in international dealings. If elections are widely seen as illegitimate, or if the state or elements of state leadership are thought to be corrupt, mobilizing the public against an external threat changes the narrative focus. This orchestration of unity involves a negotiation to produce a cult of personality: the leader offers the benefit of security in exchange for the people's demonstration of gratitude. The threat need not be real; in fact, it is frequently more politically beneficial if it is not. If events show the leader cannot deliver on his promise of security, he could face public unrest.

In contrast to autocracy, democracy is supposed to protect space for contestation of factual interpretations and voicing of differing opinions. A narrative consisting of obvious untruths should thus be exposable as false, while factual interpretations and opinions should be publicly debated on their merits. Citizens can then decide if they will actively support, acquiesce to, or oppose a narrator or the policy he advocates. The democratic process supports the distinction between leader and policy. A citizen can withhold her vote but support a politician's policy proposal, or she can vote for a candidate and protest a governmental action. Danger lurks when a leader conflates personal support with policy actions, and suppresses debate on the merits of government proposals and decisions. If his supporters are willing to suspend their concern for the accuracy of his factual claims, the leader effectively creates a cult of personality. Maintaining the collective political base of support becomes conditioned upon garnering support and suppressing doubts. In the hands of a demagogue, a counterfactual threat narrative edges the nation dangerously close to authoritarianism.

Yale historian Timothy Snyder has long warned of the dangers to democracy of condoning leaders who exercise authoritarian strategies in search of power. In his book *On Tyranny: Twenty Lessons From the Twentieth Century*, Snyder analyzes modern developments that historical precedents suggest imperil democracy.[12] Although drawing his lessons from the disastrous US presidency of Donald Trump, Snyder's observations apply to any leader who exploits the right to free speech and circumvents legal norms in pursuit of their own agenda. Among Snyder's lessons is the admonition to 'believe in truth,' and he cogently warns: 'To abandon facts is to abandon freedom. If nothing is true, then no one can criticize power, because there is no basis upon which to do so. If nothing is true, then all is spectacle. The biggest wallet pays for the most blinding lights.'[13]

Hannah Arendt maintained that even an authoritarian leader could not long sustain a consequential lie, since he is incapable of maintaining the distorted reality.[14] She cannot be faulted for failing to foresee the development of the modern information ecosystem dominated by the internet, social media, cable news networks, and those willing to embrace alternative facts in order to secure or maintain political power.[15] We need not assess the relative contributions of electronic communications and human agency in our analysis of the power of a counterfactual threat narrative. For our purposes, such narratives thrive when leaders discount veracity, followers suspend skepticism, and the truth is difficult to determine.[16] This is the environment that Israeli leader Benjamin Netanyahu exploited in constructing the Iran threat narrative that would define Israeli foreign policy and, along with it, influence Middle East and global politics.

* * *

As Israel's longest-serving prime minister and leader of the opposition when not in power, Benjamin Netanyahu played the most prominent role in the construction of a threat narrative in which Iran was acquiring the capacity to annihilate the Jewish State and wreak havoc upon the Western world. Untroubled by factual accuracy, Netanyahu's portrayal of Iran distorted history. He leveraged Israelis' uncertainty to create a vision of reality in which Jews would again become victims of a murderous regime unless Israel led a drastic preventative response. He appealed to emotion to distract from the skepticism likely to arise from a more reasoned or sober analysis of the situation.

Netanyahu's content selection entailed two negotiations. In one he crafted his identity; in the other he sought power. Negotiating his identity with powerful religious and nationalist constituencies facilitated his quest to attain and maintain power. While Netanyahu did not pretend to adopt religious orthodoxy, he aligned himself with the goals of those supporting increased Judaization as opposed to secularization of state institutions and embraced the vision of a greater Israel that encompassed the biblical kingdoms of Judea and Samaria. At the same time, he pursued policies that aimed to consolidate Jewish and Israeli identities, adding increased restrictions on the definition of what it meant to be a 'true' Israeli. He negotiated further by promising security to all Israelis if they elected and reelected him Prime Minister. His foray into identity politics mimicked the autocrat's playbook for homogenizing a population while creating a cult of personality. He conflated support for his leadership with the idea of Jewish solidarity against existential threats.

That Netanyahu could construct and disseminate a counterfactual narrative in a democracy is a testament to his political skill. As prime minister, Netanyahu was effectively Israel's national narrator for over a decade. He used his ambition, political acumen, and oratorical skills to highlight and capitalize on Israelis' insecurities. He sought out power with messages that amplified his listeners' susceptibility to fear, and as leader he made their exposure to threats large and small a central tenet of his political agenda. The threat narrative served both his policy and his power objectives. How Israel arrived at this situation and how Netanyahu achieved success in this regard are the subjects of subsequent chapters, but before examining this in detail, it is first necessary to examine the theoretical and strategic underpinnings of narrative power.

II. Internalizing Insecurity: Securitization of the Iran Threat

The capacity for a narrative to define an inter-nation conflict and produce world-changing consequences challenges conventional international relations theory. Traditional neorealism maintains that the actions of nations are based upon calculations of power, which involve an uncomplicated assessment of relative strength. Presumably, a narrative may be useful in contextualizing observable realities and providing fact-based, reasoned analyses upon which national leaders can evaluate their policy options.[17]

As Israeli leaders manipulated the situational variables and equities in a dynamic process of threat construction, they essentially created their own reality. They presented a narrative with a plausibly supportive factual predicate and assigned meaning to current uncertainties. As Netanyahu assumed control of the narrative, he recruited surrogate narrators who, like himself, had access to information sources that, in their listeners' minds, made them more knowledgeable and therefore more credible than the average citizen. In the reality of this narrative, the militarily stronger state that not only possessed a nuclear arsenal but also enjoyed an intensely close alliance with the world's most powerful nation was vulnerable to a fanatic theocratic regime with only limited military capabilities but intent on the complete destruction of all who opposed it. The Jewish State, in other words, was existentially threatened by the Islamic Republic. Saving Israel and, by extension, Judaism itself thus became a moral imperative for both the nation and the world. The threat and its attendant fear justified Israel's singular focus on preventing a nuclear Iran, as well as doing everything in its power to weaken every element of Iranian society in the hope that this pressure might precipitate the regime's downfall. This meant opposing any policy that might weaken Israel's capacity to counter Iran, no matter how tangential. For example, in this constructed reality, the perceived threat from Iran played a role in justifying Israel's refusal to engage in peace negotiations with the Palestinians, whom Israel accused of being one of Iran's many proxies.

When viewed from a power politics perspective, the narrative's powerful impact on Israeli policy and people is curious. As noted above, a reality-based assessment would reveal that not only was Iran militarily inferior to Israel and its Western allies, but also that Iran faced pressing domestic and foreign challenges that had nothing to do with the continued existence of a Zionist state. Crushing economic sanctions coupled with widespread corruption and economic mismanagement had impoverished the nation and its population. Water shortages and declining infrastructure made it difficult for Iranian domestic agriculture and industry to make up for shortages created by the sanctions. On the global level, Iran could count on few allies to support it in national defense or military campaigns abroad. It held leverage over several weaker client states and organizations but did not enjoy direct patronage from any major power.

Part of the curiosity of the Iran-Israel conflict, then, rests with Israel's use of a subjective narrative power as the basis for its foreign policy instead of a more objective showing of its military power. As Marc Lynch has noted, Israel inhabits a region that is 'one of the most realist parts of the world, with a high risk of war, deep mistrust, and fierce competitiveness.'[18] Successive generations of Israeli leaders and thinkers have embraced this belief by insisting that the country demonstrably maintain a 'qualitative military edge' over all regional opponents. This has included possessing superior weaponry and defense capabilities as well as advertising this superiority. This muscular posturing has been pursued with the aim of convincing enemies of Israel's capacity to defeat any state, group of states, or nonstate actors that may attack it.[19] This has included Israel's willingness to engage in preemptive strikes and leverage its advantage to minimize an enemy response. It has been an open secret that Israel possesses a nuclear weapon in its military arsenal.[20]

Remarkably, Israel's victimhood in the Iran threat narrative has elided a comparative assessment of the strength of the two nations.

I submit that we can understand this development by broadening the inquiry of security studies beyond relative power calculations. In a major refinement of the security studies subset of international relations theory, Danish political scientists posit that our examination of the policy calculus should go beyond the traditional definition of security studies,[21] what Stephen Walt called '*the threat*, use, and control of military force' (emphasis added).[22] In their articulation of 'securitization theory,' they argue for recognizing the power of a perceived threat as the basis for government decisions. They posit that a narrative that secures public investment in an existential threat can justify, if not compel, extraordinary action to ameliorate it, thereby giving a political leader or group immense power and authority in the process. Achieving securitization of a threat means that a substantial proportion of the public internalizes the insecurity fostered by the narrative's messages, and as a result they become active supporters of governmental actions to prevent or reduce harm. Once the population is emotionally invested in the existence of a threat, it becomes difficult to convince them merely through words that the situation may not be as dire as presented, or that the proposed response may not be justified.

The theorists view the narrative as a collection of 'political speech acts.' A narrator delivers messages targeting an identifiable audience, which are designed to inform as well as appeal to the audience's shared sense of identity, emotions, and values. The speech act carries the power to change public behavior by convincing them that their existence is threatened.[23] Importantly, this threat need not be real, or even plausible, for securitization to occur; it merely needs to be believed.[24] For our purposes, the significance of securitization is that it contributes to our understanding of the possibility and power of a counterfactual threat narrative.

The Copenhagen School maintains that the theory is applicable in many different scenarios in which an important societal value is threatened with total destruction—including nonmilitary situations—such as the threat of disaster from climate change or an amorphous threat of change to a collective identity or way of life. The danger posed by a foreign adversary is among the easiest to portray as existential. The power of a speech act is amplified by the narrator's expertise and the listeners' unfamiliarity with the details of international politics. Verification of factual claims in a situation punctuated with uncontrollable conditions and unpredictable outcomes is difficult, if not impossible. The uncertainty disposes the listener to respond to an emotional appeal.

Israel's Iran narrative provides a case study in the use of speech acts to create a securitization narrative when the existential threat is not easily identifiable, and perhaps not extant. In its purpose, the speech act resembles an emergency declaration that is invoked to justify extraordinary, perhaps even extra-legal, government actions. The fear occasioned by the danger conditions the public to accept mandates for individual and collective sacrifice.[25] Similarly, Netanyahu's narrative sought to enlist listener support for potentially extreme actions, including a preemptive strike on Iranian nuclear facilities. Since the alleged threat did not exist at the time of his invoking it, his principal prescription only indirectly addressed the problem. Simply put, he sought trust in his leadership decisions in exchange for protection from a threat that he had, through his own promotional efforts, brought to prominence. He hinted at using legally questionable military and economic actions to reduce the danger, with the end goal being regime change in Tehran.[26] The purpose behind his rhetoric, however, was largely self-promotional and threat-affirming. Action would follow only if it furthered Netanyahu's political ambitions. Even then, it would likely do little to erase the threat completely, since Israel, a small country a tenth the size of Iran, was unlikely to effect Iranian regime change on its own. Scant evidence supported the likelihood that a replacement government in Tehran would be more willing than Iran's current leaders to dismantle its nuclear program and end its support for client states and organizations that furthered Iranian strategic objectives. Moreover, the doctrine of unintended consequences holds that a future iteration of Iranian governance could be even more hardline or less pragmatic than its current leaders. Israeli action could, in other words, render its dire predictions of Iran's harmful intent a self-fulfilling prophecy.

In harnessing listeners' emotions to achieve his ends, Netanyahu also followed the prescription of securitization and psychological theorists, which notes that the interaction of cognition and emotion enables listeners to form the beliefs needed to activate their support.[27] 'Emotional beliefs' such as trust, nationalism, sense of justice, and credibility promote a collective identity.[28] This in turn promotes a consciousness in which those in the collective marginalize dissenters. Netanyahu's messaging of national peril used fear to coalesce a base willing to marginalize and exclude skeptics, further polarizing Israeli and global politics into 'with us' and 'against us' camps.[29] In his brand of nationalism, challengers of the narrative were unpatriotic, anti-Semitic, or both. As discussed in the next section, Netanyahu's manipulation of emotion to securitize the Iran threat represents a more nefarious use of the practice than the one originally envisioned by theorists.

Securitization theorists argue that a danger associated with overlooking emotion in foreign policy scholarship is that it leads to an incomplete understanding of the moral and ethical values that merit consideration in making or assessing decisions.[30] Emotion, while a murky and by definition imprecise variable, influences the formation of consequential values, which are often the product of 'messy' and internalized processes.[31] This means not only that security involves more than calculations of physical safety, but also that it reserves a role for psychology. An effective speech act should reflect the narrator's understanding of the origins and meanings of the human desire for safety and certainty. In a conflict in which security involves a zero-sum confrontation, it is important to acknowledge that the security of one group will likely create insecurity for the other.[32] Recognizing the humanity of the opponent can lead to a reasoned and proportionate response. Netanyahu did not exclude consideration of moral value from his narrative. Rather than recognize the Iranians' humanity, he vilified them as immoral, using psychological tactics to motivate his base and appealing to their emotions to breed feelings of enmity.

In understanding the power of Netanyahu's Iran threat narrative, we must emphasize that securitization requires public investment in an existential threat.[33] What qualifies a threat as existential is not a quantifiable determination, but rather involves a calculus that weighs the characteristics of obviousness, imminence, and destructive potential. The subjectivity inherent in the process of evaluating and prioritizing these variables facilitates emotional manipulation of the narrative. All politicians and passionate advocates of causes engage in rhetorical exaggeration to recruit and mobilize supporters. In modern political discourse, activists often accord urgency to societal problems by calling them epidemics or wars, such as the opioid or obesity epidemics, or the 'wars' on poverty, drugs, and crime. The existential threat calculus is more complex, and thus is fraught with greater danger.

In the existential threat calculus, obviousness refers to the individual's capacity to see and judge a threat's existence. Imminence means there is a probability that the listeners could 'soon' personally experience the harm; this characteristic relates to the urgency with which the public views the threat. The destructive potential is the capability to produce catastrophic harm; an existential threat raises the specter of permanent damage. These are malleable concepts. One challenge for the average citizen is that evaluating the characteristics of a security threat, particularly on a national or international scale, is often quite difficult. When so much information is unknown to the public, yet the consequences remain intensely personal—as with the threat of a nuclear bomb—it establishes a gap between the audience's comprehension of the situation and their fear of harm from it. To compensate, most listeners must filter their understanding through an interpretation of their leaders' words or deeds. When the danger is not evident, a narrator may manipulate uncertainty to claim it exists.

The public will not necessarily believe that an unfriendly nation developing a nuclear bomb poses an existential threat, unless they also believe that the resulting bomb will be dropped on their nation. A threat may be ongoing if the capability exists within an unpredictable timeframe. Specifying a date that harm will be dealt risks undermining belief in the threat's existence if it fails to materialize. By contrast, a threat with no set timeframe risks public fatigue and a reduced sense of urgency. If the public is not continually reminded of the threat's existence and destructive potential, even the fact that an enemy possesses a nuclear weapon may not be perceived by the public as existential.

The modern information ecosystem facilitates the construction of counterfactual narratives. The internet and social media enable the rapid dissemination of disinformation as well as the amplification of misinformation. Virtually anyone with a phone or computer can create claims that can be quickly amplified into major news events.[34] The surfeit of conflicting 'factual' claims challenges the uninformed to distinguish between fact and fiction. By contrast, those seeking to confirm their bias can find a plethora of sources that offer the information they need. The mob attack on the United States Capitol on 6 January 2021 illustrates the power of a pernicious threat narrative. President Donald Trump convinced his political base that his election loss was the result of a fraudulent election that imperiled the future of American democracy. He inspired a violent insurrection in which his supporters stormed the Capitol to prevent Congress from certifying the election results. In actuality, the election was not 'stolen,' and the end of Trump's presidency did not imperil democracy. On the contrary, the success of the 'Big Lie' and the passionate belief by a significant portion of Trump's base challenges us to think anew about protecting democratic norms.

While securitization theory explains the power of narrative and the construction process, it is less helpful in understanding how the narrator manages to secure public acceptance of a counterfactual narrative. If there is no existential threat, what purposes might the securitization speech act serve? Netanyahu's success in promoting the Iran threat and Trump's ability to create an entirely false account of election malfeasance both suggest that it would be helpful to probe how narrators of national security obtain public investment that withstands factual challenge. In the next section, I conclude this introductory discussion by expanding the securitization inquiry to add an additional explanatory dimension, which I call 'populist securitization.'

III. Public Investment in the Counterfactual Threat: Populist Securitization

Adding populism to securitization focuses attention on how the narrator secures his listeners' investment in the existence of an existential threat and their willingness to accept his ameliorative prescriptions. When we take populism into account, it enhances our understanding of the securitization process when a narrator engages in a speech act using a counterfactual threat narrative. When a narrator manufactures a threat—or exaggerates an existing one— to the extent that his audience perceives it as existential, he has a primary ulterior motive other than ending the threat.

As later chapters detail, when Netanyahu perfected his account of the Iran threat and made it the central focus of his messaging, he used the narrative not only for self-promotion but also to justify other, arguably tangential, policy decisions. Drawing upon his populist ideology, he confected a strategy of convincing his political base to conflate support for his power with public approval of state actions. This confused the public and diluted their capacity to debate the merits of his policies. Netanyahu's appeal to emotion marginalized examination of the factual claims concerning threat characteristics. For the most part, he succeeded in securitizing the Iran threat: not even his political opponents challenged the claim that Iran was actively pursuing nuclear weapons and might use them to attack Israel. Similarly, his successors in power have largely maintained the same approach to the threat which Netanyahu created.

According to Jan-Werner Müller, populist demagogues are especially adept at manipulating fear as a strategy to attract to their political base conservatives, reactionaries, and nationalists. In his 2016 book *What Is Populism?* he explains that domestic populist movements begin by pitting a cohort of the 'real people' against everyone else. Given the character of the groups attracted to the populist, 'us' is susceptible to vilification of the 'them,' who include the elites who dare to challenge the leader's power or policies.[35] What distinguishes Müller's definition is his claim that populism, unlike other approaches to politics, represents a 'particular moralistic imagination of politics, a way of perceiving the political world that sets a morally pure and fully unified—but ... ultimately fictional— people against elites who are deemed corrupt or in some other way morally inferior.'[36] The populist stifles dissent and debate over his policies and actions, and then claims that he is carrying out the will of the people.

Müller's definition of populism sheds light on Netanyahu's strategy in two ways. First, Netanyahu made common cause with a political base that he endowed with representing the nation's identity. One did not belong to his group merely because they were Jewish Israelis. His was not an organic movement but an identity shared only with those willing to support his claim on power. He invested in a few core policies that defined his leadership and solidified his base. This made his leadership personal, such that an attack on him represented an attack on the members of his support group. It also made the Iran threat narrative the central vehicle to his power since it provided the substantive material for his populist appeal.

Netanyahu transformed the Iran threat from a technical security challenge into a moral crusade, his tropes echoing the titanic and multigenerational struggle between good and evil. Israel, in this telling, was more than a frontline defense against Iran's tyranny, it was a moral beacon confronting the forces of evil emanating from the Islamic Republic. According to Netanyahu, these forces, if left unchecked, would soon overrun Europe and the entire world. This type of messaging transcended normal political discourse by creating a moral imperative for action. Faith trumped facts; debate was superfluous, if not dangerous. Within this context, Netanyahu was not just the elected leader of the Israeli nation, but a savior of the Jewish people.

Prioritizing faith and identity above accuracy enabled Netanyahu to adapt to changing circumstances without admitting any previous error. Iran's election of a bombastic anti-Zionist Holocaust denier, Mahmoud Ahmadinejad, as president in 2005 provided fodder for Netanyahu's ascription of evil intent to the nation's leaders at a key moment. Ahmadinejad's outrageous claims and confrontational style placed him in stark contrast to his predecessor, the reformist Mohammad Khatami, making Ahmadinejad the perfect avatar for the Iran Netanyahu wanted to portray.

Ahmadinejad's replacement by the moderate Hassan Rouhani eight years later indicated the possibility that Iranians were not obsessed with conflict and confrontation after all, and that they might desire a different path in international relations, which suggested that Ahmadinejad's fraught tenure was more of an exception than the rule of Iranian public opinion. Accepting this as a possibility could have changed the narrative in Israel, as it did in the West, which soon after Rouhani's inauguration began negotiations focused on placing limits on Iran's nuclear activities. Instead of changing the narrative in Israel—and despite Rouhani's overtures to the West and his sending a Jewish New Year's greeting to world Jewry on Rosh Hashanah—Netanyahu doubled down and claimed that Rouhani, like all Iranian leaders, could not be trusted. If anything, for many Israelis, Rouhani was an even less trustworthy messenger than Ahmadinejad, since his friendliness and moderation suggested a kind of duplicity which the blunt Ahmadinejad lacked.

Subsequent chapters will detail how Netanyahu's populist strategy informed his securitization campaign. He identified tropes and imagery that amplified the insecurity of his listeners, who, by virtue of their national identity, were already preconditioned to living in a perpetual state of emergency. He evoked emotional memories of the historical insecurity experienced by Jews, most especially of the Holocaust, and sought to connect those memories to a modern enemy in Iran. He recruited establishment allies to validate his message, using friends in the media, military, security services, and key constituency leaders to propagate his preferred narrative. Having planted the seed of concern among an insecure population, he sought to discredit challenges to his veracity from independent journalists, intellectuals, and political opponents within Israel and abroad. Throughout this campaign, he provided a simple, horrific vision of the consequences that would come from failing to heed his message. Netanyahu continually reassured his listeners that they need not bother with the details or nuances of the situation, because only he had the knowledge and capacity to protect them.

Netanyahu even tried extending his populist tropes to an international audience by invoking the 'us against them' archetype on an international scale over support for the Iran nuclear deal, also known as the Joint Comprehensive Plan of Action or JCPOA.[37] Netanyahu successfully used the specter of Iran to rearrange the Middle Eastern power balance along his interpretation of pro- and anti-Iran lines. As negotiations progressed, this awkwardly put Israel's Western allies, such as the United States, among the 'them' category, while anti-Iran nations in the Middle East, like Saudi Arabia, eventually began to qualify as 'us.' Later, Netanyahu would solidify this alignment in formal and informal relations with Sunni Arab states, gaining widespread recognition of Israel for the first time on the Arab peninsula.[38] Netanyahu also sought to recruit world Jewry to his cause by appealing to diaspora Jews to protest their countries' engagements with the Iranian regime. Such actions played well with his domestic supporters, who increasingly saw themselves as distinct from Jewish populations in the United States and the West.

Netanyahu did not fare as well in the international arena; at least, not until 2016 when Americans elected a fellow populist, Donald Trump, as their president, who arbitrarily abandoned American commitment to the JCPOA. He also prevented other world powers from engaging with Iran and reimposed harsh economic sanctions aimed at crippling daily life in Iran. Trump's actions, along with his close relationship with Netanyahu, helped the Israeli leader revive his narrative and retain his power. Trump also contributed to Iran hardening its resolve to withstand the sanctions, restart its nuclear enrichment activities, and adopt a more hardline stance in international relations. The consequences of these pursuits lived on even after voters forced both Trump and Netanyahu out of office in 2021.

* * *

If the political narrative is a 'communication bond' between power and public, which reflects their shared fears, hopes, and prejudices, the threat narrative is the narrative species that concentrates on the fear.[39] The narrator seeking to securitize an existential threat relies on both fact and emotion. The more ambiguous the threat characteristics, the greater the appeal to emotion. To secure public cooperation with taking extraordinary measures to ameliorate the threat, the narrator requires the public to perceive the danger as real and existential.

Theoretically, securitization of a non-obvious or counterfactual threat is harder to achieve in a democracy. When leaders respect democratic norms and that polity values political discourse, debate can expose false claims. A populist leader whose communication is exclusively targeted at the public willing to support his power has an easier path toward achieving his aims. He can discount accuracy by creating his own reality. Untroubled by truth, he can strategically merge morality, identity, and historical tropes with an emotional appeal in a way that renders facts irrelevant.

The world is rife with threats issued by foreign powers against one another. It is not inherently problematic when a fearful public seeks certitude or reassurance from its leaders. Threats to a nation's security can be real and verifiable and still provoke debate over elements of the threat calculus associated with its imminence and the extent of the danger. A threat can also be a unifying force, uniting the polity in active support of a common cause. As Ronald Krebs notes, 'Debates over national security are in fact often underpinned by dominant narratives that weave present challenges, past failures and triumphs, and potential futures into a coherent tale, with well-defined characters and plot lines.'[40] People often unreasonably expect their government leaders to offer protection and crisis resolution.[41]

The problem arises when the narrative exaggerates or fabricates a threat and then disseminates it by appealing to the public's worst instincts, in the process undermining democratic norms. Netanyahu's Iran threat illuminates the power and dangers that populist securitization poses to global security. Examining its development process, choice of content, and messaging allows us to consider how to recognize and understand the challenges of political narrative.

2

HISTORY
FROM FRIENDSHIP TO ENMITY

I. Introduction

The interaction between Iran and Israel is not a linear story. It includes accounts of peoples living within the same geographic space, of one people being ruled by another, and of two sovereign nations cooperating in pursuit of shared interests over the course of two millennia. When considering the historic timespan of their interaction, the enmity that is the subject of this study is only a recent development. If one omits this history and turns to the remaining chapters, one could be forgiven for forming a very different impression of this relationship. The modern leaders of both nations draw upon their long and rich heritages as the basis for the present hostility, yet the history they present is frequently distorted in pursuit of policy aims or some other political agenda. In Israel, particularly, it is curious to consider how Jews, who pride themselves on their learning and knowledge of their people's ancient heritage, have allowed Israeli leaders to construct narratives containing such dubious historical claims. Perhaps they consider such alternative interpretations inconsequential to modern-day realities in which the urgency of the threat justifies a more extreme reading of the past. But when the narratives serve as justifications for policy, the historical inaccuracy cannot be dismissed as inconsequential.

Ironically, what is perhaps the best known 'historic' interaction between Persians and Jews likely never happened. The story of a Persian king and his Jewish queen is told in the Book of Esther (*Megillat Esther*), which is included in the canon of the Hebrew Bible and ensured at least an annual public reading by Jews worldwide during the Purim holiday. As we shall see, although it has been passed down to us in writing, its retelling by an Israeli politician changed the story to offer a different message than the one traditionally told. This chapter begins with a look at the ancient history between Jews and Persians and its salience for today's leaders. It then briefly reviews the experience of the Jews who lived in Persia and later Iran. The 'modern' relationship, as I have defined it, begins shortly after the establishment of the State of Israel, and includes the little-known strategic cooperation between the Shah and the new State of Israel. I conclude with an examination of the early years of the Islamic Republic and the events that set the stage for the present conflict between Israel and Iran.

II. Jews in Persia and Iran

The history of what may be considered the relationship of Iran and Israel begins as one of friendship between Persians and Jews. Scholars believe that Jews dwelt within the boundaries of what is today modern Iran as far back as two centuries before the founding of the Persian Empire.[1] Significantly, the history of interactions between these two nationalities does not accord with modern narratives explaining the current conflict.

Two biblical accounts are particularly material to an understanding of the Persian-Jewish relationship, both in antiquity and modernity. One, rooted in history, tells of how Cyrus the Great, the founder of the Achaemenid Empire, liberated the Jewish people from their exile in Babylon in 539 BCE. A believer in religious freedom, Cyrus allowed Jews to practice their religion openly within his kingdom. He also allowed those who so desired to return to their homes in

Jerusalem. There he helped finance the reconstruction of the Second Temple.[2] The authors of the Hebrew Bible lauded the benevolence of Cyrus, while the Temple demonstrated the religious tolerance extended to Jews in the Persian Empire. In the text of the Hebrew Bible, God is said to refer to Cyrus as His *mashiach*, one of only five people so designated and the only gentile to receive the honorific.[3] While the Hebrew Bible's twenty-three mentions of Cyrus are all positive, not all scholars agree that Cyrus merited the credit.[4] Whatever the actual facts, however, the status of the Persian king in the Jewish canon testifies to a historic friendship that is obscured in modern accounts of the two nations' historic enmity.

The second biblical 'historical' account is better known than the deeds of Cyrus, but it is also most likely a fairytale.[5] *Megillat Esther* tells of a Persian king who spared the Jews from annihilation when his Jewish queen revealed the perfidious plot of his chief minister. The story is set in the Sassanid Empire during the reign of King Ahasuerus. A young maiden named Esther, who hides her Jewish identity, becomes queen by winning a beauty contest. Meanwhile, the King's minister, Haman the Aggagite, angered by the Jews' refusal to bow down to human royalty, convinces the king to order the killing of all the Jews in the kingdom. Esther is charged by her Uncle Mordechai to reveal her identity to her husband and implore him to save her people. According to the story, she hatches a scheme that includes risking death to approach the king without invitation and then inviting the king and his minister Haman to a private dinner party. There she reveals Haman's plot against her and her people, and she pleads with the king to spare the Jews. The story has a happy ending: the horrified king accedes to his queen's plea, orders the death of the wicked Haman, and names Uncle Mordechai to a high government post. Today, Jews continue to celebrate this deliverance in the annual festival of Purim during which they retell the story, cheering Mordechai's name and jeering Haman's.

Some accounts, both written and oral, omit certain details of the story's end. The final chapters recount how the king, unable to rescind his royal edict, allowed Mordechai to issue a second royal edict permitting 'The Jews in every city to assemble and fight for their lives; if any people or province attacks them, they may destroy, massacre, and exterminate its armed force together with women and children, and to plunder their possessions.'[6]

The story then details how the Jews both celebrated their reprieve and 'got their enemies in their power.'[7] It even includes the body count associated with the Jews' attack on 'those who sought their hurt,'[8] which numbered upwards of 75,000 deaths.[9] That some choose to omit or obscure this part of the story illustrates the power wielded by storytellers to use historical narrative to craft their particular messages.

The Cyrus and Esther stories retain a place in the history and customs of modern-day Israel and Iran. The majority of books or articles analyzing the relationship between the nations mention these stories as reference points for a historic friendship that contrasts with the present hostility. Not all scholars agree, however, that these stories have any relevance to modernity. R.K. Ramazani, who wrote an influential history of Israeli-Iranian ties during the twilight of the Pahlavi rule, challenges their explanatory value. He writes of the Cyrus anecdote, 'Such basically cultural perspectives seem less useful as a means of policy explication by way of scholars than as a vehicle of policy rationalization by statesmen.'[10] The weakness in his argument rests on his unwillingness to consider how these rationalizations not only animate policy decisions but impact their acceptance among the polity.

It is often difficult to determine whether policy decisions result from objective situational evaluation or from reverse engineering a justification from a desired outcome. Whether stemming from analysis or rationalization, historical memory has influenced the decisions of Israeli and Iranian leaders in many instances. For example, when Israel's first prime minister, David Ben Gurion, sought an alliance with Iran shortly after the Jewish State's founding, the Shah invoked Cyrus in his letter of acceptance. The Shah, who was notable for his emphasis on Persian nationalism and history, wrote, 'The memory of Cyrus's policy regarding your people is precious to me, and I strive to continue in the path set by this ancient tradition.'[11]

The influence is not always so positive, nor the memory entirely accurate. Modern Israeli and Iranian leaders have invoked the Esther story as a propaganda weapon in their rhetorical condemnation of one another's nation. To Israelis, the story cautions distrust of an Iranian enemy bent upon destruction of the Jewish people. In their retelling, Persian anti-Semitism is rooted in the pre-Islamic Persian Empire, suggesting that the story demonstrates a national or ethnic character intent on genocide. Prime Minister Benjamin Netanyahu went so far as to change the narrative to eliminate the role of King Achashverosh (the Hebrew pronunciation of Ahasuerus) in rescinding the edict of annihilation. In his controversial 2015 address before a joint session of the United States Congress on the eve of the Purim holiday, Netanyahu cited the story's significance to the present moment, declaring, 'Today the Jewish people face another attempt by yet another Persian potentate to destroy us.'[12] This was not an isolated comment. Netanyahu repeated his interpretation of the Book of Esther before the 2017 Purim holiday, when he suggested to Russian President Vladimir Putin that the story of Purim illustrates the Persian desire to destroy the Jewish people.[13]

Israeli religious leaders echoed their prime minister by drawing attention to the bombastic rhetoric of hardliner politicians in Iran, accusing former president Mahmoud Ahmadinejad of being the 'new Haman' who, like the ancient villain, threatened the destruction of Israel, this time with nuclear warheads. One rabbi predicted that 'Like Haman and his henchmen before, Ahmadinejad and his supporters would find their bows destroyed and their swords turned against them to strike their own hearts.'[14] Supposedly, a cyber weapon unleashed by Israel and the United States in the late-2000s, which sought to cripple Iran's nuclear program, referenced Queen Esther and Haman in its code.[15]

The mythologizing was not one-sided. Iranian hardliners have also reinterpreted the Esther story to justify their anti-Semitism and support their contention that the Jewish State threatens Iran. In their version of events, they challenge the notion that Jews took up arms to defend themselves and speak instead of the Jews conducting an 'Iranian Holocaust.'[16] Notably, the story has a different impact in the two countries. In Israel, everyone knows the Purim story, whether or not they accept the modern interpretation. In Iran, the story has little traction beyond the religious elite. For both countries, however, the story and its differing interpretations illustrate that factual accuracy has little to do with the power of historical narrative.

History records that the descendants of the Jews who followed Cyrus the Great back to Persia after the liberation of Babylon continued to enjoy good relations with Cyrus's successors. The Achaemenid King Artaxerxes II, who ruled Persia from 405 to 358 BCE, helped encourage a second wave of Jewish migration back to ancient Palestine, beginning with the dispatching of a royal emissary, Ezra, to help reestablish the law of the Torah in the territory of Judah.[17] Still, as they had during the reign of Cyrus, many Jews opted to remain in Persia. Later, monarchs of the Parthian Empire shielded the Jews from the harsh treatment they suffered at the hands of the neighboring Roman authorities. They allowed Jews to establish a self-governing territory within Persian lands, which included independent political, administrative, and judicial authorities. Jewish texts from this period reflect the goodwill that Persian authorities showed to Jews. There are no negative descriptions of the Persian people or their rulers in ancient Jewish texts (which cannot be said for the Greeks, Babylonians, and Romans). Instead, they depict the Persians mainly as liberators and allies of the Jewish people.[18]

This dynamic changed following the Muslim conquest of Persia in the seventh century CE. At the end of the Sassanid Empire and the beginning of the Islamic period, the Persian monarchs adopted a less tolerant position on religious freedom than their predecessors. Forced conversions to homogenize the religious makeup of the kingdom were not uncommon, although this policy met with limited success. In the early sixteenth century, following the expulsion of the Mongols from Persia, monarchs of the Safavid dynasty again pursued this strategy. This sparked a wave of Jewish emigration from the kingdom, but some Jews remained and avoided conversion. Thus, despite rulers' efforts and official policies of intolerance toward non-Muslims, Jews maintained a continuous presence in Iran. [19]

It is difficult to discern accurate numbers for the Jewish population throughout the ages. The earliest non-biblical written report on the Jewish population in Persia is from the twelfth century CE, in which Benjamin of Tudela reported the population to be around 600,000. This number decreased to about 100,000 by the

Safavid era, between the sixteenth and eighteenth centuries. It then remained stable into the nineteenth and twentieth centuries under the reigns of the Qajjar and Pahlavi dynasties. Estimates of the Jewish population in pre-Islamic Revolution Iran fall between 50,000 and 100,000 Jewish Iranians.[20]

By most accounts, the Pahlavi dynasty, the last Persian monarchy prior to the Islamic Revolution, did not mistreat its Jewish population. One commentator even described this period as a 'golden age' for Iran's Jews.[21] Such a description may be overlooking the fact that the first Pahlavi ruler, Reza Shah, was a well-known admirer of the Nazis and Adolf Hitler, although he supposedly did not subscribe to Hitler's racial views.[22] After the British and Russians forced the abdication of Reza Shah in 1941, they installed his son, Mohammad Reza Pahlavi, on the throne. Mohammad Reza was largely seen as sympathetic to the Jewish population in Iran. According to rumor, he once prayed to a Torah during a ceremonial visit to a Jewish cemetery in Isfahan, where some of the earliest Iranian Jews had settled several millennia before.[23] But in reality, the extent to which Jews were accepted within the predominantly Shiite Muslim society is unclear. Ronen Cohen, an Israeli scholar, paints a much darker picture of the prerevolutionary treatment of Iranian Jews, writing that the Jews of Iran suffered due to the Shia belief that a person who touches a Jew becomes *najes* or impure.[24]

What we do know is that a relatively small insular Jewish community called Iran home. They survived for millennia amidst a dominant culture that did not accept them as part of Persian society but also did not physically threaten their existence. Ironically, while the Jewish community was characterized by insularity and refusal to bow down to the Persian king and his courtiers—an act which had provoked Haman to seek their annihilation—the Jews not only survived in the Persian Empire, they refused to leave.

III. From Indifference to Collaboration

Prior to the twentieth century, Cyrus the Great was the last foreign ruler to encourage Jewish resettlement in their biblically ordained homeland of Israel. In 70 CE, the Romans invaded Jerusalem, destroyed the Second Temple—the building of which Cyrus had facilitated—and sent the Jewish population into exile. With the declaration of the State of Israel on 14 May 1948, that exile officially ended. It also provoked Israel's Arab neighbors—Egypt, Syria, and Jordan, with support from Iraq—to invade.

The declaration of Israel's statehood followed a vote in the United Nations the previous November, in which the British territory of Palestine was partitioned into two independent states, one Jewish and one Arab. Britain, which had administered the territory under a League of Nations mandate following the defeat of the Ottoman Empire in World War I, withdrew its forces and administrators.[25] The mandate had been marked by violence between the resident Palestinian population and Jewish emigres displaced by the Holocaust. British officials, who had sided with the Arabs to prevent the influx of Jews to the territory, also became the target of attacks from radical Jewish militants. The 1948 invasion by the Arab nations signaled their rejection of the partition plan, but the newly born Israeli state ultimately survived its 'War of Independence.' Of course, the Palestinians have a different narrative of the event. They did not achieve their state and instead annually commemorate the 'Nakba,' or 'catastrophe,' in which 700,000 Palestinians were expelled or exiled from Israeli territory. Both sides acknowledge, to a certain extent, that the 1948 conflict has yet to be fully resolved.

The war also represented a humiliating defeat for Israel's Arab neighbors, who did not want what they considered to be a political and religious anomaly in their midst.[26] Like the Iranians, many Arabs had come to loathe the British, feeling that they had betrayed them by rescinding a promise of autonomy.[27] Moreover, the Arabs lost the fight to prevent Israel's creation at the start despite having vastly superior troop numbers and natural resource advantages. This story is deeply woven into every strand of the fabric of the modern-day Middle East, as well as the mythology of the State of Israel. It also features an account of the oppression of the Palestinians, but the fate of the Palestinians themselves has been largely marginal to the narrative debate surrounding the Israeli state's legitimacy.

In Iran, the establishment of the State of Israel complicated the Shah's already difficult reign. In the UN partition vote, Iran joined with their fellow majority-Muslim countries in voting against the proposal, but it refrained from joining the Arab war effort against Israel following the declaration of the new state. Mohammad Reza Pahlavi had occupied the Peacock Throne for just seven years at that point. Having ascended to the throne solely through the will of the British, who had forced his father from office due to his German sympathies, the young Shah felt compelled to avoid entanglements that would endanger his relationship with the post-war triumphant powers.

To say the early years of rule were turbulent for a monarch still in his twenties would be an understatement. After the end of World War II, the Shah had to navigate between the competing East-West superpowers engaged in the Cold War. At the same time, he faced competing demands from his own population, which included a powerful clerical establishment in a nation with a 99% Shiite Muslim majority.[28] For the Shah, publicly supporting the fledgling Israeli state held no discernable strategic or material benefit for his reign.

It is understandable, then, that the Shah's policy toward Israel in the initial years following its creation was, according to Ramazani, one of 'calculated ambivalence,' in which the Shah avoided making any commitment either for or against Israel.[29] The wait-and-see approach enabled him to maintain the neutrality of his foreign policy in the Cold War between the Soviet Union and the West. It also allowed him to avoid taking either a losing position or one that would anger his subjects, who were by and large sympathetic to the plight of the Palestinians. Moreover, Ramazani notes that the strategy was 'in keeping in the basic tenets and thrust of Iranian nationalism' favored by the Shah.[30]

As the Cold War intensified, it became increasingly difficult for smaller countries to maintain a façade of detached neutrality. Especially in the Middle East, East and West sought strategic political and economic advantage in resource-rich nations. The competition for influence challenged the Shah. He owed his throne to the British, and Iran hosted extensive foreign investors, which were positioned to influence the country's domestic politics. The largest investment came from the Anglo-Iranian Oil Company (AIOC), the predecessor to British Petroleum, which at the time was one of the largest oil companies in the world. Granted the exclusive right to develop the Iranian oil fields in 1933 by the Shah's father, the company generated tremendous wealth for the Shah, for the company, and for Great Britain.[31] The generous terms of the concession meant the company was repatriating significant revenue to Great Britain, while still providing substantial payments to the Shah, thereby reducing his need to develop indigenous technologies for the extraction of wealth. The Shah ultimately paid a price for this arrangement: not only was he effectively surrendering some of Iran's economic sovereignty, but he was also susceptible to British pressure over his governmental decisions.[32] This arrangement challenged his ability to remain neutral in the unfolding Cold War conflict.

Three years into Israel's statehood, in 1951, a power struggle in Iran pitted the Shah against the country's prime minister, Mohammad Mossadegh. The latter assumed office determined to end British economic domination in Iran. He quickly followed through on that promise by nationalizing the AIOC and expelling its British employees from the country. His growing popularity created a rift with the Shah, which metastasized into a power struggle for control of the country. The Shah, fearing that he was on the verge of losing that struggle, eventually fled the country, mentally prepared to live out the remainder of his life in exile. In 1953, an American-engineered—and British-supported—coup d'état restored the Shah to the throne.[33] While the details of this consequential event are beyond the scope of this book, it is relevant to note that the eventual narrative ascribes responsibility to the United States for the overthrow of Iran's democratically elected leader in favor of a dictatorial ruler.

The Shah, upon his restoration to power, not only allowed the West to exploit Iran's wealth, but he also accepted its foreign policy directives. Whereas Mossadegh's government closed the Iranian consulate in Israel, albeit allegedly for budgetary reasons, the Shah's return meant that the move had little impact on relations between Iran and Israel. Ultimately, however, his actions and his capitulations to the desires of his foreign overlords fueled the popular dissatisfaction that ended with his overthrow and a rejection of his policies.

Israel, too, tried to maintain neutrality in the early years of the Cold War. The United States and the Soviet Union voted in favor of the original partition, and Israel relied on both for crucial support: financial from the Americans and military from the Soviets.[34] Rather than ally with one ideology over the other, Israel tried to navigate between the two superpowers by aligning itself with the United Nations as a global organization. As tensions rose, however, eventually culminating in the outbreak of war on the Korean peninsula in 1950, maintaining a façade of disinterested neutrality became an increasingly untenable position. The United Nations backed American forces, thereby forcing Israel into the Western camp.[35]

Thus, both Israel and Iran were aligned with the United States when, in 1955, the Soviet Union sought to actively exert its influence in the Middle East. Following an Egyptian army coup that toppled the government of King Faruq, the Soviets backed the presidency of a young, charismatic revolutionary named Gamal Abdel Nasser. To the Egyptian people who saw the old regime as corrupt, incompetent, and obsequious to British interests, and who bemoaned their defeat in the 1948 war, Nasser's message of pan-Arabism and Arab nationalism was a welcome change. He urged Arabs to unite against their enemies, most notably Israel. The Soviets saw Nasser and his message as an opportunity to gain a foothold in the Middle East. They began supplying him with equipment and funding to rebuild the depleted and outdated Egyptian military.[36]

The first test of the new alliance occurred a year later when Nasser attempted to nationalize the Suez Canal, a key passageway for maritime trade. Although located within Egyptian territory, Western powers had built and now operated the canal. France and Britain joined Israel in invading Egypt. Fearing the destabilizing effect of a regional war, the United States joined the Soviet Union in a United Nations vote condemning the attack. This was not only an odd moment in which the opposing superpowers agreed with each other, but a surprise to the invading armies who had assumed that the United States would support their action. In the end, US President Dwight D. Eisenhower pressured the invaders to withdraw and surrender the canal to Egyptian forces. In doing so, they handed Nasser a victory in both the military and the public relations arenas.

As the Arab leader willing to stand up to the Israelis and the West, his status rose. He was thus more than willing to accept the Soviets' offer of dramatically increased aid, including advanced military equipment and advisors from Eastern bloc countries.[37] Israel and Iran, although not allied with one another, now found themselves with a common enemy.

If it is true that the enemy of my enemy is my friend, it would stand to reason that in the late 1950s Iran and Israel would both have been interested in some sort of alliance. Indeed, although rarely discussed beyond academic circles, the two nations developed a relationship, which came to be known as the Periphery Alliance. One of the challenges associated with examining that alliance is the absence of public documentation associated with its origins. Israel's leaders directed little public attention to Iran, while the academic community considered Iran's relationship with Israel to be of only marginal value. If nothing else, Israel and Iran's shared alignment with the West suggested that neither nation posed a sufficiently serious threat to the other to merit serious strategic consideration.

It is also notable that few Israeli researchers had a personal attachment to or knowledge of Iran apart from their familiarity with the story of Esther. In his 2015 book examining the early alliance years, Yossi Alpher explains that ignorance of Iranian history among Israeli Middle East experts persists, such that even now most have little to no knowledge that the countries had ever been allies.[38] Whatever their exact reasons, Israeli leaders never fully recounted or left behind public documentation of their work with Iran.[39] It is, however, fair to surmise that both Israel and Iran sought a relationship that would be mutually beneficial, and that neither anticipated the attendant consequences of their actions.

Israel was not yet a decade old when the 1956 Suez Crisis highlighted its precarious strategic position. It enjoyed some support from the United States, which under the Eisenhower Doctrine opposed communist expansionism in the Middle East. Thus, it was surprising when this nominal ally handed a victory to Egypt. As a result, Israel faced an emboldened Nasser leading a pan-Arab movement sponsored by the Soviet Union. Israel, however, was not alone; other non-Arab countries in the region also faced this new threat. According to Shimon Peres, who was serving in the Israeli Parliament (the Knesset) during this period, Israel viewed Nasser as a 'new, ambitious Arab "caliph", supported by the might of a suspect power, [which] could hardly fail to rouse unhappy memories among the Turks and Iranians of dark periods in their history.'[40] Following the Suez debacle, it was with these two nations that Israel's founding prime minister, David Ben Gurion, then in his second term, pursued an alliance.

The idea had originated years earlier, shortly after Israel's founding. Ben Gurion, together with the chiefs of Israel's foreign and domestic intelligence services,[41] recognized that Israel would need strategic partners in the region.[42] They reasoned that Israel could enhance its prospects for long-term survival if it found partners with whom it at least shared the fear of a common threat. A coalition of non-Arab Middle Eastern nations could serve as a counterweight to the threat of Arab aggression.

Initially, Israel recruited three nations to join its new alliance: Turkey, Iran, and Ethiopia,[43] each of which served a strategic purpose. Turkey confronted Iraq and Syria on Israel's northern border, while in the south Ethiopia provided Israel with remote access to the Northern African plateau south of Sudan and Egypt. Israel viewed Iran as the crown jewel of the alliance: it brought geographic, diplomatic, and economic advantages key to the success of the enterprise. Geographically, its long border with Iraq positioned it to counter potential threats from one of the largest and most militarily developed Arab states. Diplomatically, the Shah's close relationship with the United States following the 1953 coup made him an invaluable resource for fostering better relations with American government officials. Economically, Iran provided access to an energy supply that was critically necessary for Israel's economic development. Moreover, with the influx of new immigrants from the Jewish diaspora, who brought with them an entrepreneurial spirit and technical expertise, access to Iran's abundant natural resources, which Israel did not have within its tiny piece of real estate, would enable the Jewish State to develop rapidly. The three nations approximated a geographic ring around almost all the Arab world; thus, Israel named the strategy the *Torat HaPeripheria*, or 'Periphery Doctrine.'

For his part, the Shah recognized that a pan-Arab alliance would interfere with his designs on extending Iran's regional influence and power. Having consolidated his authority following the CIA's engineering of his return to the throne in 1953, the Shah sought to pursue an aggressive foreign policy that would enhance Iran's stature on the world stage.[44] Since Nasser's maneuvering encroached on the Shah's ability to reach out to Arab leaders, the Shah sought opportunities elsewhere. Israel's alliance with the United States and the West presented one possibility.[45]

Initially, Iran, unlike Israel, did not consider the Arab states to be a significant military threat. Rather, Arab unification threatened the Shah's self-image and his cultivated position within the Islamic world. In his vision, he would reign over a new Persian Empire, building his image upon the prominence of Iran's Shia clerical tradition. Pan-Arabism elevated the significance of ethnic ties over those of religion, thus interfering with the Shah's plans to influence Shia-majority countries. Worse, an alliance based upon ethnicity threatened to isolate Iran in the Middle East. The Shah needed both allies and a plan to reverse this trend. His concern deepened in 1958, when the Iraqi military overthrew the Hashemite Kingdom of Iraq, Iran's immediate neighbor and historic rival. The new ruling junta, which included future Iraqi dictator Saddam Hussein, quickly entered into a series of agreements with the Soviet Union. This brought the tide of Soviet expansionism to Iran's doorstep.

Israel's proposal for the Periphery Alliance thus arrived at a propitious moment for the Shah. Although the Iranian monarch had little interest in ensuring Israel's survival, the arrangement provided him with support for countering the Soviet threat. As Ramazani put it, the Shah's decision was a 'conscious and deliberate policy [to] remain aloof from the quagmire and age-old conflict between the Arabs and the Israelis and to maintain a balancing posture between the two sides while pursuing Iran's larger foreign policy objectives.'[46]

For Israel, the Periphery Alliance represented a limited partnership for cooperative security and intelligence purposes, the efficacy of which depended on secrecy. Israel charged its foreign intelligence service, the Mossad, with coordinating and implementing the new doctrine.

Secrecy was vital to both countries, as neither leader wanted the clergy, politicians, or public to object. On one hand, Israelis would be suspicious of Iran's motives and trustworthiness, given that Iran continued to maintain active diplomatic relations with Arab countries that were dedicated to Israel's destruction. On the other, both Israeli leaders and the Shah recognized the risk to the latter posed by the potential of their cooperation being publicly revealed.[47] The Shah ruled a predominantly Muslim society guided by a clergy whose rhetoric was fiercely anti-Zionist and anti-Semitic, and they would not countenance political considerations which superseded religious faith. Moreover, the Shah owed a political debt to the principal clerical antagonist of Israel, Ayatollah Abol-Ghasem Kashani. In 1952, Kashani had publicly defected from supporting Prime Minister Mohammad Mossadegh, thus helping to bolster public support for the Shah's restoration to the throne.[48] Earlier, in January 1948, Kashani had issued a communiqué calling for jihad against Israel. This call would be repeated by Kashani's followers for years to come, including the future founder of the Islamic Republic, Ayatollah Ruhollah Khomeini.[49]

Although motivated by the desire for a strategy that would enhance his regional standing, the Shah also recognized that public revelation would not only damage his leadership aspirations but also risk his being condemned as a traitor to Islam. Even as he sought to benefit from the relationship, he needed to project an image of a ruler committed to both the Iranian nation and the Islamic world. Thus, the Shah continued his public rhetoric condemning Israel while privately seeking to benefit from the two nations' cooperation.

With the Shah having much to lose and Israel having much to gain, it was unsurprising that they viewed the secret relationship differently. For the Shah, it was a convenient arrangement. While the alliance belied his calculated ambivalence, according to Alpher, the Shah displayed a notable 'lack of emotional attachment' to the Israelis.[50] By contrast, Israel's leaders imbued the relationship with biblical significance. They saw it as the continuation of the legacy of Cyrus the Great, whose liberation of the Jews in ancient times had enabled them to return to the land that was now their independent nation. The Periphery Alliance was more than a strategic security-enhancing arrangement, it was a 'fulfillment of destiny,' a modern addendum to the biblical narrative.[51]

Despite their different perspectives, Iran and Israel agreed on the purpose of the alliance. Initially, they sought to share intelligence by convening meetings of a 'Trident' group which also included Turkey, in which each country's intelligence officials got to know one another at regular meetings held every six months. Through these interactions, Iran and Israel identified avenues of assistance beyond information exchange. In 1958, the Shah embarked on a joint covert propaganda operation alongside the Israelis to broadcast Arabic language programs that were critical of Nasser across the Arab world.[52] The Shah, having been impressed by the competency and professionalism of the Israeli intelligence apparatus, requested assistance from the Mossad in developing his own domestic intelligence service. Israel helped train the members of SAVAK, the Shah's secret police force, which spied on and terrorized his subjects.[53]

As oil prices rose, increasing Iran's financial resources, the Shah went on a spending spree for military equipment, much of which he purchased from Israeli weapons manufacturers. These sales were mutually beneficial to Israel and its GDP, accounting for a large segment of the early Israeli economy.[54] Eventually, in the mid-1970s the military element of the alliance expanded to include a more human element, beginning with officer exchange programs. These exchanges helped bring the Iranian and Israeli military closer together by establishing personal bonds of friendship between mid-level officers in both militaries.[55] The Iranian military, impressed by Israel's success in fighting Arab armies, sought to observe the Israeli Defense Force's operation and learn from its experience.[56] Given lingering tensions with neighboring Iraq, Iranian officers had reason to anticipate the possibility of a military conflict between Iran and Arab forces. The Iranians paid Israel for the consulting and training services, and the personal interaction gradually reduced Israel's suspicions of its Iranian ally. As Uzi Arad, a former national security advisor and Mossad official, explained, 'We started to identify with their struggles.'[57]

Officials in each country also recognized that the benefits could expand beyond the military and intelligence sectors. Israel lacked the energy resources to fuel the industrial development promised by the influx of human capital in the form of Jewish immigrants from the diaspora. While the Arab oil-producing countries refused to sell oil to Israel because they opposed its existence, Iran, having been excluded from the pan-Arab movement, had no such qualms. The Shah could realize the revenue from the Israeli market and, of equal importance, access Israeli technical expertise for modernizing his economy and Westernizing Iranian society.

Modernization was an imperative for the Shah. By the early 1960s, thousands of young people of the postwar generation, who had spent time traveling, studying, and living abroad, began to assert themselves in Iranian politics. They demanded liberalization and transformative changes.[58] In response, the Shah had launched what he called the 'White Revolution,' which initially centered on land reforms. Eventually, the initiative expanded to encompass a broad array of economic and social measures, including industrial privatization, infrastructure development, and the right of women to vote.[59] Among the international advisors the Shah consulted in developing these initiatives were many Israelis. As an admirer of Israel's rapid development since its founding, particularly in the agricultural sector, the Shah sought Israeli guidance in advancing Iran's farming industry and national infrastructure projects. Israelis assisted in developing a variety of high-profile projects, ranging from construction of the Darius Khabir Dam in Shiraz, to a naval base along the Persian Gulf coast, to luxury apartment complexes in downtown Tehran.[60] The Shah reportedly expressed his admiration to Uri Lubrani, the top Israeli diplomatic official in Iran, by telling him, 'Israel is a country that has the developed technology we need. Its know-how is complementary to ours.'[61] Israeli contributions to Iran's infrastructure inspired many Iranians to visit Israel to see its progress and learn its methods. Iranian farmers and engineers traveled to receive training, while businessmen sought to establish ties with Israeli firms.[62]

As Israelis developed a new understanding of Iranians, so too did those in Iran who had knowledge of the alliance come to appreciate the Israelis. Former Iranian Prime Minister Ali Amini characterized the still-secret relationship as being 'like the true love that exists between two people out of wedlock.'[63] Although the circle of knowledgeable people grew as interaction expanded, everyone who shared in the benefits—both government officials and private entrepreneurs— had an incentive to refrain from publicizing the success. When the exchanges necessitated increased consular services, the operation was disguised. Due to security concerns, the Israeli embassy in Tehran did not fly the Israeli flag or display perceptible identifying insignia, although its presence was common knowledge.[64]

An exception to the rule of secrecy was made in 1962 when Israel openly responded with assistance after Iran experienced a severe earthquake. Israel sent a team of experts to assist with recovery and reconstruction in the Qazvin region of northwest Iran. For Israel, these actions were not purely altruistic, as the Israelis then publicized the event to demonstrate to the world the proficiency of their technical expertise in disaster relief. The Shah, who was already well aware of the Israelis' capabilities, also saw value in more overt assistance, believing he could use Israel's response as an example of how his pursuit of foreign assistance was helping modernize Iran by upgrading its infrastructure, introducing advanced technology, and reforming its economy.[65]

Yet despite the strategic and economic benefits each country was realizing through their cooperation, all was not copacetic politically. In the early 1970s, Israelis working in Iran began to witness public expressions of dissatisfaction with the Shah's regime. As demonstrations against the Shah's rule intensified, Israel realized that the civil unrest could potentially force the Shah from power. The Israeli government began planning for a post-Shah Iran by instructing individuals and companies conducting business in Iran to protect themselves from future political instability. They recommended that Israelis with economic interests there try to divest those holdings. At a minimum, they suggested maintaining a negative balance of payments with Iran, so that money owed to Iranian concerns would be greater than the amount owed to Israel.[66]

While the Shah and Israeli leaders were pursuing a mutually beneficial secret relationship, Gamal Nasser continued his pro-Arab saber-rattling against Israel. Throughout the 1960s, his inflammatory anti-Israel public statements included warnings of impending war.[67]

In May 1967, reports of an Egyptian military buildup in the Sinai Peninsula reached Israeli Prime Minister Levi Eshkol, causing the Israeli military to mobilize in preparation for a potential conflict. On 5 June 1967, the Israeli military launched a preemptive attack that routed the Arab forces. Within the first hours, Israeli bombs destroyed nearly the entire Egyptian air force, annihilating their planes as they sat idle on the runway. On the ground, the Arab militaries—and especially those of Nasser's Egyptian force—proved inept. Throughout the conflict, Nasser, who had surrounded himself with sycophants and yes-men, seemed unaware of the dire situation confronting his troops and the futility of Egypt's military operations. The humiliating defeat tainted his credibility on strategic matters among Arab leaders and weakened his claim to leadership of the Arab world. For the moment, the pan-Arab threat appeared to have been quelled.

Given his aspirations as well as his alliance with Israel, the Shah was undoubtedly pleased with the outcome of the war. Nasser resigned as President of Egypt, which curtailed the Soviet Union's strategic influence in the Middle East. This gave the Shah more latitude to pursue his domestic and foreign agendas. His optimism did not last long, however. The Egyptian people reportedly demanded Nasser's reinstatement as President of Egypt. Although Nasser died of a heart attack three years later, his successor, Anwar Sadat, continued the campaign of reversing the 1967 losses. Moreover, the Soviets redoubled their efforts to resupply and rearm the Arab forces.

In 1973, Sadat joined with Syria in launching a surprise attack against the territory on the Sinai Peninsula, which had been captured by Israel. Initiated on the Jewish holiday of Yom Kippur, the holiest day of the year for Jews, the attack caused Israel to cede some of the territory it held to the invading Arab army. The conflict was now as much a regional action as a face-off between the Cold War superpowers, with the Soviets backing the Arabs and the United States supporting Israel. A massive resupply from the United States at a critical juncture in the conflict enabled Israel to regroup and counterattack.[68] Although the Soviet Union entreated Sadat to accept a ceasefire, he refused in the mistaken belief that he had the capability to defeat Israel. Eventually hostilities ended, and while neither side could objectively claim a convincing victory, neither had they provoked a larger confrontation.

Although the Shah could not appear to be pleased with the outcome, he believed himself to be in a stronger regional position than after the 1967 conflict. He had been busy in the intervening six years between the two wars. He had clamped down on domestic dissent using his powerful state security apparatus. He had also received considerable military aid from the United States, such that he possessed one of the most powerful militaries in the region.[69] Following Nasser's death and the subsequent dissolution of the pan-Arabism movement, he saw an opportunity to fill the power void in regional leadership.

During the war, the Shah had sought to profit by playing both sides while remaining officially neutral. He reasoned that an extended conflict with no decisive victor would be most beneficial to Iranian interests. Publicly, he appeared to favor the Arab cause by sending medical supplies to its armies, providing pilots to Saudi Arabia for training purposes, and allowing the Soviet air force to use Iranian airspace to ferry supplies to the Arab forces.[70] At the same time, he assisted the United States' efforts to funnel weapons to the Israelis, including small arms and heavy mortars.[71]

To the Israelis, this duplicity was a betrayal. The Shah's defiance of the Arab oil embargo or his assistance of the United States in supplying Israel with weapons meant little if Iran was also providing material aid to the Arab armies. The Shah, who had been the beneficiary of Israeli knowledge and expertise for over a decade, had abandoned them in their moment of need by assisting their enemies. At best, the Shah was a war profiteer. At worst, he was selling Israel out to enhance his claim to regional leadership. To assume the coveted role of regional powerbroker, the Shah appeared willing to abandon the Periphery Alliance.[72] Years later, a former Iranian ambassador summed up the country's position: 'We didn't have Israel as a friend to have the Arabs as enemies.'[73] Unlike the Israelis, the Shah had never embraced the idea of a shared Jewish-Persian heritage. Rather, the 1973 war demonstrated that he viewed the alliance as expendable, dependent upon fluctuating geopolitics.

In March 1975, eighteen months after the end of the Yom Kippur War, the Shah doubled down on his move away from the Israelis and toward the Arabs when he announced Iran's willingness to engage in diplomatic talks with Iraqi dictator Saddam Hussein. The two countries were not friends. They had a long-running territorial dispute between the Shatt Al Arab waterway and Khuzestan, which the Shah feared might someday become a justification for Iraq to invade Iran. More importantly, Iran and Israel had, up until the Shah's announcement, been jointly supporting an ongoing Kurdish rebellion in southern Iraq with the aim of destabilizing Saddam's regime. The effort was particularly imperative for Israel, which had used the rebellion to connect its operatives seeking to extract Iraqi Jews facing increased danger from the Baathist regime in Baghdad.[74]

In December 1975, the Shah and Saddam Hussein signed the Algiers Accord, resolving their territorial dispute and ending Iranian support of the Kurdish rebellion.[75] Israel suddenly found itself standing alone alongside the Kurds, unable to support them in their fight against the Iraqi state on its own. On behalf of an alarmed Israeli security establishment, the Israeli Defense Minister Yitzhak Rabin flew to Iran to seek a personal explanation from the Shah.[76] At least strategically, Iran's reasons for signing the accord had merit: if the Shah wanted to avoid what he saw as an otherwise inevitable war with Iraq, he had to improve relations with his neighbor. To resolve their territorial disputes, he had to stop supporting opponents of the Iraqi regime. The strategy was not without risk, which included losing the benefits of his alliance with Israel. However, the Shah had made his choice, and he effectively announced his priorities by not consulting Israel before deciding to court Iraq. Eliezer Tsafrir, the head of the Mossad in Iran, described the Shah's abandonment of the Kurds and the Israelis in favor of Saddam Hussein as akin to Chamberlain's appeasement of Hitler.[77]

From the Shah's perspective at that moment, the potential benefits appeared to outweigh the risks. He saw himself as domestically and regionally secure, and thus in a position to pursue his larger ambitions. Not only did he have conventional military might, thanks to years and years of immense expenditure on Israeli and American military hardware, but he was also now beginning to expand into the nuclear realm. Two and a half years earlier, Iran had issued its fifth five-year national development plan, in which it called for the construction of several nuclear power stations, including one on the naval base at Bandar Abbas. Officially, the program was intended purely to be a peaceful scientific and energy-related pursuit, but the Shah could not help but hint at the possibility of one day developing an Iranian bomb.[78] Without Arab intimidation or the threat of Soviet-inspired mischief, and with military and potential nuclear capability, the Shah believed he had little to lose by abandoning his relationship with the Israelis.

He demonstrated his new bravado in a 1975 interview with Egyptian journalist Mohammad Hasanein Haykal. The Shah answered a wide range of questions on numerous topics relating to Iran's foreign policy, and, for the first time, he responded directly to questions about Iran's relationship with Israel. He justified sharing military and intelligence information with Israel by claiming it was a strategic necessity for balancing the threat of Arab aggression led by Nasser. He then added, 'Now the situation has changed,'[79] implying that without Nasser's destructive influence threatening the stability of the region, Iran could reengage with its Arab neighbors based on their common religion. There was even speculation about the formation of a new regional pact in which Iran would partner with Egypt and Algeria, creating a new kind of 'moderate' pan-Arab-Iranian alliance.[80] By ending its ties with Israel and seeking an accord with Iraq, the Shah had led Iran from its regional isolation and cast himself as a powerful arbiter of stability and balance in a part of the world that had little of either.

IV. The Islamic Republic and the Jewish State

The Shah's preoccupation with his international reputation either lulled him into complacency about or altogether obscured potential domestic threats, notably the challenge posed by Ayatollah Ruhollah Khomeini. Khomeini's antagonism dated from 1953, when the CIA-backed coup d'état reinstalled the Shah as the ruler of Iran. Breaking with the tradition of clerical quietism, Khomeini became an outspoken and fiery opponent of the Shah and his policies of

Westernization and imperialism. He was particularly incensed by what he believed was a subversive infiltration by the West of Iran's Islamic culture.

The Islam preached by Khomeini included anti-Zionist rhetoric, which implied he supported a departure from the general tolerance accorded to Jews by Iran's population.[81] Iran's traditional merchant class, known as the *bazaris*, had opposed creation of a Jewish homeland in the region, invoking anti-Jewish stereotypes out of fear that a Jewish nation might challenge Iran's economic power.[82] As the *bazaris* were strong supporters of the clerics, each may have inspired the other's anti-Israel sentiments.

Khomeini used anti-Zionist messages as rhetorical devices for denouncing the Shah. He cast the Shah's cooperation with Israel and the United States as a kind of unholy and un-Islamic alliance, with all three components working hand in hand to control the Middle East, suppress popular will in Iran, and ruin the lives of Arabs. In a famous address delivered in Qom, the seat of religious power in Iran, on the eve of the Ashura holiday in June 1963, Khomeini repeatedly attacked the Shah's connections to Israel. 'Israel,' Khomeini said, 'does not wish there to be any learned men in this country. Israel does not wish the Quran to exist in this country. Israel does not wish the '*ulama* to exist in this country. Israel does not wish to see Islamic precepts in this country.' Referencing a recent attack by agents of the state on the Faiziyah religious school where Khomeini had been speaking, Khomeini accused Israel of direct participation in the assault, saying it was 'Israel that assaulted the madrasa by means of its sinister agents.' Khomeini's vitriol toward Israel continued throughout the speech, which he concluded by speculating, in true conspiratorial fashion, whether the Shah was secretly Israeli, or perhaps even Jewish.[83]

Two days after the Ashura speech, the Shah's security forces arrested Khomeini. Shortly thereafter, he was sent into exile, first in Turkey, and later Iraq and France. He continued his missives against the Shah from abroad, repeatedly citing the Shah's cooperation with the Israelis to cast him as an ineffective and un-Islamic leader, subservient to Jewish and Western interests. His supporters smuggled his lectures into Iran on cassette tapes and distributed them among the population. Khomeini's various conspiratorial narratives—which, in addition to suggestions that the Shah was secretly an Israeli, included the possibility of a mythical Israeli-Baha'i fifth column operating in Iran—fomented fear and hatred among ordinary Iranians.

Shiite clerics had long disdained the Baha'i religion, a nineteenth-century offshoot of Shia Islam, considering it a heretical faith.[84] In a 1963 communiqué, Khomeini conflated the threat from Baha'is and Jews:

> I must warn all the Muslims of the world and the nation of Iran that the Koran and Islam are in danger, and the independence of the country and its economy have fallen into the hands of the Zionists in the form of the Baha'i party. It would not take too long for them to take over the entire country and rapidly impoverish the Muslim people. Iranian television is the spy center of the Jews.[85]

Khomeini's narrative also saw the Shah's ties to America and America's support of Israel as part of an external plot against Iran. According to his account, the creation of a Jewish State in the Middle East was part of a larger American plot to partition the Islamic world. Khomeini had lots of history to work with in crafting his charges. With the Shah's popularity diminishing, the reminder of the 1953 CIA-backed coup cast America as an enemy. Moreover, in Khomeini's telling, the disclosure in 1975 of the ties between Iran and Israel returned to haunt the Shah. Khomeini accused Israel of founding and training SAVAK, the Shah's hated and feared secret police, who were engaged in spying on, imprisoning, and torturing Iranians who opposed the Shah.[86] In an interview on the eve of the Islamic Revolution, Khomeini told the French newspaper *Le Monde* that the Shah's alliance with Israel made him guilty of crimes against Islam.[87]

The Israelis were less complacent than the Shah about threats to his regime. Israeli Foreign Ministry documents from the early years of the alliance reveal concern about the emergence of Khomeini as a potentially powerful opponent of the Shah. A 1962 telegram from Israeli officials in Iran noted that Khomeini's attacks against the Shah's reforms frequently claimed that they enabled Zionist infiltration.[88] A year later, Israeli authorities again expressed alarm following Khomeini's Faiziyeh address on the eve of Ashura.[89] After the Shah exiled Khomeini in 1964 and ties between Israel and Iran grew stronger, the cleric disappeared off the Israeli radar. Like the Shah, the Israelis wrongly believed that Khomeini's exile would mitigate the threat he posed to the Shah's reign. For more than a decade, Israel stopped reporting on Khomeini's whereabouts and activities. He did not reemerge as a prominent figure of concern for Israel until shortly before the 1979 revolution.

Still, even without taking note of Khomeini, Israel's pessimism about the Shah's reliability as an ally and his future as leader of Iran deepened. In addition to his support for the Arabs in the 1973 war and his 1975 accord with Saddam Hussein, Israeli officials noted the popular dissatisfaction with the Shah's authoritarian rule. Khomeini's reemergence in official Israeli documents coincided with reports of the Shah's deteriorating physical and mental health.[90] The top Israeli diplomat in Iran, Uri Lubrani, wrote in a report to the Foreign Ministry that '[The Shah] is not the same man that we once knew, remote, sometimes astray. There's no doubt that the man is undergoing a nightmare … and what's most worrying is the feeling that he is resigned to his fate.'[91]

As popular protests against the Shah reached a fever pitch in December 1978, Israelis in Iran went into full lockdown. They feared for their safety as Khomeini's rhetoric fostered intense anti-Israeli sentiment. One senior foreign ministry official described the dire state of relations, writing,

> The extreme religious leader Khomeini's remarks in regards to [sic] the Israeli issue have turned scathing as of late. His view that Israeli soldiers are helping the Shah is well known, and that Israelis are coming to Iran to replace the striking oil industry workers, and therefore their blood is permissible [to shed].[92]

As the situation worsened, Israelis scrambled to plan for the evacuation of their facilities in Iran and the exfiltration of their nationals.

Unquestionably, the Islamic Revolution marked a fundamental change in Iranian-Israeli relations, although at the time, and in the midst of so much turmoil, many questions remained. While Khomeini's rhetoric signaled an abrupt end to formal ties, Israeli officials had no clear picture of Khomeini's intentions. His avowed support for the Palestinians could translate into military action,[93] or he might instead realize some need for covert contacts with Israel. In the immediate aftermath, it was unclear whether Khomeini and his religious fundamentalist supporters could even form a stable government or whether some reactionary or moderating force would emerge to temper or even possibly reverse the revolution. Whatever the future reality, Iran now publicly considered Israel an enemy.

Predictably, Israelis also viewed an Iran ruled by Islamic fundamentalists as an enemy. To most Israelis, who had little knowledge of prerevolutionary Iran or the secret alliance, the consequential change was the new regime's militant support of the Palestinian cause. The absence of historical perspective undermined Israel's predictive capacity.[94] Israeli leaders and analysts had considerable leeway in interpreting events and ascribing motives to Iranian leaders, and, as such, they offered different explanations. One version held that the revolution revealed the 'true' Iranian identity: Islamists driven by hatred of Jews and Israel. Others maintained that it was too early to form expectations. The initial narrative had important implications for interpreting subsequent Iranian actions. For example, some would later assert that Iran's nuclear development program was an inevitable extension of the fervor unleashed by the Islamic Revolution.[95]

In fact, far from creating solidarity, the Islamic Revolution initiated considerable turmoil in Iran and disrupted relationships with other countries. Not surprisingly, the revolutionary coalition that had ousted the Shah quickly fell apart as rival political factions vied for power. As they debated the provisions and ratification of a new constitution, they fought over the structure of the government and the extent of the clerics' power.[96] Eventually, Khomeini and his religious allies gained the upper hand and moved to consolidate control over the most powerful political institutions. They also hastily convened revolutionary courts and paraded their political opponents through show trials.[97] By executing or imprisoning officials from the

Shah's reign, they purged their political enemies from their new government and from the country.

The chaos left in limbo the Jews who had resisted Israeli entreaties to flee as well as American offers of assistance. While many left, those remaining hoped that Khomeini might temper his anti-Semitic conspiracy theory accusations by distinguishing Iranian Jews from Israelis.[98] When he secured his leadership, however, Khomeini did not abandon his attacks on the Iranian Jewish community. Revolutionary authorities arrested several Jewish leaders during their initial purges. The most infamous case involved Habib Elghanian, who was sentenced to death in 1979 for 'treason by maintaining a connection with Israel and Zionism.'[99] In response, Israel issued only a terse statement of condemnation. It sounded both nostalgic and a bit hopeful, stating that 'there has never been a conflict of interest between the State of Israel and Iran, irrespective of the regime in various periods.'[100] Remarkably, despite these notable and often violent exceptions, Khomeini moved to assure Iran's Jews that he would not harm them based upon their religion, nor did he intend to interfere with the community's practice of Judaism.[101]

The effect of the political shockwave in Iran was exacerbated when taken in the context of Israel's recent political watershed. It was not inconsequential that the Islamic Revolution occurred two years after the Israelis had elected the first non-Labor government in their nation's history. The victory of the right-wing Likud party not only represented a dramatic political change, it brought to the seat of prime minister a former terrorist and reactionary in the form of Menachem Begin. Begin, who had been a member of the underground Irgun movement that had fought the British and Palestinians to secure Israel's independence, was considerably more hawkish than his predecessors. He believed that military conflict with Israel's neighbors was the inevitable result of centuries of tension between Muslims and Jews. This belief in the intractability of regional conflict made him less inclined to negotiate with the Palestinians and skeptical about peace initiatives with the surrounding Arab states.[102]

Keeping in character with his suspicious view of Israel's Muslim-majority neighbors, Begin was thus unwilling to give the new Islamic Republic the benefit of the doubt regarding its intentions. When

Khomeini, in his initial diplomatic act, offered the vacated Israeli embassy building in Iran to the Palestine Liberation Organization, Begin was not shy in criticizing the move. Acknowledging the provocation, he called it an 'alliance between two phenomena of blind, deep hate,' and he urged Israelis to 'grasp and appreciate what it is we face, what kind of enemy we confront.'[103] He took to referring to the revolutionaries as 'Khomeini's mob,' even using the epithet in a toast at an April 1980 White House dinner hosted by President Jimmy Carter.[104]

Begin's toast that evening was more than a critique of the Iranians; it was an implicit criticism of what he considered the United States' passivity in response to American citizens being held as hostages by Iran. After the United States had admitted the deposed Shah for medical treatment at an American hospital, Iranian students had stormed the American embassy in Tehran, taking the remaining staff as hostages. Five months into the crisis, when Begin gave his toast at the White House, he noted that the United States, unlike Russia, was trying 'every avenue, accepting patience and pain' to free the hostages.[105] Later, in an interview with ABC television, Begin elaborated on his disapproval by imagining how Russia would have responded in the same situation: 'They would have marched on Tehran and captured it.' He claimed that a military intervention would have succeeded 'because the Khomeini army is no match to any other army at all. It's a mob, an armed mob, but still a mob.' To make his point perfectly clear, Begin then mocked the United States: 'As for Iran—the Americans are humiliated. This great nation, with all the massive power at its disposal, feels itself to be humiliated and does not know what to do.'[106]

Israeli officials, taking their cue from Begin, continued to direct an aggressive war of words at Iran even as Khomeini secured his grip on power. Notably, their critiques often took the form of personal insults and references to cultural stereotypes. For example, Defense Minister Ariel Sharon—who would two decades later become Israel's prime minister—told the *Wall Street Journal* in 1982 that Iran's approach to warfare was 'naïve,' and he spoke of Iranians as 'all these Mongols riding horses.'[107] Two years later, Sharon's successor as defense minister, Moshe Arens, labeled Iran as one of the Middle

East's four 'mad regimes,' the others being Libya, Syria, and Iraq.[108] As the American hostage crisis dragged on, some Israeli officials expressed sympathy for the United States, while at the same time demonizing the Iranians as immoral savages. In a January 1981 speech to the World Jewish Congress, Foreign Minister Yitzhak Shamir noted that 'Israelis understood the pain and fear of hostages being held by inhuman beings.'[109]

On 22 September 1980, Iraq invaded Iran. In a serious miscalculation, Iraqi President Saddam Hussein believed that the leadership struggle in the new Islamic Republic rendered Iran vulnerable to Iraqi expansionism.[110] But rather than securing a quick victory, Saddam's troops met with fierce opposition from the Iranians. For a second time, Iranians of all walks of life rallied around Khomeini in defense of their nation. Initially, the Iranians were able to reverse the tide of the war and push the Iraqi invaders back. But, rather than sue for peace, the Iranian military—spurred on by their leader's religious fervor—pressed their luck. Now it was Khomeini's turn for miscalculation. Sensing strength and momentum in the Iranian war effort, Khomeini employed his charisma and crafted a martial narrative aimed at justifying an invasion of Iraq. His massive counterattack initiated an eight-year struggle that cost hundreds of thousands of lives and ended in a stalemate.

For Israel, the war was an unsettlingly positive development. Two large and menacing Muslim-majority countries fighting one another meant that they were distracted from attacking the Jewish State. However, the looming threat of a victory by one side threatened to upend the regional power structure, creating a constant sense of impending instability. Menachem Begin publicly described the conflict as a 'very dangerous event' that 'concerns Israel because it is in the periphery of the Middle East.' Years into the war, when the Labor Party resumed a role in Israel's government,[111] Defense Minister Yitzhak Rabin was more open about the advantages of a prolonged war. He observed,

> Iraq is tied down in its war with Iran, and there is no doubt that the lengthy war, which is now entering its seventh year, has exacted a high price in human lives, and in terms of Iraq's

national morale and its economy, and its end is not yet in sight. Even if it ends, tension will remain. It's hard for me to see Iraq being anxious for an additional military adventure against Israel after such a long and wearing war.[112]

Even as the war continued, Israel needed to calculate its strategic interests in different outcomes. An Iraqi victory was likely to provide Saddam with additional territory and more access to natural resources while increasing his regional power. It could also validate the military prowess of the Iraqi army, emboldening the leadership to pursue other military objectives. On the other side, the consequences of an Iranian victory were less clear, but also risky for Israel. Khomeini's vitriolic rhetoric and the idea that the extremist elements of his government might seek to extend their victory unnerved Israeli leadership. In particular, they worried about Iran's support for the Palestinian Liberation Organization and other anti-Israel organizations, as well as Khomeini's vow to 'export' the Islamic Revolution beyond Iran's borders. Israel feared that its regional presence would become even more uncomfortable if other Muslim-majority states followed Iran's path toward theocratic governance. Hence, Israel faced the proverbial conundrum: an Iraqi victory would embolden a known historical enemy state, while Iran's triumph would subject Israel to an emerging enemy state with uncertain motives.

Israel's calculations eventually led it to side with Iran for several reasons. Despite the rhetoric coming from Iran's new theocratic rulers, Israeli officials viewed Iran as the lesser of the two evils. They reasoned that, if Iran was fighting for survival, it might not have the luxury of engaging in anything more than a rhetorical war with Israel. Somewhat more optimistically, Israeli strategists believed that their shared Iraqi threat might even create space to develop a back-channel relationship with their erstwhile Iranian allies. By contrast, Iraq was, according to Defense Minister Ariel Sharon, the foremost 'extremist' state in the region. Sharon explained that this assessment did not mean Israel was comfortable with Iran, but rather that, while Iran posed the larger strategic challenge, the Iraqis were by far the greater threat.[113]

Inherent to Sharon's assessment was another influential factor, namely uncertainty regarding the future of postrevolutionary Iran. In Israel, few senior defense and security officials had much knowledge of Iran, and scholarship focusing on the modern nation was sparse. Both the distribution of power within the government and the depth of the debate in the decision-making process were limited. According to Ronen Cohen, a professor at Ariel University who has written several books on Iran, there was some academic debate about the logic of supporting Iran, but the future of Israel's relationship with Iran was never discussed in government forums.[114] Yossi Alpher, a young officer in the Mossad at the time, confirms the dearth of knowledge about Iran in the halls of Israel's military and intelligence services. In the introduction to his book on the history of the Periphery Alliance, he describes how following the revolution he was assigned Mossad's Iran Desk, despite having no prior experience with the country.[115]

The Israeli public similarly had little understanding of Iran's internal dynamics and its future position vis-à-vis Israel. In his study of Israeli 'Iranophobia,' Haggai Ram posited that Israelis were confused by the Islamic Revolution and its aftermath.[116] As a people who had thrown off colonial rule, Israelis were initially quite sympathetic to a revolutionary ouster of an oppressive monarchy, believing that such change could be progressive. Filtering the uprising through their own independence narrative in which their nation had achieved modernization and democratic governance, they could hope that Iran's 'popular' movement would create openings for more liberal forms of government, including a possible democracy.[117] Ironically, Ram speculates that Israelis were slower to recognize the negative consequences associated with the clerics' consolidation of power due to blind spots with regard to their own experience following the election of a conservative Likud government two years prior. They had not seen, for example, how Israel's leaders—once a bastion of secularism and socialist values—were slowly becoming more beholden to policy demands from Israel's religious establishment.[118]

Whether because of or despite the absence of knowledge about present-day Iran and its future, once Israelis realized the danger of a revolutionary theocratic government taking hold, they hoped that the Khomeini government would be only a temporary holdover until something more stable, and potentially more enlightened, emerged. While wishful thinking is human nature, in Israel's case it was grounded in experience. Since the founding of the state, Israelis faced a continuing struggle between those who would impose theocratic governance and those who maintained a secular Judaism. Israel had muddled through the tensions while maintaining fealty to democratic values and international alliances. So too, they believed, would Iranians reject theocratic dictates that disrupted their lives and hindered the nation's advantageous international ties.

Yossi Alpher coined the term 'Periphery nostalgia' to describe Israelis' rose-tinted visions of their past. He explained that the term referred to

> The presumption that because Iran has historic tensions with the Arab world and because one Iranian regime, that of the Shah, seemingly aligned itself strategically with Israel over the course of two decades, this pattern of alliance and shared strategic interests must through some form of historical determination or strategic norm, continue to manifest itself in Israel's relations with Iran.[119]

Such nostalgia, however, created a cognitive bias that engendered a false understanding of the situation and prevented Israelis from recognizing their own ignorance.

Understandably, those Israelis who had had the closest ties to the Shah's regime experienced the strongest cognitive dissonance. This cohort included representatives from powerful organizations at the top levels of government, intelligence agencies, the military, and the business community who, based upon their experience, opined that the new theocratic dictator did not represent the feelings or interests of the 'true' Iran. They argued that Israel should somehow seek to maintain the Periphery Doctrine, including information exchange and economic development assistance, despite the temporary regime change. In a true act of fanciful thinking, Ariel Sharon even put forth a plan to reinstall the Shah with the help of the Israeli military.[120] The Iran-Iraq War kept alive the hopes of a continued Israel-Iran relationship. Thus, Israel determined it was in their best interest to help supply the Iranians with arms in their fight against Iraq, and as late as 1986 Israeli Defense Minister Yitzhak Rabin justified the continued shipments by claiming that Iran was 'Israel's best friend.'[121] Of course, it helped that some Israelis were realizing considerable profits from the arms sales. Israeli investigative reporter Ronen Bergman explained that 'More than anything else, the weapons industry wanted to make money.'[122] According to Bergman, when Israel commenced its secret sales to Iran, one military official told him that there was never a discussion of the ethics of these weapons sales, or what they would mean politically for Israel if the deals became public.

Israel's role in transferring weapons to the Islamic Republic eventually came to light as part of what became known as the Iran-Contra Affair. A full exploration of this scandal goes beyond the scope of this book, but Israel's role in creating the plan and facilitating the process is worthy of consideration in light of what it reveals about Israel's relationship with Iran after the revolution.

The scandal, which involved the sale of American arms to Iran in exchange for the release of American hostages held in Lebanon, as well as the use of the proceeds by the United States to fund an anti-communist guerilla insurgency in Nicaragua, was the biggest foreign policy crisis of President Ronald Reagan's administration. The Israeli government did not participate extensively in the public hearings in the United States that followed the disclosure of the program, nor did it hold a hearing of its own. In his autobiography published after he left office, Reagan wrote that the idea for the weapons transfers had originally come from the Israelis. He called Israel the 'prime mover' of this arrangement, stating that the Israelis had promised that the weapons would only be supplied to Iranian 'moderates' and not to Khomeini hardliners.[123] Reagan's personal account is likely self-serving, but the congressional report on the affair at least partially corroborates his claim. In addition to the release of American hostages, the Israelis had suggested that providing arms to the Iranians could potentially bring with it the prospect of improved American relations with Iran.[124]

Ultimately, the initiative proved unsuccessful at either securing the release of the hostages or improving US-Iran relations.[125]

Nevertheless, the Israelis were so eager to continue selling arms to the Iranians that they offered to accept full responsibility, as well as to absorb all financial and material losses should the plan not succeed. The Israelis' magnanimity effectively offered to indemnify the United States against any negative repercussions should the arrangement come to light. US Secretary of State George Schultz pointed out to National Security Advisor Robert McFarlane that Israel, unlike the United States, had no policy against selling arms to Iran, and that, given the hostility of most of its neighbors, Israel might be more willing to gamble on the prospect of future changes in the Iranian government.[126]

At the same time, Israel's motivations included a desire to maintain the conflict between Iran and Iraq for as long as possible. While the United States and Israel were both eager to avoid a decisive victory by either side, the Israelis further hoped that the fighting would drain the resources of two of their publicly identifiable 'enemies,' thereby reducing the possibility that either would redirect their hostility toward Israel once hostilities ceased.[127]

The protracted war between Iraq and Iran ended in 1988 when the United Nations brokered a ceasefire and sent peacekeepers to enforce it. After eight years of fighting, the combatants had achieved little except for sustaining millions of casualties. Each side retreated to their prewar borders. Ironically, while Saddam Hussein's invasion of Iran had sought to exploit the instability of the new regime, he actually contributed to saving it.

Khomeini's capacity to rally the Iranian people to repel the Iraqi invasion solidified his power. His subsequent ill-fated invasion of Iraq, which prolonged the conflict, did not undermine his leadership. Instead, fueled by memories of Iraqi atrocities—which had included chemical weapons attacks—and angered by the United States supporting their enemy, the Iranian people supported government efforts to secure the nation from future threats. They approved efforts to rebuild the Iranian military and strengthen defense capabilities. At the same time, they feared that Iraq might develop nuclear weapons.[128]

For Israel, the war did not last long enough. Although the war initially helped Khomeini secure his leadership, the Israelis calculated that a long and costly conflict would eventually destabilize the government and lead to an internal revolt. Not only did this not happen, but both Khomeini and Saddam Hussein remained in power. Moreover, Saddam appeared to have the capacity to rebuild Iraq's nuclear capacity, as well as to expand its chemical and biological weapons program.[129]

Unexpectedly, Iran soon posed an even greater threat than Iraq. The country had developed a new military apparatus, known as the Iranian Revolutionary Guards Corps (IRGC), whose members were committed to enforcing the fundamentalist religious principles of the Islamic Revolution. The IRGC assumed both the principal police and military functions throughout the country. It supplanted the traditional army, which had included the Israeli-friendly officer corps from the days of imperial Iran. Most of those men, who had personal or professional contacts among the Israelis, or had engaged in exchanges with the Jewish State, had died or been killed in battle or purges. For members of the IRGC, opposing Israel and exporting the Islamic revolution were core values.

Iran focused on Lebanon as an initial target for securing a regional foothold, in particular the Israeli-occupied south. Israel invaded South Lebanon in 1982 during the Lebanese civil war in order to expel the PLO forces operating in the area. Allied with Christian militia forces, they established a buffer zone between Lebanese and Israeli territory.[130] Iran commenced to exploit residents' discontent with an oppressive occupation, the predominantly Shiite region providing fertile recruiting ground for Iranian agents looking to support coreligionist opposition groups. Iran gradually extended its influence over the Hezbollah and Amal organizations by providing them with weapons, training, and logistical support for their fight against the Israelis. Meanwhile, Israel appeared to underestimate this developing threat on its northern border as it struggled to maintain control over the local population.[131]

For Israel to acknowledge Iran as a 'real,' and not merely rhetorical, enemy meant that many of its government officials and analysts had miscalculated the significance of the Islamic Revolution and its aftermath. Israel's support of Iran during its war with Iraq had not produced the hoped-for moderation in Iran's opposition to

Israel's existence. On the contrary, with the war over, Iran engaged in arming paramilitary groups hostile to Israel while it openly embraced the Palestinian cause. Moreover, Iran's active opposition to Israel created a shared interest with countries in the region, with which it otherwise had little in common. Clearly, Israel and Iran had begun a new chapter of their history.

V. Conclusion

The messy and erratic history of the relationship between Persians and Jews and Israel and Iran is as much a story about the actions of external forces as it is about choices made by the nations' leaders. From ancient times through the founding of the Islamic Republic, there was never any consistent narrative that made the next development obvious or inevitable. Not even the geopolitical and religious conflicts between the two nations and peoples fit within conventional historical understanding. The Persians did not oppress the Jews; the Iranians were not part of the pan-Arabist Soviet-supported orbit. Both peoples had a long, proud, and distinct heritage that did not include a legacy of enmity toward one another.

Key parts of the history of Israeli-Iranian interaction are not well known. The mythical story of the Persian king and his Jewish queen is a book of the Hebrew Bible. Similarly, the chronicles of Cyrus's patronage on behalf of his Jewish subjects are detailed in Jewish historical accounts, meriting only passing mentions in general histories of the period. During the twentieth century, Iran and Israel conducted their Periphery Alliance, by which the new state of Israel and the re-enthroned Shah secretly helped one another enhance their nations' security and economies. The two nations' cooperation is a testament both to how states engage in mutually beneficial cooperation, and to how public rhetoric may contradict private relations.

History is always important as a descriptive record of events that contributes to our present. It aids our understanding of why events happen and produce particular consequences. When historical accounts are incomplete or inaccurate, their value is not only diminished, but they can also be misused. Such is the challenge presented by the history of Israel's relationship with Iran. History would suggest that the new Israeli state might develop a working relationship with a non-Arab state on the periphery of a hostile region. Israeli officials thus endowed the alliance with historical significance and miscalculated the strength of Iran's commitment. Few had studied Iran's own history or uncovered the nuances that would influence its future development and inform its international relations.

The chapters that follow detail how Israeli officials revised their understanding of the historical relationship as Israel and Iran became increasingly fierce enemies. Eventually, the new version of their relations would serve as the backdrop for a narrative that cast Iran as an existential threat to Israel. The power of the narrative detailing this threat obscured Israeli officials' absence of knowledge, mistakes in foresight, and misreading of Iranian intentions. In this version of history, the Islamic Republic is the modern incarnation of Israel's historic enemies.

3

POLITICS
EMPLOYING THE THREAT

I. Introduction

It is notable that Israel and the Islamic Republic have never engaged in a hot war.[1] For decades, their leaders have hurled murderous insults at one another; their officials have engaged in a war of words; they have recruited and trained effective military forces; and they have inflicted damage on one another using proxies, yet their animosity has never escalated to the scale of full-fledged military conflict. While this does not make their enmity unique, it does necessitate a deeper look into their hostility toward one another so as to understand how their conflict has shaped each other's perspectives and policies.

In terms of historical parallels, the Israel-Iran conflict contains some similarities to the Cold War. The United States and the Soviet Union cast one another as existential threats that justified the investment of massive resources in maintaining a continuous war readiness, expanding political and military advantages, and engaging in nuclear brinksmanship. Unlike the superpowers' standoff, which emerged from the ashes of World War II, the origins of the Israel-Iran conflict are not as obvious. Theirs is not a competition to extend territorial and ideological hegemony into the same geographical space, nor is it a global struggle that extends into every conflict in every corner of the globe.[2] In fact, as many commentators have noted, Iran and Israel have no significant strategic interests that overlap.[3] Moreover, they both share an animosity to Sunni terrorist organizations, including Al Qaeda and the Islamic State of Iraq and Syria (ISIS), which could have, at least theoretically, provided some basis for strategic coordination.

It is also notable that their enmity has been largely asymmetrical. Each country has vilified the other, but this has rarely occurred with the same intensity on both sides. The difference has been most pronounced in recent years, in which Israel's security posture and international relations strategy has been reoriented to deal almost exclusively with the Iranian threat. The same is true for the policy focus of each state's leaders. Israel's fear of Iran penetrates deeper into its policymaking than Iran's concern with Israel, even though, of the two 'combatants' in this conflict, only Israel currently possesses nuclear weapons capability. Iran, meanwhile, continues to espouse its familiar anti-Zionist refrain, usually in relation to issues related to Palestinian rights, but its leaders stop short of calling for military operations, regime change, or all-out war.[4]

This chapter examines how Israel's foreign policy evolved from viewing Iran as a peripheral threat to treating it as a primary strategic challenge. Building upon the history examined in Chapter 2, I analyze how the conduct and messages of Israel's political leaders and intellectual elites have framed Iran as an existential threat to Israel's nationhood. The basis for this study is the public record, in particular the words and media reports that comprise the narrative defining the threat to Israel posed by Iran. I submit that analysis of this material, composed for Israel's domestic public and for Western international audiences, reveals how leaders generated the support for an Iranian threat narrative built in larger part upon a social and political construct as opposed to a realistic threat of annihilation.

As a preliminary matter, it is curious that there is no consensus on the origins of their conflict. Some Israeli experts have sought to identify an event that marked the beginning, a transformative moment that marked the end of the era of Israeli-Iranian cooperation and the plunge into enmity.[5] For many, the obvious choice was the

Islamic Revolution's installation of a theocracy avowedly dedicated to the destruction of Israel. Although disproved by the arms sales during the Iran-Iraq War, this explanation has gained acceptance over time as Israel's hostility toward Iran has intensified and memories have faded. It is, however, an incomplete explanation; it relies upon words but does not take into account the actual behavior of the players involved. As the previous chapter details, although the Islamic Republic's first Supreme Leader, Ayatollah Ruhollah Khomeini, excoriated Israel for supporting the Shah and oppressing the Palestinians, he also readily accepted its military assistance in his war against Iraq.[6] While Khomeini considered the Jewish State to be a foe, he did not consider it as great a threat as the hostile, aggressive, Sunni-led Baathist nation equipped with a powerful military situated along Iran's western border. Similarly, Israel's leaders calculated that Iran was less threatening than Iraq, as evinced by their decision to provide assistance to a country led by a ruler with a lengthy history of denouncing Israel. The Islamic Revolution signaled a dramatic change in the status quo and created uncertainty about the future, to be sure, but arguably the strategic concerns that had brought the two nations together still existed, even in the wake of the Shah's demise and the end of the Periphery era.

It is questionable whether there is value in finding the precise historical moment,[7] but, if we were to try, it is notable that the candidates for a genesis point almost always involve a moment in which Iran is actively threatening Israel, the Jewish people, or global stability. For example, some experts point to bombings perpetrated by Iran-supported surrogates, singling out such high-profile attacks as the 1992 bombing of the Israeli Embassy in Argentina or the 1994 bombing of the Asociación Mutual Israelita Argentina building. Others offer a vaguer explanation, suggesting that the official and unofficial ties severed by the Islamic Revolution simply withered away over time.[8] One influential Israeli politician cited Iran's decision to train and supply Hezbollah and Amal forces in Lebanon beginning in the 1980s.[9] Others, still, argue that the permanent severance of a relationship came with the resurrection of Iran's nuclear program in the early 1990s, or perhaps its public revelation a decade later.[10] One Israeli investigative journalist argues that the enmity between the two nations predates the news of Iran's nuclear program going public. Still others claim that the 2006 Lebanon War and subsequent events served as a 'wake up call' for Israelis to the secret war Israel had been fighting with Iran over the course of several decades.[11]

Iran's postrevolutionary words and deeds indisputably represent a break with its past policies regardless of the particular moment. More significant to understanding Iran's confrontational posture with Israel are the reasons for the present hostility. Despite its prominence in the current international relations discourse, very few scholars have studied this conflict in isolation. There are two notable extant theories that attempt to identify a specific genesis. One advanced by Trita Parsi holds that the convergence in 1991 of the dissolution of the Soviet Union and the American-led defeat of Saddam Hussein created a power vacuum in the Middle East, which in turn caused Israel to restructure its threat perception and reorient it around the Iranian threat.[12] The second is Haggai Ram's psychology-based argument that the Israeli fear of Iran—and, hence, the Iran-Israel conflict—flowed from Israel's Ashkenazi Jewish majority perceiving the non-European Mizrachi population as a threat to their hold on power. Ram maintains that the Ashkenazi establishment projected their fear of losing power onto Iran, which subsequently proliferated into the current conflict.[13] For our purposes, Ram's reasoning is less important than the idea that the conflict originated within Israelis' collective psyche rather than from specific actions taken by Iran.

I believe that while both scholars contribute to our understanding, neither of these theories provides a full explanation, especially considering recent turmoil. Parsi correctly identifies that the early 1990s were a key turning point for Israel's framing of its security concerns, both regionally and specifically vis-à-vis Iran. Ram's argument that fear, rather than rational strategic thinking, was a principal driver of Israel's decision to identify Iran as a top security threat also has merit. The missing element in the discussion is how each nation's leaders, operating within internal political and cultural frameworks, constructed narratives of the 'other' as a potential combatant. This characterization then drove development of their respective national foreign policies.

II. The Emergence of the Threat Narrative

Despite Israeli leadership's disappointment that the Iran-Iraq War had ended, the end of hostilities received little attention among Israelis, although it raised considerable uncertainty about the future of the region and their own security. Remarkably, a nearby war that had lasted eight years and caused millions of casualties had little effect on Israelis' daily lives. The disclosure that Israel was selling weapons to Iran in the middle of the war caused a minor stir, but ultimately it catalyzed no public debate over the wisdom of the decision to do so in the first place. Defense Minister Rabin had once characterized the conflict between Iran and Iraq as a 'balance of threat,' in which the best outcome for Israel would be a 'no win situation.'[14] Although in the end neither side did win, at least in the technical sense of the term, in Israel's viewpoint the end of fighting spelled the end of the 'distraction' that had kept them from potentially targeting their true sworn enemy, Israel.

One reason the war's end was peripheral to Israel's concerns was that Israelis were at that moment far more preoccupied with the security challenges within and along their borders. The initiation of the first Palestinian Intifada in December 1987, a year before the end of the Iran-Iraq War, surprised most Israelis. Beginning as a leaderless and disorganized uprising, it grew into a sustained campaign of civil disobedience, public protest, and, eventually, acts of violence that would disrupt Israeli life for the next six years. Importantly, it created an immediate and imminent sense of personal insecurity among Israelis, who felt they could at any moment be victims of a random terrorist attack.

At the same time, the Israeli army was still engaged in military operations in South Lebanon. Israel had inserted itself into the Lebanese civil war in 1982 when it invaded and occupied southern Lebanon seeking to root out Palestinian Liberation Organization (PLO) operations there. It continued its advance northward, stopping just short of the capital Beirut. Although by the late 1980s the Israeli Defense Forces (IDF) had withdrawn to a small strip of land along Israel's northern border, it remained an occupying force that was heavily enmeshed in the daily lives of Lebanese citizens.[15]

Together with its ally the South Lebanese Army, a Christian militia, the IDF had control over nearly 100,000 Lebanese civilians, the vast majority of whom were Shiite Muslims.[16] Although the IDF had been originally welcomed as liberators upon their arrival in 1982, their sustained presence and apparent disregard for religious customs sparked fierce resistance and drove many new recruits into the ranks of budding resistance movements such as Amal and Hezbollah. Hezbollah, in particular, enjoyed significant backing from Iran, including financing, materiel, and training support.[17] In November 1988, amidst the ongoing turmoil, Israel held national elections in which Prime Minister Yitzhak Shamir and his Likud Party narrowly held on to power by winning a razor-thin plurality.[18]

The Islamic Republic may have been a nascent problem in South Lebanon, but during this time Israel was not paying much attention to the domestic goings-on in Iran itself which included the first—and, to date, only—Supreme Leadership transition in the revolutionary regime's history. On 3 June 1989, less than a year after the end of the war with Iraq, the Islamic Republic's Supreme Leader and founder Ayatollah Khomeini died. Knowing that Khomeini was in declining health, officials had prepared a succession plan that called for the elevation of President Ali Khamenei to the position of Supreme Leader.[19] In elections held the following month, voters chose Akbar Hashemi Rafsanjani to replace Khamenei as president.[20] Initially, Israelis had no reason to see the change of leaders as a significant shift in Iran's policies or attitudes toward Israel. They knew Khamenei to be a fiery, hardline cleric, who shared the fundamentalist conservatism of his predecessor, but his views on Israel were not well known on the world stage.[21] Presumably, his close ties with his predecessor meant that Khamenei shared Khomeini's view of Israel as an illegitimate state that was usurping Palestinian lands and oppressing Muslims throughout the region, but this view was not unique for a leader of a Muslim nation during the late 1980s.

Israel got a sense of the direction of the new Iranian leadership when it learned of the Islamic Republic's plans to host a gathering of representatives from Fattah, Hezbollah, Amal, and the Popular Front for the Liberation of Palestine. Dubbed the 'terror summit' by Israeli officials and the press, Israel feared that the gathering in

Tehran with the new Supreme Leader aimed to formulate a unified strategy for confronting Israel, prompting predictions of doom and gloom stemming from an impending 'terror wave' that would wash over Israel in the near future.[22] Such predictions of Iranian-inspired mayhem would become more commonplace in years to come.

Iran, however, was sending confusing signals on the world stage. While the Supreme Leader planned for the convening of his summit, President Rafsanjani called for improved relations with the West. What did it mean for the religious leader to strategize on alliances with armed groups accused of terrorist acts while the elected leader signaled an interest in improving the nation's international standing? For some Israelis, it suggested at least the possibility of a back-channel opening. Quietly, officials began to explore the possibility for a resurrection of cooperation with Iran based on a mutual-enemy strategy. Iran still feared Iraq, believing that Saddam Hussein was continuing to stockpile chemical and biological weapons. Israeli officials, too, suspected Saddam of having hostile intentions, harboring fears that the Iraqi strongman might someday decide to attack their country. Thus, according to Israel's security and political establishment—including elements of the country's political right—Israel would benefit from Iran's normalization of relations with the West. Such a development would grant Israel a modicum of protection from Iraq while providing Israel's allies with leverage to restrain Iranian aggression. As the *Jerusalem Post* editorialized, 'A strong, stable Iran is the best available antidote to Iraqi threats.'[23]

Israel's decision to reengage made more sense once it emerged that Israel had not actually severed all ties with Iran, even after the Iran-Iraq War. In December 1989, the US State Department revealed that Israel had quietly resumed purchasing oil from Iran. The deal—arranged by Uri Lubrani, an Israeli Defense Ministry official who had been head of mission in Tehran during the last days of the Shah—meant that the two countries were continuing the tacit economic cooperation they had developed during the war. In a continuation of the logic that had partially driven the Iran-Contra affair, the strategy also enabled Israelis to hope that they could secure Iran's help in facilitating the release of IDF hostages being held in Lebanon by Hezbollah and Amal.

The disclosure of the oil sale produced several different public narratives, each meant for a different audience. Iranian elites wanted to assure the world of its enduring enmity toward Israel. *The Tehran Times*, Iran's English daily, ran an inflammatory story decrying the sale of oil to the Zionists and pledging that 'enmity will continue as long as this cancer exists in the heartland of the Islamic Land.'[24] By contrast, Israeli leaders cited the sales as evidence of a difference between Iran's public rhetoric and strategic interests. Defense Minister Rabin implied that the only barrier to economic cooperation with Iran was the latter's attitude, which could be surmounted. He did not think that Iran's boycott of Israeli products meant that they would refuse to use Israeli weapons.[25] Significantly, he did not voice concern that Iran might someday use these weapons against Israel.

As the twentieth century entered its final decade, the public enmity between Israel and Iran was mostly asymmetrical. While Iran's rhetoric was far more belligerent, its strategic interests did not appear to include initiating active confrontation with Israel. The Israelis were engaged with other foes, and Iran—despite its public and, in some cases, material support for some of these enemies—did not merit much attention, let alone any kind of threat narrative that the general public would understand, much less worry about in existential terms. Rather, there remained the hope among Israeli political and military elites that, despite Iran's inflammatory rhetoric, there might still be avenues of cooperation open for the mutual benefit of the two nations.

If the Iranian threat narrative in Israel has a distinct birth date, it is 20 January 1993.[26] On that day, a tendentious public exchange by Israel's highest officials indicated that all hope of cooperation between Israel and Iran was lost. The drama began when Labor Minister Ephraim Sneh[27] rose in the Knesset to pose a parliamentary question about Iran to Prime Minister Rabin. This question designated Iran as a concern separate and apart from that posed by other states of the region, implying that Iran had become one of Israel's most disconcerting adversaries, one that deserved prioritization among the nation's security threats.

Notably, Sneh became the first Israeli government official to use the phrase 'existential threat' (איום קיומי) to describe the magnitude of the danger posed by Iran. From the Knesset floor, Sneh methodically outlined a case against Iran as an enemy that Israel 'can't ignore.' He identified three characteristics that made the country a danger to Israel: its ideology, its efforts to spread its influence regionally and globally, and its desire to acquire weapons of mass destruction. In support of the latter claim, he cited statements made by CIA director Robert Gates. Finally, Sneh raised the issue of Israel's newly discovered vulnerability by invoking the memory of Saddam's cruise missile attacks as evidence of what a remote but dangerous tyrant with a 'lack of inhibition' is capable of doing. Addressing the Iran threat, he maintained, went beyond economic concerns: 'To us, this is not a matter of oil, it is a matter of blood.'[28]

The prime minister's response did not challenge Sneh's claims, although he sounded a more cautious note. He too believed that Iran was pursuing purchase of nuclear weapons as well as beginning to develop its own nuclear industry, but he characterized the danger as somewhat less immediate. Instead, Rabin presented Iran as a medium- to long-term threat. While he acknowledged that Iran held the potential to become more dangerous than Iraq, he added a caveat: while Israel was right to be concerned about these developments, Rabin noted, it would be wise not to allow Iran to inhibit Israel's ultimate foreign policy goal of advancing the cause of regional peace.[29]

Rabin's Knesset speech represented a change in his public position as an advocate for engagement with Iran. In 1987, Rabin had portrayed Iran as Israel's natural geopolitical ally.[30] Two years later, he had defended Israel's decision to do business with Iran following the disclosure that Israel had been secretly purchasing oil from the Islamic Republic.[31] Now, with recent developments suggesting that interaction between the two countries was politically inadvisable, Rabin pivoted to a position foreclosing future engagement. Although he admitted the threat from Iran was not imminent, he nonetheless prioritized it in Israel's security matrix.[32] Iran was no longer peripheral to Israel's existence. As Yossi Alpher later observed, Rabin's shift in tone was the highest-profile indication that Israel had finally shed its nostalgia for the Iran of the Periphery era.[33]

The policy change implied the need for a different depiction of Iranian society. Israelis should no longer picture Iran as a multipolar society, in which not all elements of its government shared the religious fervor of the clerical elite. According to Trita Parsi, after 1992, the foreign policy of Israel's ruling Labor Party rejected the notion that there existed a 'moderate' Iranian political faction.[34] Moreover, the party line associated Iran's pursuit of weapons of mass destruction with its Islamic ideology. For Israel, this portrait of a theocracy with nuclear ambitions was incompatible with the possibility that it might also pursue diplomatic solutions. From this followed the non-debatable proposition that Israel was the intended target of Iran's nuclear weapons. As Rabin later explained, 'Iraq tried to develop nuclear weapons. Iran is trying to do this. Against whom, if not against Israel?'[35]

Although Iran's pursuit of nuclear weapons made news, the leadership's pivot from Iraq to Iran as the state they considered the major threat to Israel did not garner significant public concern. Sneh and Rabin clearly identified a threat, but otherwise offered confusing details as to why that threat mattered. Moreover, their reasons for advancing the new narrative remained opaque. Even a decade later, Sneh offered no further clarification. In his 2004 book, *Navigating Perilous Waters: An Israeli Strategy for Peace and Security*, he characterized his Knesset speech as the moment that first 'placed this danger on Israel's national agenda,' and he argued that the Iran of 1993 was the 'most salient strategic threat to Israel's existence.'[36] Yet he failed to explain what prompted his call to action.

When asked again for such an explanation in 2015, Sneh claimed that he had felt a duty to bring the issue to the attention of the Israeli public. He elaborated by recalling how, as a field commander in South Lebanon in the early 1980s, he had witnessed the influence Iran wielded in their support of Shiite resistance against the Israeli occupation. He explained how in 1982 he was particularly disturbed to witness Iran's role in helping terrorists establish a base for guerilla attacks against Israel.[37] After becoming a member of the Knesset and serving on the Intelligence Subcommittee of the Defense and Foreign Affairs Committee, he read intelligence reports that led him to conclude that Iran was an unrecognized growing threat to Israel. By January 1993, he felt compelled to issue a warning.[38] Sneh indicated that he believed that Rabin's presence in the Knesset that day, and his decision to validate Sneh's concerns, contributed to raising the profile of the Iran threat.[39] This, then, was the moment that the Prime Minister, who was also serving as his own Defense Minister, adopted the alarmist position from which he would not retreat for the remainder of his time in office.

Although few noticed, Rabin differed from Sneh in his understanding of the primary danger. For Rabin, the threat lay primarily in Iran's insidious support of terrorism. While he agreed with Sneh that Iran was targeting Israel, its actions also represented a direct threat to the international community. Thus, following the reelection of Akbar Hashemi Rafsanjani as Iran's president, Rabin declared that Iran was a global danger.[40] In a meeting of the Knesset Foreign Affairs and Defense Committee, he added that Iran's ideologically driven expansionist aims included establishing a 'terrorist infrastructure in Europe.' This, he claimed, made Iran a unique foe, since 'even the Palestinian organizations never possessed such a ramified international infrastructure of terror.'[41]

For Rabin, the terrorism threat went beyond targeting Israel. He claimed that Iran harbored 'imperialist aspirations,' and thus it sought to export its 'Khomeinist ideology.' This ascribed to Iranian leaders an ambitiously subversive agenda. According to Rabin, Iran would not seek to overthrow governments, but rather would 'adapt its message to the local conditions and character of the society,' thereby undermining them from within.[42] With ideology doing the heavy lifting, Tehran could strategically extend its influence without having to invest in costly armed opposition. At the same time, it could avoid being faulted for disrespecting a nation's sovereignty while working to, in a sense, overthrow the established order.

While Rabin and Sneh identified the same enemy, which they agreed could potentially become an existential threat to Israel, they appeared to disagree on the means—and the likely timetable—for achieving the intended harm. This led to an extended debate over the nature, scope, and meaning of the threat Iran posed to Israeli society.

The 1993 Knesset colloquy raised an issue it did not settle. Fifteen months later, Rabin responded to a similar question about the relative danger posed by Iraq and Iran with the same answer but slightly different reasoning. He asserted, 'No doubt I place more importance on Iran because it is the source of spreading extremist fundamentalist movements all over. They endanger all the moderate regimes in the Arab world.'[43] As a consequence of directing attention to Iran, Rabin and his military establishment concluded that one method by which Iran was targeting Israel was by using its influence to disrupt Israeli efforts to establish a dialogue with Arab states.[44]

Rabin did not advance a specific Iran policy, but rather used the threat of Iran to justify his overall foreign policy objectives. He reasoned that seeking to make peace with Israel's Arab neighbors would neutralize the Iranian threat. The peace Rabin imagined would reduce the appeal that Iran's revolutionary ideology held for Arab states; it would weaken the connections between Iran, a non-Arab nation, and Arab terrorist organizations. If Israel could defuse the tension with those living within and along its borders, Iran would not have a receptive audience for its belligerent, anti-Israel rhetoric.

Sneh, who had positioned himself as the most hawkish of Iran hawks, did not entirely agree with this assessment. While he concurred that the Iranian threat gave urgency to the Arab issue, he did not believe that an Israeli-Arab peace accord would fully resolve the Iranian threat. Sneh instead saw the advantage of a quick peace with the Arabs in that it would enable Israel to redirect its full attention to Iran, where a potential nuclear conflict loomed.[45] Whereas Rabin saw Iran as engaged in spreading its revolution through rhetoric and strategic assistance that might someday jeopardize Israeli security, Sneh viewed Iran as directly targeting Israel itself. For Sneh, resolving the Arab threat did little to neutralize the real enemy. Rather, peace with the Arabs was merely a temporary reprieve that might prevent Iran from arming Israel's more proximal enemies with conventional and nonconventional weapons alike.

In 1994, Rabin pursued his version of the Iran policy by working quietly with Foreign Minister Shimon Peres to set up what they called the 'Peace in the Middle East Department.'[46] They tasked it with leading an international diplomatic campaign against Iran by portraying the country as a globally destabilizing force driven by fanatical Shiite fundamentalism. Their goal was to isolate Iran from the international community,[47] and they reportedly attached great significance to the new initiative. Typical of the new narrative was a newspaper account describing Iran as 'the greatest risk Israel has ever faced' and explaining how Iran was a global menace and a destabilizing force for the entire region.[48]

Despite seemingly full government support for adopting an increasingly aggressive posture toward Iran, this narrative of Iran as an emerging menace did not meet with universal acceptance in Israeli society. Skeptics took issue with both the government's rhetoric and their portrayal of the Iranian threat. Rabin's concern about Iran generated extensive debate in the military and intelligence establishments, as well as in the academic community. Since analysts had up to that point largely ignored or overlooked Iran as a strategic priority, many were engaging with the topic for the first time knowing relatively little about Iranian history, society, or political intentions. They recognized that the Iranian military buildup, which was no longer preoccupied with waging war against Iraq, raised troubling questions regarding the regime's intent, but many questioned whether this development represented a significant threat to Israel, let alone an existential one.[49]

In particular, military and intelligence officials worried that the increase in the intensity of rhetoric portraying Iran as a danger could become a self-fulfilling prophecy. Chief among the skeptics was IDF Chief of Staff Ehud Barak. He sought to scale back public discussion of the Iranian issue,[50] reportedly instructing his generals to refrain from publicly discussing Iran's nuclear efforts. He feared that speculation about the nature of the program would fuel perceptions of potential risk unsupported by military or intelligence assessments. Notably, the annual intelligence assessment for 1993–4 submitted to the chief of the general staff did not list Iran among the direct threats facing Israel.[51]

Independent analysts and commentators also expressed doubts about Rabin's Iran rhetoric. One important voice at the time, Ephraim Kam, then a researcher at Tel Aviv University's Jaffee Center for Strategic Studies,[52] contradicted many of the assertions made by the Labor government based upon a close inspection of Iran's economy and society. Writing in a 1993–4 report, Kam characterized the threat as 'of very limited scope and nature.'[53] He explained that Iran's military had limited technological capability, and that without surface-to-surface missiles capable of reaching Israel, Iran could not pose a direct military theat. Importantly, he challenged claims about Iranian intentions, maintaining that Iran perceived itself to be facing danger from its immediate neighbors and thus was not concerned with Israel. Moreover, Iran was, in his view, 'a decade away, if at all, from obtaining [nuclear] capabilities.'[54]

Kam's analysis was significant because it examined conditions in Iran rather than simply ascribing motives to its leaders. He saw Iran's serious economic problems and social unrest as being key motivators for Iran's leaders to moderate the nation's foreign policy. He distinguished Iran's nuclear ambitions from those of Iraq, implying that, unlike Saddam Hussein, Iran would not be driven to join the nuclear club at any cost. He pointed out that Tehran's investment in nuclear development was still far below what it had been under the Shah in the 1970s and 40% below Iraq's spending on its nuclear development program.[55]

Political analysts also challenged Rabin's version of the Iranian threat narrative. Dore Gold, who would later become a top advisor to Prime Minister Benjamin Netanyahu,[56] penned an editorial in the *Jerusalem Post* challenging the 'virtual left-right consensus targeting Iran as one of the major Israeli strategic challenges in the 1990s.'[57] In his column, entitled 'Putting the Iranian Threat in Perspective,' he argued that a 'military clash between the two countries is not inevitable.' Like Ehud Barak, he saw even the tone of the discourse surrounding Iran as dangerous, because 'the talk of the Iranian threat might become a self-fulfilling prophecy.' Iran, he reminded readers, takes note of Israeli media, and a 'recent spate of articles in the local press has been filled with lists of Iranian weapons acquisitions.' He also agreed with Barak's assessment that, while Tehran's support of terrorism threatens Israel, it 'does not at this stage constitute a threat to Israel's civilian rear.'[58]

Ultimately, the Rabin-Sneh narrative proved salient and resilient, over time convincing many skeptics. One prominent new adherent was Ehud Barak. Speaking to the Knesset Foreign Affairs and Defense Committee in August 1994, Barak disclaimed his earlier dismissals of the strategic significance of Iran, describing it as the 'key threat right now.' In what amounted to a direct reversal of his statements from a year earlier, Barak stressed that Iran was continuing to pursue a nuclear capability that included developing missiles with sufficient range to reach Israel. He also echoed portions of the Sneh doctrine that stated that concluding a separate peace with the Arab states would not mitigate the threat stemming from the periphery.[59]

A second official reversal came from former skeptic Uri Saguy, Chief of Israeli Military Intelligence.[60] A *Jerusalem Post* profile printed in October 1994 of Saguy and Ya'acov Ami-Dror, the right-wing head of the research division of military intelligence, described the two men as agreeing that Iran was a serious threat to Israel. The story noted that, while the two men opposed one another on most threat assessments and responses, they totally agreed that Iran was a key security concern and a primary driver of the spread of Islamic fundamentalism across the region.[61]

Together, Barak and Saguy offered a compelling picture of the Iran threat. By juxtaposing Iran's 'nuclear capability' with its missile development program, Barak attempted to highlight Israel's relative vulnerability in the face of a motivated and highly ideological foe. By indicating that the threat narrative transcended intra-Israeli partisanship, Saguy cast the Iran narrative as a significant policy rather than a mere political maneuver. Moreover, as both men were high-ranking members of the military establishment—traditionally considered one of, if not the most, trustworthy institutions in Israel— they were able to leverage their credentials to add more weight to their newfound acceptance of the urgency of the Iran concern.

By the mid-1990s, Israel's political leaders were well on their way to establishing a narrative that portrayed Iran as an existential threat to Israel. While most Israeli citizens focused on recent Palestinian terrorist attacks and the loud public protests seeking to undermine the Israeli-Arab peace process,[62] the Iran threat also secured a place on the political agenda. Israel's narrative both echoed new concerns in the United States and contributed to the emerging US policy regarding Iran and Iraq. The United States had abandoned its approach of balance-of-power politics, in which Iran and Iraq countered one another, in favor of a more confrontational approach that relied upon sanctions and threats of force. The Clinton administration called this policy 'dual containment.' Under pressure from a Republican Congress to take a tougher line on the Islamic Republic, President Clinton signed Executive Order 12959 in 1995, which prohibited all US trade with Iran.[63] Congress went further and passed the Iran-Libya Sanctions Act, dictating harsh penalties for foreign companies doing business in Iran.[64] The coincidence of Israel's intensified rhetoric and the United States' sanctions led the Iranian leadership to accuse Israel of pressuring Washington to adopt sanctions.[65] It also furthered the conspiratorial belief in Iran that Israel was secretly in control of American policy in the region.

Whether Israel had enlisted or joined the United States in a new Iran policy was less important than that the two countries now shared a common understanding.[66] Present within this understanding were several key themes. These included: (1) Iran could not be trusted to tell the truth about its development of nuclear capacity, which was not limited to peaceful energy purposes; (2) the timetable for the development of nuclear weaponry was relatively short; (3) Israel would be the target of Iran's deployment of a bomb; and (4) a response against Iran's malicious behavior was imperative.

Iran's insistence that its nuclear program was for civilian purposes enabled their opponents to portray Iranian officials as dishonest at best, malevolent at worst. It set the stage for Israel and the United States to argue that Iran would be technologically capable of covertly upgrading its facilities for bomb production. Iran could not credibly contradict any claim regarding its production timetable. The time until Iran produced its nuclear weapon would, in subsequent years, be the subject of numerous alarming predictions. Ironically, few would note that all previous predictions had proved incorrect.[67] A January 1995 article in the *New York Times* headlined 'Iran May Be Able to Build an Atomic Bomb in 5 years' was only one such example.[68] Prior to its publication, most experts believed that Iran was at least a decade away from weapons production. In offering the accelerated prediction, the story omitted the fact that, although Iran had acquired 'dual use' technology, it had conducted no tests, nor had it taken any overt actions that could confirm it was building a bomb.

While not all experts agreed that Iran would target Israel with its bomb, the importance of this claim to the emerging threat narrative was that it ascribed indisputable intention to Iran's leaders. Whether or not it was true, the idea of Israel as the target of Iran's nuclear ambitions added a sense of urgency to the issue. At a minimum, it implied that Iran intended to go to war with Israel in some form. Although this trope would be repeated continuously over the years by politicians and 'experts,' it had the least evidentiary support.[69] Nearly two decades after Ephraim Sneh's speech on the Knesset floor, Dr. Daniel Kurtzer, a professor of Middle Eastern Policy Studies at Princeton University and former US ambassador to Israel and Egypt, summed up the skeptics' position: 'If Iran developed a bomb, it would not waste it on Israel.'[70]

It was around this point that the emphatic imperative for action began to emerge in Israeli discussions around Iran. War, of course, was out of the question, but what should something more than talk but less than war look like? Hawkish politicians in Israel publicly speculated about the feasibility of a preemptive strike on Iran similar to the 1981 Israeli bombing of the Osirak reactor in Iraq, although most military experts concluded that such a strike would not be as effective against the Iranian nuclear program as it had been in Iraq.[71] To those invested in establishing the salience of an Iranian threat, nuclear deterrence offered no strategic value, since Iran could not be trusted to act rationally and Israel would not admit to having a nuclear weapon. The imposition of economic sanctions on Iran offered the optics of an immediate and punishing response, as well as the opportunity to keep Iran on the policy agenda. American politicians could both demonstrate their support for Israel and curry favor with Jewish constituents by proposing to toughen sanctions. The United States could exploit consideration of a United Nations resolution to enlist new supporters, indirectly providing Israel with new allies. The problem for Israeli hawks, however, was that the sanctions would not reduce the danger Iran posed as they described it. Specifically, economic sanctions could not quell Iran's fanaticism, which Israel believed would continue to drive the Islamic Republic forward in its military pursuits. To satisfactorily address the threat, they needed to go further.

For Israeli officials, crafting a comprehensive policy position to justify putting Iran's nuclear bomb at the top of their list of security priorities was easier than gaining public traction. The debate over

Rabin's Arab peace initiative had turned ugly, with his enemies resorting to inflammatory personal attacks. With the public's attention focused elsewhere, it was difficult for those sounding the alarm on Iran to make themselves heard or to be considered anything other than a distraction from more immediate concerns. Rabin's assassination by a far-right Jewish extremist on 4 November 1995 did not materially change the narrative surrounding Iran.[72] His successor, Foreign Minister Shimon Peres, adopted the bulk of Rabin's Iran policy and rhetoric, even adding hawkish flourishes and taking advantage of the international stage to draw attention to Iranian malfeasance. This was hardly surprising, given Peres's extreme criticisms of Iran while he served as Rabin's foreign minister. During a joint press conference with Egypt's foreign minister approximately two months before Rabin's assassination, Peres said that 'Iran thinks of us as a collective Salman Rushdie,' referring to the fatwa issued by Ayatollah Khomeini calling for the author's death.[73]

In early 1996, Peres doubled down on his rhetoric by expanding the danger presented by the impending bomb to include Iran's support of 'terrorism, fundamentalism, and subversion.'[74] Calling upon European leaders to stop 'flirting' with Iran, he became the first Israeli prime minister publicly to compare Iran to Nazi Germany, claiming that Iran was potentially more dangerous than the Nazis since the former sought to acquire nuclear weapons.[75] Significantly, he issued these denunciations at a joint anti-terror conference in Egypt, which was officially called the Peacemakers' Summit. Peres's emphasis on Iran's connection with terrorism increased the immediacy of the security threat it presented to Israel. It also added a justification for an active Israeli response. Shortly after the summit, Peres warned Iran that Israel would retaliate with air strikes for any terrorist attacks in Israel or against Jewish targets abroad. The Iran threat had now become concrete.

III. The Entrenchment of the Threat Narrative

One indication that the Iran threat narrative had not penetrated public consciousness was its near total absence from public discourse in the 1996 Israeli national election campaign between Shimon

Peres and Likud challenger Benjamin Netanyahu. There are several explanations for this. For one, the election cycle was dominated by the disagreement over Labor's pursuit of a peace process with the Palestinians and the signing of the Oslo Accords in 1993. At the same time, Iran offered less space for distinction between the Likud and Labor positions on security. Both candidates saw Iran as a threat, which devalued it as a wedge issue within the context of the campaign. Yet the failure to mention Iran indicated that it remained a concern primarily of the elites, relegated to esoteric discussions between politicians, military officials, and security experts.

Broadly speaking, both Peres and Netanyahu were Iran hawks, but Netanyahu had taken slightly longer to convert. In his first book, *A Place Among the Nations*, published in 1993, Netanyahu barely mentioned Iran in his rundown of Israel's adversaries. Despite Saddam's defeat in the First Gulf War, Netanyahu continued to insist that Iraq was the primary nuclear threat in the region. He argued that 'Saddam's Iraq was, and still is, a menace of the sort that has previously only been the stuff of suspense novels: a terrorist state with a leader seeking to graduate from car bombs to nuclear bombs.'[76]

By 1995, however, Netanyahu had changed his position, taking to the floor of the Knesset to deliver a lengthy speech indicating his agreement with Prime Minister Rabin's assessment of the Iran threat. Netanyahu colorfully warned of a coming 'Islamic wave' that would flow over the Middle East if outside forces did not act swiftly to prevent Iran from acquiring nuclear weapons capability.[77] The speech received validation from Labor member Raanan Cohen, who added that World War II would look like 'child's play' in comparison to the 'new world war that Iran will lead.'[78]

In his second book, published in 1995, Netanyahu devoted a chapter to the looming nuclear crisis.[79] While in full agreement with the government's assessment, Netanyahu raised two notable points. First, he effectively admitted that Israel possessed nuclear weapons when he argued that Iran had become the primary threat to Israel's nuclear monopoly in the Middle East. The admission was also implied by Netanyahu's questioning the value of relying upon a strategy of deterrence rather than a preemptive strike. He claimed that 'There is no way of knowing whether Iran can be deterred from

91

using its nuclear arsenal, as the Soviet Union was for more than four decades, or whether it would actually be willing one day to plunge the world into the abyss.'[80]

Additionally, Netanyahu skillfully conflated the issue of terrorism and nuclear weapons, describing a catastrophic 'best-case scenario' in which Israel would experience a significant increase in conventional terrorism perpetrated by Iranian-supported groups, who would be protected from reprisal by Iran's nuclear arsenal. This 'nuclear umbrella,' Netanyahu argued, would effectively indemnify terrorist groups from harsh Israeli reprisals, the implication being that Iran's willingness to deploy the bomb made escalation far too risky. In other respects, Netanyahu echoed more familiar themes: Iranian leaders could not be trusted; the intended target of their nuclear weapons program was Israel; and Iran's acquisition of a bomb was imminent. Looking toward the future, he gave Israel less time to deal with the looming Iranian threat than most previous assessments, offering an accelerated timetable claiming that a weapon was only three to five years from completion.[81]

Notwithstanding their agreement on the issue, it is notable that neither candidate in the 1996 elections saw fit to discuss Iran as a looming security threat.[82] It is unlikely that their silence was an oversight but rather a reflection of a lack of public interest in the topic. There was no evidence that the public saw the Iran threat as a priority. While a pre-election poll registered voters' concern about terrorism, pollsters did not inquire about voters' attitudes toward Iran and its nuclear program, or their perception of the threat posed by the country.[83] Unsurprisingly, Iran did not see the election outcome, in which Netanyahu narrowly defeated Peres, as consequential.[84] In what was by then a familiar refrain, Iranian media called the candidates 'two sides of the same coin.'[85]

After his victory, Netanyahu revived his Iran narrative. He raised the issue in a visit to the United States during which he sought to reaffirm the strong Israeli-American partnership. This appeared to be a strategic move with dual purpose. It highlighted the two countries' shared concern regarding Iran while overshadowing the United States' opposition to Netanyahu's abandonment of his predecessors' peace initiatives. In a 1996 speech to a joint session of the US Congress, Netanyahu employed remarkably strong language in describing the Iranian regime as 'the most dangerous' of the 'unreconstructed dictatorships whose governmental creed is based on tyranny and intimidation.' Iran, he maintained, was a country that had 'wed a cruel despotism to a fanatic militancy,' and he warned that 'if this regime, or its despotic neighbor Iraq, were to acquire nuclear weapons, this could presage catastrophic consequences, not only for my country, and not only for the Middle East, but for all mankind.'[86] Netanyahu's audience extended beyond American politicians. Instilling Israel's fear of Iran in American Jewry enabled him to seek their support for his leadership, even among those who disagreed with him on the peace process.

Upon his return from the United States, Netanyahu did not prioritize continued engagement in peace process negotiations.[87] Instead, he focused his foreign policy pronouncements on Iran by repeating the message he had delivered to American politicians and world Jewry. Curiously, however, as he publicly promoted the idea of a preemptive strike, his allies were quietly exploring a change in tone toward Iran. This new approach held that the Labor government had been too aggressive toward Iran and too soft on Syria.[88] From a strategic standpoint, the focus on Syria enabled Netanyahu to oppose Rabin's peace initiative. Rabin had linked the pursuit of an Arab peace to the Iranian threat. By decoupling the Iran issue from peace negotiations with the Arabs, Netanyahu was indicating that his opposition to the peace process was stronger than his conviction about the immediacy of the challenge posed by Iran, regardless of statements made in prominent public speeches.

It is questionable whether Netanyahu's policy modification was anything more than a tactical move. The Labor hardliners noted Netanyahu's reticence to criticize Iran and attacked him for it, pressing him to take a more confrontational approach.[89] Developments in Iran in the late 1990s had certainly provided Netanyahu with the opportunity to modify the narrative if he chose to do so. In May 1997, the victory of Mohammad Khatami, an avowed reformer, in Iran's presidential elections shocked the world. A few Israeli officials floated the idea of revising their entrenched hostility toward the Islamic Republic, seemingly questioning momentarily their perception of Iran's national ideological fervor.

For example, days after the Iranian election, Minister of Foreign Affairs David Levy claimed in a speech to the Israeli parliament that 'Israel has never determined that Iran is our enemy.' He expressed hope for a changed relationship: 'We would be very happy to see Iran joining the regional efforts to lessen tension, stop terrorism, and search for ways of cooperation and peace.'[90] Reports also surfaced that Netanyahu had authorized contacts with the Iranians to investigate the possibility of starting a dialogue.[91] Israel failed to seize this initiative, however, ultimately ignoring the opportunity to modify, in any meaningful sense, the general image it held of Iran as a nation in the grip of religious clerics committed to Israel's destruction. Mirroring Iran's response to Israel's election the previous year, Israeli officials concluded that Khatami's victory did not represent a meaningful change.

In contrast to Netanyahu, the original coterie of Iran hawks never wavered in their conviction that reconciliation with Iran would be dangerous for Israel. In advance of Khatami's first major international interview on CNN in January 1998, Ephraim Sneh warned Israelis not to put too much stock in what the new president said, since it would have no impact on the decisions made by either Iran's ruling regime or its Supreme Leader.[92] Following the interview, Foreign Ministry spokesman Aviv Shir-On added, 'We did not find signs of conciliation or a desire for compromise in the Iranian president's words … It does not appear from them that Iran's position has changed.'[93] Netanyahu used the interview to rebut rumors about pursuing a policy reset. In a speech shortly afterwards, he amplified the nature of the Iranian threat by claiming that since its founding Israel had never faced a more concrete threat to its existence.[94] Not only was the speech a stark departure from the carefully phrased diplomatic language of his government ministers, it was also a full-throated return to the rhetoric of the Rabin government and its policy of centering Israel's long-term security around Iran.

The vehemence of Netanyahu's rhetoric contrasted sharply with the international optimism that followed Khatami's surprise election. While suspicion of Khatami's ability to effect change was understandable, Netanyahu's decision to adopt the hawks' message about the new Iranian president signaled an unwillingness to explore any new possibilities. Israel's right-wing media reinforced this posture by running old news footage of hardline mullahs addressing crowds chanting 'Death to Israel,' thereby stunting all momentum for a shift in the Iran narrative away from one of inexorable threat. Meanwhile, Iran continued its nuclear development program, albeit without any evidence to suggest that it was doing so in the interest of attacking and eliminating its Israeli adversary.[95]

IV. Uncertainty

For anyone paying close attention to the development of the Iranian threat narrative in Israel, Khatami's election highlighted a shift in the rhetorical asymmetry, in which Israel was now more alarmist about Iran than vice versa. An astute observer might have wondered how far the fear of Iran's potential nuclear capability had permeated into the Israeli public's consciousness. Since the 1979 Islamic Revolution, Iran's clerical leaders had included Israel, or the 'Zionist regime,' among Iran's enemies, charging it with oppressing Palestinians, illegally occupying Lebanon, and aligning itself with the United States, among other sins. By contrast, since 1993, Israeli leaders had aligned their public messaging on Iran toward instilling fear in Israelis by convincing them that they were the intended victims of Iran's nuclear weapons development program. The continuous repetition of this particular version of Iran as insidious obscured its inherent problems: did Iran in fact have a weapons program; would it actually use such a weapon; and, as noted by Israeli skeptics when this theory was first advanced, might Israel's promotion of the Iranian threat narrative prove to be a self-fulfilling prophecy?

In a way, it was understandable that Israelis were incredulous of Iran's denial that it was pursuing the development of nuclear weapons, given Israel's own reluctance to admit that it was doing the same thing. Moreover, there could be no proving or disproving the intention ascribed to Iran's leaders; and, since few Israelis closely followed Iranian internal affairs, there was no educated debate regarding the claim. Merely floating the idea that the Islamic Republic, a sworn enemy of Israel, had a nuclear program was sufficient to instill in many Israeli minds the idea that Iran must secretly harbor ambitions for nuclear domination, or, perhaps, even an apocalyptic fantasy of nuclear Armageddon. As this narrative slowly took hold in the Israeli psyche, it prompted ever more repetitions and overlayed all Iranian actions with a lens of suspicion. Most problematic, however, was the question of whether Israeli calls for action against Iran in order to mitigate the growing threat would prompt the latter to escalate a conflict that heretofore for had been confined predominantly to words.

In the final two years of the twentieth century, three developments moved the Israel-Iran hostilities beyond the rhetorical, increasing the stakes for both nations. But by the century's end, the nature of the Iran threat and Israelis' perception of it still remained surprisingly murky. The first development was a January 1998 story in the *Jerusalem Post* claiming that the paper had obtained documents that definitively proved Iran had successfully acquired several nuclear warheads from Kazakhstan shortly after the collapse of the Soviet Union.[96] The second was Iran's testing of its first ballistic missile. Finally, political developments in Israel, including the 1999 ouster of Netanyahu as prime minister and the withdrawal of Israeli forces from Lebanon the following year, demonstrated the country's vulnerability.

The story of the pilfered nuclear weapons appeared credible at first glance. It included numerous specifics about the sale, including the price—$25 million—as well as the details of the smuggling operation by which the warheads had reached Iran.[97] Readers were not informed that the facts largely came from a 1992 Report by the American House of Representatives' Republican Research Committee, which by then had been debunked by various experts.[98] Israeli politicians also ignored the veracity of the claims, as they insisted, using hyperbolic and fatalistic rhetoric, that the 'evidence' validated Israeli fears and justified taking immediate action. Netanyahu castigated the international community for its indifference and suggested that it might already be too late to thwart Iran's nuclear weapons and ballistic missile development.[99]

Whether or not intended as provocation, Iran conducted a test of its first ballistic missile on 22 July 1998. It exploded 100 seconds into flight.[100] Faced with the proverbial choice between reporting the glass as half-empty or half-full, the Israeli press interpreted the test as largely successful and a harbinger of a dark future. Barry Rubin, a prominent Israeli academic and researcher, wrote in an opinion piece that 'Iran's successful launch of a medium-range missile last week makes assessing the Iran issue much more urgent.'[101]

Although Iran never provided an official strategic rationale behind its missile test other than the standard explanation of national defense, statements by Iranian government officials implied that one motivation was Iran's fear of a potential attack from Israel. From Iran's perspective, the test was part of an initiative to enhance its domestic military deterrence capability. Iran, too, could picture itself as a victim of foreign aggression. Iranian Defense Minister Ali Shamkhani voiced such concern in an interview with the Saudi Arabian daily *al-Wasat*, pointing out, 'You would notice that no other country has been as bullied or threatened as Iran.' He continued, 'Israel, for instance, menaces Iran more than it menaces any other country.' President Mohammad Khatami then emphasized Iranians' concern for their safety by noting the salient fact that had largely gone unmentioned, namely that Israel possessed a stockpile of nuclear weapons. This, he claimed, made Israel the foremost threat to regional stability.[102]

Predictably, Iran's actions intensified the public rhetoric coming from Israeli officials, precipitating a new round in the war of words. Once again, Ephraim Sneh fired the first verbal salvo by declaring that it was time for Israel to consider a preemptive strike against Iran.[103] As a member of the political minority, Sneh was not speaking for the government, which had thus far resisted such a specific proposal. Nevertheless, Sneh intended to elicit a response from Iran that would support his characterization of the country's leaders as dangerous.[104] He succeeded, but he also provoked significant pushback from Israeli critics.

In response to Sneh, Iranian Defense Minister Ali Shamkhani promised that Iran would respond in a 'stunning way' if Israel attacked the Iranian nuclear reactor.[105] Additionally, however, officials in Netanyahu's government—who were critical of Iran's nuclear program—criticized Sneh for taking things one step too far with his rhetoric. For example, Israeli Defense Minister Yitzhak Mordechai called his statement 'redundant and harmful.'[106] Ephraim Kam resurrected his concern that ill-conceived policies built upon rhetorical claims rather than evidence could become a self-fulfilling prophecy.[107] He authored a report explaining how Israel's perception of Iran was gradually overtaking the reality of the danger it actually posed. As he had in an earlier analysis, Kam disputed the hawks' characterization of the threat by arguing that 'Iran was a cause for concern, not alarm.' He also criticized Israeli leadership and its willingness to contribute—'not always with excessive wisdom'—to the perception that Iran was a significant enemy. This perception, he warned, would prove difficult to change, especially when so many Israeli leaders had publicly embraced a goal of trying to halt Iran's weapons development efforts. Kam urged Israeli leaders to moderate their tone on Iran to demonstrate that Israel did not regard Iran as a primary enemy.[108]

Kam's arguments should have engendered debate among politicians who appeared largely to agree on the Iranian threat, but, as he predicted, too many Israeli politicians from different parties had already invested in supporting the narrative. Despite their divergent stances on other policies and mounting criticism of Netanyahu, few leaders were willing to risk the political price of disputing the existence of a threat resting on their constituents' fears.

Netanyahu, having collected too many critics, could no longer survive a vote of no confidence, and he was forced to call for elections.[109] As had been the case in the 1996 elections that had elevated him to power, the Iran nuclear threat did not figure prominently among the issues that caused his downfall, and it made only cameo appearances in the election campaign.[110] Once again, the 1999 elections demonstrated that Iran was primarily a concern of Israel's elites, with the majority of citizens focused on the issues closer to home and their daily lives.

Netanyahu's successor, former IDF Chief of Staff Ehud Barak, wasted no time in signaling that he did not share his predecessor's fixation on Iran.[111] Although he did not take the initiative to address the issue directly, shortly after his election victory he responded to a direct question about Israel's Iran policy by stating, 'We are for a kind of a very cautious and careful approach to the Iranians.'[112] He then equivocated by notably omitting reference to Iran in his response to a follow up question about what he considered the 'main threats' to Israel's existence. Barak replied that Israel lived in a 'very tough neighborhood,' before pivoting to a discussion on what he considered Israel's most urgent problem: a stagnant domestic economy.[113]

The Barak government demonstrated its decision not to embrace the aggressive position on Iran pioneered by Netanyahu and Sneh by its muted reaction to Iran's second ballistic missile test in July 2000. In a marked contrast to earlier claims that Iran intended to attack Israel, Director General of the Defense Ministry Amos Yaron was even willing to admit that Iran's military development was understandable, given its tumultuous history and ongoing enmity with its neighbors. Choosing empathy over belligerence, Yaron explained that 'Iran developed these capabilities as a result of the lessons they had learned from the wars of the past, which is to say from its big war against Iraq. Iran didn't develop this missile against the State of Israel.'[114]

After barely two years in office, Israeli politics unrelated to Iran brought down the government, forcing Barak to call for new elections.[115] That year, both Israel and Iran held elections with sharply contrasting outcomes. Barak lost decisively to his Likud challenger, Ariel Sharon, signaling a rightward shift away from Barak's pragmatism.[116] Meanwhile, Iranians reelected President Mohammad Khatami in a landslide victory, giving him 77% of the vote with 67% voter turnout.[117] Sharon had shown little regard for world opinion, while Khatami's reelection suggested Iranians remained interested in global reengagement, including the possibility of negotiation and reconciliation with the West. Still, Israelis again refused to acknowledge that Iran had changed in a way that might warrant any reconsideration of their overarching views of the nation.[118]

* * *

It is a trite understatement to say that the security profile of the world changed on 11 September 2001, when a group of Sunni Muslim terrorists commandeered airplanes to attack targets in the United States. While the terrorists accorded Israel a relatively minor role in their justification for the attacks—and did not mention Iran—Israel used the occasion to highlight its own insecurity in the face of all Muslim opposition.

The attacks thrust terrorism to the top of the world's threat agenda with President George W. Bush declaring a 'Global War on Terror.' If nonstate actors could inflict death and destruction in a surprise attack on the United States, no country could feel safe. If the previously unimaginable spectacle of flying airplanes into iconic American buildings could now be imagined, so too could a rogue nation providing nuclear weapons to terrorists willing to use them.[119] What had been a catastrophic event to a large nation like the United States could mean the cataclysmic destruction of a small state such as Israel. What might Muslim extremists do if they ever gained access to such destructive potential?

In declaring common cause with the United States in the wake of the attacks, Israel sought to capitalize on the fervor of the moment to enlist American assistance in enacting a more aggressive policy toward Iran. To sum up the danger of Muslim extremism in a single concept, Israel had to ignore the distinction between Sunnis and Shiites, between Arabs and Iranians, and between nonstate terrorist actors and a sovereign nation. It also needed the United States to recognize Iran as a greater threat than Iraq. To Israel's disappointment, in the aftermath of the attacks, the Americans chose first to focus their desire for revenge on Afghanistan and, shortly thereafter, Iraq.[120] To further complicate matters, Iran's leaders had quietly reached out to the United States to offer assistance in its fight against the Taliban in Afghanistan.[121]

Notwithstanding the absence of evidence linking Iran with any of the 11 September events, Israeli leaders persevered in belaboring their claims of Iran's connection and the urgent need for confrontation.[122] The new feeling of insecurity introduced new reasons for fear.[123] It also presented opportunities to capitalize on the strain of anti-Muslim sentiment that was taking root in response to the terrorist attacks among audiences who were not yet acquainted with distinctions between Sunnis and Shiites or Arabs and Persians. Former Prime Minister Benjamin Netanyahu undertook a busy schedule of writing and speaking to reinvigorate public awareness of the Iranian nuclear project, in which he revisited familiar tropes while trying out new ones. He reimagined the clash of civilizations in which Iran and its allies would 'devour the West,'[124] and he warned that a nuclear bomb was far more devastating than '300 tons of jet fuel.'[125] Depending upon his audience, he compared Iran, Iranian ideology, or its revolutionary movement to Nazism[126] or communism.[127]

Prime Minister Sharon did not leave the narrative formation to Netanyahu, although he focused on Iran as 'a center of terror.' Speaking at a press conference alongside British Prime Minister Tony Blair in November, Sharon emphasized the terror threat coming from Iran and Syria while expressing support for the new US- and British-led campaign to combat global terrorism. He left the criticism of the Western powers to his Defense Minister, Binyamin Ben-Eliezer, who accused the United States and its partners of ignoring the threats from Iran and Syria in building its coalition against bin Laden.[128]

It is difficult to know whether Netanyahu and Sharon would have succeeded in their mission to securitize the post-11 September Iran threat narrative without two unintended contributions by the Iranians. In December 2001, former Iranian President Ali Akbar Hashemi Rafsanjani delivered the annual Al Quds Day lecture at Tehran University.[129] The address largely focused on the traditional themes associated with the formation of the State of Israel and the suffering it has caused the Palestinians. Rafsanjani added a single musing about what the Islamic world might do with a nuclear bomb: 'If one day, the Islamic world is also equipped with weapons like those that Israel possesses now, then the imperialists' strategy will reach a standstill because the use of even one nuclear bomb inside Israel will destroy everything.'[130]

Not surprisingly, this line caught the attention of Israeli leaders. Although Rafsanjani was no longer a government official—and despite the elected Iranian government officials' current efforts to improve relations with the United States and the West—Israel had just heard a prominent Iranian muse, in public, about one potential endgame of the Iranian nuclear program that had included speculation about an attack on Israel.[131] In Israel's repetition of the Al Quds Day remark, Rafsanjani, a founding father of the Islamic Republic, was characterized as a 'moderate' by Iranian standards. This implied that his thinking was both mainstream and indicative of the 'Ayatollahs'' worldview. The Israeli reaction again overlooked salient facts that might have enabled a more accurate interpretation. At the time of his speech, Rafsanjani was not only out of favor with some members of the clerical establishment,[132] but he had also sought to delegitimize Iran's political and spiritual leadership. One could have seen his provocation as being directed at Iran's rulers rather than at Israel. Regardless, the quote became a favorite citation for Israeli officials and media figures seeking proof of Iran's true nuclear ambitions.

A month after the Al Quds Day speech, Iran arguably supplied more fodder for Israel's narrative when the Israelis seized a cargo ship off its coast, which they alleged was carrying Iranian military equipment to the Palestinian Authority. In Israeli media accounts, Prime Minister Sharon stood before the seized ship, the *Karine A*, to demonstrate how Iran was an enabler of terrorism, working with the Palestinians to 'sow ... death and destruction throughout the entire world.'[133]

While most of the West was focused on going to war against the perpetrators and alleged sponsors of the 11 September attacks, these two incidents enabled Israel's leaders to remind its population, as well as the world, of the danger posed by Iran. By linking nuclear weapons, terrorism, and Israeli victimhood with Iranian words and deeds, Israel made its case for taking action against Iran rather than seeking resolution of the Palestinian 'issue.' More importantly, it enabled Israel to keep Iran in the public consciousness at a time of extreme Islamophobia in the West.

Israeli efforts realized their greatest success several months after the 11 September attacks, when President George W. Bush included Iran among the members of the 'Axis of Evil' in his January 2002 State of the Union Address to the US Congress.[134] The utterance of this phrase, which would become a defining moment of his presidency and a seminal moment in United States foreign policy, linked Iran with Iraq and North Korea as global threats. President Bush reportedly inserted the reference to Iran at the last minute for strategic reasons. He rejected his advisors' suggestion to remove Iran from inclusion, allegedly to deflect attention from US plans to invade Iraq.[135] Whatever his rationale, he had offered Israel validation and leverage in arguing for military action.[136]

V. *Conclusion: Image or Imagination*

This chapter's examination of the intensifying enmity between Israel and Iran reveals two features of the process by which one nation, Israel, invested in a foreign policy based upon the characterization of the other, Iran, as an existential threat. First, Israel's characterization of Iran's hostility seemingly had all the elements needed to create the sense of fear to achieve securitization of the issue: historic religious enmity, cultural stereotypes that painted Iranians as nefarious and untrustworthy, and location in a geographic region beset by chaos and intrigue. Its principal arguments invoked emotional themes ascribing destructive intentions to leaders who would, according to numerous publicly presented timelines, imminently possess nuclear weapons. Still, between 1993 and 2002, the issue did not dominate Israeli national discourse, but remained limited to discussion among elites. The public did not perceive Iran as an existential threat dictating Israel's policy decisions. Second, sometimes events beyond the control of those constructing the narrative can contribute to the 'success' of the securitization process. This study illustrates how a narrative is essential but may not be sufficient to achieve securitization.

Although the securitization process concerns the conduct of nations toward one another and the impact of world events, we can also learn two lessons about the role of human behavior. First, in addition to emotion playing a large role in the process, a concomitant feature of securitization is ignorance. For a threat that is evidently apparent and lacks immediacy, its resonance depends upon its audience's credulousness, and their inability to verify the factual predicate of the claimed danger. Second, where the securitization process unfolds amidst global uncertainty, the narrative arc of a conflict is never inevitable. The political, military, academic, and, occasionally, religious actors all play critical roles in securitizing the conflict and elevating it to a place of prominence in the national discourse. Their motives, credibility, and political acumen, among other human characteristics, will affect how information is interpreted, and the manner of its presentation to their audience. In short, securitization is a process directed by humans to other humans.

Thus, Israelis and world leaders accepting Iran as an existential threat was neither a foregone conclusion nor an inconsequential myth. It did not emerge from a linear development process in which Israeli leaders consistently constructed a case for acting to eliminate the danger posed by Iran. Most often, the accusations were not coordinated with specific strategies for taking action. The nature of the confrontation between the foes was also asymmetrical: Israeli leaders felt far more threatened by Iran than Iranians were concerned about Israeli actions, although this does not mean that Iran did not play any role in the creation of the conflict. Iranian leaders' propensity for colorfully bombastic language targeting the 'Zionist Regime,' along with its stated support for Palestinian groups, inflamed tensions and exacerbated its image as an out-of-control, ideologically driven nation in the eyes of many Israelis. For those with no prior knowledge of Iran or its history with Israel—both during the final decades of the Pahlavi monarchy and in the early years of the Islamic Republic—these statements, diligently repeated by Israeli leaders and reported by the press, generated a sense in Israel that the Islamic Republic was irredeemable, even as domestic politics in the country shifted in unexpected and occasionally promising directions. Still, in the early years, some Israelis worried that Israel's accusatory rhetoric might act as a self-fulfilling prophecy and compel Iran to put their words into action, empowering hardliners at the expense of what some Israelis still saw as the moderate, 'true' Iran.

The examination of the consequential historical events in this chapter shows how at key inflection points Israeli officials interpreted facts and addressed uncertainties to fashion an image of an Iran intent on ending Israel's existence. They brought to their narrative their imagination—informed by personal experience, bias, and ambition—thereby creating an image that relied less on facts than on the narrators' interpretations of their own experiences and preexisting beliefs. The narrators' identities, their positions in society, and how they located Israel in the Middle East, as well as their view of global politics, all affected their capacity to secure widespread concern over Iran's actions and intentions.

Significantly, expertise on Iran's politics, governance, and military strategy were all in short supply in the public discourse about Iran, frequently taking a back seat to overtly political considerations. In most cases, even if Iran's actions could arguably be interpreted as signs of weapons development, there was no definitive evidence that Iranian leaders intended to target Israel directly, let alone engage in an apocalyptic nuclear war. Interestingly, few Israelis noticed when their leaders' dire predictions about the completion date of Iran's bomb were proved wrong. The timetable kept shifting, but the fear of Iran's imminent deployment of a nuclear weapon did not.

While Israeli leaders occasionally discussed preemptive attacks and sought to enlist countries in sanctioning Iran, the confrontation between Israel and Iran remained largely rhetorical. Only a handful of Israeli leaders spoke openly about regime change or preemptive destruction of Iran's nuclear infrastructure, and even fewer believed such efforts would succeed. Nevertheless, the narrative implied that these were the only options for neutralizing the Iran threat. [137]

It is ironic that the 11 September terrorist attacks contributed so substantially to the securitization of the Iran threat narrative since Iran had no part in those events. Whether the continuous and escalating repetitions of the Iran threat narrative by Israeli officials to a primarily domestic constituency would have, without the increased publicity created by the attacks, achieved acceptance among the polity is a matter of conjecture. The post-11 September climate of fear enabled Israeli officials to adapt their narrative, and thus to raise the profile and immediacy of the Iranian threat both at home and abroad. Portraying Iran as a 'center of terrorism' cast it as an enemy in the new Global War on Terror. The US President assigned Iran membership in his Axis of Evil. With Israelis and the world fearing Iran's support of terrorism, all that remained to do was to portray Iran as a nuclear-armed global menace, one that no country in the world could ignore.

4

ACTIONS
CONSTRUCTING AN ENEMY

I. The Threat of Diplomacy

When Benjamin Netanyahu arrived to address the United Nations General Assembly in October 2015, he had a specific agenda. Three months earlier, after years of negotiations, the five permanent members of the United Nations Security Council plus Germany (P5+1)[1] had reached an agreement with Iran. The latter had agreed to limit its nuclear program in exchange for relief from economic sanctions. Netanyahu had vociferously opposed the negotiations, and he now came to the UN to denounce the agreement. He believed that Iran was misleading the world and that the P5+1 were naïvely being led into a disastrous deal negotiated in bad faith with an immoral partner.

Netanyahu was incensed by the details of the deal, known formally as the Joint Comprehensive Plan of Action (JCPOA) or, more commonly, as the 'Iran deal' or the 'nuclear deal.' It placed strict limits on Iran's nuclear enrichment capabilities, restricted the number of centrifuges, and imposed a threshold on the amount of enriched uranium that could be present in the country at any one time.[2] It provided for enforcement through rigorous inspection and oversight by international watchdog authorities, led by the International Atomic Energy Agency (IAEA). In exchange, Iran would receive relief from the harsh economic sanctions that had crippled its economy.[3] Yet even more than the details of the JCPOA, Netanyahu was furious about what the deal signaled. Although it was not overtly written into the agreement—but perhaps more importantly than certain details that were—the JCPOA afforded Iran an opportunity after decades of isolation to rejoin the world community as an active economic and diplomatic participant.

Netanyahu's opposition to Iran long predated the agreement to which he was objecting from the UN podium. He had opposed even exploring the possibility of negotiations with Iran, preferring instead to float the possibility of a preemptive military strike to halt Iran's development. Reportedly, he had been on the brink of ordering such an action three years earlier.[4] Now, in front of the world, he settled for rhetorically attacking his allies, including the United States, while joining with several of Israel's historic enemies to oppose a diplomatic solution. Based upon their shared distrust of Iran, Israel and several Sunni Arab states opened new channels of communication. They shared the view that any deal with Iran would only embolden the Islamic Republic in its quest for regional hegemony and strengthen a global menace.

In his speech, Netanyahu spared no aspect of the deal, nor anyone involved in it, from his criticism. He employed inflammatory imagery and rhetorical flourishes as he methodically attacked the terms, the negotiators, the signatories, and those who credulously celebrated the accord as a triumph of international diplomacy. He claimed that the Iranian character precluded their acting in good faith. The Iranians, he said, were incapable of adhering to the terms of the agreement, no matter their stated position. In Netanyahu's view, Iran was as methodical as it was maniacal, its goals simultaneously chaotic and focused. Iran posed an existential threat to Israel, and it endangered global peace and prosperity.[5]

Netanyahu began his address by warning his audience to 'check your enthusiasm at the door,' setting the stage for his dark remarks. Over the next forty minutes, he employed familiar tropes and added some new ones. As he had in many previous speeches, he invoked the memory of the Holocaust as an overarching theme, admonishing the world leaders for their complacency. 'And now,' Netanyahu said, 'another regime has arisen, swearing to destroy Israel.'[6] He warned the assembly that the missiles Iran was building were not only for Israel, but for Europe and America as well. Iran was engaged in a war of civilizations and developing a nuclear program 'for raining down mass destruction—anytime, anywhere.'[7]

The most unconventional element of his speech came halfway into his address, when Netanyahu unexpectedly paused for forty-four seconds. He stood at the podium glaring at the audience, which sat in total silence. Apparently, he intended this moment to be symbolic of the global leaders' lack of objections to Iran's promises to murder the Jewish people, another reference to the world's silence in the face of a potential Holocaust. Netanyahu also employed a form of plain speaking in his delivery, which was unusual for such a formal address. Invoking cultural stereotypes, he used the term 'mullahs' as a pejorative catchall for Iran's leadership and indicated that they were intent on deception. Iran, he insisted, must not be allowed to sweep its violations of its nuclear commitments 'under the Persian rug.'[8]

He ended with a breathtaking flourish in which he positioned Israel as the world's savior, and its last line of defense against Iran:

> Ten miles from ISIS, a few hundred yards from Iran's murderous proxies, Israel stands in the breach—proudly and courageously defending freedom and progress. Israel is civilization's front line in the battle against barbarism ... Ladies and Gentlemen, stand with Israel because Israel is not just defending itself. More than ever, Israel is defending you.

In the 42-minute speech, he had mentioned Iran 67 times.

The tropes invoked in the New York speech had been years in development, but the position in which Netanyahu found himself was new. He had crafted his original Iran strategy during his first term as prime minister in the late 1990s and polished the tropes he relied on in the preceding six years of his second term of service, which began in 2009. Yet Netanyahu's address highlighted the divergence of the goals he had pursued in building this image of Iran as Israel's mortal enemy. At first, Netanyahu had sought to convince Israelis that they should fear the Islamic Republic. While he wavered on solutions to the challenges posed by Iran, he sought to capitalize on the public's sense of insecurity by urging them to support his leadership and foreign policies. At the same time, he sought to convince world leaders that they should support his case and join forces to oppose the radical regime led by the 'mullahs' and 'ayatollahs.' By the time of the 2015 UN speech, Netanyahu could emphasize that he had the support of the Israeli public, but he stood in opposition to many of the member nations of the UN Security Council and Germany.

Back home, Netanyahu had succeeded in convincing the 'vast majority' of Israelis to oppose the JCPOA. An August 2015 poll showed that 72.7% of Israelis agreed with Netanyahu that Iran posed an 'existential threat' to Israel.[9] In that same survey, a substantial majority of respondents expressed doubt that Iran would abide by the terms of the accord. A mere 16.8%—one-sixth of the population—expressed confidence that Iran would uphold its end of the bargain.

An objective analyst could be excused for being confused by the vehemence and intemperance of Netanyahu's opposition to the JCPOA. The overwhelming majority of nuclear experts agreed that the terms of the deal effectively made it impossible for Iran to produce a nuclear weapon for at least the next decade.[10] Moreover, it imposed the most sophisticated monitoring mechanisms devised to date, thus minimizing Iran's ability to cheat on its denuclearization commitments. Iran would also face severe sanctions for violating the agreement's terms, including the 'snap back' of the harsh economic sanctions that had helped bring Iran to the negotiating table.[11] Beyond the good feeling engendered by the accord, there remained an undercurrent of threat to the arrangement. The language of 'all options are on the table' hovered over the negotiations, and the implied threat of military action persisted even in the wake of the historic accord. At the very least, the agreement ensured that for the foreseeable future Israel would remain the sole nuclear-armed power in the region, although this seemed to be of little comfort to its politicians and population.[12]

To be sure, the deal did little to alleviate the enmity between Iran and Israel. Iran was not a benign neighbor to Israel's security, but rather a strategic opponent to several nations in the region, which included several Sunni Arab states along with Israel. The deal would not do anything to erode Iran's large military force and network of proxy groups, which had proven themselves capable of maintaining order at home and facilitating strife on foreign soil.[13] Israel remained a target for terrorist groups funded and supplied by Iran, including Hezbollah, which controlled the Lebanese territory along Israel's northern border. Iran still had hardline leaders in its government and prominent politicians espousing inflammatory anti-Israel messages, including Supreme Leader Ayatollah Khamenei.

But, by any objective criteria, the nuclear deal did nothing to increase the threat Iran posed to Israel. Using conventional measures, Iran could not match Israel's significant military advantages. On strictly economic terms, Iran's military budget paled in comparison to Israel's, as well as all of Iran's regional rivals, including Saudi Arabia.[14] Both the Saudis and Israelis enjoyed close relations with the Americans, with their nations being among the top global recipients of military funds and equipment from the United States. Historical precedent suggested that such support would increase as compensation or inducement for allowing Iranian sanctions relief.

Moreover, for the present and foreseeable future Iran would be unable to focus much attention on Israel. It was effectively tied up in Syria's bloody civil war, where the Iranian Revolutionary Guards Corps Quds Force—led by Qasem Soleimani—and Iran's Lebanese client Hezbollah were engaged in maintaining the regime of Syrian President Bashar Al Assad. Iran could do little more to challenge Israel's existence than occasionally conduct a missile test or issue a provocative statement.[15] These realities, combined with the terms of the nuclear agreement, seriously undermined the image of Iran as an urgent and potentially apocalyptic threat Netanyahu had so assiduously crafted and advanced over the years.

This chapter and the next examine how Netanyahu arrived at the pivotal moment in 2015 where he attacked his international allies for supporting a deal that, by any objective measure, blocked Iran's capacity to produce a nuclear weapon while at the same time he convinced a majority of the Israeli people to fear Iran as an existential threat. This chapter details how two seminal events in the mid-2000s—namely the 2005 election of Mahmoud Ahmadinejad as Iran's president and the 2006 Lebanon War—contributed to the popularization, and thus the full securitization, of the Iran threat narrative.

It is counterproductive to speculate whether without these two developments there would have been sufficient support to sustain Iran as a securitized issue on Israel's agenda. Admittedly, Iran's nuclear development program and the prospect that the country might acquire the capacity to produce a nuclear weapon was cause for deep concern. Nevertheless, as discussed in the previous chapter, the initial fear expressed by Israeli leaders, with media support, did not induce the same fear in the public. Ahmadinejad's heightened rhetoric threatening Israel and the Second Lebanon War both served to intensify the power and durability of the threat narrative. Consequently, these events profoundly affected the public's political understanding, leading Israelis to question their leaders' capability to respond to their fears. Benjamin Netanyahu would exploit this concern and, using a populist political strategy, offer his leadership as a response to the looming dissatisfaction.

To set the stage for this discussion, this chapter begins with a look back at the development of Iran's nuclear program, starting with its origins under the Shah's regime. It turns briefly to the impact of the United States' invasion of Iraq in 2003. From there, it looks at how the election of Mahmoud Ahmadinejad contributed to the salience of the Iran threat narrative.[16] Finally, it concludes with an examination of how the Second Lebanese War strengthened the general sense of a burgeoning Iranian threat while simultaneously weakening the sitting Israeli government. This series of events resulted in a public that was primed to accept an explanation that the primary source of their insecurity came not from Israel's traditional opponents, but rather from Iran, which Israelis came to accept as their existential enemy. This shift in public perception set the stage for the election of new leadership and, ultimately, a new phase of the Iran conflict.

II. Iran's Nuclear History

The world witnessed the destructive force of nuclear weapons when the United States dropped bombs on Japan to end World War II. Since that time, select countries have sought to increase the deadly capability of such weapons while most of the world has searched for ways to deter their development and use. Even as scientists were developing the technology for nuclear weapons during World War II, they worried about the destructive impact of their invention. After the war, political movements and civic activists publicized and politicized these fears, and public culture reflected the concerns.[17] A paradigmatic 1964 film, *Dr. Strangelove or: How I Learned to Stop Worrying and Love the Bomb*, imagined a rogue bomber crew triggering a nuclear apocalypse that the world's bumbling leadership was powerless to prevent, and in 1983 a made-for-TV movie, *The Day After*, cemented fears of a potential doomsday scenario involving global nuclear war.[18]

As world leaders negotiated agreements to limit and destroy nuclear weapons, public discourse and imagination concerning their threat abated. The dissolution of the Soviet Union ended the superpowers' nuclear standoff policy of mutually assured destruction, but it also raised concerns about the fate of Russia's nuclear arsenal, as well as the employment prospects for the scientists who had built it. Officials and analysts worried about a market for nuclear material, technology, and weapons experts, which could allow rogue nations and terrorist organizations to acquire nuclear capacity.[19]

The development of nuclear technology as an energy source complicated global nonproliferation efforts. In addition to the risk of catastrophic accidents, a state could in theory disguise a weapons program by claiming to be building a nuclear power plant. The logic was easy to follow: such an explanation might provide cover to the leader of a poor nation seeking to enhance his standing by acquiring a nuclear weapon. He could justify the commitment of scarce resources to the costly venture by claiming that it would provide vital energy or nuclear-related research. He might also attempt to convince his citizens that nuclear capability would be a deterrent of enemy hostile actions as well as a source of national pride.[20]

Saddam Hussein's decision to invest in a nuclear program and his failure to hide it demonstrated the inherent risk in such behavior. In 1981, Israel launched a surprise bombing raid that destroyed Iraq's nearly completed nuclear reactor at Osirak. Israeli leaders reasoned that an Iraq led by Saddam Hussein armed with nuclear weapons posed an existential threat to their nation, and that the reward of preemptively eliminating the threat more than compensated for the risk involved.[21] Although world powers, including the United States, publicly condemned the action, there were surely many leaders who breathed a sigh of relief following the setback to Saddam's nuclear ambitions. During the Iran-Iraq War, he had targeted civilians with chemical weapons. When the war had ended, Iraq still retained a powerful military. No one familiar with the Middle East believed Saddam could be counted on to act rationally in his own or his country's best interest. The world assumed that Iraq would continue to defy international behavioral and legal norms governing the use of unconventional weapons.

Israel's development of nuclear weapons provides a contrast to the situation with Saddam Hussein. Israel has never admitted possessing such weapons, although almost no one questions that they do, in fact, have them.[22] Notably, the nation is not among the 190 signatories to the Nuclear Non-Proliferation Treaty (NPT) that took effect in 1970.[23] As a general rule, Israel eschews the Cold War strategic doctrine of mutually assured destruction, preferring instead to pursue a policy of keeping all other nations in its neighborhood from obtaining nuclear weapons.

Despite Israel's desire for a nuclear monopoly in the Middle East, it did not initially register Iran's development of nuclear power as a significant threat. Iran launched its program with the assistance of the United States in 1957. Shah Mohammed Reza Pahlavi signed a nuclear cooperation agreement with the Eisenhower Administration—part of the Atoms for Peace Initiative—under which the United States assisted Iran in constructing a five-megawatt nuclear reactor in Tehran. The program aimed to provide countries with established civilian nuclear capabilities in the hope that would prevent them from developing militarized nuclear programs through their own efforts.[24] Later, the Shah sought to enhance Iran's nuclear capacity with the construction of a second, much larger reactor near the town of Bushehr, although this project would not be completed before his downfall.[25]

The Shah maintained his ambitions throughout the 1960s and 1970s, his love affair with advanced weaponry leading up to his nascent attempt to develop a nuclear weapon. He made no secret of his desire to expand his nuclear capacity and obtain membership in the exclusive nuclear club. His desires met domestic resistance from opponents who strongly criticized him for having misplaced priorities as he diverted resources from the country's other needs, particularly since he already possessed a large, well-trained, and well-equipped military.[26] Nevertheless, the Shah continued to press the American government for more nuclear technology and expert assistance while sending dozens of Iranian students to the United States to study nuclear engineering. Although Iran had signed the NPT in 1970, under which it agreed to restrictions on its nuclear development, including foreswearing acquiring nuclear weapons, American intelligence officials questioned the Shah's intentions. One major skeptic was President Jimmy Carter, who, after assuming office in 1977, voiced his concern that the Shah aimed to build an atomic bomb.[27] The project fit the Shah's self-image: it would secure Iran's place in the top tier of the global power structure while drastically altering the balance of power in the region.

When Ayatollah Khomeini assumed the leadership of Iran following the 1979 Islamic Revolution, he suspended Iran's nuclear program.[28] Khomeini claimed that it was a waste of resources and an immoral pursuit of the excesses of the West. He allowed the Bushehr reactor to sit idle. Even after the Iraqi invasion of Iran, Khomeini resisted the pleas from military advisors to reconsider his position on nuclear development. Iran's enemies suspected, however, that the ban would not last, and Iraqi forces went so far as to bomb the now empty Bushehr site as a precautionary measure.

In later years, Khomeini reversed his prohibitory edict, but his reasons for doing so remain unclear. Facing power shortages occasioned by the war with Iraq, Khomeini allowed work on Iran's nuclear infrastructure to restart, but he reportedly once again resisted his advisors' urging to adapt the nuclear program for possible military applications. Despite the presence of Iraqi soldiers on Iranian soil, Saddam's use of nonconventional chemical weapons against Iranians—including civilians—and the enormous human toll of the war, Khomeini maintained that nuclear weapons violated Islamic jurisprudence and were, therefore, out of the question.[29]

Yet despite Khomeini's steadfastness, there remained valid reasons for skepticism about Iran's intentions. Its work on developing the nuclear fuel cycle and expanding capacity allowed for 'dual use' as both energy and weapons production. By creating the perception of technological advancement in nuclear proficiency, Iran could develop the intellectual capability to build a weapon should it choose to do so. Still, throughout the 1980s, Israeli leadership appeared largely unconcerned about Iran's nuclear activities. Only once during this period did an Israeli politician even refer to Iran's nuclear program in public debate.[30] A transcript of a Knesset discussion about French arms sales to Saudi Arabia briefly mentions that France had sold nuclear materials to Iran.[31] A broader review of the Israeli Foreign Ministry Historical Documents archive during this period reveals that Israel was far more concerned about the plight of Iranian Jewry and the strategic value of arms sales than it was about the Shah's nuclear machinations.[32] It seemed the specter of a nuclear-armed Iran simply did not merit much by way of public discourse.

Conversely, Israelis did believe that Iraq and its unpredictable leader posed a threat to Israel's security. This fear proved warranted when Iraq launched ballistic missiles at Israeli targets in the hopes of expanding its 1990 invasion of Kuwait into a regional conflict.[33] Although the action caused few casualties, it had a powerful psychological impact on Israeli society.[34] Saddam had used long-range missiles to attack Israeli territory, which Israel feared could one day carry chemical weapons in their payload, and this engendered a new type of vulnerability among Israelis. The state-wide issuance of gas masks to all residents shortly thereafter forced Israelis to realize the uncomfortable fact that warfare had moved beyond conventional military confrontation and that even non-neighboring enemies could now pose a significant—and, importantly, non-abstract—threat to human life.

Israel's recognition of its increased vulnerability coincided with the disintegration of the Soviet Union and the uncertainties associated with both the fate of Russia's nuclear stockpile and the world's nonproliferation regime.[35] The chaos in the east as the USSR crumbled sparked fears of worst-case scenarios in which Russia's massive nuclear stockpile, left unguarded and unsecured as soldiers abandoned their posts, fell into the hands of the highest bidder at the global arms bazaar. Israel's regional enemies—including Syria, Algeria, Libya, and Iraq—reportedly had indicated an interest in purchasing nuclear material and employing displaced scientists from the former Soviet Union. The possibility of an enemy armed with nuclear weapons now appeared to be a real threat, at least in the public imagination. Reports on burgeoning nuclear powers were everywhere. A 1991 report on Algeria suggested that the country could be only a 'very few years' away from building a nuclear bomb,[36] while a newspaper editorial entitled 'The Real Middle East Problem' noted that Iraq, Libya, and Iran were all in a 'scramble for nuclear capability.'[37]

With Saddam's defeat in 1991 by the United States and its allies following his invasion of Kuwait, Iraq could no longer compete in this post-Soviet market. At least for the foreseeable future, Saddam would be preoccupied with maintaining control over his own country rather than planning invasions of others.[38] Over the next ten years, Saddam would seek to make a comeback, and eventually his weapons development activities would again come under suspicion. For reasons that remain unclear, however, Saddam Hussein refused to dispel enemy notions that he was attempting to rebuild his nuclear program or developing other weapons of mass destruction. The United States took his obstinance as its principal justification for leading an invasion of Iraq in 2003 that ended Saddam's reign.[39]

Although Saddam remained in power after the First Gulf War, Israel nevertheless recognized that the threat he posed to their country had significantly diminished. This necessitated reprioritizing the remaining threats it faced. Such decisions involved more than merely debating classified military assessments and contingency plans. Given Israel's political culture, government officials would need to make a case to the public and rally popular support for new policies targeting identifiable enemies. One obvious candidate for filling the threat vacuum left by Iraq was Iran.

In the beginning, the Israeli media took the initiative in increasing awareness of Iran. Stories not only frequently mentioned Iran as a potential black-market customer for Soviet nuclear material, but also ascribed motives to Iran's leadership for wanting to buy it. While reports of Arab buyers generally focused on factual accounts, discussion of Iran included analyses of how the country's acquisition of nuclear 'know-how' would change the region's balance of power and complicate the security picture. Media reports increasingly called into question the intentions behind Iranian nuclear development efforts, echoing earlier critiques of Saddam Hussein's program. They spoke of Iran's leaders as irrational and lacking in self-restraint. Adding the new dimension of religious fanaticism, they implied that Iran's leaders would not be inhibited from using a nuclear weapon as a means of achieving their goals of destroying the Jewish State.[40] Famously, Yitzhak Rabin, who had just a few years earlier described Iran as 'Israel's best friend' in the region, now called it a nation with 'megalomaniac tendencies.'[41]

In early 1992, the *Jerusalem Post* ran a series of stories focusing on Iran that offered an object lesson in how the tone and manner of coverage of the Iranian issue in Israel had changed. The content of these stories and their placement on the front page emphasized to readers the urgent need to address the threat posed by Iran's nuclear ambitions. The news element had been previously reported in stories about how Iran was in the market for Soviet leftovers, but these details were secondary to the emotional alarmism inherent in the possibility of weapons of mass destruction finding their way into the hands of an ideologically driven enemy.[42]

The first story spoke of how the Iranians were buying Soviet weaponry at a 'breakneck pace.' It then added a variety of speculative items, including where ex-Soviet scientists might be and how Iran's leaders intended to fill the vacuum left by Iraq following its defeat in the First Gulf War.[43] A subsequent story reported that Iran was on a 'single-minded campaign to become a regional power,' before adding new accusations that the country was pouring money into ex-Soviet Muslim republics, including Tajikistan, Uzbekistan, and

Kazakhstan, and that Iran 'made no secret of its intention to become a nuclear power.' It concluded by warning, 'It is a mistake to assume that post-Khomeini Iran is more moderate. The present leadership in Teheran is simply more sophisticated.'[44]

If read carefully, the stories highlighted how changes outside of Iran—namely those in Iraq and the Soviet Union—were affecting Iran and, by extension, Israel. The news was not that either country had changed; Iran was known to have a nuclear development program, and Israel still had plenty of enemies in the Middle East. Rather, it reported how the disintegration of the Soviet Union reportedly provided Iran and its fanatical leadership with new opportunities for influence and weapons acquisition, while Saddam's defeat reduced Iraq's threat to Israel. What these developments actually portended, however, was pure speculation, but there was no shortage of speculation from many quarters. Former Mossad official Yossi Alpher, in an interview with the *New York Times* days after Bill Clinton's 1992 presidential election victory, declared that Iran was now Israel's 'Enemy No. 1.'[45]

The U.S. also voiced new concerns about Iran. In late 1992, the United States House of Representatives Republican Research Committee claimed in a report that it believed 'with 98% certainty' that Iran had already acquired 'all or virtually all of the components required for the construction of two to three nuclear weapons.'[46] In what would become a predictive ritual over the next twenty-five years, the committee claimed that 'it was likely that these [Soviet-supplied nuclear] weapons would be operational by February to April 1992.'[47] Similarly, a *U.S. News and World Report* story reported that three nuclear warheads, which had gone missing from Kazakhstan, had been sold to Iran.[48] These claims could not be verified.[49]

Undoubtedly aware of the increasing frequency and intensity of Iran news, Israeli officials signaled a shift from reacting to reports provided by others to generating their own case against Iran. In January 1993, as discussed in the previous chapter, a public exchange in the Knesset between Labor Minister Ephraim Sneh and Prime Minister Yitzhak Rabin initiated the characterization of Iran as an existential threat. Over the years, Israeli leaders would go on to construct a threat narrative that would serve as the basis for the country's foreign policy. In this effort, it mattered less to Israel whether the claims highlighting Iran's dangerousness were verifiable so long as they were difficult to refute. Israeli officials sought to build a compelling narrative that showcased Iran's leaders as steadfast in their commitment to destruction, Israel's in particular.

On 14 August 2002, a spokesperson for the National Council of Resistance of Iran (NCRI),[50] an anti-Iranian government opposition group based in France, held a press conference in Washington to announce it had discovered two undeclared nuclear sites inside Iran. According to the NCRI, Iran was secretly building these facilities unbeknownst to the IAEA and international inspectors. NCRI's spokesman, Alireza Jafarzadeh, claimed that the organization had made these discoveries as a result of 'extensive research and investigation.' Few familiar with the organization, however, believed that it had the resources to develop this intelligence, which led to speculation that the NCRI was failing to disclose a source of secret help.

The announcement, which was impressively specific about Iran and its nuclear activities, seemed calculated to raise suspicion along with public awareness about Iran's possible intentions. The heretofore secret sites at Natanz and Arak appeared to have been chosen for their strategic defensive position. The Natanz facility was located deep underground inside a bunker ringed by a thick concrete wall, rendering it impervious to conventional bomb damage. The heavy water reactor at Arak could arguably be used to produce material for building nuclear weapons. The NCRI's message was clear: the clandestine construction of nuclear facilities fortified to withstand attack coupled with Iran's lack of candor about its nuclear activities proved that Iran was hiding something. The only logical conclusion, therefore, was that Iran was building a bomb.

Although the NCRI intended its report to generate intense concern, the revelations were not particularly shocking to United States intelligence, nor was the evidence conclusive. Throughout the 1980s, the CIA had not found evidence of a military component in Iran's nuclear pursuits. Although it changed this assessment shortly before the NCRI announcement, by the time of the press conference, it had compiled the information and submitted it to the

IAEA.[51] Many suspected that it was the Americans' evidence leaked by the Israelis which had provided the basis for the NCRI's polished presentation. These suspicions likely explain the uncharacteristically muted reaction from Israel, where the revelations did not trigger a major outcry from public officials, intellectuals, or the media.[52] Oddly, Israel's prime minister at the time, Ariel Sharon, offered no official statement following the press conference.[53]

Either unknown or unacknowledged as part of the discourse surrounding the NCRI revelations was the fact that Iran was about to end all activities associated with military applications of its nuclear program.[54] Months later, in 2003, it did so, although it continued its development of nuclear energy, including its efforts to master the nuclear fuel cycle and advance its uranium enrichment capabilities. Iranian officials were steadfast in their conviction that Iran's status as a signatory to the NPT entitled it to the continuation of a peaceful nuclear program as a sovereign right.

Iran undoubtedly knew that this decision would not end the accusations concerning its nuclear ambitions. Even an unequivocal assertion of its intention to comply with the NPT and direct its limited resources to economic development could not challenge the widely disseminated narrative that included claims that Iran's leaders could not be trusted to tell the truth.

Moreover, as Iran continued to enrich fuel, scientists archived research materials that could be utilized in the future should the country's leaders change their minds about including a military dimension to the nuclear program. By creating a sense of ambiguity and leaving the door open, if only just a crack, to weapons development, Iran was inviting its enemies to fear the worst regarding its nuclear program. It fed the claim that Iran was something beyond a conventional enemy; in short, Iran was an 'existential' threat.

III. Phase I: Israel and the 'Axis of Evil'

The United States' invasion of Iraq in 2003, although not obvious at the time, was a transformative moment for Israel's relationship with Iran. The administration of US President George W. Bush had pivoted away from its military invasion of Afghanistan, the country supposedly harboring the terrorists responsible for the 11 September attacks, in favor of invading Iraq. The goal of the invasion was not subtle. Bush wanted to correct the mistake of his father's war with Saddam and sought to eliminate the Iraqi dictator along with his regime. Several of the president's given explanations for his attack on Iraq could subsequently be contradicted by facts, including that its leader, Saddam Hussein, had aided the attacks on 11 September.[55] Other justifications included that Saddam had a weapons of mass destruction program that threatened the security of the United States, or that his ouster promised a democratic transformation of the Middle East. Whatever the reason, Israel fully supported the US decision because it represented the operationalizing of a regime change policy in the Middle East. In making the case for war, Bush had characterized Iraq as part of an 'Axis of Evil,' comprised of enemies of the United States who were dangerous on account of their development of nuclear weapons and sponsorship of terrorism.

Israel had lobbied hard in favor of Saddam's removal, and many Israelis hoped that a quick military victory against the Iraqis would prove a stepping-stone for future military action against neighboring Iran, a fellow member of Bush's Axis of Evil. At the very least, the American invasion of Iraq served as a serious warning to Iran: reconsider your nuclear ambitions, or else. There were additional rationales, as well. Benjamin Netanyahu, then a private citizen, testified before the United States House of Representatives, during which he argued that toppling Saddam could initiate a process of creating a safer, stabler, and more democratic Middle East.[56] Ephraim Inbar, head of the Bar-Ilan BESA Center, advanced the economic case for invasion, arguing that Israel would save 'billions of shekels' in defense costs.[57]

For most Israelis, as well as for President Bush, the ultimate fate of Iraq was less important than removing Saddam and dismantling his supposed weapons program. Neither the Americans nor the Israelis gave much thought to the feasibility of Iraq becoming a Western-style democracy or whether its future leaders would be any more sympathetic to Israel than its current one. The Israelis were primarily interested in the invasion sending a clear message: the same fate could await any Middle East leader who sought to produce weapons that could threaten Israel or the West.

The ease with which the United States initially dispatched the Iraqi conventional forces and toppled Saddam's government added to Israel's optimism about the potential for reshaping the region by force. Debate about whether it was logical to take military action against Iran gave way to discussion of timing and logistics, implying that the decision was a foregone conclusion. After all, if Iraq's weapons program threatened global peace and stability, so too did Iran's alleged development of nuclear weapons.[58] The renewed discussion included speculation about the ease with which regime change in Iran could be effected.[59] In a column entitled 'It's Mullah Time!' commentator Mark Steyn dismissed concerns about popular support on the ground, emphatically claiming that toppling the Islamic Republic would be easy since 90% of Iranians already desired change.[60]

Subsequent events in Iraq dampened Israeli optimism. However, for advocates of moving to bring about regime change in Iran, the genie was out of the bottle. They had committed to a strategy involving the use of force, and, having already dismissed less dramatic options, they saw no alternative plans left to pursue.

The remarkable feature of the Iranian threat narrative initiated by Ephraim Sneh and amplified by Netanyahu is that it was grounded mainly in speculation. During the 1990s, no one knew with certainty the nature of Iran's nuclear program or its strategic intentions. As mentioned earlier, few Israelis had much knowledge about Iran at all.[61] As the United States got bogged down in the Iraq quagmire, it became increasingly harder to make the case for war with Iran. That is not to say that some did not try. Developments in Iran contributed to a robust debate in Israel that focused on four main issues: what was happening at Iran's nuclear facilities;[62] how long would it take Iran to build and test a nuclear weapon; what were Iran's intentions vis-à-vis Israel; and why was Israel cutting its defense budget at this precarious time?

Many Israelis had believed that toppling Saddam would enable Israel to reduce its defense expenditures. Facing budget problems, Israel had decided to cut its defense spending after the United States invaded Iraq. Ironically, it was Benjamin Netanyahu, Israel's finance minister at the time, who had advanced that recommendation.[63] Iran hawks sharply condemned the decision. Ephraim Sneh, now a Labor Knesset Member (MK) led the opposition, accusing Ariel Sharon's government of complacency in the face of what he claimed was the real—and growing—threat to Israel's security.[64]

The alarmists received new ammunition in August 2003 when the IAEA reported finding trace amounts of highly enriched uranium at the Natanz nuclear facility. The revelation drew very different responses from Israeli and Iranian leaders. The latter dismissed the significance of the finding, claiming that the traces were left on used components that had been obtained from overseas.[65] For many Israelis, however, this was the first hard evidence proving Iran was secretly producing a bomb. The hawks dismissed or ignored Iran's negotiation offer, which they considered untrustworthy,[66] and they renewed calls for Israel to take action sooner rather than later. When the IAEA issued another report claiming that there was no evidence of a secret nuclear weapons program in Iran,[67] it apparently made no difference in the Israeli position.[68]

As discussion of the Iranian threat in Israel accelerated, more officials came under pressure to offer their analyses. As is frequently the case with assessments of long-term military strategies, this often took the form of various timelines for when the threat would escalate. In the case of Iran, the near universal concern among Israelis was its alleged march toward a nuclear weapon. Notable among the Israeli officials now offering their opinions on Iran were military leaders, who in the past had been hesitant to assign concrete dates to Iran's nuclear progress. Israeli military intelligence chief Major General Aharon Ze'evi, despite previously having refused even to discuss the possibility of Israeli military action against Iran, said that he estimated that Iran was just two years away from building its bomb.[69] The day after the November IAEA report came out, Israel's Defense Minister, Shaul Mofaz, reduced this estimated production time to less than a year.[70] Although officials offered their predictions without much evidence to support them, the mere speculation of a terrifyingly short wait until Israel faced a nuclear rival had an important effect on Israeli perceptions of the imminence of the Iranian threat.

Precision in estimation was less important than the idea that the deadline was creeping ever closer, by which point Israel would need to act if it was to retard or destroy Iran's nuclear capabilities. Failure to act within the established timeframe would leave Israel facing severe anxiety at best, and annihilation at worst. The continuous sounding of alarms over Iran's impending completion of the bomb also ignored the fact that previous predicted deadlines had come and gone. No officials had faced public questioning over their inaccurate predictions, and few had publicly revisited their previous assessments or questioned the wisdom of continuing such speculation without evidentiary support. Instead, officials revised and reissued their warnings of imminent or short-term bomb completion, each time seeking to emphasize the sense of urgency.[71]

Warnings of the consequences Israel would suffer if Iran realized its nuclear ambitions also continued as part of the political discourse. Speakers offered rhetorical depictions of the destruction that would be inflicted by Iran's irrational, ideology-driven leaders. Knesset Foreign Affairs and Defense Committee Chair Yuval Steinitz provided a characteristic example, claiming that Iran was a 'totally irresponsible and unpredictable totalitarian regime that is ready to sacrifice millions of people for its crazy ideology.'[72] Israeli officials directed this message to the global community as well. At the United Nations in 2004, Foreign Minister Silvan Shalom asserted, 'Iran has replaced Saddam Hussein as the world's number one exporter of terror, hate, and instability,' and reminded the assembled leaders that Iran's missiles could now reach London, Paris, Berlin, and Russia.[73]

Iranian President Mohammad Khatami's government, meanwhile, generally refrained from engaging with Israel over its incendiary accusations. But conservative hardliners—including the Supreme Leader, who opposed the reformist Khatami's popularity—often provided comments that were sufficiently provocative to validate Israel's threat narrative.[74] However, with few exceptions, Iran's leaders for the most part did not exhibit the same fear of an Israeli threat as Israelis exhibited toward Iran. As noted earlier, securitization efforts in this conflict were asymmetrical: Israeli officials maintained that Iran posed an existential threat, while Iran's elected government was actively pursuing improved relations with the West. One of the few exceptions to Iran's practice of not responding to Israeli accusations came in 2005 when Israel threatened military action against Iran's nuclear facilities.[75] That year, an explosion at a government facility in Iran prompted speculation among the Western press that Israel had carried out its threatened raid. Iranian officials insisted that the explosion had been a controlled demolition at an Iranian dam construction site, although doubts remained.[76]

Yet for all the discussion of Iran—including the potential for taking military action against it—within the Israeli government, military, and media, by early 2005 it remained unclear whether the Israeli public was significantly fearful—or even aware—of their leaders' concerns over the Islamic Republic.[77] Public opinion surveys on national security often did not think to include questions about Iran's nuclear program, whether the public believed that Iran posed a threat (existential or otherwise), or whether Israelis favored using military force to halt Iran's nuclear progress. For the most part, polls continued to reflect the public's concern with the traditional security threats, including Palestinian unrest and the activities of neighboring Arab states.[78] The ambivalence of the Israeli public would soon change, however, when a controversial new Iranian leader emerged, bringing Iran to the forefront of Israeli public consciousness.

IV. Phase II: The Case Against Iran

Mahmoud Ahmadinejad's surprise victory in the Iranian presidential election in 2005 was a gift to Israeli hawks. His predecessor, Mohammad Khatami, had sought negotiations that, at a minimum, disproved the charges that Iran was singularly focused on building a bomb to destroy Israel. The situation, however, was far from clear. Supreme Leader Ayatollah Khamenei grew suspicious of the popular Khatami during the latter's second term in office and precipitated a conflict between the reformists and the conservatives, with the nuclear program as its battleground. Thus, while Khatami's government explored possible diplomatic solutions with the West, Khamenei and the IRGC disrupted discussions by issuing belligerent public statements punctuated by an occasional missile test. Although the Second Intifada and its attendant security problems commanded Israel's immediate attention, the remarks of the Iranian hardliners were sufficient to support Israeli hawks' warnings that Iran was a danger to Israel, and to keep the issue in the news.[79]

By 2005, as Iran prepared for a presidential leadership change, Israel could not be optimistic about prospects for international action against Iran. It was clear by now that the overthrow of Saddam Hussein was not going to transform the Middle East into the envisioned democratic utopia. If anything, the United States' war in Iraq appeared to be worsening.[80] In June elections in neighboring Lebanon, Hezbollah—an insurgent organization that was one of Israel's sworn enemies—won fourteen seats in the national parliament, as well as all twenty-three seats in southern Lebanon.[81] The 7 July 2005 terrorist attacks in London and the November 2005 hotel bombings in Jordan highlighted how civilians anywhere in the world were vulnerable to the spread of terrorism. The optimism that Western determination could reshape the Middle East was, if not gone, at least fading quickly.

In the midst of this turmoil, Iranians went to the polls to select a new president. Mahmoud Ahmadinejad's victory in a runoff election on 24 June 2005 represented a significant change of leadership. His mix of hardline conservative politics, bombastic style, and virulent anti-Semitism made him the perfect villain for Israelis who sought to portray Iran in monolithic terms. That he came to power through ostensibly democratic elections reinforced many of the stereotypical characteristics that Israeli leaders had attributed to the Iranian public at large.[82]

Ahmadinejad, a former member of the Revolutionary Guards who had played a role in planning for the 1979 storming of the United States embassy compound in Tehran, surprised observers by making the runoff following the first round of elections.[83] At the time, he was a relative newcomer to electoral politics in Iran, having served only two years as mayor of Tehran.[84] His subsequent defeat of Akbar Hashemi Rafsanjani, a two-term former president and one of the most powerful politicians in Iran, came as a shock. As mayor, Ahmadinejad had rolled back many of the liberalizing measures implemented by his more moderate predecessors, and during his presidential campaign he had sharply criticized the reforms instituted by the Khatami government. Backed by conservative and hardline factions, Ahmadinejad promised a more confrontational approach to the West, and in particular the United States.[85]

Israel—or, in Iranian political parlance, the 'Zionist Regime'— did not figure prominently in the Iranian presidential campaign. Likewise, as it focused primarily on the shortcomings of the Khatami presidency, the election did not garner much attention in Israel until Ahmadinejad's unexpected victory. Once the Israeli media introduced the public to the controversial president-elect, however, listeners were quick to seize on Ahmadinejad's radicalism in an attempt to tie him to Iran's nuclear threat.

In a cabinet meeting two days after the election, Foreign Minister Silvan Shalom claimed that Ahmadinejad's victory proved that Iran was not actually interested in reform or conciliation, but rather valued only conservatism and extremism. He said Israel was greatly concerned about Ahmadinejad's promises to increase nuclear development, which, he argued, had 'one purpose in mind: to obtain nuclear weapons.' He continued by saying it was now 'more probable than ever' that Iran would arm terrorist organizations with nuclear weapons and bring the nuclear threat to the world's doorstep. Shalom suggested that Israel seek to have the United Nations Security Council take up the issue of Iran's nuclear program.[86]

Those weighing in on the meaning of Ahmadinejad's election offered two related messages, one primarily for domestic audiences and the other for the international community. First, Israelis, who had long propagated the danger of Iran, declared themselves to be vindicated and their critics—particularly those experts who had argued against them—proved wrong. Second, the selection of a hardliner to the highest elected office in Iran prompted Israeli leaders to challenge the complacency of the Western nations who had sought to engage with Iran. They criticized the West's previous softness on Iran, especially since Israel saw it as according the Islamic Republic a level of international legitimacy that they now claimed was not justified.[87]

Israeli hawks claimed that the election results validated their warnings. Ironically, in justifying this claim they adopted two cognitively dissonant arguments. While some maintained that Ahmadinejad's election represented the 'real' Iran, others claimed that the elections were 'clearly rigged,' and that the Islamic Republic was finally abandoning the pretense of electoral legitimacy.[88] In a stinging opinion piece entitled 'The Mask Is Off and No One Cares,' columnist Caroline Glick wrote that the elections were a 'democratic farce.' She called Ahmadinejad a 'global terrorist who was actively seeking nuclear weapons.'[89] One Israeli hardliner sarcastically noted the weakness of the argument that Iran's elections had democratic legitimacy, saying, 'Even Hitler was democratically elected.'[90] Some who had been previously skeptical of Iranian intentions adopted revisionist claims about their previous views.[91] For those who had long been denouncing Iran, Ahmadinejad's election did not represent a significant change. Rather, it was just the latest chapter in Iran's inexorable march into darkness, although this new installment did mean that now they possessed the ammunition necessary to prove their former critics wrong. Ahmadinejad, they believed, would be a difficult man to defend on the global stage.

Israeli leaders wasted no time in employing the election results to castigate nations, especially in the West, for their willingness to treat the Islamic Republic as a legitimate state. Ahmadinejad's victory conclusively showed that Iran deserved confrontation, not engagement. How could one even engage with a man such as him? By criticizing Ahmadinejad as undeserving of respect as a head of state, Israeli leaders advocated for Iran's ostracization from the rest of the international community. Undoubtedly, some Israelis hoped that the United States would find Ahmadinejad so objectionable as to warrant potential military action against Iran, although few expressed optimism that this would happen.[92]

Somewhat counterintuitively, Ahmadinejad's rise to power initially did not materially alter the nature of the nuclear threat, at least in terms of the official Israeli position. Ariel Sharon chose to exclude Iran's nuclear activities from his remarks in his fall 2005 address to the United Nations General Assembly. In fact, the speech was noticeably light on mention of Iran in general. Only once did he refer to Iran as a threat to global stability, and he did not even explicitly mention the country by name.[93] Believing that he could secure broad international opposition to Iran's nuclear activities and prevent any compromise, Sharon pursued his Iran agenda primarily outside of the public's view.[94] Upon his return from New York, Sharon reported to his cabinet that he had discussed the need for transferring the Iranian nuclear issue from the IAEA to the United Nations Security Council, and that he had stressed his desire to see the world powers 'prevent any agreement or compromise with Iran.'[95]

On that front, at least, Sharon need not have worried. In his first few months on the job, Ahmadinejad did not disappoint those who expected him to manifest the danger they claimed he represented. In an effort to provoke Israel—and, by extension, the rest of the Western world—the Iranian government hosted an international conference in October 2005 entitled 'A World Without Zionism.' Ahmadinejad used the occasion to refer to Israel as the 'occupying regime' and declare that it should be 'wiped off the map,' a statement which would follow Ahmadinejad throughout the remainder of his presidency and, more generally, would haunt Iran beyond that.[96] Matching Sharon in his resistance to any compromise concerning the other nation, Ahmadinejad stated, 'We cannot compromise over the issue of Palestine.'

While it is difficult to say with certainty to what extent Ahmadinejad had intended to create a global controversy with his remarks, once they were picked up by international media outlets, Israelis were quick to amplify them. Israeli officials cited multiple reasons for the escalation in rhetoric. Former Israeli President Shimon Peres called for Iran to be expelled from the United Nations for committing a crime against humanity.[97] Foreign Minister Silvan Shalom reminded the French foreign minister that Europe should remember that their cities were within range of Iranian missiles, and that it was important for the 'whole Western world to stand united in its position' against the Iranian threat.[98] He also reminded Israelis that Ahmadinejad's election as president represented a reaffirmation of Iran's long-held desire to destroy Israel.[99]

Coverage of Iran exploded in the wake of Ahmadinejad's election victory and subsequent machinations, with Israeli media seizing the opportunity to cast Ahmadinejad as Israel's primary adversary. In one analysis, the average number of news articles mentioning Iran

Figure 4.1: *Jerusalem Post* articles mentioning 'Iran' (1989–2015)[102]

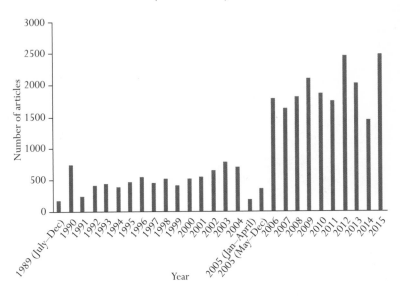

Source: Author's analysis of *Jerusalem Post* archives (via Newsbank)

more than tripled during the Ahmadinejad era, rising from 43.1 articles per month before his election in May 2005 to 154.1 per month after (see Figure 4.1).[100] The percent change was even larger when limited only to the opinion section, where the number of pieces mentioning Iran increased by more than 500%, going from 10.4 per month in the period before his election to 53.1 after (see Figure 4.2).[101]

Ahmadinejad's bombastic style and combative rhetoric made for easy comparisons to Hitler, Haman, or other would-be destroyers of the Jewish people. Increasingly, those invoking this history also claimed that the threat of annihilation as it currently stood would be even greater if Iran could use nuclear weapons to achieve its genocidal goal.[103] The frequency of distinct articles mentioning both 'Iran' and 'Holocaust' spiked following Ahmadinejad's ascendancy to Iranian national politics, as did various other combinations of 'Iran' and Holocaust-related lexicon, including 'Hitler,' 'Nazi,' and 'genocide'

Figure 4.2: *Jerusalem Post* articles mentioning 'Iran' (opinion section only)

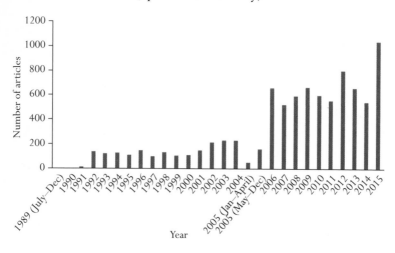

Source: Author's analysis of *Jerusalem Post* archives (via Newsbank)

Figure 4.3: Keyword analysis in *Jerusalem Post*

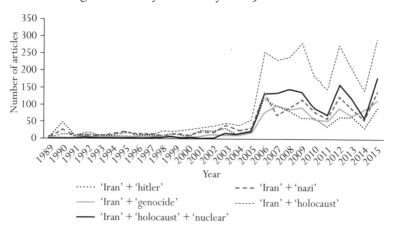

Source: Author's analysis of *Jerusalem Post* archives (via Newsbank)

(see Figure 4.3).[104] A significant proportion of these articles—nearly half, on average—also mentioned Iran's nuclear program. Between 2005 and 2008, there were more than 200 articles per year using the words 'Iran' and 'Holocaust' in the same text, with many making direct comparisons between the Nazi Final Solution and the Iranian nuclear program under Ahmadinejad.[105]

Security experts and military officials seized upon this shift in public attention to advance the case for action. Avi Dichter,[106] a former director of Israel's domestic intelligence agency, the Shin Bet, declared to a pro-Israel American audience that if Iran were to reach an 'irreversible point' in its nuclear program, America would have to do to Iran what Israel had done at Osirak in Iraq.[107] Lieutenant General Dan Halutz, Chief of Staff of the Israeli Armed Forces, declared that sanctions alone would not be sufficient to deter Iran. 'In general,' he said, 'for people who are used to eating olives and pita bread, sanctions which won't let them have cream with their caviar is not something that is too bothersome.'[108]

Halutz's comments were notable for two reasons. First, that a senior military officer was willing to speculate openly about the potential necessity of military action against Iran emphasized to the public the seriousness of the threat. Second, his evocation of cultural stereotypes about Iranians—their simplicity, poverty, and general orientalism —implied a key feature of the Israeli political discourse on Iran. In this view, Iranians were either fanatics or simpletons who did not value life as much as Israelis. Iranians would readily make personal sacrifices for the aggressive military ambitions of the state. Another Israeli general, Amos Yadlin, articulated a similar sentiment when he described the Iranian threat as 'ideological in origin,' which created an 'arc of evil that stretches between Teheran and Damascus.'[109]

It is difficult to know whether Israel's leaders had orchestrated and coordinated their response to Ahmadinejad or whether individual leaders each independently seized the opportunity to offer dire messages about Iran's future. Either way, these messages created an argument for unilateral preemptive action by Israel if the international community failed to mount a collective response. Reflecting years later on the Ahmadinejad era, Israeli journalist and political advisor Yaakov Katz observed that Ahmadinejad had been a significant public relations victory for the Israelis because he embodied and articulated the threat characteristics that Israeli politicians had previously attributed to Iran and to which they were already accustomed.[110] Ahmadinejad's status as an elected official—as opposed to an appointed religious cleric—added to his usefulness in this regard since it made the entire country appear at least somewhat complicit in Ahmadinejad's plans to commit horrible crimes against humanity in the name of a divine mission.

Despite Ahmadinejad's provocations, convincing world leaders of the need for action remained a challenge for Israel. By the late 2000s, global enthusiasm for expanding the wars in Iraq and Afghanistan beyond their borders had withered, even among the most aggressive and war-hungry members of the Bush administration. Regime change in Iraq had gone so badly that it served as a warning to anyone paying attention. Iran, many were suddenly noticing, was a much larger, more capable, and more difficult country to contend with than a raggedy Iraq, and few outside of the political fringes believed it could be dealt with without a significant expenditure of blood and treasure, which neither the United States nor any other Western nation was willing to pay. Israeli leaders had no response to this reluctance on the part of the West, and they gave no indication that they had considered the potential repercussions of Iran retaliating for any attack within its borders.[111]

Still, the Israeli public relations campaign against Iran churned on. Military officials, as noted above, expressed contempt for the idea that softer measures, such as economic sanctions, would successfully deter Iran, while other prominent public figures doubled down on imagining the consequences of Israeli inaction. One such alarmist, Israeli television presenter Chanan Azran, published a book in March 2006 entitled *To Die of Fear: The 'Dirty Bomb'—Nightmare Scenarios.*[112] In an interview, Azran explained that the comments of IDF Chief of Staff Halutz concerning how Iran might provide Al Qaeda with radioactive material for a dirty bomb was one of his main sources of information about the seriousness of the threat. He called it 'the first time a senior military person has called a spade a spade—or in this case, a dirty bomb.'[113] He added that it was only a matter of time before Israel was the victim of a nonconventional weapon attack on its soil.[114] Chief of Israeli military intelligence Ze'evi Farkash also offered a particularly vivid image of the impending danger. He professed that 'The Middle East is currently standing before a global jihad tsunami.'

The diffusion of the Iran threat narrative to the Israeli public and its impact on the public psyche remained matters of speculation until April 2006. If a tenet of war theory is the requirement of public support—which in Israel is particularly essential due to its mandatory military service requirement—it is notable that the first major public opinion polls regarding public attitudes toward Iran were so long in coming. Shortly after Israel's national elections,[115] the monthly Peace Index poll asked Israelis about their perceptions of the threat posed by Iran. The responses revealed that an overwhelming majority, 78%, of the Israeli public believed that Iran constituted a real strategic danger to Israel.[116] The majority, however, did not favor a unilateral military response by Israel against Iran's nuclear facilities as the solution to this problem. Only 37% answered favorably while nearly half, 47%, opposed such action.[117] The overall lack of public support for the military intervention advocated by many prominent political and military leaders suggested that, despite the national concern over Iranian behavior, many did not share such a dire view of the threat. Still, this represented a solid base upon which to build a campaign for future offensive action.

The absence of public enthusiasm for military action against Iran did not deter those who believed it was the proper course of action. The internal debates between those wanting to pursue a diplomatic solution and those advocating stronger measures became public in May 2006 following the speech delivered by Prime Minister Ehud Olmert to the US Congress. Although Olmert invoked the familiar themes in condemning Iran's nuclear program and support for terrorism, many on the Israeli right attacked his strategy as insufficient. Caroline Glick of the *Jerusalem Post* called the speech 'weak,' declaring that the situation had gone well beyond the point where words alone would sway Iran.[118] Another column entitled 'Religious Fanatic at a Persian Bazaar' epitomized the overall tenor of the emerging debate. In it, Amir Taheri argued that the time for diplomacy with Iran was over. The real problem with Iran, he claimed, was that the Ahmadinejad government believed in its messianic vision backed by the Hidden Imam, a messianic figure whom Twelver Shiites believe will return to lead the forces of good in an apocalyptic battle shortly before the Day of Judgment. With Ahmadinejad claiming to have divine authority on his side, he would thus view concessions in the international arena as unnecessary and illogical. Negotiating with such an individual, Taheri wrote, would be akin to appeasement with Adolf Hitler.[119]

Even as the United Nations Security Council imposed new sanctions against Iran, Israel continued to argue that Iran could be neither engaged nor deterred. The embrace of Holocaust rhetoric among a growing segment of the political right signaled a shift in the argumentation from strategic assessment based upon relatively conventional security measures to a case grounded increasingly in moral considerations. The proponents of action replaced rational calculations with warnings of existential danger and impending doom. In addition to hardline politicians, some of Israel's leading moral authorities began weighing in with concerns about the continued survival of the Israeli—and, by extension, the Jewish—people. In May 2008, Elie Wiesel, a Holocaust survivor and one of Israel's moral leaders, said in reference to Iran that it was mandatory for Israelis to 'act against evil.' He added that it was the duty of 'everyone who has a heart' to stand in opposition to Iran.[120] Israel's religious leaders, who had been initially reticent to reject a diplomatic solution, joined in making the moral case.[121] Notably, this chorus grew louder as Israel confronted what would turn out to be yet another transformative event in the Iran-Israel conflict: the Second Lebanon War.

V. Phase III: Fighting Iran in Lebanon

In 2006 Israel invaded Lebanon, thus launching the Second Lebanon War. Tensions between Israel and Hezbollah had been slowly simmering along Israel's northern border in the six years since Israel's abrupt withdrawal from southern Lebanon. Israeli strategists were well aware of the role Iran had played in developing and supporting the Shiite militia forces operating in Lebanon, most notably Hezbollah, which had developed and strengthened during Israel's eighteen-year occupation of the country. Still, for those preoccupied with the Iran threat, there was a delay in connecting the violence that erupted in June 2006 with Iran. The invasion followed the abduction of two Israeli soldiers who had been patrolling along Israel's northern border. In response, Israeli forces promptly reoccupied southern Lebanon with the intent of rooting out Hezbollah forces by eliminating their base of operations.

By most accounts, the conflict proved complicated and confusing.[122] Israeli troops were uncharacteristically disorganized and struggled to identify and engage an enemy whose members had burrowed deep into the societal structure of South Lebanon.[123] With the memory of the IDF's harsh occupation still fresh in their memories, the local population proved extremely hostile to Israeli forces, making it difficult for the IDF to gain any actionable intelligence on enemy operations. Israeli intelligence proved unprepared to counter Hezbollah's bunker-based defensive tactics and insurgency-style operations, and IDF ground troops struggled to coordinate their movements with air support.[124]

The fighting concluded just a few weeks later with both sides declaring victory. Israeli leaders touted the damage they had inflicted on southern Lebanon—including a superior body count— as evidence that they had dealt Hezbollah a severe blow. Meanwhile, Hezbollah claimed a strategic victory, noting that not only had they repelled the Israeli invaders, but they had survived the full force of the Israeli military's power, thereby disproving the invincibility of the IDF.

In retrospect, the Lebanon war changed the political landscape, not because of what happened or did not happen during the brief encounter, but because it produced a new chapter in Israel's Iran narrative. It prompted Israeli leaders to reconsider both the meaning of the Iran threat and its role in Israel's lengthy history of conflict with its neighbors. The soul-searching conducted in the wake of the Lebanon conflict would lead to a complete rethinking of the Iran threat, and would subsequently lead many in Israel's political and security establishment to decide that their prior thinking about Iran as a peripheral or secondary challenge had been incorrect all along. In fact, they concluded, Iran was and had been Israel's primary challenger going back decades. This enhanced view of Iran as a pressing issue, together with the increasingly moralistic tone of Iran's security discourse, would lay the groundwork for an enterprising politician to seize on that fear and use it to serve his political agenda.

The long-term significance of the Second Lebanon War would not be determined on the battlefield but rather revealed in the analyses that followed. These postmortems began with the military and strategic reviews of Israel's conduct. Both internal and third-party appraisals concluded that Israel had actually accomplished very little of what it had intended to achieve during the fighting. One scathing internal review called the war 'a serious missed opportunity' in which the region's most powerful and technologically advanced military force had failed to best a force of several thousand men. It cited Israeli political and military leaders' 'grave failings.'[125] Many in the IDF agreed. They had assumed they would quickly dispatch Hezbollah forces, whom Israelis regarded as second-rate terrorists capable of fighting only low-level guerrilla battles. Instead, like many militaries throughout history, they were unexpectedly defeated by an enemy whose quality they deemed far inferior to their own. Israeli forces returned home surprised by their foe's competence, the quality of their weapons, and the sophistication of their tactical operations.[126]

Importantly, the results of these inquiries were not kept secret. They quickly worked their way into international news, dispelling the myth—which had been only halfheartedly propagated by Israeli military officials and members of the Ehud Olmert government— that Israel had won a decisive victory in Lebanon. While it took some time before public discussion of the conflict in Lebanon recognized a direct Iran connection, eventually opponents of the Olmert government began raising the issue of there being a link. Benjamin Netanyahu, then the leader of the Likud opposition, was among the first to condemn Iran's role in the conflict. Netanyahu claimed that the Lebanese opposition had been 'conceived, organized, trained and equipped by Iran, with Iran's goal of destroying Israel and its fantasy ideology of building a once-glorious Muslim empire in which we are the first pit stop.' He went on to declare Iran 'the source of everything that is happening here now.' Invoking the Nazi analogy, he said, 'These people [the Iranians] are stark-raving mad, but there is a method to their madness, just like Hitler.' According to Netanyahu, Iran could be found lurking behind nearly all of Israel's enemies.[127]

Netanyahu's accusations not only initiated discussion of Iranian involvement in—if not responsibility for—the war with Hezbollah, but it also transformed Iran from a passive threat into an active belligerent in the conflict. It was now directly responsible for Israeli casualties. Israeli media was quick to seize on this theme and broadcast the identification of Iran as public enemy number one throughout the country and beyond. The *Jerusalem Post* captured the new development days after the end of fighting with its editorial entitled 'A Wake-up Call':

> This struggle, in the end, has little to do with Lebanon, and even with Hezbollah, but with the true existential threats facing Israel, first and foremost from Iran … Our job now is to better prepare ourselves at every level: societal, diplomatic, governmental, and military; and, as the nation on the front line, do our utmost to mobilize the free world to collectively and effectively defend itself.[128]

Interestingly, while Ahmadinejad and other Iranian officials celebrated Hezbollah's victory over Israel, they disclaimed responsibility for helping them in the fighting. In Ahmadinejad's telling, the Israelis had been defeated by a 'unified, patient, and stable people.' In an ironic turn-about, Iranian MP Hussein Najat called on UN Secretary General Kofi Annan to seek a war crimes indictment against Israel for its conduct during the fighting.[129]

Meanwhile, the claim that Iran bore responsibility for Israel's inability to root out Hezbollah in Lebanon gained traction as Israel struggled to account for the failure of its mission there. One explanation held that Israel had not understood its enemy in the conflict. Israel had not just been fighting Hezbollah, it had engaged in a war against Iran as well. Defeat of the former, therefore, could not have been possible without a direct engagement with the latter. Eventually, those seeking to rationalize Israel's performance during the war settled on a consensus that enabled them to pivot attention away from Lebanon in favor of an explanation that centered on a bigger, more capable enemy. Accordingly, the true opponent of the

Lebanon War had not been a simple terrorist organization operating along Israel's northern border, but a sovereign country with a large, well-equipped army and aspirations of becoming a nuclear power.

In the new account, this type of conflict could not be resolved by a month-long skirmish in a third country against a few thousand members of a terrorist organization acting as a proxy on behalf of the real enemy. Moreover, the fact that Israel had engaged in a hot war, which involved Iran, changed the nature of the threat calculus, allowing Israel to counter international criticism of its aggression by recasting itself as a victim. With Israel now seeing itself through this prism of victimhood, it followed that the rest of the world was insufficiently sympathetic to Israel's plight.[130] This new understanding of Iran as the overarching enemy proved appealing to politicians, military officials, and—most importantly—a public who were searching for certainty amidst a jarring moment of unease. This narrative began working its way through Israeli media and eventually permeated its way into other realms of political and social discourse, including both fiction and nonfiction popular literature.

A novel authored by Shabtai Shoval, a former Israeli intelligence officer responsible for devising and gaming hypothetical nightmare scenarios for Israeli security, is one such example. Originally published in 2003, *The Chosen One: The Mossad in Iran* gained renewed attention in the immediate aftermath of the Lebanon War. The story tells the tale of a fictional coup d'état that forces Iran's religious leadership to abandon Tehran and take refuge in a secret bunker near the city of Qom.[131] Faced with imminent defeat and certain death, the Iranian clergy—led by Supreme Leader Ayatollah Khamenei, the only real-world figure named in the book—decide to launch a nuclear attack against Israel, fulfilling their murderous ambitions. A long-shot clandestine Mossad operation is the only hope for Israeli redemption.

The book is filled with racist and Islamophobic stereotypes portraying Iranians as bloodthirsty and untrustworthy. In one of the book's climactic moments, Khamenei gives a sermon to his 'possessed' followers. As he announces the decision to launch the nuclear strike, he preaches,

The events at hand will open the eyes of those countrymen of ours who have resigned to the path of treason. I believe that once we unleash the fire bolts of Salah al-Dīn upon the Zionists, these traitors will cease their imbecilic war on God's messengers and return to the patronage of the Qur'an and the holy Ayatollahs.

The author graphically pictures the crowd's response:

The bunker's personnel chanted after him, their throats parched, as they stamped their feet in an ever-growing rhythm. A hypnotic power permeated the space, like a rolling thunder washing over the packed crowd in overwhelming and dense waves of resolve, crushing all resistance. Masses clamored for their foreseen death, driven by sheer faith.[132]

After the Lebanon War, Shoval, who had become a prominent counterterrorism authority at an Israeli university, explained in an interview that he had written the book hoping that it would 'bring the looming danger [of Iran] to the forefront of public consciousness.'[133]

A year later, another book purporting to tell the real story behind the Lebanon War met with much greater commercial success. Ronen Bergman's *The Point of No Return* sold nearly 100,000 copies, which, by Israeli standards, was an impressive number.[134] It was subsequently published in English under the more revealing title, *The Secret War With Iran: The 30-Year Clandestine Struggle Against the World's Most Dangerous Terrorist Power*. The book offers a grim portrait of Israeli military and intelligence efforts to counter and contain Iran. Going beyond the book's primary focus on the failures of the 2006 Lebanon campaign, Bergman delves into Israel's military past to construct a history of conflict with a heretofore unrecognized Iranian enemy.[135] In the book's introduction, Bergman explains the challenge this poses:

The problem is that after three decades of trying to meet the Iranian challenge with a variety of strategies, covert negotiations, arms deals, critical dialogue, containment, direct political confrontation, and indirect action against its proxies, we still do not understand Iran. We do not know what its leaders want to do, and we do not know how to stop them from doing it, or at least, we do not know enough.[136]

Despite his absence of knowledge of Iran's intent, Bergman was sharply critical of Israel's complacency in facing off against Iran. According to Bergman, the conflict involved 'a titanic struggle between an aggressive, ideology-driven Islamic revolutionary regime, assisted by a no less brutal ideological ally that is willing to do its bidding, and a complacent, satisfied society that thought it had put its existential fears behind it.'[137] For Bergman, Israel's ignorance of Iran was a critical shortcoming. Thus, it is significant that Bergman, an investigative journalist for the Israeli newspaper *Yediot Aharonot* renowned for his connections to Israel's intelligence community,[138] lamented in a subsequent interview that the Israeli establishment had failed to understand virtually every aspect of its conflict with Iran.[139]

In 2007, two additional publications made notable contributions to the public discourse. An influential essay in *The New Republic* noted that 'For over two decades, since the era of former Prime Minister Menachem Begin, the Holocaust was rarely invoked, except on the extremes, in Israeli politics. In recent months, though, the Iranian threat has returned the Final Solution to the heart of Israeli discourse.'[140] Authors Yossi Klein Halevi and Michael Oren, a future Israeli ambassador to the United States, captured the growing fear represented by Ahmadinejad's anti-Semitic rhetoric and Israel's sense of vulnerability to a nuclear Iran. At the same time, the article crystalized the transition of concern from Ahmadinejad's view of history to a narrative in which the Holocaust served as a model for understanding Iranian behavior.[141] The article, which received considerable attention, mentioned a poll in which '27 percent of Israelis said they would consider leaving if Iran went nuclear.'[142] The prominence of the essay and its widespread circulation and discussion among Israeli elites contributed to the ever-increasing normalization of Holocaust discourse in the public debate.[143]

As the Iran threat intensified in Israel, the domestic media landscape was changing in ways that both reflected and exacerbated the new atmosphere of terror and paranoia in Israel which stemmed from an ever-present fear of destruction. A new Israeli newspaper emerged to take advantage of the lack of ready information on Iran and the growing emotional tenor of public discourse. Unsurprisingly, *Israel Hayom* (or 'Israel Today') capitalized on this fear to quickly become one of the most widely read newspapers in the country.[144] Financed by the staunchly conservative American billionaire Sheldon Adelson, who derived his fortune from the Las Vegas casino industry, the enterprise promoted right-wing policy proposals and championed the causes of conservative Israeli politicians, including Likud leader Benjamin Netanyahu and Yisrael Beiteinu leader Avigdor Lieberman.[145] It was free to the public, a first for an Israel newspaper, and it accorded prominence to Iran in both its reporting and opinion pieces.[146] Whether the paper reflected an already present political shift in the Israeli public or it influenced them in that direction is unclear and less important than its reporting and commentary on the security threats facing Israel.

The sharp increase in readership that followed its release allowed the paper to frame the debate of ideological issues and set the tone for debate nationwide. Security issues, in particular, reflected the paper's right-wing, hawkish ideological bias. It evinced this bias on Iranian issues shortly after its debut by publishing inflammatory and alarmist articles on Iran's nuclear program. In November 2007, *Hayom* quoted Yossi Baidatz, the head of the Israeli military's research division in the intelligence branch, as claiming that international pressure had failed to stop Iran, and that in the worst-case scenario Iran would have the capability to produce a bomb in under two years.[147]

The paper's focus on the Iran narrative followed a series of new sanctions which the United Nations had imposed against Iran earlier that year.[148] Prime Minister Olmert hailed these measures as an 'important, encouraging step by the international community.'[149] He added that Israel would 'continue to act to the best of our ability ... in order to strengthen this international front.'[150] While sanctions fit within Israel's Iran containment strategy, for the hawks they were insufficient. Thus, when evidence emerged that the sanctions might have had an impact, *Hayom* stood ready to refute the conclusion.[151]

In December 2007, the United States released its National Intelligence Estimate (NIE) for the past year, which reported that since 2003 Iran had suspended its military nuclear program and that, despite its ongoing nuclear development projects, Iran was no longer actively seeking to build a nuclear weapon.[152] The NIE, which is released annually both in classified and unclassified versions, offers a rundown of all the national security threats facing the United States and the intelligence community's assessment of each.[153] For years, Israel had relied heavily on American intelligence reporting to bolster their claims about Iran's nuclear activities. Consequently, the revelation that Israel's most important and powerful ally did not agree with the alleged facts underpinning Israel's justification for its Iran assessment had an outsized impact in Israel.

In the following day's edition, *Israel Hayom* carried several pieces about the NIE with a feature story on the front page headlined, 'In Tehran they died laughing.'[154] The newspaper juxtaposed pictures of the air defenses located around Iran's Natanz nuclear facility with pictures of the building itself, implying illegal activity within. Another headline highlighted the joy of the Iranian president at seeing the report, claiming that Ahmadinejad hailed the NIE as 'the nation's victory.'[155] The paper ran an editorial written by Ya'acov Ami-Dror, a former major general who would become National Security Advisor to Benjamin Netanyahu, asking why Iran would even need to produce their own uranium if not for a bomb. 'Why should the Iranians have to hide and risk the threat of sanctions, if they do not mean evil?' Amidror wrote.[156] This, he claimed, was reason enough to redouble Israel's efforts to stop the activities Iran was hiding.

Hayom argued that the NIE's failure to find evidence of a weapons program was not proof of absence; it meant only that Iran had succeeded in hiding the evidence that the paper insisted was there.[157] By emphasizing the uncertainty inherent in an esoteric and scientifically complex topic, as well as playing to its readership's well-established anti-Iran biases, the paper effectively used the NIE's conclusion that Iran had ended its weapons program to maintain that this only proved the opposite. The Israeli reaction to the NIE also indicated that some of Israel's most prominent military figures and security advisors were prepared to distrust American intelligence and factual assessments in favor of relying upon their own moral judgment of Iran's dishonesty.

The views expressed in *Hayom* were not outliers; many others voiced similarly skeptical views about the report's findings. It became something of a national mission to cast doubts on the accuracy of the report's conclusions. One popular tactic involved pointing out the historical inaccuracies of past American intelligence findings, such as the claim that there were weapons of mass destruction in Iraq, which Israel had vocally supported at the time as justification for invasion of that country.[158] Amos Regev, *Israel Hayom*'s editor in chief, penned an op-ed entitled 'American Intelligence—A Tradition of Mistakes.'[159] Defense Minister Ehud Barak joined in the chorus of those rejecting the NIE, saying that Israelis 'cannot allow ourselves to rest just because of an intel report from the other side of the earth.' Avigdor Lieberman, the Strategic Affairs Minister, was equally dismissive, invoking the uncertainty theme by claiming that 'No one knows when Iran will have the bomb.'[160] The manipulation of uncertainty contrasted with the certitude of those who had invested significant personal capital and credibility in the existence of the Iran threat. The idea that Iran was doing anything other than developing a bomb was so contradictory to their worldview that the only possible response was to reject the American assessment out of hand. In short, Israel was unwilling to be proven wrong.

The NIE came out at a particularly awkward time for Israeli leaders. Since the end of the Second Lebanon War, Iran had been steadily gaining steam as a matter of national importance. Politicians across the political spectrum had carved out a space of rare consensus over the urgency of the issue. In addition, Israel's academic and policy community had recently joined the conversation in support of publicizing Iran as an existential threat. For example, in 2007, The Institute for National Security Studies (INSS) published nineteen reports on Iran, a new record.[161] In the Knesset, speeches by Labor members had become nearly indistinguishable from those of more conservative party members.[162] There was general agreement that Iran was an increasingly dangerous opponent and that the next conflict was right around the corner. Most thought, although not all admitted publicly, that the government's containment policy of working to build an international coalition for the imposition of economic sanctions would prove inadequate in reducing the threat.

Meanwhile, although it had been brief, the Lebanon War nonetheless provided the catalyst for new ideas and additional actions from politicians. Everyone wanted to be part of the solution, even if this only meant offering symbolic proposals. For example, one Kadima MK proposed adding Iran to an anti-infiltration statute that barred illegal entry into Israel from countries hostile to the national interest, a list that included Syria, Lebanon, Saudi Arabia, and Yemen. The amendment, adopted with only one dissenting vote,[163] was largely meaningless as illegal entry into Israel by Iranian citizens was not a real concern.

Likud opposition leader Netanyahu advanced a more ambitious idea, demanding that the United States, among other countries, prevent the transfer of funds to companies that operate and invest in the Iranian private sector.[164] According to Netanyahu, such companies, which were primarily located in Europe, must be shunned by Israel and the United States to ensure that money did not indirectly reach 'the Iranian death machine.'[165] Netanyahu and his colleagues knew it was highly unlikely the United States would boycott European companies doing business with Iranian firms not connected to the government. Nevertheless, these and similar moves demonstrated that most Israeli politicians wanted to be seen as doing something proactive to counter the Iranian threat. There were also curious indications that Israel was open to broader engagement with countries in the region that shared its opposition to Iran: Kadima Party leader Tzipi Livni floated a reference to 'moderate countries of the region' with whom Israel might work to counter Iran.[166]

The plethora of attention heaped upon Iran began to bear fruit in subsequent measurements of Israeli public opinion. An April 2008 poll showed that a plurality of Israelis (38%) viewed the Iran nuclear program as the largest threat facing Israel.[167] They ranked it ahead of concerns about a possible Israeli-Arab rebellion (17%) or ongoing struggles against the Palestinian population (12%).[168] In one sense, the results were hardly surprising given the steady stream of fear-inducing speeches and reports coming from many different sources. It is understandable that the highly publicized threat of imminent mass destruction would capture the public's imagination more than intermittent terrorist attacks. On the other hand, the response was remarkable given that the factual predicate for the fear had been seriously challenged by Israel's own ally's intelligence assessment.

Significantly, the NIE had also contradicted Washington's Iran narrative.[169] A month after the report's release, President Bush travelled to Israel to reaffirm the United States' commitment to protect Israel from Iran. With the Iranian issue topping the agenda, Bush and Olmert both sought to portray Iran as a continuing threat. In their joint press conference, Olmert explained, 'The President of the largest power in the world, the most important power in the world, is standing right here, and he has said in no uncertain terms that Iran was a threat and remains a threat.'[170]

Rhetoric notwithstanding, all world leaders had been put on notice that there were serious doubts about the key components of Israel's public relations campaign against Iran. Crucially, the NIE had challenged the notion that Iran's development of a deadly bomb intended for Israel was imminent. Thus, if Iran was to remain atop Israel's foreign policy and military concerns, the nature of this threat needed to be expanded beyond its current scope. The discussion had to shift from a focus on esoteric and technical analysis of centrifuges and breakout timelines to something more abstractly nefarious. The obvious choice was to enlarge the narrative.

The debate spawned by the NIE over the imminence of the Iran threat generated a wedge issue to separate Israel's Iran hawks' position from those who were inclined to turn their security concerns elsewhere. Thus, Netanyahu, as the leader of the opposition bent on a return to power, seized the opportunity to construct a new version of the Iran narrative that would enhance its appeal to a populace primed for eternal conflict. At the end of the first decade of the twenty-first century, as Netanyahu prepared his run for prime minister, he creatively linked the present government's policy objectives with the burgeoning fear of Tehran. Netanyahu claimed that a divided Jerusalem would invite Iran to fill the vacuum left by Israeli withdrawal. He suggested that a weak Palestinian government would allow Hamas, under the direction of Iran, to operate freely within Israel's borders.[171] This injection of Iran into domestic politics hit many of the resonant proverbial buttons that provoked Israeli fears. It invoked Israelis' concerns for their immediate personal safety from unpredictable terrorist attacks. It also invoked the emotional issue of the fate of Jerusalem, which spoke to Jews worldwide. Finally, it raised disturbing visions of Israel's future.

VI. Conclusion

The election of Barack Obama as the forty-fourth President of the United States on 4 November 2008 marked the beginning of a new era of Israeli-US relations. For the previous eight years, Israel had worked closely with the George W. Bush administration to reshape the Middle East. Israeli leaders had encouraged the US invasion of Iraq and the removal of Saddam Hussein from power. They had also pressed for increased action against Iran, but on that front Israel could only claim partial victory. Although the United States supported imposing increasingly stricter economic sanctions against Iran, it had stopped short of endorsing military action against the other Middle Eastern member of the 'Axis of Evil.'

Iran had changed in important ways during this era as well. The US invasion of Iraq had strengthened Iran's strategic position in the region. The toppling of Saddam Hussein effectively eliminated a principal enemy that had checked Iran's activity along its western border, enabling Iran to exert influence on Iraq's newly empowered Shia majority. Domestic politics in Iran had taken a hard turn to the right with the election of Mahmoud Ahmadinejad as president in 2005, which did not benefit Iranians at home or abroad. Given his anti-Semitic and threatening rhetoric, Israeli leaders had found in Ahmadinejad an avatar for the Iran they pictured and propagated in their threat narrative.

Israel's case for taking extraordinary action against Iran to reduce or eliminate the threat, however, met with mixed success. Some national leaders amplified their condemnation of the nation and its leaders, but Israel was unsuccessful in excluding Iran from the United Nations or barring Ahmadinejad's recognition as a head of state. Not only was the West reluctant to consider military action, but world leaders also would not rule out seeking a diplomatic solution to reduce the threat of a nuclear armed Iran. The agents promoting the Iran threat narrative met with more success at home, meaning that it permeated Israeli political discourse and resonated with large segments of Israel society. Politicians, opinion leaders, the media, and popular culture fueled the public's imagination, offering doomsday scenarios that incited feelings of fear and insecurity. Experts, military officials, and other respected establishment figures added details such as the imminence of Iran's bomb development, the dishonesty of the Iranian regime, the justification for taking active measures against Iran, and—importantly—the options for action.

Israel's invasion of Lebanon in 2006 demonstrated the power and adaptability of the Iran narrative. Israeli political and military leaders turned an ill-conducted military campaign with an unsatisfying outcome into a validation and escalation of the threat posed by Iran. In the aftermath of the war, many Israeli leaders skillfully retrofitted their rhetoric to match their new reality. By identifying Iran, rather than Hezbollah, as their primary enemy, Israel concretized for its public the danger of Iran as something more than an abstract enemy tinkering with a nuclear program. The war also served as a precedent for holding Iran responsible for any belligerent action perpetrated against Israel. Hence, when Israel went to war in Gaza two years later, a chorus of Israeli leaders joined in blaming Iran for the renewed hostilities.[172] This not only reaffirmed and expanded the threat narrative, it highlighted for the public the consequences of inaction against Iran.[173]

The narrative proved its durability when the Israeli public continued to identify Iran as the top security threat to Israel despite the NIE and other experts concluding that Iran was not, in fact, pursuing nuclear weapons. While many, if not most, Israelis dismissed this assessment as incorrect, sustaining the general public's fear of imminent existential danger nevertheless required reshaping how Israel framed its conflict with Iran. Given the challenges associated with new developments in a continually changing social, political, and international environment, a skillful politician who succeeded in crafting a salient narrative could also succeed in promoting himself and his agenda. To do so, he would need both compelling rhetoric and a political strategy to advance and sustain a sense of threat, even in the face of contradictory evidence. Unfortunately for Iran, one potential leader was ready and waiting for just such an opportunity.

5

MESSAGING
NETANYAHU'S IRAN

I. Introduction

In 2009, Netanyahu was reelected prime minister after a ten-year hiatus. His campaign message was 'strong on security, strong on economy.' Although he narrowly lost the popular vote, he was given the first opportunity to form a governing coalition.[1] Netanyahu's first coalition in his return to power was surprisingly diverse, including right-wing parties Yisrael Beiteinu and Jewish Home, the ultra-orthodox parties Shas and United Torah Judaism, and the center-left Labor Party.

As detailed in the previous chapter, in the period between Netanyahu's first and second terms, events had conditioned Israelis toward being highly receptive to Netanyahu's promotion of Iran as a threat to Israel's existence. The experience of two wars, the Second Intifada, and periodic incidents of violence both within and along Israel's borders had heightened Israelis' fears for their safety. Netanyahu added to voters' worries by regularly voicing concerns about the looming threat of a nuclear Iran, launched by its unhinged and apocalyptic leader Mahmoud Ahmadinejad. To this threat, he offered himself as his country's protector.

As a national leader, Netanyahu had again secured a global megaphone to reach an international audience for his threat narrative, and in doing so he promoted his status at home. In a world now partially defined by the fear of terrorism, fueled by two large-scale wars in Iraq and Afghanistan—as well as America's ongoing global War on Terror—adding the specter of a state that sponsored terrorists acquiring a nuclear weapon fit neatly into the feelings of fear and anger in the West directed toward Muslim-majority countries. President George W. Bush had declared Iran to be part of an 'Axis of Evil' in 2002, and since that time Iran had not been able to shake the image created by that designation.[2]

Domestically, Netanyahu's use of the Iran threat narrative served two purposes. First, it enabled him to avoid more contentious foreign policy issues by concentrating on Iran as the primary security issue from which all others followed. By tying the Palestinian question to the conflict with Iran, Netanyahu claimed that Israel could not address the occupation until the world solved the crisis created by Iran's malign activities. Second, it provided a unifying principle for positioning himself as a strong leader who merited voter support. He would invoke a counterfactual claim that it was his hardline policies and bellicose rhetoric that deterred Iran from attacking Israel. This eternal brinksmanship provided a best-case scenario for the new prime minister: he could continue to stoke Iranian anger and provoke threats from Iranian officials while claiming credit for keeping Israel safe and out of war. He did not intend to lose another election anytime soon.

This chapter deconstructs Netanyahu's narrative by examining the tropes and the strategy he used to sustain Israelis' belief in the existential threat posed by Iran. It begins with a brief overview of events in Iran to provide context for Netanyahu's messaging. As it happened, the antics of Iranian President Ahmadinejad facilitated Netanyahu's narrative development and dissemination efforts, but the subsequent election of Rouhani challenged the narrative's sustainability. By embracing strategic populism Netanyahu was able to overcome both this challenge to his securitization of the Iran threat as well as, eventually, the challenge posed by Iran's agreement to suspend its nuclear development program in 2015. The chapter provides the foundation for understanding the power of Netanyahu's narrative to promote his leadership and political agenda and, as detailed in the next chapter, to change history.

II. Ahmadinejad's Facilitation and Rouhani's Contradiction

As Netanyahu assumed the mantle of power in 2009, Iran projected a complex and perplexing image to the world. Iran transitioned slowly into a postrevolutionary society with a highly educated population of mostly young people, a considerably flawed but marginally democratic electoral process allowing voters to choose their civil government officials from a slate of candidates vetted by religious authorities,[3] and a diverse and energetic political scene with multiple competing power centers. This nuanced picture clashed with the lingering perception among Israelis of Iran as a brutal, backward, and totalitarian theocratic police state. Netanyahu's return to power coinciding with the controversial reelection of Mahmoud Ahmadinejad as Iran's president in 2009 arrested Iran's ability to project the newer image.[4] In fact, Ahmadinejad's antics provided Netanyahu with considerable material for intensifying his warning of Iran's intentions to destroy Israel.[5]

By the time Netanyahu assumed office, Ahmadinejad had already established himself as a bloviating contrarian. On the international stage, he was the source of derision and ridicule. He trafficked in conspiracy theories, openly questioning the historical accuracy of both the Holocaust and the American account of the 11 September terrorist attacks. In 2006, he had hosted the International Conference to Review the Global Vision of the Holocaust, which brought together some of the world's most prominent Holocaust deniers and revisionists, including the American white supremacist and former Ku Klux Klan Grand Wizard David Duke.[6]

Ahmadinejad was not particularly popular among Iranians. During his first term his administration bungled attempts at an economic stimulus, and its disastrous distribution of direct cash payments led to widespread inflation and unemployment.[7] The government's economic mismanagement and perceived widespread corruption sparked occasional protests and riots.[8] While citizen activism indicated the emergence of a postrevolutionary society, the US allowed Ahmadinejad to shrug off responsibility for his contribution to the nation's economic difficulties.[9] To disguise his insecurities and corruption, Ahmadinejad targeted the United States and Israel as scapegoats for Iran's economic woes as a tactic to unite citizens against foreign powers and distract them from his leadership failures.[10]

Given Ahmadinejad's lack of popularity, it was not surprising that his reelection aroused accusations of fraud. What was unexpected, however, was that his victory generated a wave of public protests, including a nascent opposition movement that came to be known as the Green Revolution.[11] This civil society action complicated traditional perceptions of Iran. Since Iran was an authoritarian regime in which only the Supreme Leader's decisions mattered, manipulation of election results should have been expected rather than an impetus for public protest. Although the government responded with a crackdown on the protesters, which resulted in several dozen deaths and thousands of arrests, the incident suggested the presence of Iranian activists and widespread dissatisfaction among the population with the current direction of the country, which might have been emboldened by international condemnation.

Ahmadinejad also complicated the global perception of Iran's government by publicly questioning the power of the country's religious establishment.[12] This not only shattered the picture of Iran's government as a unitary militant theocracy by highlighting a leadership divide within conservative circles, but it also echoed the discontent of many Iranians who railed against the power of unelected elites.[13] This disunity did not resolve; in 2012, Iran's parliament, the Majles, in a historic move summoned Ahmadinejad to answer questions concerning his presidency.[14] This development suggested further reasons for foreign governments to reconsider policy options.

Netanyahu ignored the complexity of Iranian politics in favor of claiming that Ahmadinejad validated the image of a police state governed by religious fanatics. When asked by an American television reporter during the Iranian protests whether the election had been a fraud, Netanyahu seized the opportunity to vilify 'the

Iranian regime' and belittle the idea that Iran could ever have truly meaningful elections.[15] In multiple interviews, he stressed the 'true nature' of the Iranian regime, its lack of legitimacy, and its threat to world peace. Netanyahu cited the protests and the government response to reiterate the criticisms he had advanced during his days as opposition leader:

> This is a regime that represses its own people, supports terrorism worldwide and openly denies the Holocaust, while calling for the elimination of Israel. This regime is not only a great threat to our existence, but also to moderate Arab countries, the safety of Europe and to the peace in the world.[16]

Ahmadinejad's most valuable 'contribution' to Netanyahu's messaging was his active Holocaust denialism. Netanyahu frequently analogized the threat Iran posed to Israel with the Nazis' murder of six million Jews during World War II, invoking the rallying cry of 'Never again.'[17] Netanyahu appropriated this expression of defiance to call for preemptive action against Iran's nuclear facilities. The Iranian president's Holocaust denialism further highlighted the linkage in Netanyahu's messaging. For different reasons, both men used it as a provocation.

For Netanyahu, attacking purveyors of anti-Semitic messages was a strategic decision. While such behavior is reprehensible, publicly denouncing the messenger of hate directs attention toward him, which can, in some circumstances, prove counterproductive.[18] In political and foreign policy settings, it can also escalate controversy and prolong the visibility of the issue. The challenge might even lend credibility to the denialist's claim, building an otherwise ridiculous statement into an issue deserving of widespread attention and action.

While it is understandable that Israel is extremely sensitive to Holocaust denialism, especially when it comes from national leaders, Netanyahu's response to Ahmadinejad did not reflect a coherent strategy to isolate him for his purveying of anti-Semitic conspiracy theories. Rather, he prominently featured Ahmadinejad's claims as conclusive evidence that Iran intended to destroy Israel at its first opportunity.[19] Ignoring Ahmadinejad's publicity-seeking buffoonery, Netanyahu merged Iran's Holocaust denialism with the threat it posed as a nuclear power to amplify his messages of fear and danger, especially for Jewish audiences.[20]

In hindsight, Ahmadinejad's Holocaust denialism was but one of many ways in which his antics contributed to Netanyahu's narrative and gave him occasions to publicize it. The Iranian president also facilitated Netanyahu's effort to enlist the attention of world leaders in hopes that they would take more aggressive action against Iran. In 2010 and 2011, the United States and the European Union adopted a series of measures that completely cut off Iran from the international banking system, thus disabling the country from participating in international money transfers.[21] This action increased Iran's already substantial economic problems and intensified domestic pressure on Ahmadinejad and his administration.

For Netanyahu, Ahmadinejad's rhetoric provided the basis for escalating his accusations against Iran and advocating action against it. Sanctions, he claimed, were ineffective and insufficient. Even if he could not compel the international community to do more, he urged his government officials to consider a military response. However, this ran the risk of making the dire predictions he had made and the narrative he had promulgated come to fruition. By 2012, Israel had plans for a preemptive strike against Iran's nuclear facilities, which it reportedly scrapped only when US President Barack Obama refused to back such an operation.[22]

Few international leaders regretted Ahmadinejad's departure from the presidency when Iranians elected new leaders in June 2013. The election of Hassan Rouhani—a comparatively moderate cleric, career government official, and former National Security Advisor— surprised most observers. Rouhani campaigned on a platform that proposed to increase diplomatic engagement and called for an end to Iran's international isolation. Shortly after his inauguration, he began a global campaign to improve Iran's image. Dubbed by the international press as a 'charm offensive,' Rouhani stressed the new moderate direction Iran would take under his leadership, one that valued diplomatic and economic engagement over the provocative threats of his predecessor.[23]

These developments directly challenged Netanyahu's messaging, in which he had built up the Iranian threat scenario in part by casting Ahmadinejad—and, by extension, all Iranian leaders—as its primary villain. By Netanyahu's telling, Iran would always be led by a 'madman' or 'villain' who would keep the Middle East in a state of perpetual crisis until the world united to change the regime. Rouhani did not just change Iran's rhetoric, he presented an entirely new image of an Iranian leader. He was erudite and friendly, a religious cleric but with a modern view of the world. He attended the World Economic Forum in Davos, where he again called for 'constructive engagement' with the rest of the world.[24] Importantly, he encouraged the United States and its Western allies to negotiate a deal over Iran's nuclear program. That such an agreement might end Iran's crippling economic sanctions was an anathema to Netanyahu's strategy of keeping the Islamic Republic isolated, desperate, and angry.

Not surprisingly, Netanyahu and his supporters were unwilling to be charmed by Iran's new president. While skepticism and suspicion of Iran were understandable responses, Israeli leaders immediately dismissed Rouhani's overtures. Within days of the election, Deputy Foreign Minister Zeev Elkin said in a Knesset speech that Iran was a 'joke of democracy.' He said the idea of considering Rouhani's election to be a significant change in that country was 'funny.' Elkin attacked the new president's credibility, claiming that Rouhani had determined that the best way to move forward with the Iranian nuclear program was to 'delude the West' into thinking Iran was seriously negotiating while secretly continuing with its technological development.[25]

Israel's response to the Iranian elections capitalized on the uncertainty inherent in change. Assertions of potential worst-case scenarios are difficult to refute, especially when entrenched messaging and policies were built upon pervasive distrust. Echoing Netanyahu, Israeli media and policy elites refused to credit Iran's new leader with sincere motivations. News stories resorted to *ad hominem* attacks on Iran's new leader, mocking his sincerity and referring to 'Rouhani and his shy, sweet smile.' Israel arms control experts publicly reminded officials to remain vigilant and steadfast, especially 'when your adversary is smiling.'[26]

Rouhani's diplomatic demeanor required Israelis to pivot away from utilizing the Iranian president as an avatar of its governing regime. Without acknowledging the contradiction, commentators asserted that the post of president in the Islamic Republic was as a figurehead rather than a chief executive. This new version of the narrative was equally misleading. By maintaining that the levers of political power rested entirely with the Iranian clerical establishment, Israeli critics again ignored the complicated political dynamics at work in Iran as it transitioned from a revolutionary government to a postrevolutionary society.[27] Their picture discounted the reality that Iran had a young and educated population contributing energetically and creatively to the development of a vibrant civil society. They also attacked the legitimacy of the diplomatic initiatives being pursued by Iran's newly elected 'figurehead.'

Netanyahu now confronted new difficulties in maintaining his threat narrative, which he constructed in order to prioritize Israel's protection from Iran's dangerous and irrational leaders, and simultaneously to bolster his own leadership credentials. Rouhani's election had the potential to compel an amendment of the factual predicate for Netanyahu claiming there was an ongoing and imminent crisis. The possibility of change in Iran also eroded Netanyahu's ability to muster support from world leaders for isolating the Islamic Republic, which could take a 'military option' off the table. Rouhani not only presented a different face for Iran, but his soft-spoken manner and affability opened space for the world to learn more about Iranian society. He made it tenable for international leaders to engage with Iran in a meaningful way. They would no longer risk embarrassment by trying to negotiate with the unpredictable Ahmadinejad. Most importantly, in both word and action, Rouhani disproved the claim that Iranians blindly supported government officials who were openly intent on eradicating the Jewish State.

III. Netanyahu's Tropes

A. Narrative Strategy

Like most Israeli politicians, Netanyahu embraced protecting the nation's security as the top issue on his political agenda, while employing messages that heightened Israelis' sense of insecurity. Israelis had lived in a state of emergency since the country's founding, experiencing both periodic war and terrorist attacks. While some of Netanyahu's political opponents held out visions of peace, including ending hostilities with regional neighbors and accommodating the mutual interests of the Palestinians and Israelis, Netanyahu spoke almost exclusively of the urgency of Israeli security. He positioned himself as the leader who would address Israel's principal threat: Iran.

Netanyahu's strategy for retaining power focused on two audiences. Domestically, he employed a populist strategy to secure Israelis' belief that Iran posed an existential threat. This included promoting the perception of a crisis, highlighting his capability of leading the nation in responding to this challenge, and minimizing opposition. Internationally, he recruited allies for this crusade. With a perfect command of English,[28] he accepted speaking opportunities that would enhance his visibility at home[29] as well as attract international support for his cause. As prime minister, he secured meetings with the US president and other Western leaders in which he could make his case. In addition, he was always welcome to address major Jewish organizations, where he could urge members to influence their government's policies.[30]

In framing his messaging and constructing his narrative, Netanyahu relied on three principal tropes upon which he grounded his populist strategy. First, he set up Israel's conflict with Iran as a moral crusade. In his telling, the clash between the two nations represented a struggle between a morally superior democratic state, which was fighting for its survival, and a depraved and untrustworthy regime, which should not be allowed to participate in the community of nations. Moreover, those questioning the legitimacy of the Iranian threat would be setting themselves apart from the struggle to ensure that good triumphs over evil. Second, he ensured that Iran's nuclear program created a perpetual crisis marked both by fear and uncertainty. Israel required muscular leadership to confront this crisis. Third, he positioned himself as uniquely qualified to lead this modern crusade against Israel's would-be destroyer.

Netanyahu's messaging required minimal alteration when presenting it to his two audiences. To Israelis, he maintained that the morally branded crisis demanded unity. Those who challenged his factual accuracy or his analysis—including professional analysts, political opponents, and even dissenters within Israel's military and national security establishments—were unpatriotic. To the international community, he warned listeners not to be duped into believing they could reduce the danger posed by Iran through the use of conventional strategies of diplomacy and compromise. His advocacy for direct action was largely tactical posturing, but implicit was the possibility that the Iranian threat could become a viable contingency warranted by changing conditions.

B. Setting the Stage

Significantly, on the day of his second-term inauguration, Netanyahu chose an English-language media outlet for his first interview outlining his foreign policy vision and proposals for enhancing Israel's security. Sitting down with *The Atlantic* magazine's Jeffrey Goldberg, Netanyahu debuted the tropes that would come to define his Iran narrative. Having largely convinced Israelis to see Iran as a danger, he now aimed to persuade Americans that they should not only fear for Israel's security, but for the safety of the world if Iran were allowed to produce a nuclear bomb. Concomitantly, by emphasizing the existential risk posed by a nuclear Iran, Netanyahu implied that the criticisms lodged by progressive Jews of Israel's policies, such as the treatment of the Palestinians and human rights violations, should be dismissed as lesser concerns.

Netanyahu's published remarks on Iran focused on two themes: first, the threat of a nuclear Iran was real and unprecedented; and second, the United States should honor its strong relationship with Israel by joining in some as-yet-undefined confrontation with Iran.[31] Netanyahu stressed that complacency about Iran was dangerous, dismissing critics who questioned his foreign policy priorities and focus. Now, in a one-on-one interview with a familiar and sympathetic journalist,[32] Netanyahu sought to control the exchange to expand upon these themes. He addressed the moral dimension of the conflict with Iran using what Jan-Werner Müller refers to as 'the moral imagination of politics.'[33] Netanyahu pictured Israel as engaged in a moral crusade against a corrupt regime. This represented an evolutionary refinement from his first term when he had defined Iran as being a foreign policy issue, but not the singular danger. The conflict was now a clash of civilizations, in which Israelis were defending not only themselves but the entire Western world. Netanyahu threatened preemptive military action and warned other nations against engaging diplomatically with Iran.[34] According to Netanyahu, Iran not only embraced a death wish, but it also willingly accepted its own destruction in its quest to destroy others. He claimed that Iran was a nation that 'glorifies blood and death, including its own self-immolation.'[35]

Netanyahu hyperbolically argued that Iran had been remorseless about its conduct during its eight-year war with Iraq. In Netanyahu's retelling, the great human cost of that conflict had meant nothing to Iran, which had 'wasted over a million lives without batting an eyelash.' Contrary to reality, he asserted that the costly war 'didn't sear a terrible wound into the Iranian consciousness.'[36] By Netanyahu's reckoning, Iran was not entitled to justify either its nuclear program or its military buildup, including its missile arsenal, by citing its own security concerns. He dismissed the idea that Iran might see itself as a victim of enemy aggression and, hence, could fear future attacks. Rather, Iran sought weapons—and specifically nuclear weapons—to engage in immoral and apocalyptic aggression against other nations.

Implicitly, Netanyahu distinguished Iran's putative quest for a nuclear weapon from Israel's possession of a nuclear arsenal. Israel's nuclear weapons, though undeclared, were necessary, since Israel had a historical need and right to defend itself given its history and location in a hostile region. Also left unsaid was the implication that Israel possessed the moral rectitude to responsibly possess weapons of mass destruction. Goldberg did not press Netanyahu for the source of his confidence that Iran intended to produce a weapon. When challenged on his certitude about the danger Iran and its drive for nuclear weapons posed, Netanyahu questioned Iran's rationality and claimed their 'unbelievable fanaticism' meant that normal containment measures would not work against them.[37]

Netanyahu also invoked his self-aggrandizing trope in which he portrayed himself as the only politician willing to speak the ugly truth. Addressing Americans, he pressed his case that confronting Iran represented a 'great mission,' both for himself and President

Barack Obama. Ridding the world of the Iranian threat would serve as a 'hinge of history' for the future of Western civilization. Netanyahu did not say whether he expected that the newly inaugurated President Obama, who had recently received the Nobel Peace Prize, would engage in another military conflict. He undoubtedly knew Americans were weary from years of unproductive wars in Iraq and Afghanistan, the loosely defined War on Terror, and a financial crisis that made even the cost of posturing too expensive.

Netanyahu had his opportunity to raise the issue with Obama in their first face-to-face meeting the following month. When pressed by Obama, who was interested in addressing the Palestinian issue, Netanyahu invoked Iran as a bargaining chip with the noncommittal response: 'We want to move simultaneously and then parallel on two fronts: the front of peace, and the front of preventing Iran from acquiring nuclear capability.'[38] Netanyahu would use this evasive tactic frequently in the years of his tenure. By prioritizing the imperative to resolve the Iran threat, he would deflect efforts to force Israel to negotiate with the Palestinians. While Netanyahu knew he had supporters for this position among American lawmakers and many American Jews, he did not want to risk alienating the new US president. If Obama became less receptive to Israel's future entreaties and more willing to criticize Israeli actions, he might also exclude Netanyahu from deliberations over Iran policy.

C. Operationalizing the Tropes

The simple basis of Netanyahu's morality-based message pictured Iran as intent on doing evil. Embedded in this message were complex implications. The images he conjured in his inauguration day interview with *The Atlantic* became staples of his rhetoric: Iran's leaders comprised a 'messianic apocalyptic cult'; 'When the wide-eyed believer gets hold of the reins of power and the weapons of mass death, then the entire world should start worrying'; 'Since the dawn of the nuclear age, we have not had a fanatic regime that might put its zealotry above its self-interest.'[39] Netanyahu intended these descriptions to act as warnings against trusting evil Iranian leaders: 'People say that they'll behave like any other nuclear power. Can you take the risk? Can you assume that?'[40]

For Netanyahu, the intentions of Iran's leaders created a moral imperative for action. The world needed to address the threat and do so quickly. This was the segue to his Holocaust analogy by which he urged national leaders, unlike their predecessors who failed to protest or prevent the murder of Jews, not to remain silent about the danger of the renewed existential threat. Netanyahu's message also raised the specter of anti-Semitism. In his first speech to the United Nations General Assembly in fall 2009, Netanyahu admonished the world leaders for their willingness to listen and talk to Iran, as well as for their criticism of Israel. He dramatically asked them, 'Have you no shame?'[41]

While Netanyahu was subtle in the ways he accused those who disagreed with him of anti-Semitism, he was much more blatant about displaying the anti-Islam bias that animated his criticism of Iran's leaders. In his United Nations speech, Netanyahu attributed the source of Iran's evil intentions to the extreme fanaticism which 'has swept the globe with a murderous violence and cold-blooded impartiality of its choice of victims.'[42] Israel's right-leaning media, which regularly reported Netanyahu's speeches and comments, amplified Netanyahu's disparagement of Islam as embraced by Iran. Columnists and editorial writers of the *Jerusalem Post* and *Israel Hayom* increasingly turned the Islamic honorific titles into epithets by referring to Iran's zealous 'mullahs' or 'ayatollahs.'[43]

A textual analysis of *Jerusalem Post* opinion pieces and articles that quoted Israeli officials shows a steady increase in usage of these terms as derogatory descriptors of Iranian leaders (see Figure 5.1), reflecting the intensity of Netanyahu's efforts to vilify Iran's leadership. The sharp rise in 2006 coincides with Netanyahu becoming the leader of the opposition in anticipation of another run for prime minister. The peak of 228 articles in 2015 is notable not only because this was the year of the signing of the Iran nuclear deal but also because it is two years after Rouhani initiated his global 'charm offensive' in a bid to change Iran's image. As an English-language paper, the *Jerusalem Post* disseminated Netanyahu's message to a broad readership that included an international audience as well as recent immigrants, *olim*, many of whom were fervent Zionists inexperienced in Israeli politics.

Figure 5.1: 'Ayatollahs' / 'Mullahs' usage in *Jerusalem Post* text

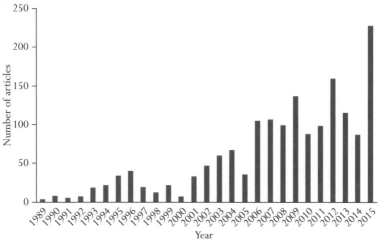

Source: Author's analysis of *Jerusalem Post* archives (via Newsbank)

For the first three years of Netanyahu's second term, Ahmadinejad's antics arguably validated Netanyahu's morality trope. By the time of Rouhani's election, Netanyahu's continuous repetition of the trope effectively allowed him to foreclose recognizing Iran's potential for change. Instead, he was able to explain why the election of a new Iranian leader, regardless of his message, was inconsequential.

Israel's intellectual establishment provided source material to back up Netanyahu's distrust of Rouhani's outreach efforts. Scholars preternaturally inclined to suspect Iran's intentions cited the concept of '*taqiya*' as the proof text for distrusting Iranian motives underlying their seemingly conciliatory statements: they claimed that *taqiya* was a lie that was permitted by Islam if it was intended to deceive one's enemies.[44] This allowed Netanyahu to pivot from critiquing Iran's leaders to discrediting Iran's negotiators, whom he deemed also likely to be deceitful and dishonest in their dealings with the heathens in the West.[45]

A close Netanyahu advisor, Dore Gold,[46] in his book *The Risk of Nuclear Iran: How Tehran Defies the West*, the publication of which coincided with Netanyahu's return to office, argued that dishonesty was a key feature of Iranian behavior. According to Gold, Ayatollah

Khomeini had invoked *taqiya* to hide Iran's nuclear development program and its support for terrorist groups.[47] Similarly, influential author Ronen Bergman, whose book *The Secret War With Iran* contributed to the Israeli public's understanding of the Iranian challenge, noted that *taqiya* was an important part of the Iranian psyche. Bergman explained that 'This blatantly cunning style of leadership would have a significant impact on the conduct of government in Iran after [Khomeini's death], and on the conduct of Shiites all over the world.'[48]

Netanyahu's critique of Iranian Islam served two purposes. First, it enabled him to distinguish between the ruling Islamic theocracy and Israel's religionists in positions of political power. Netanyahu undoubtedly understood that in a state founded upon a single religion there are fundamentalist factions that must be accommodated. His coalition partners included some men who sought to impose religious-based policies on nonbelievers. There was no reason for Netanyahu to ignore a similar political dynamic in Iran. Second, as discussed above, his simplistic portrait of Iran's Islam as corrupt also allowed him to discount as untrustworthy or untrue any 'inconvenient' statements made by Iranian leaders.

To the objective observer, Netanyahu's representation of Iran's leaders was shortsighted. His version of morality not only failed to account for the nuances of Iranian politics but also refused to acknowledge Iran's post-revolution societal evolution. It left no space for recognizing—or indeed for working toward—change that could reduce the risk posed by Iran. But then, a less-threatening Iran was not in Netanyahu's subjective interest.

Rouhani's election posed the greatest challenge to Netanyahu's narrative. Netanyahu maintained that Israel's clash with an erratic and unpredictable enemy regime in possession of a nuclear bomb amounted to an ongoing crisis, and manipulating his domestic audience's uncertainty of Iran's intentions sustained their fear. Making the case to world leaders—who were skeptical of Netanyahu's factual predicate—was harder, as Iran had yet to produce a weapon or a delivery system capable of reaching Israel.[49] Netanyahu pressed for action to prevent this from happening, hinting that it would likely require direct military intervention. In a May 2012 private talk, he went so far as to concede he was willing for Israel to suffer collateral damage from an American attack if it would guarantee the end of Iran's nuclear threat. He maintained that such an outcome was 'preferable to an atom bomb over our head.'[50] Following Rouhani's election and the initiation of talks on a nuclear deal, reality intruded on his claims of an ongoing crisis. Still, Netanyahu did not abandon his outreach to international audiences. Although he risked undermining his credibility, he may have believed that world events would reinvigorate his position. At a minimum, reports of his uncompromising speeches abroad declaring his hardline stance on Israel's safety would likely enhance his stature at home.

Netanyahu's strategy for maintaining his political power required preserving Israelis' collective crisis mentality. To an audience fearful of unpredictable violence, Netanyahu deftly conflated the existential threat of Iran's nuclear program with its more immediate reprehensible conduct of sponsoring terrorism. In effect, each of these threats were two sides of the same coin: one side was abstract yet conceivable, while the other was familiar. He sought to convince Israelis that both were believable. Those skeptical of Iran's present capacity to bomb Israel should still fear that it might do so in the not-too-distant future. At the same time, Israeli citizens should not only fear the immediate unpredictability of an Iranian-sponsored terrorist attack, but they should see the present hostile rhetoric as a sign of Iranian intent to eradicate Israel.

Netanyahu further merged the two risks by claiming that Iran's acquisition of a nuclear weapon would embolden terrorists.[51] He argued that a nuclear-armed Iran would protect terrorists by placing them under a 'nuclear umbrella,' in that Israel would be prevented from responding to terrorist attacks because it could provoke a more dangerous Iranian retaliation.[52] Not only could a relatively small act lead to a disastrous escalation of hostilities, but Israel's advanced missile defense systems would be less effective against a guerilla-style attack.

Iran's intention to produce a bomb and target Israel was the distinguishing element of the crisis trope. Sporadic or even frequent terrorist attacks were neither existential nor novel. They remained terrifying but were also an accepted feature of living in Israel. They did not threaten the stability of the state. Netanyahu's narrative pictured a crisis based both on the certainty that Iran would produce a weapon and the indeterminacy of when it might use that weapon against Israel. Representative of this conceptualization of crisis was his 2009 speech to the gathering of Jewish Federations of North America. He stated that 'The Iranian regime tyrannizes its people, sponsors and supplies terrorists, and openly pledges to wipe Israel off the map. Now just imagine how much more dangerous this regime would be if it had atomic bombs.'[53] He cited as proof text a 2001 quote from former President Hashemi Rafsanjani about the effects a nuclear bomb might have on a small territory like Israel. The Iranian leader observed that one bomb would completely destroy Israel, while a similar bomb could not annihilate the Muslim world, even if it caused massive damage.[54]

Netanyahu used the Rafsanjani quote to serve two purposes: to remind Israelis of their vulnerability, while also obfuscating any difference between Iranian hardliners and more moderate voices. In fact, it ascribed the same voice to all present and future Iranian leaders. 'It's instructive,' Netanyahu said in his address at the American Israel Public Affairs Committee (AIPAC) meeting in 2010, 'that the ingathering of Jews to Israel doesn't deter them. In fact, it whets their appetite.'[55]

As noted above, Ahmadinejad facilitated both Netanyahu's crisis rhetoric and its resonance with the Israeli public. In August 2012, Ahmadinejad delivered a series of highly inflammatory speeches in the lead-up to the annual celebration of Quds (Jerusalem) Day on 17 August. To a gathering of ambassadors from Islamic countries, Ahmadinejad argued that the key to solving the Palestinian problem was the elimination of the Zionist regime. Invoking a variety of anti-Semitic tropes, he maintained that 'a horrendous Zionist clan has been ruling the major world affairs' for 400 years. Zionists were 'behind the scenes of the major power circles, in political, media, monetary, and banking organizations in the world.'[56] According to the Anti-Defamation League, the address was Ahmadinejad's 'most anti-Semitic assault to date.' This was remarkable given that the ADL carefully monitored anti-Semitism and Ahmadinejad's many pronouncements. Two weeks later, on Al Quds Day, Ahmadinejad reiterated his calls for the destruction of the Jewish State by claiming it was time to 'remove the cancerous tumor of Israel' from the region.[57]

Israeli officials amplified Ahmadinejad's remarks, according them international attention by directing the Israeli ambassador to the United Nations to demand that the organization respond. The Israeli ambassador opened his letter to the president of the UN Security Council by claiming that recent statements and actions by Iran's leaders 'mark a new phase in its war against the State of Israel.' The letter extended the geographic reach of Iran's violence by claiming that Iran had sponsored acts of terror in Bulgaria, Delhi, Georgia, Thailand, and Azerbaijan.[58]

The following month, Netanyahu dramatically delivered a similar message in person. During his address to the United Nations General Assembly, he held up a diagram of a cartoon bomb meant to symbolize Iran's progress toward building a nuclear weapon. He then drew a red line to illustrate the point at which Israel and the world would no longer be able to prevent Iran from developing the bomb. He repeated his claim that 'Nothing could imperil our common future more than the arming of Iran with nuclear weapons.' He enlarged the threat by warning that the danger lay in the probability that Iran would provide such weapons to terrorists. 'Imagine the world with a nuclear armed Al Qaeda,' he added.[59]

In addition to providing imagery that represented imminent disaster, Netanyahu omitted discussion of contingencies likely to deter use of a nuclear weapon. In particular, he ignored the long history of nuclear deterrence that has prevented any nuclear power from using such a weapon. Similarly, he did not discuss the collateral consequences that would follow from its use, including the destructive impact, radiation contamination, and regional disruption. He neither admitted nor alluded to the fact that Israel, a non-signatory to the NPT, possessed a nuclear weapon.

By appealing to emotion rather than reason, Netanyahu also sought to insulate his crisis from being deactivated by developments that would challenge its sustainability or ease the crisis mindset. Less than a year before the Iranian elections that ended Ahmadinejad's presidency, polls had showed that over half of Israelis believed there was a real possibility of being harmed by an Iranian attack.[60]

As discussed above, the messaging used by Netanyahu to convince Israelis of their insecurity enabled him to avoid materially altering his crisis tropes after Rouhani took office. Counterintuitively, as Figure 5.2 shows, Netanyahu's warnings of the danger posed by Iran increased following Rouhani's election, although it is likely that he also tried harder to make his case to a less receptive audience. In 2013 alone, Netanyahu raised the Iran threat on forty separate occasions, more than double that of the previous year.[61] His pronouncements spiked again in 2015 (thirty-one statements, twenty more than the previous year) as negotiations produced the deal that limited Iran's enrichment activities in exchange for the Islamic Republic receiving relief from sanctions.

Additionally, a textual analysis of transcripts of Netanyahu's speeches (see Figure 5.3) shows that Netanyahu increasingly focused on Iran at the same time as the West was increasing its diplomatic engagement. Given Netanyahu's vociferous opposition to the negotiations, his focus on Iran was exclusively negative. Ironically, Netanyahu averaged more attacks on Iran in his speeches and public statements during the Rouhani administration than during the Ahmadinejad years, suggesting that he was more concerned about a deal that would reduce the intensity of the crisis he had machinated than he was about the antics of a man who sustained it. The density plot of his Iran references in Figure 5.3 also indicates that Netanyahu increased his attacks as negotiations progressed toward critical milestones in reducing the nuclear threat.

As Netanyahu expanded his sustained attacks on Iran to include his opposition to a nuclear deal, he situated himself to assume an additional role. In addition to securing his leadership at home, he positioned himself as the leader of global opposition to negotiations with Iran.

Netanyahu did not need to amend his self-promotional tropes from his early campaigns to fit his new populist strategy. He had never lacked self-confidence, and nothing in the intervening years gave him reason to modify what Eyal Arad, his former advisor, called 'a messianic notion of himself.'[62] He believed he was the best leader for Israel and the best representative of Israel in global affairs. He was the leader bold enough to confront Iran and condemn those who

Figure 5.2: Public pronouncements on Iran by year

	2004	2005	2006	2007	2008	2009	2010	2011	2012	2013	2014	2015
Mofaz		2										
Shalom	3	4	1									
Sharon		1										
Ze'evi		1										
Olmert		1	5	4	6	2						
Hanegbi		1										
Livni			6	1								
Peretz			2									
Hirschon			1									
Shalev/Bielski/Porat				1								
Netanyahu						10	12	8	15	40	11	31
Unnamed								2	1			
Cohen									1		1	1
Peres										2		

Source: Author's analysis of Prime Minister's Office archives

Figure 5.3: Dispersion plot of 'Iran' in Netanyahu speeches (2009–15)

Jan 2009   Dec 2015

Time

Source: Author's analysis of Prime Minister's Office archives

refused to do so; he was prepared to take whatever steps he deemed necessary and to convince others to join his effort.[63]

Netanyahu grounded his leadership agenda on a selective recounting of history. The principal lessons for the modern age dictated that the Jewish people not wait for their enemies to attack first before seizing the opportunity to strike against those who sought their destruction.[64] His priority was to prevent another Holocaust. Iran represented the potential for history to repeat itself: Iran's leaders were Adolf Hitler, and its nuclear development program represented the modern incarnation of the Nazis' Final Solution. Netanyahu buttressed his calling with references to earlier existential challenges the Jewish people had faced. As discussed earlier, he suggested there was a direct connection between the account in the Hebrew Bible of the threat posed by Persia to the ancient Jews and the threat posed by modern-day Iran to the Jews of Israel.

To fit his narrative, Netanyahu offered a simplified and simplistic version of the biblical story of Esther in which Persians were the sole villains, leaving out details such as the Persian king's collaboration with Esther that enables her to save her people.[65] One might argue that the edit was negligible, since it did not detract from Netanyahu's point that he was the successor of the heroic Esther, destined to intervene to prevent harm to his people. Still, it is remarkable that Netanyahu began an address on 'the grave threats of radical Islam and Iran,' delivered to a joint session of the US Congress on the day before the 2015 Purim holiday,[66] with the misstatement that a 'powerful Persian viceroy named Haman … plotted to destroy the

171

Jewish people some 2,500 years ago.'[67] He concluded his remarks by returning to the biblical narrative: 'Today the Jewish people face another attempt by yet another Persian potentate to destroy us. Iran's Supreme Leader Ayatollah Khamenei spews the oldest hatred, the oldest hatred [sic] of anti-Semitism with the newest technology.'[68] Even Russian President Vladimir Putin rebuked Netanyahu for this analogy.[69] In a surreal twist, the incident also elicited a response from Iranian Foreign Minister Javad Zarif, who took to Twitter to lecture Netanyahu on biblical scripture and accuse him of 'selling bigoted lies against a nation which has saved the Jews.'[70]

Netanyahu's speech to the US Congress represented the evolution of his leadership trope from a self-image as a head of state to that of a savior. Back in 2012, Netanyahu had told an audience at the American Israel Public Affairs Committee conference that 'As Prime Minister of Israel, I will never let my people live in the shadow of annihilation.'[71] Now in the shadow of an international agreement that had the potential to reduce the risk of annihilation, he set three related goals for his leadership. First, he vowed to oppose a 'bad' and 'dangerous' diplomatic agreement that would be powerless to reduce the Iran nuclear threat. Second, he sought to prevent normalization of Iran in the international order. Finally, returning to his message conflating the nuclear threat with Iran's support of terrorists—which presented the threat as being larger than Iran's nuclear program, thus highlighting the inadequacy of the nuclear deal—he vowed to ensure that Israelis were protected from the ongoing danger of Iran.

While Netanyahu failed to prevent the signing of the JCPOA (also known as the 'Iran nuclear deal'), his threat narrative resonated with Israelis. One of the more interesting adaptations of his message took the form of a book purporting to reveal a history of secret Israel-Iran proxy conflicts. Authored by prominent Israeli journalists Yaakov Katz and Yoaz Hendel and published in 2012, *Israel vs. Iran: The Shadow War* imagines Iranian nuclear strikes against Israel and preemptive Israeli military missions against Iran.[72] Several years after its publication, Katz explained that the inspiration for writing the book came from observing the 'Israeli panic' over Iran's nuclear program. He admitted to expecting considerable public interest in reporting and speculating about these topics.[73] At the time of the book's publication, not only did a majority of Israelis see war with Iran as a real possibility,[74] a majority (56%) expressed skepticism about the sincerity of Western diplomatic efforts to stop Iran from acquiring a nuclear weapon.[75] Three years later, after the exit of Ahmadinejad and the election of Rouhani, Israelis reelected Netanyahu to a third term as prime minister.[76] Several commentaries described his governing coalition as the 'most right-wing' in the country's history.[77] Netanyahu had achieved his primary goal of retaining power.

IV. Conclusion: Narrative vs. Reality

It is hard to know whether Netanyahu believed in the justness of his crusade against Iran or whether he was engaging in strategic posturing. Since Netanyahu's tropes did not rely upon accuracy, his strategy for disseminating his narrative did not require him to believe what he was saying. It was important that voters perceived Iran as an existential threat, which required him to sustain their fears and minimize challenges to the accuracy of his claims.

Intelligence leaks have revealed that Netanyahu knowingly overstated the danger Iran posed to Israel. The 'Mossad spy cables,' which covered the years 2006 through 2014, included five years of Netanyahu's second term as prime minister.[78] They reveal that Netanyahu presented an accelerated timetable for Iran being likely to produce a nuclear weapon at the same time that intelligence officials informed him that they did not believe Iran was producing weapons. The files also show that Netanyahu's advocacy of military intervention contradicted the advice of his generals, who reportedly expressed their concern that starting a regional war with Iran could prove detrimental to Israel. Top military officials also indicated that a conventional military response would be futile in stopping Iran's nuclear program.[79]

Cabinet meeting minutes reveal Netanyahu's unwillingness to accept any negotiated agreement with Iran, even if it were to reduce the risk of a nuclear strike against Israel. Rather, he continued to claim that such a deal would 'enable Iran to arm itself with nuclear weapons.'[80] In a display of what Richard Hofstadter called the 'fundamentalist mind,'[81] Netanyahu refused to allow changing circumstances to influence his positions. He blurred the distinction between nuclear technology and weaponry by maintaining that even if Iran was not actively engaged in producing a bomb, it would remain a 'nuclear threshold state.'[82] According to this argument, there was no functional difference between Iran's nuclear energy program and the technological knowledge for producing a bomb. If the military could not destroy Iran's nuclear reactors, there was no solution to the Iran threat short of regime change.

There were also public challenges to Netanyahu's position, some of which required a different type of response. Whereas with his subordinates he dismissed or obfuscated facts that contradicted his claims, he sought to discredit the challengers.[83] Invoking his populist strategy, Netanyahu manipulated the fractures in Israeli society to create an Israeli polity in which those rejecting his message would be excluded. Like most of his Iran messaging, his appeal was emotional rather than factual. Israelis, and by extension all Jews, were bound by the Jewish imperative of solidarity when threatened with annihilation. Thus, secular and religious Jews should recognize their shared danger and minimize any criticism of his narrative, which meant refraining from public disagreements that could embolden their enemies.

In appealing to secular Jews, Netanyahu recognized that he could not compromise his fealty to the religious factions that comprised his core base. The political power of his religious constituency resulted from what Michael Walzer called the 'paradox of liberation.'[84] Walzer observed that Israel's secular founders, having eschewed religious orthodoxy and historic Jewish victimhood to create a modern state, had effectively instigated a backlash among the religious communities. The latter resented their exclusion from the vision of the new state,[85] and subsequently sought to reestablish their religious authority in the 'Jewish State.' They had grown in number due to their high birthrates and the immigration of religious Zionists, and they had become politically savvy. They also secured the support of many non-orthodox Jews, who were offended by the idea that the founders had denied Jewish history and tradition.[86]

The religious parties proved to be astutely practical. In enlarging the political space for their messages, they accepted the personally secular but politically ambitious Netanyahu as their leader. With no strongly held domestic agenda of his own, Netanyahu was open to promoting policies embraced by Israel's right-wing religionists. By yielding to the religionists' domestic policy demands and by offering foreign policies that they could enthusiastically embrace, Netanyahu could create the illusion—if not the reality—of a large following. With his co-religionists, Netanyahu could construct a morally superior 'Jewish Peoplehood' that both embraced his Iran narrative and refused to tolerate dissent. That his challengers were largely elites and experts from non-orthodox or secular institutions—including think tanks, universities, and civil society organizations—facilitated accusations that they were not 'of the people.' As intellectuals who resisted Netanyahu's emotional appeal to fear, they were willing to brave public rebuke; but their power to impact public opinion proved limited.

Although Netanyahu's narrative succeeded in enlarging his support at home and securing his position as Israel's leader, it was rejected by the world's most powerful leaders. As the latter engaged with Iran's government officials, they began to increasingly isolate Netanyahu from the deliberations.

6

IRAN AND ISRAEL IN THE AGE OF POPULISM

I. Introduction: The Triumph of Diplomacy

Although the JCPOA will forever be associated with Hassan Rouhani and Barack Obama, it is really the fulfillment of a decades-long ambition to reach a negotiated settlement on Iran's nuclear capabilities. The history of this effort is long and complicated and includes multiple promising starts, missed opportunities, and failures. While a comprehensive understanding of this history has been and will continue to be a study for scholars for years to come, it is beyond the scope of this book. Still, it is worth taking a few moments to examine the key elements of the JCPOA to understand why it succeeded where so many other attempts failed, as well as the conditions of the agreement that allowed Benjamin Netanyahu to incorporate it into his threat narrative. While most of the world celebrated the agreement that experts proclaimed would verifiably prevent Iran from acquiring a nuclear weapon, Netanyahu portrayed the moment as a colossal failure, one that would significantly increase the risk to Israel, the Middle East, and the Western world.

In the final months of Mahmoud Ahmadinejad's second term in early 2013, a small group of American and Iranian diplomats gathered in Oman to explore the possibility of restarting negotiations over

Iran's nuclear program. This was not the first time American and Iranian officials had quietly convened to discuss this topic. Despite decades-long animosity dating back to the 1979 Islamic Revolution, the two adversaries had several times explored direct negotiations. In the early 2000s, during the presidency of Mohammad Khatami, the Iranians had made several entreaties to the United States to gauge its interest in resolving their disputes—including, most notably, the scope of Iran's nuclear program—but each time they were rebuffed by the George W. Bush administration. The arrival of the Obama administration offered another chance, but here, again, early attempts at diplomacy with Iran were derailed by a combination of factors, including domestic political concerns in both countries.[1] In 2013, they tried again.

Given the two countries' history, the first few rounds of discussions took place in extreme secrecy. The meetings were tense, and progress was slow. It was difficult for the American representatives to find common ground with Ahmadinejad officials, who had spent the past eight years demonizing the United States and being demonized in return. The change in Iran's leadership following the June 2013 presidential election improved prospects for negotiations. Hassan Rouhani had campaigned and won on the promise to end Iran's international isolation. The new negotiating team, led by Foreign Minister Mohammad Javad Zarif, understood they had a mandate from the president to pursue negotiations, which included talking directly to the United States. Significantly, Zarif's team did not possess the built-up hostility to the West borne by their predecessors, nor were they stigmatized by a history of collaboration with Iran's hardliners who had long decried America as the 'Great Satan.' Zarif himself had received most of his secondary, graduate, and postgraduate education in the United States, including a PhD in international law and policy from the University of Denver.

In September 2013, just weeks after Rouhani took office, Zarif met briefly with US Secretary of State John Kerry on the sidelines of the United Nations General Assembly, in the first meeting of high-level American and Iranian officials since the 1979 Islamic Revolution. During the trip, Zarif presented a new Iranian proposal for a diplomatic agreement that Kerry described as 'very different in tone and very different in vision ... with respect to the possibilities for the future.'[2] Two months later, Iran signed an interim agreement with the United States, Great Britain, France, Russia, China, and Germany—the permanent five members of the UN Security Council plus Germany, or the P5+1—in which Iran agreed to place a short-term freeze on its nuclear program in exchange for limited sanctions relief while the parties continued to negotiate. Nearly two years of intense negotiations followed, culminating in the signing of the final accord in Vienna on 15 July 2015.

At the core of the JCPOA was a simple exchange: limiting nuclear development actions for sanctions relief. Iran agreed to reduce by two-thirds its number of working centrifuges, as well as halt development of newer, more efficient next-generation centrifuges. It also agreed to convert or disable parts of its nuclear reactors at Arak, Fordow, and Natanz, and limit these facilities to civilian use, including industrial and medical research. To prove they intended to comply with the accord, Iran submitted to a uniquely intrusive inspection and monitoring system. The International Atomic Energy Agency, working alongside a joint commission at the United Nations, would have unimpeded access to Iran's nuclear facilities, as well as the ability to request permission to visit other 'undeclared' sites. In return, Iran gained relief from the nuclear-related sanctions imposed by the United Nations, the European Union, and, most significantly, the United States.[3]

The JCPOA was historic in both its scope as well as its intrusion on Iran's sovereignty. Though the deal did not address all the West's concerns with Iran's behavior—particularly its ballistic missile capabilities and its support for actions fomenting regional unrest, topics which Iran insisted were essential for its self-defense and not open to negotiation[4]—it was the most comprehensive diplomatic agreement to limit a nation's nuclear capability ever reached. The level of transparency Iran had agreed to provide was burdensome, thus many of the provisions had set time limits. These limits, known as 'sunset clauses,' would expire after a specified number of years of Iran's compliance.[5] Importantly, even after the restrictions expired and the extraordinary inspection regime ended, Iran would remain subject in perpetuity to other restraints on nuclear weapons development, including its commitment to the NPT and the IAEA's additional protocol.[6]

The temporary nature of the deal's more onerous restrictions represented an important condition for the Iranians: fairness. In their view, Iran had been unfairly singled out for its nuclear activities. The West's presumption that Iran was attempting to weaponize its nuclear program—an assumption that Iran admittedly had at times encouraged or at the very least not refuted—was both incorrect and unfair. Iran did not want to be seen as 'giving up' legitimate parts of its nuclear program as allowed by its participation in the NPT. At the same time, Iran had to prove to the United States that it was not interested in weaponizing its nuclear program. Iran's negotiators frequently noted that, despite the extraordinary punishments their country had endured, Iran's program should not be considered special. Under the NPT, Iran was allowed to operate a civilian nuclear program. Iran's most vocal opponent, Israel, not only was not a signatory to the NPT, but it had received international assistance in secretly developing a nuclear arsenal.[7] While this was not exactly equal treatment, Iran insisted on protecting this concept of fairness in negotiations, especially given its willingness to allow intrusive inspections.

Also important to the Iranian negotiators was that the structure of the deal was such that they could claim that Iran had entered into the agreement by choice rather than under duress. The deal had to respect Iran's national dignity and recognize its legitimate rights, both of which were key elements of Iranian national security strategy.[8] In exchange, Iran accepted coercive measures designed to compel their compliance. These included 'snap back' provisions that would instantly restore sanctions should Iran be found in breach of the agreement. This arrangement served the self interest of both parties. In the short term, Iran realized economic rewards of sanctions relief, while the world powers averted a Middle East arms race. If successful over time, the deal could establish a foundation of trust, which might lead to future negotiations to address other areas of concern.

Netanyahu saw things differently. As he portrayed it, the negotiations and the resulting agreement were part of an elaborate

Iranian ploy to secure sanctions relief while secretly maintaining, or perhaps even progressing toward, a capacity to build a nuclear weapon. At best, the deal offered a beleaguered regime a much-needed economic lifeline. At worst, the JCPOA was a shroud of legitimacy under which Iran could continue its illicit pursuits. Netanyahu argued that the P5+1 had erred by granting the Iranians a reprieve rather than pushing the regime closer to collapse, which could have initiated regime change.

Moreover, Netanyahu maintained that, as the temporary components of the deal expired, Iran would gradually bring its nuclear program back online until, by the end of the deal, it emerged as a revitalized nation with an unimpeded path toward building a nuclear weapon. Netanyahu dismissed the enhanced inspection mechanisms as insufficient, given Iran's reputation for duplicity and cunning. As long as Iran maintained operation of nuclear facilities, it had the expertise to build a weapon. Combined with its religiously inspired imperative to destroy the Jewish State, this meant that even under the deal Iran remained an existential threat to Israel. Netanyahu argued that progress toward the bomb would never stop; it would just move out of sight.

The element of truth in Netanyahu's argument is that Iran had already achieved most of the capabilities required for building a nuclear weapon. That genie had long been out of the bottle. Past setbacks, including assassinations of its lead scientists and sabotage campaigns against its facilities, had resulted in temporary delays, but they had not halted Iran's knowledge acquisition or technological capacity. By 2015, many nuclear experts agreed that Iran possessed the resources, knowledge, and capabilities required for weaponization of their nuclear program.[9] Most believed that Iran had chosen not to do so. What the nuclear deal added was a verifiable delay to the 'breakout period,' the time between initiation and completion of a bomb-building project, should Iran choose to embark on such an endeavor. For at least the next decade, the length of this period would be one year, giving the world time to respond should Iran suddenly decide to weaponize its program. The P5+1 nations believed Iran could be convinced not to make that choice; Netanyahu maintained that the Islamic State had already made it.

The fundamental question underlying the JCPOA was whether a period of enforced safety from a nuclear Iran was more valuable than an uncertain present. Netanyahu's answer went beyond even an emphatic no. Incorporating his objections into his public Iran threat narrative, Netanyahu dismissed the efficacy of the inspections regime, conflated Iran's ballistic weapons development with its nuclear ambitions, and ascribed to Iran's leaders the intention to produce a nuclear weapon specifically for use against Israel. In his telling, the P5+1's misplaced faith in the Iranians had significantly heightened the danger to Israel and, by extension, the entire world. Netanyahu's narrative disguised his objectively counterintuitive argument that the JCPOA was thus far riskier and more dangerous than no deal at all.

With the signing of the JCPOA, Iran signaled to the world that it was open for business. Iran's leaders sought to attract foreign investment and tourism to the country. Throughout 2016, European and Asian delegations arrived in Tehran to explore the possibilities for expanded trade. Highly publicized deals with Boeing and Airbus promised to upgrade the country's outdated and unsafe civilian aircraft fleet, initiating Iran's efforts to rectify the damage caused by decades of harsh economic sanctions.[10] Iran's leaders hoped that these deals, coupled with Iran's improving reputation, would initiate a tourism boom. However, despite these lofty expectations, the promised benefits to the daily life of ordinary Iranians were slow to materialize.

Iran faced several political and operational obstacles, both at home and abroad, in realizing its goals. Domestically, Rouhani's hardline opponents objected that the deal allowed foreigners to exercise undue influence on Iran's politics. They denounced his government for placing trust in the word of American negotiators, and they decried the economic opening of the country as being an opportunity for foreign infiltration.[11] Some members of Iran's religious and military establishments, who had used Iran's isolation to capture and control key parts of the national economy, feared that greater transparency would expose the dishonesty, mismanagement, and corruption that had become endemic in the Iranian business climate under sanctions.[12] Investors faced abstruse commercial regulations and uncertainty regarding the returns on their investments.[13]

Resistance in the United States, from Republicans opposed to an Obama initiative as well as Democrats loyal to Israel, had tried and failed to undermine the deal, but a presidential election loomed in November 2016.[14] While the United States' adherence to an international agreement should not have been an issue of concern, the Republican frontrunner and eventual nominee had voiced his opposition to the deal and signaled that he might not respect traditional diplomatic norms. Thus, the US election held potential consequences for Iran, including the possibility of sanctions being either lifted or reimposed, depending on whether voters chose Donald Trump or Hillary Clinton.[15]

Trump's promise to dismantle the accord brought with it some uncertainty, but few considered him likely to win the election.[16] However, Trump was also courting financial support from several powerful Jewish donors who had embraced Netanyahu's leadership and who shared his antipathy for Obama.[17] Trump secured large investments from those who saw Hillary Clinton, Obama's first Secretary of State, as a continuation of the Obama administration. Despite her expression of strong support for Israel, she had also declared her intent to maintain the JCPOA.[18]

As Iranian leaders faced numerous challenges in implementing the JCPOA, they likely accorded only limited attention to Netanyahu's opposition or Trump's budding candidacy. With Trump still a long shot for the White House, Netanyahu appeared to be an isolated agitator. He had a platform but few friends, and he had virtually no power to overturn the deal unilaterally. While Rouhani offered hope to Iranians, Netanyahu continued to preach fear to Israelis, world Jewry, and the West, conjuring images of Armageddon. Western leaders, who had invested in diplomacy to reduce the risk of a 'nuclear Iran,' largely accepted Rouhani as credible and acting in good faith, and consequently they ignored Netanyahu's predictions of disaster. Israelis may still have believed that Iran was untrustworthy, but the larger international community trusted that Iran's agreeing to the terms of the JCPOA meant it would forego acquiring a nuclear weapon.

The remainder of this chapter examines Netanyahu's 'campaign' to convince President Trump to withdraw from the JCPOA. It details how the two men, each pursuing a personal agenda, coalesced to end an international agreement negotiated by seven countries and endorsed by numerous others. In adapting Netanyahu's Iran threat narrative as their justification for doing so, they both ignored its inherent contradiction. Trump echoed Netanyahu's claims that Iran's nuclear capability represented an existential threat to Israel, but he also followed Netanyahu's imperative to end the diplomatic agreement aimed at preventing Iran's acquisition of a nuclear weapon. The threat narrative pictured a crisis, which each man in turn used for political self-promotion. It is impossible at this writing to know the exact motives behind Netanyahu's course of action, nor can we know what strategic considerations led Trump to accede to Netanyahu's agenda and then continue to provoke Iran up to the brink of war. At best, we can parse rhetoric, deconstruct messaging, describe the events that provide context, and examine the actions taken and their consequences.

Previous chapters examined how Netanyahu had carefully constructed a narrative in which a nuclear Iran threatened Israel and the world. This threat served as the central element of his populist securitization enterprise by which he maintained his hold on power. While most of the international community recognized the JCPOA deal as an opportunity to mitigate the immediate risk of a nuclear Iran, Netanyahu counterintuitively maintained that the Iran deal amplified the threat. This chapter details how Trump's election rescued Netanyahu from isolation on the global stage and revitalized his narrative. When Trump eventually agreed to end the United States' participation in the JCPOA, he effectively reincarnated what the agreement had rendered a negligible threat. The renewed crisis meant Netanyahu could remain positioned as savior and protector of the State of Israel and, by extension, the Jewish people. However, Netanyahu had not foreseen that this time, although Israelis still believed in the existential Iran threat, they no longer saw his leadership as indispensable to confronting it.

The next section describes Netanyahu's courtship of Trump in an attempt to convince him to abandon the JCPOA. With only minimal tinkering of his threat narrative, Netanyahu manipulated Trump's obsession with the 'nature of the deal' not only to maneuver the United States toward withdrawing from the accord, but also to convince the US president to adopt Netanyahu's rhetoric in support of Israel's desired policies.

The third section then explores the early years of Trump's presidency, which effectively amounted to another disconnect, this time between Trump's rhetoric and action. This intermission between the presidential campaign and the announcement of the United States' withdrawal from the JCPOA suggests that, at a minimum, there were Trump advisors who were skeptical of the accuracy of Netanyahu's threat assessment. Section four describes Netanyahu's 'success' in bringing Trump over to Israel's way of seeing things, validated by his ending the JCPOA as a functioning mechanism for ensuring limitations on Iran's nuclear program and returning to open hostility between Iran and the United States.

The chapter concludes with an examination of the consequences of Netanyahu's populist securitization achievements. Predictably, neither Israel nor the world achieved greater security once Iran, with no incentive to continue adhering to the deal after the United States had backed out, began deliberately violating its terms. Moreover, Iran's resolve to withstand the economic sanctions did not weaken the regime, but rather resulted in the consolidation of power within a much more hardline sect of leaders. Ironically, going by the approval of their respective electorates, neither Netanyahu nor Trump benefitted politically from this effort, and both men lost their offices in early 2021. Less than a year after Netanyahu's defeat, many high-ranking Israeli officials began publicly stating that his efforts to upend the JCPOA and reinitiate conflict with Iran had been among his most costly policy failures for Israel and, perhaps, the world. Still, even if there was an emerging degree of regret within some circles, Israel's new leaders continued to advocate against a resurrection of the deal. In a way, it was as if Netanyahu had never left.

II. The Courtship

The signing of the JCPOA represented a significant challenge to Netanyahu's narrative, which had the potential to damage his leadership. Although unable to prevent the agreement, he had reason to believe that his cause was not permanently lost. As countries around the world embraced populist leaders, Netanyahu saw an opportunity to make common cause with new allies who were willing to see Iran as a threat. The success of the Brexit campaign, in which voters in the United Kingdom supported a referendum to leave the European Union, demonstrated the appeal of a political movement built upon themes of moral indignation, xenophobia, and a perception of constant crisis. The fact that Donald Trump was a serious presidential candidate in America meant that populist messaging also resonated with a major American political party. Trump denounced Muslims and Obama, from which it followed that he would also oppose the JCPOA. Like Netanyahu, Trump had only a loose affiliation with the truth, and thus his attacks on Iran often echoed those of the Israeli leader and his wealthy donors.[19]

While Netanyahu benefitted from Trump's candidacy, he would be best served by an against-the-odds victory that could resurrect his and Israel's international standing. Netanyahu had personal connections to Trump, which would likely provide him access to the White House and the publicity of having a close personal relationship with the American president. His long-standing ties with the family of Trump's son-in-law, Jared Kushner, meant he would have the ear of a high-ranking advisor.[20] While Trump was unfocused about his intentions for the JCPOA, Netanyahu had reason to believe he could prevail on Trump to withdraw American support. Netanyahu understood that Trump did not operate on principle; whether he abandoned an American obligation would depend upon his own personal impulse and ego. For example, Trump might find it difficult to endorse a deal he had not negotiated, perhaps impossible given it was his predecessor's signature foreign policy achievement. Trump was also mercurial and uninformed. On various occasions, he had appeared drawn to the business potential of an untapped market in Iran, criticizing Obama for not lifting the remaining sanctions that would facilitate commercial dealing.[21] Days later, he voiced his determination to tarnish his predecessor's legacy by destroying the signature policy achievement that had ended Iran's international isolation.

If Netanyahu saw a risk in openly supporting Trump's candidacy, he also understood it potentially held a large reward. With

Netanyahu's guidance and influence, Trump could be convinced to echo the Iran threat narrative and include Netanyahu in the strategic decision-making of his administration. A Trump victory would mean that Netanyahu would no longer be the lonely voice opposing a deal that the rest of the world was wholeheartedly embracing. Netanyahu had endangered his standing with Western allies by embracing the illiberal populist forces that darkened the future of international diplomacy. If Trump won, Netanyahu would make the American president both audience for and ally of his threat narrative.

Ironically, while both Netanyahu and Trump invoked metaphors of darkness, future Israeli Ambassador to the United States Ron Dermer observed that Trump's victory represented Israel's 'light at the end of the tunnel.'[22]

* * *

Netanyahu's Iran narrative did not require significant editing to capture Trump's attention, as its themes generally fit neatly within Trump's preexisting beliefs. Netanyahu understood that Trump's intense dislike of Obama could be leveraged to enlist the president into undoing much of his predecessor's policy, particularly if the policy was a defining achievement of Obama's. By appending a claim that the JCPOA increased rather than reduced Iran's nuclear threat, Netanyahu and Trump could amplify the danger while affixing the blame on Obama's shortcomings. Netanyahu also recognized that the best strategy for moving Trump to action would be an appeal to his ego. He played to Trump's self-professed deal-making capability, flattering Trump as the only leader capable of resolving the crises created by Obama and the global elite. Moreover, the Islamophobia, morally charged panic, and warnings of Iranian duplicity in Netanyahu's original narrative neatly played to many of Trump's prejudices.

For Trump, who was frequently guided by instinct, vilifying an enemy often proved a substitute for action rooted in policy or strategy. Certainly, his position on US-Iran relations would not be the product of a strong commitment to national or global security. Iran was not an issue of concern for the majority of Trump's political base. His followers would, however, approve of his undoing a key piece of Obama's legacy. Meanwhile, some of his wealthy donors, like casino magnate Sheldon Adelson, would applaud Trump's protection of Israel. Netanyahu's major challenge was that Trump's reputation for unreliability meant that it was never certain whether he would follow through on his rhetoric with action. Thus, Netanyahu knew he needed to allow Trump to choose which narrative theme would compel him to act.

Like Netanyahu, Trump had embraced populist messaging that discounted facts and expertise in policy discourse. The Brexit campaign was a harbinger of what economic analyst Esfandyar Batmanghelidj recognized as 'a change in mindset' from the time of JCPOA negotiations.[23] While Iran had no official position on the impact of Brexit,[24] Batmanghelidj discerned a troubling message for the country. In a blog post, he wrote that the Iran deal 'seemed a triumphant example of cooperation and vision where the national interests of seven different countries, representing the global community, eventually produced a single robust agreement.' Brexit now signaled a 'rejection of [that] type of politics.' Hence, he argued, Iran might be coming back into the 'community of nations. But … that community will seem less welcoming and less hopeful.'[25] What he did not note was that if Netanyahu was successful in his campaign to destroy the agreement, Iran might not be allowed reentry into that global community.

Netanyahu's formal courtship of Trump began in September 2020, six weeks before the presidential election, in the penthouse of Trump Tower in New York City. Although a Trump victory still seemed unlikely, Netanyahu sought to preemptively shape the Republican candidate's amorphous ideas about Middle East policy. He offered Trump his vision of a Middle East political realignment built upon increasing confrontation with Iran.[26] Trump advisor Steve Bannon reportedly admitted that the attendees were 'blown away' by Netanyahu's ideas. Since no one in Trump's inner circle had substantial knowledge of either Iran or the Middle East, Netanyahu presented a plan that appealed to Trump's preconceived biases, which denigrated the Islamic Republic and favored Israel. One unnamed attendee succinctly summed up the meeting: 'Israel just had their way with us.'[27]

When Trump won the election, Netanyahu demonstrated his loyalty by immediately positioning himself as a high-profile Trump defender. Before the inauguration, Netanyahu publicly disputed claims that Trump or his advisors were anti-Semitic. In an interview on the CBS news show '60 Minutes,' Netanyahu insisted, 'I know him very well. And I think his attitude, his support for Israel are very clear.'[28] The flattery worked. A mere two days after taking office, Trump invited Netanyahu to visit Washington. For Netanyahu, the invitation represented an end to his estrangement from the center of American power.

Ahead of his arrival in Washington, Netanyahu launched an intensive messaging campaign that put the Iran deal in the political spotlight. Liberally employing Twitter, Trump's favorite communication medium, Netanyahu focused on the inadequacy of the JCPOA terms, which he claimed had been insufficiently scrutinized by the Obama administration. According to a Netanyahu tweet, the deal itself was a danger: 'Stopping the Iranian threat, and the threat reflected in the bad nuclear agreement with Iran, continues to be a supreme goal of Israel.'[29]

It did not take long for Trump to reinvigorate the conflict with Iran. A week and a half into his presidency, Trump allowed his National Security Adviser, Michael Flynn, to place Iran 'on notice' because Iran conducted a missile test which had not been prohibited by the JCPOA.[30] The meaning of the announcement was not self-evident, and Trump provided no explanation. While international inspectors continued to verify Iran's compliance with the terms of the nuclear deal, Trump used the Flynn warning to highlight the deal's omissions.[31]

By the time Netanyahu arrived in Washington in February, Trump had fully embraced a hardline position on Iran. Reiterating his support for Israel's security, Trump characterized the Iran deal as '[o]ne of the worst deals I've ever seen.'[32] Netanyahu responded by noting their shared commitment to 'preventing Iran from getting nuclear weapons' and by praising Trump for acting immediately after taking office to impose new sanctions on Iran in response to its ballistic missile tests. Conflating Iran's missile capabilities with the nuclear issue enabled Netanyahu to emphasize Trump's leadership in challenging Iran. He also positioned Trump as the defender of Israel by twice reminding the President that Iran had inscribed its test missiles with the words 'Israel must be destroyed.'[33]

The meeting in Washington assured Netanyahu that his Iran narrative had an attentive audience in the White House, but it did not conclude with the outcome Netanyahu sought. Trump echoed Netanyahu's fierce rhetoric, but he was more subdued in his desire for active confrontation. Realistically, Trump had limited policy options as long as the nuclear deal remained in effect and Iran remained compliant. But Netanyahu was not satisfied with press conference bromides, and he was aware of Trump's unreliability when it came to turning promises into action. Thus, following the meeting, Netanyahu increased the pressure on Trump to push the United States closer to a conflict with Iran.

A central feature of this campaign involved the continuous repetition of the threat narrative in multiple public forums. One significant venue was the Fox News channel, a source Trump trusted for general information and private advice.[34] A month after the White House visit, Netanyahu secured an interview with Sean Hannity, a popular prime-time show host and unofficial Trump confidant.[35] The 'softball' interview featured questions that enabled Netanyahu to speak to Trump through the trusted Hannity. Netanyahu invoked the fear trope, portraying Iranians as bloodthirsty zealots and adding that even Arabs believed that 'Iran will cut their throats, and they are right.' He glibly noted that the nuclear deal meant 'No bomb today, 100 bombs tomorrow.' Hannity then tied Trump's executive order banning visas for travelers from certain Muslim countries, including Iran, to Netanyahu's narrative by asking whether he agreed that 'radical Islam is the evil of our time, and Iran represents the biggest threat.'[36] Netanyahu's response amplified his warning to Americans: 'When you couple a radical Islamic regime that says, 'Death to America,' with the weapons of mass death, then you have a much, much bigger problem.'[37]

Two months later, Hannity again provided a forum for Netanyahu to repeat his warning to Trump during a broadcast from Jerusalem. Netanyahu described Israel as a 'mini-United States right here in the Middle East,' underscoring the larger danger associated with Israel's vulnerability to a weapon of mass destruction in the hands of 'radical mullahs.' He added a strategic appeal to Trump by mentioning his predecessor. Obama's deal had 'pave[d] the way for Iran to get the bomb,' while granting them 'untold billions of dollars with which they can not only fund their nuclear arsenal but also fund their aggression.' By contrast, Netanyahu praised Trump for recognizing the danger and initiating an 'important change' in the United States' posture.[38]

Trump's growing embrace of Netanyahu's threat narrative provided the Israeli prime minister with the opportunity to increase his international presence and enlist allies in his campaign. Having antagonized the signatories to the JCPOA, Netanyahu broadened his travel agenda. Prior to August 2015, he had made no more than eleven international trips during any of his three terms as prime minister. In this fourth term, he took over fifty trips, including first visits by an Israeli prime minister to Kazakhstan, Azerbaijan, Singapore, Australia, Brazil, and Chad, among others. He made the first trip by an Israeli prime minister to Africa in three decades and opened diplomatic relations with several Arab nations.

Netanyahu also returned to Europe and Russia, where he tried to convince leaders to take a harder line on Iran. He made six trips to the United States to meet with Trump and administration officials, which included multiple private meetings with Trump himself. His entreaty to Prime Minister Theresa May during a visit to the United Kingdom typified his messaging during these sojourns. During the February 2017 meeting, he told May, who had assumed the office seven months earlier, that 'Iran seeks to conquer the Middle East. It threatens Europe. It threatens the West. It threatens the world.' He then praised Trump for his 'assistance of new sanctions against Iran' and added, 'I think other nations should follow suit, certainly responsible nations.'[39]

With this investment of time and energy in global relations, Netanyahu sought more than favorable rhetoric from Trump; he wanted the US president to act to destroy the JCPOA. Netanyahu had three reasons to be concerned about his political future. First, while Netanyahu's historic travels and newfound alliances enhanced his image among Israelis, they were relatively marginal achievements that were unlikely to compensate for the reputational damage he would suffer if the JCPOA continued to operate as intended. Trump's failure to end the Iran deal would diminish the criticality of Netanyahu's narrative. If Iran did not move toward a nuclear weapon, Netanyahu's rhetoric would eventually ring hollow. Trump's delay in ending the agreement also opened space for those willing to challenge the accuracy of Netanyahu's claims. Iran's continued compliance with the terms of the agreement would undermine Netanyahu's characterization of the threat as existential and imminent. Meanwhile, Iran would be able to expand trade, strengthen its economy, and build trust with Western nations, which would be difficult to undo absent actual wrongdoing.

Second, Netanyahu's strategic populism needed an ongoing crisis for him to remain the protector of Israeli and global security. The longer the JCPOA remained in effect, the greater the likelihood that his contradictory logic would be challenged. Although he insisted that the deal was dangerous, its demise would remove the restraints on Iran's restarting its nuclear program and render moot the argument of those who saw the JCPOA as ameliorating the threat of a nuclear Iran. Netanyahu needed the United States to withdraw in order to justify his investment in undoing the deal and validating his leadership credentials.

The third reason for Netanyahu's intense focus on changing the status quo of the Iran deal involved domestic Israeli politics. The existence of the Iran threat allowed Netanyahu to evade serious engagement in more controversial and politically fraught challenges, such as settling Palestinian claims and ending Israel's ongoing occupation of the West Bank and Gaza Strip.[40] Many interests proffered 'peace proposals,' and even more critics challenged Israel's treatment of the Palestinians. Netanyahu's political base opposed negotiations, fearing that they might result in compromise and Israelis having to withdraw from already settled regions of the West Bank. If Netanyahu wavered in his opposition to compromise, there were other Israeli politicians willing to assume leadership on this issue. Netanyahu's elevation of the Iran threat as the overarching security concern of the state accomplished two objectives: it allowed him to distinguish his leadership credentials while excusing his evasion of addressing complaints about Palestine.[41]

In addition to in-person visits and media entreaties, Netanyahu's strategy recognized that his target audience was a prolific Twitter user. He thus embraced social media as a vital tool for disseminating his message. During the Obama years, Netanyahu had tweeted only sparingly mostly from his official prime minister account. His usage spiked on the two occasions when Iran had commanded significant public attention: in November 2013 when the parties signed the interim nuclear agreement, and again in early 2015 anticipating the implementation of the JCPOA. Seeking to reach an international audience, Netanyahu tweeted attacks on the agreement in English rather than Hebrew. For example, on 10 February 2015, he posted, 'I'm determined to speak before Congress to stop Iran,' and he urged his followers to demonstrate their support by retweeting.[42] Against President Obama's wishes, Netanyahu addressed a joint session of Congress the following month, but his speech had no impact on the administration's determination to complete the deal.

Taking his cue from Trump's success, Netanyahu harnessed the power of social media in 2016 for self-promotion. While Iran was a frequent topic, Netanyahu also touted his accomplishments, attacked his enemies, and, importantly, courted Donald Trump with lavish compliments. Like Trump, Netanyahu personalized his Twitter posts, preferring the handle @netanyahu over the official state account @IsraeliPM. Knowing that Trump valued loyalty and craved adulation, Netanyahu knew this was a way to let Trump know that he had personally sent those tweets of gratitude and praise.[43]

III. Engagement: Trump's First Year

In the first year of his courtship of Trump, Netanyahu had learned it was easier to convince Trump to issue a rhetorical attack than it was to move him to definitive policy or military action. Trump had embraced Netanyahu as an ally and friend, frequently and publicly voicing his support for Israel and its prime minister. Yet tangible efforts to punish Iran and hinder implementation of nuclear deal had not followed from this, and Trump's true intentions remained unpredictable. It would require an even more concentrated effort to push Trump to take the action Netanyahu desired.

Although Trump avoided active confrontation with Iran, he took several measures early in his term which appeared to reward Netanyahu's loyalty, effectively depriving Netanyahu of reasons to complain. With all that Trump was doing for Israel, Netanyahu could not risk criticizing his inaction on Iran.[44] A week after his inauguration, Trump issued an executive order banning entry of travelers from seven Muslim countries, including Iran, to the United States.[45] In fulfilling his campaign promise, Trump incorporated his Islamophobia into a heavy-handed policy that initially failed to pass judicial scrutiny.[46] When he engaged in the 'obligatory' presidential duty to acknowledge the Palestinian issue, he did so without distressing Netanyahu. His idea for a peace initiative was to charge Jared Kushner with crafting the 'ultimate deal' between Israelis and Palestinians. And although Trump invited Palestinian President Mahmoud Abbas for a White House visit, months later he officially recognized Jerusalem as the capital of Israel.[47] The announcement of his intention to relocate the US Embassy from Tel Aviv to Jerusalem, an action long sought by Netanyahu, so enraged Abbas that he severed all communications with administration officials, including Trump, Kushner, and Vice President Mike Pence for the remainder of Trump's presidency.[48] Trump effectively abandoned any pretext that America would serve as an unbiased broker in settling Middle East disputes. Given Trump's embrace of Netanyahu and his messaging, it did not appear to matter that Kushner's efforts to craft a peace plan between Israel and the Palestinians contradicted Netanyahu's longtime claim that the Iran threat prevented Israel from resolving the Palestinian question.[49] Netanyahu had little fear of being coerced into territorial compromise from Trump's idea that the Palestinians would settle their long list of disputes with Israel in exchange for economic incentives.

Still, by early 2018, the United States remained committed to the Iran deal. Since taking office, Trump had twice recertified Iran's compliance with the terms of the JCPOA.[50] Reports emerged that several high-ranking advisors, including Secretary of State Rex Tillerson and Defense Secretary James Mattis, had urged the President to remain in the Iran deal despite its imperfections.[51] By accepting, however grudgingly, the conclusions of the nuclear inspectors and US intelligence agencies that Iran was abiding by the terms of the agreement, Trump implicitly disproved Netanyahu's claims that Iran could not be trusted and the deal must be destroyed. Trump took a symbolic step in Netanyahu's direction in October 2017 when he refused a third recertification, although there was no evidence that Iran had changed its behavior or weakened its commitment to compliance. He justified his decision with hyperbole that had no factual basis: 'We will not continue down a path whose predictable conclusion is more violence, more terror and the very real threat of Iran's nuclear breakout.' Trump then ordered his aides to work with Congress and US allies to 'address the deal's many serious flaws so that the Iranian regime can never threaten the world with nuclear weapons.'[52] Still, American noncertification of Iran's compliance had no legal significance for the JCPOA's implementation, and the United States remained a party to the deal.

Rather than announce his intention to abandon the accord, Trump promoted himself as a 'dealmaker' willing to renegotiate and expand the terms of the agreement. On 11 January 2018, Trump declared that he would 'fix' the Iran deal, demanding that it incorporate prohibitions on long-range missiles and eliminate 'sunset clauses.'[53] Since Iran had repeatedly deemed these issues unacceptable during the original negotiations, it is unclear what Trump's intentions were in issuing this demand. Observers debated whether Trump was engaging in political theater, edging closer to abandoning the agreement, or expressing confidence in his capability to negotiate a better deal. The following day, Trump dodged decisive action when he chose not to impose additional broad-based sanctions on Iran and instead authorized Treasury Secretary Steven Mnuchin to impose targeted sanctions against individuals.[54]

As Trump publicly addressed amending the JCPOA, reports emerged of the disagreement among his advisors.[55] On one side, those who ascribed to the 'traditional' Republican party perspective argued that foreign policies should further the best interests of America, which in this case included recognizing the potential for diplomacy and honoring the nation's commitment to international agreements. On the other side was a small cadre of extreme nationalists and isolationists, who disagreed with the traditional assessment of America's global interest and were unconcerned with honoring commitments made by previous administrations. Joining the latter were influential voices outside the administration, including the cohort of billionaire Jewish Republicans whose financial support during the campaign had been instrumental in Trump's victory.[56]

Internationally, America's allies were also split on the deal. The United Kingdom, France, and the European Union strongly favored preserving the agreement, while Sunni-majority Middle East states, such as Saudi Arabia, opposed any arrangement that normalized Iran's standing in the world. The parties advanced reasoned opinions based upon their differing values, priorities, and perspectives, which guided their evaluation of both the facts and the uncertainties. They were, however, arguing to a decision-maker who was not particularly interested in detail, contingencies, nuances, or expertise. To Trump, the principal question often concerned how a decision would affect him personally. Netanyahu, who was allied with the JCPOA's opponents, understood Trump's approach to politics and decision-making better than those who sought to preserve the deal.[57]

Personal considerations inclined Trump toward withdrawal. No matter what Trump did, the JCPOA would always be Obama's deal. If it succeeded in deescalating the Iran threat, Obama would get the credit. Even if Trump renegotiated what he considered a flawed agreement, he would still be adhering to the framework of a deal credited to a man he detested.[58] He needed to make the deal his own or abandon it. Netanyahu, who had invested in causing the latter action, recognized that since the JCPOA was a multilateral arrangement, Trump lacked the leverage to change the terms unilaterally. Thus, both men could speak the language of fixing the agreement, but Trump's only power was to withdraw the United States completely, reimpose sanctions on Iran, and threaten the other parties with punishment should they attempt to circumvent America's will. Still, neither Iran nor Netanyahu could provide Trump with a principled basis for abandoning the agreement. Netanyahu's morality-based argument that Iran was a bad actor would not work for a man who traditionally shunned moral considerations in negotiations. Trump had a long history of business dealings with disreputable characters and had already shown favor to America's adversaries, such as Russian autocrat Vladimir Putin.[59]

Trump's refusal to certify Iran's compliance with the deal was more than a public relations gesture, as it effectively put the JCPOA on life support. By not reimposing sanctions, he preserved his flexibility to maneuver and continued to test the impact on his political fortunes. He had no basis for demanding that Iran agree to new terms, no support from the other signatories for such a demand, and no reasons for expecting Iran to accede to his demands. With Netanyahu's help, he had confected a procedural set up for withdrawal, but Netanyahu would still have to wait.[60]

IV. The Union: Success

Netanyahu had one thing in common with Iranian leaders after a year of the Trump presidency: they were both impatient with Trump's inaction on the JCPOA. Iran's leaders, seeking an indication that the United States remained committed to the deal, chose to limit their hostility even as Trump's rhetoric grew increasingly aggressive. They pivoted their focus from the United States to Europe, imploring the European Union to maintain its promise to increase trade with Iran. If the United States withdrew from the JCPOA, Iran's leaders understood that they would need to find a workaround for the US economic sanctions that were sure to follow.

Even without the United States' withdrawal, Trump's threats and the potential for the reimposition of sanctions were negatively impacting Iran. A British parliamentary report in October 2017 following Trump's decertification noted that 'U.S. Administration hostility to the JCPOA and to Iran in general may add to the uncertainty of foreign investors because of the possibility of new sanctions.'[61] The threat of 'secondary sanctions'—penalties targeting third-party enterprises conducting business with sanctioned countries or entities—discouraged European companies considering business ventures in Iran.[62] Given the likelihood that Iran would refuse to reopen negotiations, the Europeans explored whether they could preserve Iran's compliance with the existing agreement while protecting investment opportunities.[63] For Rouhani's government, attracting foreign capital was critical. After staking the success of the deal on Iran's realization of economic gains, if he failed to deliver he would find himself facing the ire of citizens.[64] If Rouhani could not improve people's lives, his opponents could capitalize on the anger and frustration among voters to force an end to Iran's compliance.

As Iran worked quietly to salvage the deal, Netanyahu intensified his campaign to end it by adding a performative element to his political offensive. On 10 February 2018, Netanyahu claimed that Israel had shot down an Iranian drone in Israeli airspace. Military officials initially explained that the Iranians had launched the drone from Syria, and they accused Iran of 'dragging the region into a situation in which it doesn't know how it will end.'[65] Although Iran called the accusation 'ridiculous,'[66] Israel immediately responded with a 'large scale strike' against Iranian targets in Syria, during which one of its F-16 fighter jets was downed by Syrian anti-aircraft fire. Two days later, the Israeli military dialed back its accusations when a high-ranking Israeli Air Force officer admitted uncertainty about the purpose behind the incursion of the Iranian drone. Expressing puzzlement, he said, 'I can't say for certain what the mission was.'[67]

The following week, Netanyahu used the occasion of a prominent speech to an international security conference in Germany to stage a dramatic 'show and tell.' Toward the end of a fourteen-minute speech in which he mentioned Iran forty-one times, he held aloft a piece of the downed drone, which he claimed was 'what's left of it after we shot it down.' He challenged Iran's Foreign Minister, Javad Zarif, who was present at the conference but not in the audience for Netanyahu's speech, 'Do you recognize this? You should. It's yours.' He then warned Zarif, 'You can take back with you a message to the Tyrants of Tehran: Do not test Israel's resolve.'[68]

Earlier in his speech, Netanyahu had preemptively denied that he was comparing Iran to Nazi Germany before proceeding to do exactly that. He drew historical analogies between the Third Reich and the Islamic Republic, noting that 'One advocated for a master race, and the other advocates a master faith.' He admitted that Jews in Iran were not sent to gas chambers, but he maintained that 'Iran openly declares its intention to annihilate Israel with its six million

Jews.' Pivoting to the subject of European culpability, he added, 'Just as was true 80 years ago, an agreement that was seen as appeasement has only emboldened the regime and brought war ever closer.'[69] When Zarif took the stage several hours later, he characterized Netanyahu's antics as a 'cartoonish circus,' stating that his speech 'does not deserve the dignity of a response.'[70]

Cartoonish or not, Netanyahu's narrative appeared to be reaching his targeted audience. In early 2018, Trump shifted his cabinet membership, replacing his more traditionalist Secretary of State, Rex Tillerson, with the hardliner Mike Pompeo, who had until that point been serving as Trump's Director of the Central Intelligence Agency. On 29 April, three days after being sworn in as the new Secretary of State, Pompeo met with Netanyahu in Tel Aviv. At their joint press conference. Pompeo echoed Netanyahu's narrative claim that the greatest global threat is 'the marriage of militant Islam with nuclear weapons and specifically the attempt of Iran to acquire nuclear weapons,' and he repeated Trump's refrain that the JCPOA was 'very flawed.' He then announced that President Trump had 'directed the administration to try and fix it, and if we can't fix it, he's going to withdraw from the deal.'[71] For Netanyahu, the press conference was a setup for a grand finale the following day.

On 30 April 2018, in a made-for-television event aired from Jerusalem, Netanyahu dramatically revealed what he claimed was a cache of documents recovered from a covert Israeli raid on a document depository in a Tehran warehouse. Speaking English, he asserted that the documents confirmed Iran's intention to produce a nuclear weapon. Over the next eighteen minutes, Netanyahu stood in front of a screen emblazoned with the words 'Iran lied' in giant letters and staged a slow reveal of bookshelves and a wall of compact discs that he maintained contained a trove of secret information related to Iran's nuclear program.

At one point, he pretended to 'debate' with a video clip of Iran's Foreign Minister Javad Zarif asserting to an interviewer, 'We never wanted to produce a bomb.' Pausing the tape, Netanyahu mockingly retorted, 'Yes you did. Yes you do.'[72] He then insisted that the nuclear deal provided a 'clear path' to Iran's production of a nuclear arsenal. The performance ended with a direct appeal to Trump's egotism, in which Netanyahu stated he was certain Trump would 'do the right thing for the United States, the right thing for Israel, and the right thing for the peace of the world.'[73]

Netanyahu was not done; the same day he prevailed upon the Israeli Knesset to give the prime minister and defense minister the extraordinary power to declare war in 'extreme situations.'[74] This represented the culmination of Netanyahu's populist securitization process. He had not only convinced Israelis of Iran's existential threat, but he had also orchestrated the handing over of authoritarian war-making power to the prime minister's office. He had achieved the status of protector and savior of Israel and minimized opposition to his policies on Iran. Yet he still had an unrealized objective: to convince Trump to withdraw from the JCPOA. The next day Netanyahu doubled down on his campaign to target Trump with an appearance on the popular Fox News morning show *Fox & Friends*, a favorite of the US president which he always made a point of watching.[75] On the show, Netanyahu declared that 'The person who is going to make the decision for the United States is one person, and that's President Trump.'[76]

Netanyahu had given a masterful performance. One news site summed it up by noting that 'Netanyahu's two-day lobbying blitz shows that he has a savvy understanding of how Trump receives and processes information.'[77] Others were similarly complimentary of Netanyahu's insight into Trump's decision-making process.[78] It did not matter that Netanyahu's performance was a charade, nor was it relevant that the content had already been briefed to Trump in secret two months earlier.[79] The ominous tone and the accusations of wrongdoing on Iran's part were what ultimately mattered to Trump. Most experts would eventually conclude that, while the documents were authentic, they did not contain any new revelations about Iran's recent behavior.[80] Although there were references to Iranian intentions in the early years of its nuclear development program, there was no evidence that Iran had violated or intended to violate its commitment to the JCPOA. The facts, however, did not matter in Netanyahu's appeal to an ill-informed, instinct-driven decision-maker whose ego prevented him from questioning the correctness of his opinions.

The following week, on 8 May 2018, Trump formally ended America's participation in the JCPOA. Six days later, Israel celebrated its Independence Day with the grand opening of the new United States embassy in Jerusalem. The move affirmed Netanyahu's 'success' in achieving his foreign policy goals. Netanyahu likely also saw it as affirming a partnership with the United States in a new strategy to confront Iran. Meanwhile, Iran acknowledged Netanyahu's power over the Americans. As one daily news outlet, *Jamhuriye Islami*, put it, blame rests with the 'fraudulent Zionists,' adding that 'President Trump's role here is nothing but that of a frightening scarecrow.'[81]

* * *

If Netanyahu's primary concern was the existential threat to Israel posed by Iran's nuclear development, it is curious that he invested considerable energy and political capital into undoing an agreement aimed at imposing strict limitations on that program. Netanyahu could have used the JCPOA as a tool to rally domestic support and build international alliances without also seeking its demise, but this was not the path he chose. Complaints that the deal did not address the full scope of Iran's reprehensible behavior—including its human rights abuses, support for proxy forces in regional conflicts, and ballistic missile production—had merit. Yet it was unclear how abandoning a diplomatic mechanism that sought to reduce the threat Iran posed to Israel would be more effective than intrusively monitoring Iran's suspension of its nuclear program and seeking to negotiate further concessions. Iran had not established a relationship of trust with the United States, but there was still a potential for an improved rapport if the deal held, whereas virtually any scenario in which the deal failed presented increased danger. In the end, the belligerent instability of the past overshadowed any vision of a less threatening future.

Netanyahu also did not explain why he believed that regime change in Tehran would produce a new government that was any less hostile to Israel than its current leadership. Nor could he adequately explain why or how economic sanctions and the accompanying social turmoil would sufficiently destabilize the Iranian government to facilitate the regime change he wanted. He likely understood that Iran's hardliners would expand their power should Rouhani's attempts at moderation conclusively fail. The withdrawal of the United States from an international agreement at the very loud and public urging of Israel further fueled Iran's perception that Israel controlled American foreign policy, thus undermining America's credibility with Iranians of all political persuasions. At the end of May, the state news agency IRNA ran an editorial accusing the United States and Israel, along with Saudi Arabia, of forming a 'new Axis of Evil.'[82]

The intensity with which Netanyahu advocated his strategy of machinating American withdrawal from the deal contrasted with the uncertainties of its success. In the months that followed, Netanyahu hinted that he wanted to take more aggressive action against Iran, including fomenting revolution or possibly a military strike. In June, he posted a video message on Facebook praising the Iranians' 'courage' in recent anti-regime protests.[83] Speaking at the United Nations General Assembly in September, he unveiled what he said was another 'secret' Iranian nuclear facility in which Iran was stockpiling nuclear material in violation of the JCPOA.[84] Objectively, Netanyahu's strategy was a dangerous one, and it risked destabilizing Iran and the greater Middle East. But from his perspective, it was preferable to maintaining a status quo in which Iran's compliance with the JCPOA could result in Netanyahu, as Trita Parsi termed it in a book of the same name, 'losing an enemy.'[85]

Netanyahu's hope of a US military engagement was not entirely fanciful. A month prior to the withdrawal announcement, Trump had appointed as his new National Security Adviser John Bolton, a known proponent of regime change in Iran as well as of using military action to force an end to Iran's nuclear program. During the 2015 JCPOA negotiations, Bolton had called for an air strike against Iran in a *New York Times* op-ed entitled 'To Stop Iran's Bomb, Bomb Iran.'[86] Bolton had also identified an Iranian exile group, the Mujahadeen-e-Khalq (MEK) as a potential government-in-waiting, despite there being a near-total absence of support for the group inside Iran.[87]

For Netanyahu to realize his vision, Iran had to behave in a fashion consistent with Israel's depiction of it. In Netanyahu's telling, Iran was dominated by militant, Israel-hating religious zealots. This overly simplistic portrayal of Iranian politics failed to account for the complicated political landscape of competing power centers, each with its own goals and strategic vision for Iran's future. Netanyahu understood there were Iranian hardliners who actively opposed the JCPOA, but he also knew they had lacked the power to block Iran's original entry into the agreement and its ongoing compliance with the terms.

In May 2017, one year before Trump's withdrawal, Iranians had reelected the moderate Hassan Rouhani as president, rejecting his conservative opponent, Ebrahim Raisi. Rouhani, whose administration had negotiated the JCPOA, campaigned on this achievement and won in a landslide. He received 57% of the votes cast in the first round of balloting, which obviated the need for a runoff.[88] By reelecting him, Iranians had affirmed their hope that diplomacy and engagement with the West still held out the promise of a better life. When Trump announced the withdrawal of the United States from the JCPOA in May 2018, Rouhani chose restraint over belligerence in his initial response, indicating that Iran would remain compliant with the terms of the deal.

Rouhani set out to salvage the deal and its benefits for Iran by continuing negotiations with the Europeans. Seven months later, in January 2019, Iran and the European signatories announced, with considerable fanfare, the establishment of INSTEX, a special-purpose financial vehicle to facilitate 'legitimate trade' between European enterprises and Iran 'within the framework of the efforts to preserve' the JCPOA.[89] Technically, the purpose of INSTEX was to provide European companies who wished to do business with Iranian organizations a safe haven for exchanging payments beyond the reach of US sanctions. The mechanism was complicated, and it was ultimately unable to insulate investors from secondary sanctions. For most enterprises, it was not worth the risk of losing business with the United States for the uncertain benefits of the Iranian market. Eventually, Iran realized that the Europeans could not defy United States pressure, and Tehran moved to consider a new strategy of noncompliance.[90]

If Iran was not living up to its image in his threat narrative, Netanyahu still hoped Trump's promised 'maximum pressure' campaign would inflict significant pain on the Iranian people and destabilize the government.[91] Trump's ultimate objective was more difficult to discern. Unquestionably, the sanctions had a disastrous impact on Iran's economy. Oil exports fell from a high rate of 2.1 million barrels per day to a total of 260,000 barrels.[92] Foreign companies cancelled business deals that had been negotiated after the signing of the JCPOA, including the Boeing and Airbus sales of civilian airliners.[93] Yet even with the pain the sanctions brought to Iranian daily life, the regime did not appear closer to collapse, nor was Iran about to 'reform' its behavior. Rather, Iranians directed their anger at the foreign oppressors who were making their lives so difficult. Although frustrated with their leaders' incompetence and corruption, Iranians banded together in defiance of the United States. Within the regime itself, the sanctions had no apparent effect on Iran's foreign policy; its support for militants operating in Syria, Iraq, Lebanon, and Yemen continued unabated.[94]

Turmoil within the Trump administration also created uncertainty regarding America's policy goals. During Bolton's seventeen-month tenure as National Security Adviser, he had reportedly clashed with Trump over major foreign policy issues, including his Iran strategy.[95] When he left the administration in September 2019, the *New York Times* reported that one point of recent tension had arisen from Trump's expressed willingness to meet with President Rouhani 'under the right circumstances.' The story noted that Trump had even considered extending short-term financing options to Iran as an economic lifeline for sanctions relief.[96]

Faced with an 'uncooperative' Iranian response and a mercurial Trump, Netanyahu realized he needed more potential allies at hand than just the United States. Since Iran was seeking common cause with western Europe to save the deal, Netanyahu looked east to Hungary and Poland in hopes of garnering support for his Iran threat messaging. It was remarkably odd for the leader of the Jewish State to court Europe's far-right leaders, whose nationalist rhetoric included anti-Semitic tropes, rendering them political outcasts in Europe, and whose nations had been complicit in the murder of Jews during the Holocaust.[97] For this cohort of Eastern European leaders, a relationship with Israel could help efforts to 'rehabilitate' their nations, bringing them out from the shadow of their treatment of Jews during World War II, as well as countering accusations that that they or their supporters were anti-Semitic.[98] To make common cause with these fellow populists, Netanyahu—who frequently referenced the Holocaust as the basis for his moral indignation and often conflated criticism of Israeli policy with anti-Semitism—had to overlook both their problematic past and their present conduct.

As a political strategy, Netanyahu's theatrics were defensible, but when put in context they bordered on the bizarre. In a 2018 visit to Israel by Viktor Orbán, Hungary's illiberal, autocratic leader, Netanyahu embraced him as a 'true friend of Israel.' Orbán reciprocated by defending Netanyahu's government and admonishing his fellow European leaders for not aligning more closely with Israel. Netanyahu's Foreign Minister Gabi Ashkenazi asked his Hungarian counterpart to present Israel's case against Iran at a 2018 meeting of the International Atomic Energy Agency (IAEA).[99] Similarly, Netanyahu invited Poland's right-wing populist prime minister, Mateusz Morawiecki, along with Orbán and the leaders of the Czech Republic and Slovakia, to Jerusalem, offering to play host to the first foreign meeting of the Visegrád Group.[100] The Israeli newspaper *Haaretz* described the meeting as part of 'Netanyahu's efforts to shake up the EU consensus on issues related to the Palestinians and Iran.'[101]

In February 2018, Netanyahu further promoted his narrative with Trump's help at an international security conference in Warsaw. Although the meeting had been officially requested and organized by the United States, Netanyahu's influence over the event was evident. Billed as a meeting on 'Mideast Security,' the agenda focused almost exclusively on Iran, leading several observers to conclude that it was actually an 'anti-Iran conference.'[102] Representatives of Russia, China, France, Germany, the higher ranks of the European Union, and Iran did not participate.[103] In a performative, if amateurish, pre-meeting event, Trump confidant Rudolph Giuliani spoke at an anti-Iran rally to declare that Iranians are 'assassins, they are murderers, and they should be out of power.'[104]

When Netanyahu arrived, he announced, 'I am going to a meeting with 60 foreign ministers and envoys of countries from around the world against Iran ... [T]his is an opening meeting with representatives of leading Arab countries, that are sitting down together with Israel in order to advance the common interest of war with Iran.'[105] The reference to 'war' engendered significant controversy until the Prime Minister's Office clarified that the appropriate translation should have been a more benign 'combating.'[106] Ultimately, the conference achieved little except for enraging the Iranians. Kamal Kharrazi, a former foreign minister who was head of Iran's Strategic Council on Foreign Relations, characterized the event as an 'insult to the Europeans' identity.'[107]

Netanyahu's delicate balancing of Holocaust politics with his embrace of Europe's far right took place against a backdrop of a rancorous dispute within his governing coalition. When they were unable to resolve the issue of military service by Yeshiva students, the Knesset voted to dissolve and move the general elections to April 2019 from their originally scheduled date later in the year.[108] Consequently, Netanyahu had to turn his attention to campaigning with the expectation that the success of his Iran policies would help him get reelected. Polls showed that half of Israeli Jews believed that Israel should attack Iran if it chose to resume its nuclear activity. An additional 10% of respondents said Israel should launch a military assault even if the United States did not approve or participate in the attack, while another 10% said that Israel should 'work toward replacing the Iranian regime.' Only 4% believed that Israel should consider 'establish[ing] a diplomatic channel vis-à-vis Iran.'[109]

Throughout the campaign, Netanyahu emphasized his strong relationship with Trump. Billboards sprung up around Israel displaying a smiling Netanyahu and Trump shaking hands.[110] Trump's brand of populism and his common cause with Netanyahu were more popular in Israel than in the United States. Weeks before the vote, Trump sought to help Netanyahu's campaign by recognizing Israel's sovereignty over the Golan Heights, a gesture long sought by the Israeli right. And the day before the election Trump sweetened the deal by designating the Iranian Revolutionary Guard Corps (IRGC) a terrorist organization, marking the first time the label had attached to a nation's official military organization. Both moves were primarily symbolic, but they appealed to Netanyahu's base and bolstered his security credentials, suggesting that Israel would benefit from Netanyahu's continued leadership and his close association with Trump.

Netanyahu's opponent was Benny Gantz, a retired army general in his first campaign for public office. Gantz's career military service fortified his national security credentials such that he could not be easily attacked as being 'weak' or a 'dove' for having cautiously supported the JCPOA. There was otherwise little daylight between the two men on key foreign policy issues, which blunted the force of Netanyahu's narrative. What distinguished them were their respective scandals. Netanyahu was the subject of a criminal investigation for corruption relating to his conduct in office, while Gantz's cell phone had been hacked by the Iranians several weeks before the election. Media reports claimed that the hack revealed that Gantz had engaged in a 'lurid' adulterous affair.[111] Shamelessly, Netanyahu unleashed a series of tweets attacking Gantz as a pawn of the Iranians. In one post he wrote: 'Gantz, what material does Iran hold on you? The State of Israel needs a strong and non-blackmailable prime minister who will stand firm against our enemies.'[112] The irony that he was attempting to use an Iranian hack to bolster his reelection campaign was presumably lost on the incumbent.

The election ended in a tie between Netanyahu's Likud Party and Gantz's Blue and White Party.[113] Each won thirty-five seats, far short of the sixty-one required to form a government.[114] Netanyahu hadn't lost, but, despite his achievements and years in power, the results showed that he was politically vulnerable. Israel's president designated Netanyahu as the first to try forming a governing coalition. When he was unable to secure sufficient partners, the Knesset voted to dissolve itself on 29 May before Gantz could be given the opportunity to try. It set 17 September as the date for the second election.

In the interregnum between the first and second elections, Netanyahu continued propagating his Iran threat narrative and pressing world leaders to intensify their confrontation with Iran. He held discussions with Japanese Prime Minister Shinzo Abe, British Prime Minister Boris Johnson, French President Emmanuel Macron, and Russian President Vladimir Putin. On 24 August, three weeks before the election, Israel claimed that it had conducted an air strike in Syria where Iran was plotting to use 'killer drones' to attack targets in northern Israel.[115] Following the operation, Netanyahu tweeted, 'If someone rises up to kill you, kill him first.'[116] The action heightened Israelis' sense of insecurity, while the response highlighted Netanyahu's strong leadership. In the days before the election, Netanyahu orchestrated yet another dramatic presentation in which he revealed a secret site south of the Iranian city of Isfahan where, he claimed, Iran 'experimented on nuclear weapons development.'[117] The source backing up his claim was the same trove of documents used in his May 2018 press conference, but this time he spoke in Hebrew before switching to English. The event featured Netanyahu's mastery of political theater: its timing, style, and substance were all calculated to amplify Israelis' fear at a crucial political moment.

But Netanyahu's strategy did not produce its intended result. The September election ended in another stalemate between the same two parties. In what was perhaps a reflection of growing voter fatigue and frustration, each party's share of the vote actually decreased from the first election in April.[118] Netanyahu's Likud Party secured 32 seats, one fewer than Gantz's Blue and White. Nevertheless, this was a small 'victory' for Netanyahu as he continued to defy efforts to remove him from office.

At the same time, the election did not dispel perceptions of his vulnerability. One weak point was the united opposition of Israeli Arab voters and the possibility that their party would join an anti-Netanyahu coalition.[119] However, Netanyahu's campaign had anticipated this possibility and incorporated it into to his Iran narrative. Five days before the election, a chatbot on Netanyahu's Facebook account urged supporters to go to the polls to stop 'a dangerous leftwing government' that would rely on Arab politicians 'who want to destroy us all ... and enable a nuclear Iran that would wipe us out.'[120] Facebook suspended the chatbot for twenty-four hours. Netanyahu denied responsibility for the message, blaming it on a campaign staffer.

As Netanyahu and Gantz maneuvered to form alliances that would give them the requisite parliamentary majority, the only two things they agreed on were that they wanted to avoid a third election and that they did not want to serve together in a government. Gantz said he would join with Likud so long as Netanyahu was not involved. Netanyahu accused Gantz of dragging Israel into an unnecessary election while it currently faced an existential threat from Iran.[121] Sequentially, each man received the designation to attempt to form a government; both failed. In December, the Knesset set a third election for 2 March 2020.[122]

As 2020 began, Netanyahu was still prime minister. Since he had been indicted on corruption charges the previous November, his only hope of avoiding prosecution was if he remained in that post.[123] Retaining that office, in other words, had become an existential imperative for his political future. Ironically, Trump confronted a similar challenge. He too faced a reelection campaign and possible legal jeopardy if he lost power.[124] And although foreign policy rarely dominated American voters' concerns, Trump had no singular foreign policy achievement winning him universal praise, despite his many efforts to find one. He did not have the equivalent of Obama's bragging rights for killing Osama Bin Laden or negotiating the Iran deal. Rather, it appeared that his foreign policy legacy would be cozying up to foreign dictators for photo-ops.

We may never know why, on 3 January 2020, Trump ordered a drone strike targeting the Iranian military commander Qasem Soleimani, a leading figure in regional politics and a respected military leader. Similarly, we are unlikely to learn Netanyahu's motivations for contributing to the attack. The killing was a daring move. Soleimani, the leader of Iran's Quds Force—the foreign operations branch of the IRGC—had achieved a certain mythical status; he was beloved by Iranians and feared by his enemies.[125] His death prompted a massive outpouring of grief across Iran coupled with fury at the United States. The act allowed Iranian officials to accuse America of 'state terrorism' and empowered Iran's ambassador to the United Nations to argue, not implausibly, that the killing was a 'clear example of a gross violation of the principles of international law.'[126] Iran's parliament designated the United States armed forces as a terrorist organization.[127] Trump offered several rationales for ordering the strike, including the possibility that Soleimani was planning to 'blow up our embassy' in Baghdad, but he offered no specific evidence to support his claim of preemptive self-defense.[128]

While Americans were skeptical, puzzled, and divided regarding whether killing Soleimani had been a prudent act, Israelis were overwhelmingly positive in their public praise. Political rivals Netanyahu and Gantz both lauded the action, and across the board Israeli officials contended that it lessened the danger of a terrorist attack on Israel.[129] Both men dutifully commended Trump for his 'determination' and 'bravery' in ordering the strike.[130] At the same time, no Israeli official admitted to taking part in the operation. Netanyahu, seeking to avoid an Iranian reprisal, instructed his security cabinet to emphasize how it was within the United States' rights to defend itself.[131] There was reason to believe that Netanyahu had been informed of the strike before it happened.[132] He had cryptically mentioned to reporters that 'very, very dramatic things' were happening in the region, while offering his support of the United States 'and its full right to defend itself and its citizens.'[133] Only much later did reports suggest that Israel had helped identify and track Soleimani's cell phone.[134]

When considered without the benefit of hindsight, it is questionable whether the killing of Soleimani served Israeli interests. Iran's Foreign Minister Javad Zarif declared that 'American terrorist forces ... will undoubtedly make the tree of resistance in the region and the world more prosperous.'[135] Iran's parliament voted an immediate €200 million increase in funds for the Quds Force to 'boost their defensive power.'[136] Neither Trump nor Netanyahu had the prescience to know whether the action would initiate a war, and, if it did, what the potential consequences of that war would be. While Trump often acted impulsively with a narrow focus on how that action might impact his personal interests, Netanyahu certainly understood the danger to Israel of a military escalation. Nearly two years later, after leaving office, Trump complained to an Israeli reporter that Netanyahu had been 'willing to fight Iran to the last American soldier.'[137] He stated that he had felt betrayed by both the Israelis and their prime minister for the insufficient support they had been willing to offer against Iran, although he did not clarify what he had expected of Netanyahu in the first place.

Fears of a massive Iranian retaliation proved overblown. For its part, Iran resisted the urge to escalate in favor of what it characterized as a measured counteraction: a week after the killing of Soleimani, Iran launched rocket attacks on two American military bases in Iraq. To emphasize its restraint, the Iranians issued a warning of the impending attack, which prevented the loss of American lives.[138] Significantly, the Iranian government also announced it was abandoning the 'final limitations in the nuclear deal' and would resume uranium production and enrichment beyond the limits established by the JCPOA.[139] This latter action, which had been expected since May 2018, when the United States had withdrawn from the agreement, prompted Trump to issue additional bellicose threats. Regardless of intent, the escalating reciprocal threats from Iran heightened the risk of war between the two countries.[140] Perhaps realizing this risk, at the last minute both sides stood down and a cold peace ensued.

It is unlikely that either Trump, by his provocative action, or Netanyahu, by capitalizing on the killing of Soleimani and using it to reify his Iran narrative, enhanced their political fortunes. Subsequent events, unrelated to Iran's nuclear program and unforeseeable at the time, overshadowed memories of the incident and debates over its significance. But even in the immediate aftermath of the assassination, little changed: Netanyahu's narrative lived on, and Iran remained a dangerous and volatile enemy.

V. Conclusion

On 21 February 2020, Iran held its scheduled parliamentary elections. Four years earlier, the moderate and reformist 'List of Hope' coalition had won 125 seats, which accounted for 43% of the 290 seat Iranian parliament, known as the Majles. The hardliners, meanwhile, secured just 82 seats after receiving 29% of the vote.[141] The results from the February 2020 election underscored how events had impacted the collective Iranian psyche during the intervening years, as well as the shifts in strategic thinking within the regime's leadership. Reformers won only 20 seats compared to the hardliners' 221, while voter turnout plummeted nearly 20 points to 42.5%, the lowest level since the 1979 Islamic Revolution.[142]

Iranians had many reasons to feel dissatisfied and frustrated. The Guardian Council—the governing body that approved candidates based on their 'Islamic' and 'revolutionary' credentials—had disqualified the majority of the reformists' registered candidates, reflecting a stated desire of Iran's unelected conservative elite to push the country back toward a more hardliner stance. In the prior parliamentary and presidential elections, voters had indicated that they were still hopeful that Rouhani's coalition could deliver the promised benefits from the JCPOA. However, since that time, their lives had only become more challenging. The United States had shown itself to be untrustworthy, which diminished Iranians' faith in international diplomacy and reinforced their suspicions of there being a foreign conspiracy aimed at suppressing Iran's advancement. The American president appeared beholden to the Israeli prime minister and his narrative that ascribed evil intentions to Iran's leaders, offering only domestic revolution or foreign intervention as a possible solution.

Iranians resented not only the callous disregard of Western leaders who claimed to care about the welfare of the 'Iranian people' but also the gullibility of their own government officials who had trusted in the West's willingness to help a nation that they had spent decades demonizing. The results were predictable. Voters voiced their frustrations by supporting candidates who offered new, more confrontational solutions to Iran's problems, or by simply refusing to vote. The election represented the fulfillment of a long-held goal of the United States and Israel: it was a 'regime change,' though not one that brought a friendlier, safer Iranian legislature to power.

The 2020 Iranian parliamentary election was arguably the first step toward an Iran that more closely matched the one depicted by Netanyahu's narrative. Still, even with his self-fulfilling prophecy come at last to fruition, the results in Iran did not materially affect the outcome of Israel's third election on 2 March, which ended in yet another stalemate. Netanyahu's Likud party won 4 more seats than it had in the second election, garnering nearly 3% more of the vote than Gantz's Blue and White. But, once again, neither party had an obvious path toward forming a governing coalition.

Compelled by voter fatigue and the imperative to forestall a fourth election, the parties at last engaged in intense negotiations to form a unity government. Gantz 'blinked' first. Despite his avowed political mission to defeat Netanyahu, he agreed to join with him in forming what they dubbed an 'emergency coalition' government. Under their arrangement, Netanyahu would retain the office of prime minister for the next eighteen months before transferring the office to Gantz in November 2021. Observers of Israeli politics quickly noted that such a fragile coalition was unlikely to last that long, and that Netanyahu would likely break the coalition and call for new elections before he handed over the reins to Gantz. With a corruption indictment looming over him, the incumbent understood that the only path out of his predicament was to remain in power. For the moment, however, it appeared that Netanyahu had again emerged victorious.

As Israeli politicians conducted their post-election negotiations, the world around them was radically changing. A novel virus, which proved to be both contagious and deadly with no known prophylaxis or treatment, honored neither geographic boundaries nor political ideologies as it infected people worldwide. Iran was among the first nations to suffer a widespread outbreak of the disease, which was dubbed COVID-19 and likely originated in China.[143] US sanctions increased Iranians' suffering by impeding the nation's access to drugs and specialized medical equipment.[144] On 7 March 2020, Foreign Minister Zarif accused the United States of engaging in 'medical terrorism' by refusing to grant exemptions to allow lifesaving aid.[145] Secretary of State Pompeo responded ten days later that the United States would seek additional sanctions to 'further Iran's economic and diplomatic isolation.'[146]

The global pandemic created domestic crises for both Netanyahu and Trump as rising case numbers and mortality rates dominated the public's attention. Both Israel and the United States, not unlike the rest of the world, proved unprepared to respond. As citizens clashed over whether and how government should protect their lives and livelihoods, there was little room for other issues, especially manufactured threats and crises based on hypothetical nuclear bombs.

With the American presidential elections scheduled for 3 November, Trump struggled to control the virus, the narrative surrounding it, and its impact on people's lives and health. He sought to position himself as uniquely deserving of reelection, despite an approval rating that had rarely exceeded 50% in any poll, and he began to cast doubt on the democratic process in general. The details of Middle East politics became a secondary concern, and Iran rarely entered public discourse during the campaign. On occasion, Trump's opponent, Joe Biden, who had served as Obama's vice president, argued that Trump's maximum-pressure campaign was a failure and indicated that he would seek to resurrect the JCPOA.[147] In August, the Trump administration sought to extend the United Nations arms embargo against Iran, but the Security Council rejected the proposal.[148]

Without the Iran issue to bind Trump and Netanyahu, and with both men's political careers facing more pressing threats, their strategic coordination and shared policy focus lost prominence. Subsequently, their relationship began to fray. When Trump unveiled Kushner's long-awaited Middle East Peace Plan in early 2020, the White House was reportedly stunned when Netanyahu upstaged Trump at the public ceremony to claim that it supported annexation of large portions of the West Bank. Netanyahu then felt betrayed when the Trump administration—and, specifically, Jared Kushner— refused to endorse the Israeli annexation plan.[149] Netanyahu defiantly announced he would proceed with the plan anyway, but later abandoned it in exchange for official recognition by the United Arab Emirates.[150]

As the year progressed, Netanyahu, aware that Trump could and likely would lose the election, avoided any involvement in the American campaign that might be read as an endorsement of Trump. Although the Democratic nominee Joseph Biden had been Obama's vice president, Biden and Netanyahu maintained a cordial relationship. They had known each other for decades, dating back to Biden's long tenure in the Senate and his service on the Foreign Relations Committee. Six weeks before the election, Netanyahu allowed Trump to stage one final performance. He traveled to Washington for the signing of the Abraham Accords, an alliance between Israel and several Sunni-majority Gulf Arab states that were willing to join with Israel in opposing Iran.[151] Netanyahu allowed Trump to claim much of the credit for the achievement,[152] which avoided the question of whether the agreement represented more than an acknowledgment of the regional rearrangement of strategic alliances occasioned by mutual suspicions of Iran.[153] Trump's presence highlighted the symbolic nature of the Accords, which he emphasized by presenting Netanyahu with a gold 'key to the White House.' The two men effusively praised each other throughout the ceremony.

This would be the last hurrah of Trump and Netanyahu's populist alliance, and the end of their shared obsession with an Iran threat constructed and disseminated to further their personal political fortunes. Netanyahu, likely subconsciously, summed up his journey with Trump to a reporter when asked whether Israel currently felt globally isolated. He responded with an emphatic 'Heck no!' before adding,

> We're breaking out to the entire world because we have a strong, free economy, because we have a strong military, and because we have a strong relationship with the President of the United States and the American people. I think the people who feel isolated are the tyrants of Tehran because of the pressure that the President has applied on them.[154]

CONCLUSION

Unlike Queen Scheherazade, the fabled narrator of *The Thousand and One Nights*, who used her collection of stories and dramatic narration to avoid execution, Benjamin Netanyahu's narrative was ultimately not strong enough to save him. Whereas Scheherazade spun tales to capture the attention and win the affection of her audience, King Shahryar, Netanyahu was no longer so beloved by the Israeli electorate.

Ironically, both Netanyahu's Iran narrative and Scheherazade's stories focused on content unrelated to their true motivations. While Scheherazade used storytelling to save her life and the lives of other Persian women from an enraged monarch, Netanyahu ultimately could not retain his claim to power by portraying himself as the savior of his people from the Iranian leaders he pictured as bloodthirsty tyrants. As storytellers, Scheherazade and Netanyahu both had drawn upon myth and history to create compelling and impactful narratives. The power of their stories outlived their reigns.

The March 2021 Israeli election—the fourth in two years—represented both an end and a continuation of Netanyahu's narrative. It marked the end of Netanyahu's service as prime minister, but not of his narrative. This time, his Likud party secured the largest share of the vote, outpolling the second place Yesh Atid ('There Is a Future') party by 24% to 14% and winning 13 more seats.[1] While it initially looked as if another Netanyahu-led government was a foregone conclusion, after several weeks of negotiations he still

217

lacked the necessary sixty-one seats to form a coalition. While some of his closest allies continued to stand by him, Netanyahu's years of political maneuvering, backroom dealmaking, and backstabbing had taken a toll on his credibility, serving ultimately to alienate several of his ideological brethren. The mandate to form a government then passed to Yair Lapid, the leader of Yesh Atid, who confected a national unity government consisting of eight parties that that shared a single unifying principle: ending Netanyahu's reign as prime minister.

To reach the required threshold, the new government brought together a diverse array of politicians and interests, putting hardline religious nationalists in league with the remnants of the Israeli left. For the first time in the history of the State of Israel, the governing majority included an Arab political party.[2] If Netanyahu's tenure as prime minister had been guided primarily by the desire to retain power, even at the expense of ideological purity or a consistent policy agenda, his ouster ironically came at the hands of a government in which the participants agreed on few issues other than the need to remove him from office.

The fourth election and its aftermath highlighted the distinct contributions of securitization and populism to the construction of Netanyahu's Iran narrative. He had crafted a narrative that portrayed Iran as an existential threat to Israel, prioritizing believability over factual accuracy and appealing to emotion over reason. By manipulating the vulnerabilities—both geographic and historical— of Israel and the Jewish people, he generated a fear that proved more powerful than rationality. The threat reached securitization when Israelis, perceiving it as truth, endorsed efforts by leaders who proposed policies to protect them from Iran's harm, which naturally followed from their calculated promotion of insecurity.

Unlike threats that are proximal or have visible manifestations, the Iran threat was not imminent or self-evident. Israel's leaders established their superior knowledge of this foreign policy matter by claiming to have access to classified information and expertise upon which they based their assertions about the purpose of Iran's nuclear endeavors. Israeli leaders used this framework to establish a scenario in which Iran's nuclear program was not simply an exercise in technological achievement in the face of Western opposition, but rather a top-secret endeavor fated to end in chaos and destruction for Israeli citizens. In a robust democracy, the uncertainty regarding Iran's behavior and intentions should have, at the very least, stimulated debate, particularly within the top echelons of state officialdom. The polity would then have had the opportunity to evaluate both the proposed actions of their candidates for leadership and their support of those officials' actions.

Netanyahu's embrace of populism was a strategy for minimizing this debate. He built his claim to leadership on the promise to protect Israelis' security, and he manufactured a demand for that protection by promoting their insecurity with tropes that optimized his narrative's emotional appeal. Grounded in a mythologized history, he traced the enmity between Iran and Israel from Biblical times, while analogizing the modern Islamic Republic to the Third Reich. Using Islamophobic tropes, he ascribed evil aspirations to Iran's leaders. His narrative served and was served by his foreign policy: Iran contributed to all terrorist acts against Israel; it was the force behind the disastrous Second Lebanon War and subsequent Gaza wars; it provided the excuse for avoiding negotiations to recognize the rights of Palestinians; and it was the source of an ongoing existential nuclear crisis. In the absence of a world willing to confront the Iranian challenge directly, these threats required bold Israeli leadership.

Netanyahu's populist strategy for maintaining his power also included discrediting those who would challenge his narrative. Manipulating the political and religious fractures in Israeli society, Netanyahu skillfully incorporated a vision of a society of believers— the 'us'—opposed by skeptics not of the people—the 'them'—into his messaging. In this way he insulated his narrative from public debate, in which it would run the risk of being challenged by national security experts, historians, and policy analysts, among others. Most especially, he silenced rival politicians afraid of being seen as weak on protecting the nation's security. In international forums, Netanyahu used accusations of anti-Semitism to divert attention from would-be critics of his narrative and policies.

The salience of Netanyahu's narrative received assistance from developments outside of Israel. Mahmoud Ahmadinejad's

Holocaust denialism during his tenure as President of Iran reinforced Netanyahu's fear-based tropes. The election of Donald Trump as President of the United States in 2016 marked the apex of the narrative's power, paving the way for Netanyahu to engineer the destruction of the JCPOA. With this act, he effectively made his narrative self-fulfilling. By causing the demise of the nuclear deal, Netanyahu diminished Iran's incentives for refraining from restarting its nuclear enrichment efforts. As it increased its stockpile of enriched uranium, Iran grew ever closer to producing a bomb. Netanyahu responded both with narrative tropes emphasizing the imminent danger as well as clandestine activities, such as sabotage and assassinations of Iranian nuclear scientists. These assassinations, as many have noted, showcased Israel's long military reach, but they had only marginal impact on Iran's nuclear capabilities.

The collective effect of Netanyahu's actions influenced the outcome of Iran's 2021 general elections, which marked a repudiation of Rouhani's engagement with the West.[3] America's withdrawal from the JCPOA caused Iranians to lose faith in Rouhani's pursuit of diplomatic compromise and revived their distrust in Western powers, especially their suspicions about American subservience to Israel. Faced with the disastrous consequences occasioned by Netanyahu's convincing Donald Trump to reimpose harsh economic sanctions, the regime responded by engineering a leadership change that positioned a devout, ultra-conservative hardliner as the leading presidential candidate. Ebrahim Raisi, who had been Rouhani's main opponent in the 2017 presidential elections, was in many ways the polar opposite of his predecessor.[4] While he was not as flamboyant or bombastic as Mahmoud Ahmadinejad, Raisi had run on a platform that staunchly opposed compromise with the West.[5] To ensure his victory, Iran's Guardian Council—the group tasked with reviewing the credentials of all candidates for office—had preemptively disqualified all major reform or moderate opposition candidates. Voters, faced with a choice between a hardliner or not voting, opted in historic numbers for the latter option. The dismal turnout of 48.5% was the lowest in national history and nearly twenty-five percentage points below that of the 2017 election.

The contribution of the political developments in Iran and the United States, when combined with Netanyahu's populist securitization of his narrative, made it difficult for his successors to effect policy change. A poll conducted by the Israel Democracy Institute in November 2021, six months after Netanyahu left office, affirmed the narrative's entrenchment. Of those polled, 62% of Israeli Jews said that they believe Iran poses an existential threat to the state, and 58% said they would support an attack on Iran's nuclear facilities, even without American consent.[6] It would be extremely challenging for a leader of an Israeli right-wing party, whose overall numbers had grown stronger during Netanyahu's tenure as prime minister, to meaningfully alter the narrative.

Although the centrist Lapid had finished second to Netanyahu and had led the formation of the governing coalition, he allowed Naftali Bennett—the leader of the right-wing Yamina Party—to serve as the initial prime minister of the new government. Lapid likely recognized that Bennett, as the leader of a religious nationalist party and former Netanyahu ally, would be sympathetic to the status quo, but as the face of the new government he would be responsible should events challenge the correctness of Israel's Iran policy. Bennett had only a tenuous hold on power in the eight-party coalition.[7] He had to appease a political base already skeptical of his coalitional associations and simultaneously avoid alienating his government partners, knowing that the defection of any one group could prematurely end his tenure as prime minister and bring down the government. Policies upon which all agreed—or at least which were sufficiently uncontroversial—were rare. As Bennett assumed office, Netanyahu's version of the Iran threat fit within that narrow space. Still, Bennett sought to distance himself from potential consequences of Netanyahu's actions, observing that his predecessor had bequeathed him 'a situation in which Iran is at the most advanced point ever in its race to the bomb.'[8]

Bennett effectively mimicked Netanyahu's anti-Iran rhetoric even as he claimed his approach would be different.[9] Ahead of his first visit to the United States following Trump's defeat in the 2020 US presidential election, Bennett noted that he was planning to present a 'new strategic vision on Iran.' When he elaborated on this vision, however, its components sounded nearly identical to Netanyahu's approach.[10] Part strategic alliance with Sunni Arab nations, part diplomatic and economic sanctions, and part clandestine operations to sabotage and obstruct Iran's nuclear progress, Bennett's plan had little that was new to offer other than a slightly softer tone.

Bennett also utilized the United Nations to disseminate his message to a global audience. During his first trip to the General Assembly meeting in September 2021, he made Iran the focal point of his speech. He accused the Iranians of seeking to 'dominate the region' and 'destroy my country,' and he even employed derogatory phrases like the 'Mullah touch' to describe how 'every place Iran touches—fails.' Like Netanyahu, he lobbied for regime change, arguing that Iran's regime is 'rotten' and 'much weaker [and] more vulnerable than it seems.'[11] If there was any substantive difference between Bennett and Netanyahu, it was only that the former eschewed the latter's dramatic use of visual props.[12]

Bennett also used Netanyahu's imagery as he affirmed Israel's resolve to challenge what he believed to be the world's, and especially the United States' unwillingness to confront Iran more aggressively. Thus, he pictured Iran as being driven by a 'radical Islamist' philosophy in pursuit of 'Shi'ite hegemony,' and he spoke of the specter of a 'nuclear umbrella' under which terrorists would operate freely and without fear of repercussions.[13] In a speech days before the reopening of negotiations between Iran and the P5+1, Bennett said, 'We hope the world won't blink, but even if they do, we don't plan to blink.'[14] Two weeks later, as the JCPOA signatories met in Vienna, the Israeli government resumed its public saber-rattling when Defense Minister Benny Gantz announced that he had ordered the Israeli military to prepare for a possible military strike against Iran.[15]

While the narrative remained strong, without Netanyahu's populism there was new space for Israelis—particularly those within the national security community—to challenge the actions the narrative had supported. Some critics began pointing to mistakes in Netanyahu's Iran strategy, publicly questioning its wisdom and efficacy. Former Mossad chief Efraim Halevy called Netanyahu's government a 'dismal,' 'unfortunate,' and 'historic failure.'[16] Danny

Citrinowicz, the former head of the Iran branch of Israel's military intelligence division, described Israel's clandestine efforts to sabotage Iran's nuclear program as a 'strategic failure.'[17]

Former Prime Minister Ehud Barak, who during the Netanyahu government had been a strong supporter of military strikes against Iran,[18] published an op-ed stating that the time had come for a 'sober assessment of the situation,' adding that 'hollow public threats … may impress some Israeli citizens, but not the Iranians or their negotiating partners.'[19] In calling for 'a realistic view of the reality and … mistakes made by our leaders,' Barak directly challenged the foundational fear that had defined Netanyahu's message. In a change from his position when he served as Netanyahu's defense minister in 2012, when he had argued in favor of a preemptive strike on Iran's nuclear program, Barak now admitted that Israeli threats of a military operation were not feasible. In a direct contradiction of the narrative threat, he wrote, 'Iran seeks to have nuclear weapons, not to use them against the U.S., Israel or any other neighboring nation.' He added, 'The Iranian ayatollahs are extreme in their ideology, but they are not fools. They want to solidify their hegemony in the region, but not to bring their nation back to the stone age.'[20]

These critiques were important because they signaled the introduction into public discourse of informed analysis, reasoned opinion, and debate within the national security community about Iran's intentions. Politicians and the public heard something more than alarmist predictions about looming nuclear annihilation. They could now hear about mistakes made and the lessons learned, and they could consider alternative futures that included the possibility of accepting a diplomatic agreement as the wisest course of action for Israeli security. They would, however, have to suppress their fear in order to listen. They would have to ask questions, engage in debate, and develop the capacity to respond with skepticism when leaders promised protection. Since the public still perceived the threat as real and the story as ongoing, it would take more than a few expert voices to change direction.

In general, political narratives are foundational to the quest for and exercise of power. Narratives shape our perception of the world and the problems within it. For politicians, narratives are the justification for their leadership; they are the predicate for forming policy; and they provide the rationale for their actions. Narratives are products of human ingenuity and are therefore susceptible to the same biases, emotions, and flaws in judgment that affect human thinking. A narrative can be a simple recounting of facts and an explanation of the inferences drawn from available information, or it can be a total fabrication. A deft politician can construct a narrative that achieves believability among his supporters because they have invested in his leadership and his message and are unwilling or unable to challenge his claims. Security narratives, grounded in predictions of potentially dire consequences about which the public has limited access to information, can be particularly powerful tools for creating and concentrating power. Narratives embedding a message of fear and insecurity often obscure the public's concern about accuracy; they facilitate the narrator's pursuit of his policy with support of the polity.

The narrative that warned Israelis that Iran posed an urgent existential threat is a version of what Timothy Snyder calls the 'politics of eternity.' It sought to seduce Israelis by creating a 'mythicized past [that] prevents … thinking about possible futures.'[21] Snyder warns of the dangers of this practice: 'The habit of dwelling on victimhood dulls the impulse of self-correction. Since the nation is defined by its inherent value rather than by its future potential, politics becomes a discussion of good and evil rather than a discussion of possible solutions to real problems.'[22] In Netanyahu's telling, the Holocaust was the past that prevented Israel from even debating how best to mitigate the Iranian threat in the present, let alone resolve it. By appealing to the fear of annihilation, he paralyzed policymaking aimed at creating a less combative and safer future, one not based upon us versus them, or the 'good' Israel versus the 'evil' Iran. The existential threat instead created an 'eternal present' in which the crisis foreclosed both constructive consideration of reasoned solutions to the Iranian nuclear threat along with the resolution of other controversial issues that might undermine Netanyahu's power.

Even with the disruption of Netanyahu's populist hold on Israeli society, Israel still has not freed itself from its eternal present. The structural changes that have taken place in Israeli and Middle

Eastern politics point increasingly toward sustained hostilities with Iran. Snyder maintains that a better understanding of history can both enlighten the past and suggest alternative futures. Netanyahu has made this harder by distorting history, directly linking Iranian nuclear development with the emotional resonance of 'Never Again.'

The historical relationship between the Jewish people and Persia has a long history of co-existence and conflict. By contrast, the modern relationship of Israel and the Islamic Republic is marked by nearly continuous tension, at times subdued and at other times intense, but always including a rhetorical war waged by the nations' leaders. The ideas that these officials embedded in their verbal salvos were directed less toward influencing the actions of the enemy state than they were in sustaining national allegiance at home and building global allies abroad. Moreover, the conflict was asymmetrical: the frequency, characterization, and putative consequences of Iran's threat to Israel were not matched by the concerns of Iran's leaders for Israel's conduct. Still, the national leaders' words did not exist in isolation, nor were they simply chronological markers in a long-running conflict. The words, and the actions they inspired, had consequences far beyond the moment they were addressing.

In understanding the course of the Israel-Iran conflict, it is important to acknowledge that words have consequences. The historical record prioritizes examining actions, but political narratives have the power to shape and, significantly, reshape history both as a description of the past that justifies current policies and as a foundation for future actions that are history-making. But history can also disrupt a narrative's power: events can intervene, or powerful voices can emerge to correct the record or offer new narratives. Our understanding of the relationship between Israel and the Islamic Republic of Iran in the first two decades of the twenty-first century requires us to acknowledge the power of Netanyahu's threat narrative on the events that affected this conflict. As time passes, the question will be whether Netanyahu's narrative simply played a role in the historical moment or whether it defined the history of this era.

NOTES

INTRODUCTION

1. Al-e Ahmad's work denouncing Western cultural influence in Iran would play an important role a decade and a half later during the Islamic Revolution led by Khomeini, providing part of the ideological foundation for the Shah's overthrow.

2. Al-e Ahmad professed a fascination with the founding of the Jewish State, in particular its socialist roots and religious ethos. Socialism, in particular, was a point of interest for Al-e Ahmad. In *Gharbzadeghi* (Westoxification), he condemned the capitalist 'machine' of the West and Iran's exploitation at its hand.

3. There are different interpretations of the title of Al-e Ahmad's book. The Persian title that appears on the original book—سفر به ولایت عزرائیل—incorporates a deliberately misspelled version of the Persian word for 'Israel,' using an 'Ayn instead of an Alif and a Zeh instead of the usual Sin. This means that while the title remains technically 'Journey to the Land of Israel,' the final word is only a transliteration of the country name. Literally, the title translates to 'Journey to the Land of the Angel of Death.' This title, which is far more tongue-in-cheek than the commonly known English translation, suggests Al-e Ahmad held a more ambivalent, or perhaps even pessimistic, view of his visit to Israel, possibly the result of his later disenchantment following the 1967 Six Day War. Hamid Dabashi, *The Last Muslim Intellectual: The Life and Legacy of Jalal Al-e Ahmad*, 1st edition (Edinburgh: Edinburgh University Press, 2021), 233.

4. Dabashi again critiques Al-e Ahmad's use of the term *velayat* and some of its common portrayals. Instead of interpreting the *veyalat* descriptor as a compliment, Dabashi suggests the possibility that Al-e Ahmad was being somewhat sarcastic in his writing. By using *velayat* rather than 'state' to refer to Israel, Al-e Ahmad may have been subtly subverting Israel's legitimacy by refusing to confer on it the legitimacy of statehood as that term is commonly understood, i.e., 'Palestinians ruling over Palestine.' Dabashi, 228.

5. Ruhollah Khomeini, *Islamic Government: Governance of the Jurist*, 1970.

227

6. The timing of Al-e Ahmad's trip and subsequent praise of Israel was also surprising considering the already growing atmosphere of discontent in Iran surrounding the Shah's alliance with Israel. Khomeini would denounce the Shah as an Israeli stooge at a speech at the Faiziyeh religious school in Qom just a few months after Al-e Ahmad's trip. The speech would spark widespread protests followed by a brutal crackdown, and Khomeini was arrested and subsequently exiled by the Shah.

7. Jalal Al-e Ahmad, *The Israeli Republic: An Iranian Revolutionary's Journey to the Jewish State*, trans. Samuel Thrope, Translation edition (Brooklyn, NY: Restless Books, 2017), chap. 1.

8. In support of this proposition, he cited the trial of Nazi war criminal Adolf Eichmann. Israeli courts convicted Eichmann of mass murder of Jews during the Holocaust. His execution was the only case of capital punishment in Israel. Al-e Ahmad believed that this event demonstrated that Israel's leaders were acting in the name of guardianship of Judaism rather than simply of the state itself. He argued that by mounting a massive operation to kidnap Eichmann for trial in Israel the country's leaders had engaged in 'something loftier than human rights declarations.'

9. This idea of the 'muscular Jew' was deliberately meant to contrast with the post-World War II image of Jews as the weak and vulnerable victims of Nazi Germany.

10. The group visited kibbutz Ayelet HaShahar situated adjacent to the border with the Syrian-controlled Golan Heights. Israel later captured that territory in the 1967 War, four years after Al-e Ahmad's visit.

11. Al-e Ahmad, *The Israeli Republic*, chap. 4.

12. The other non-signatory nations are India, Pakistan, South Sudan, and North Korea. All, save for South Sudan, are known nuclear-armed states.

13. The Cold War, the India-Pakistan standoff, and the confrontation between North Korea and the West offer instructive examples.

14. Ronen Bergman's highly influential book *The Point of No Return* (original Hebrew title) will be discussed in Chapter 4.

15. While official Israeli documents involving strategic security debates remain classified, older state records and other historical studies detail the early years of the relationship between Iran and the new Israeli State. In addition, Israel allows access both to unclassified archival materials on relatively recent policy matters as well as the document collections of the Prime Minister's Office, the Knesset, and the Israeli Foreign Ministry. Transcripts of parliamentary debates that discussed Iran provided useful insights into how members of different parties viewed the urgency of the Iranian threat across the country's diverse political spectrum.

16. Unfortunately, many current or former government officials were unwilling to speak on the record about Iranian issues.

17. While I would have liked to have conducted more research in Iran, I was not able to do so due to visa restrictions and other safety concerns. I was, however, able to visit Iran for two weeks as a tourist in 2016. At the time, Iran-US relations were improving following the implementation of the Iran nuclear deal. I was able to

discuss, informally, perceptions of Israel with many Iranians during my trip, but I was not able to travel freely, set up interviews, or investigate archival material while there.

18. To the extent Iranians feared an attack by Israel, they believed it would be aimed at its nuclear facilities or would consist of some other targeted action. This fed the Israeli narrative, which portrayed Israel as refraining from targeting civilians and seeking to minimize collateral damage while Iran exercised no such reservations.

1.   THE POWER OF NARRATIVE

1.   It was not until November 2021, eight months after Netanyahu left office and over three years removed from Donald Trump's decision to take the United States out of the 2015 JCPOA, that many former top Israeli officials began speaking out against the decision. In addition to Barak, Netanyahu's former Defense Minister Moshe Ya'alon, former Mossad Chief Yossi Cohen, and former IDF Head of Military Intelligence all spoke publicly about the failure of Netanyahu's Iran policy. Jacob Magid, 'He Led IDF Intel Gathering on Iran, Was Ignored and Fears Israel Is Now Paying Price', *The Times of Israel*, 30 November 2021, https://www.timesofisrael.com/he-led-idf-intel-gathering-on-iran-was-ignored-and-fears-israel-is-now-paying-price/; 'Ex-Mossad Chief Admits: Iran Enriching More Than Under Nuke Agreement', *Haaretz*, 21 November 2021, https://www.haaretz.com/israel-news/watch-one-on-one-with-the-man-who-led-israel-s-covert-iran-war-1.10403338; '"The Iran Deal Was a Mistake. Withdrawing From It Was Even Worse"', *Haaretz*, 21 November 2021, https://www.haaretz.com/israel-news/the-iran-deal-was-a-mistake-withdrawing-from-it-was-even-worse-1.10403339.

2.   Peter Brooks, *Reading for the Plot: Design and Intention in Narrative*, Revised edition (Cambridge, MA: Harvard University Press, 1992), i.

3.   In this context, 'listeners' is a generic concept that refers to those exposed to a candidate's appeal for support delivered in oral or written form. All who are willing to consider the messages are deemed listeners. As conceptualized by the securitization theorists, narrative content is created for and delivered by a 'speech act' making polity to which its messages are aimed the listeners.

4.   Hannah Arendt, 'Truth and Politics', *The New Yorker*, 18 February 1967, https://www.newyorker.com/magazine/1967/02/25/truth-and-politics.

5.   Psychologist Jonathan Haidt explains that when people are 'confronted with facts that contradict their values, the common response is for people to reject the facts and try to justify the beliefs.' Cited by Tom Nichols, *The Death of Expertise: The Campaign Against Established Knowledge and Why It Matters* (New York: Oxford University Press USA, 2017).

6.   Annette Gordon-Reed writes that origin stories 'inform our sense of self; telling us what kind of people we believe we are, what kind of nation we believe we live in … much of the concern with origin stories is about our current needs and desires (usually to feel good about ourselves), not actual history.' Annette Gordon-Reed, *On Juneteenth* (New York: Liveright, 2021), 58.

7. The term is adapted from W. Lance Bennett and Murray Edelman, 'Toward a New Political Narrative', *Journal of Communication* 35, no. 4 (December 1985): 156–71.

8. An enemy army amassed on a country's border is an obvious threat. A report that a country is harboring terrorists requires more information about the capability and intention of the terrorists.

9. The belief in another country's willingness to use nuclear weapons can be as or even more powerful than the possession of the weapons themselves. During the Kennedy administration, the United States learned that the so-called 'missile gap' between its own nuclear stockpile and that of the Soviet Union was, rather than the deficit it had believed itself to have, actually an enormous surplus. Paradoxically, this led some experts and military officials to conclude that their superiority in arms posed an even greater threat to American security, since the Soviets' relative weakness could make them more likely to seek a first-mover's advantage in the coming nuclear showdown between the two superpowers. Eric Schlosser, *Command and Control: Nuclear Weapons, the Damascus Accident, and the Illusion of Safety*, Reprint edition (Penguin Books, 2013), 269.

10. Under international law, the absence of an imminent threat limits a country's right to claim self-defense as a justification for preemptive use of military force to eliminate the threat. The issue has been subject to considerable debate in recent years with respect to targeted killings and the claim by the United States that there is a right of anticipatory self-defense. The decision of whether to take preemptive action is rarely debated in public, but the public may come to expect 'some' such action. Israel's bombing of the Iraqi nuclear reactor raised the question of whether the Israelis would take similar action against Iran. The decision of whether to act is strategic, but an elected government will want public support. Hence, the threat narrative matters.

11. Leslie E. Gerwin, 'The Challenge of Providing the Public With Actionable Information During a Pandemic', *The Journal of Law, Medicine & Ethics* 40, no. 3 (1 October 2012): 630–54.

12. Timothy Snyder, *On Tyranny: Twenty Lessons From the Twentieth Century* (New York: Tim Duggan Books, 2017).

13. Ibid.

14. Arendt, 'Truth and Politics'.

15. By amplifying inaccurate information, social media posts, internet sites, and cable news personalities can sufficiently change reality by creating bubbles in which untruths are sustained until it is too late to prevent their damage. Rebecca J. Rosen, 'Truth, Lies, and the Internet', *The Atlantic*, 29 December 2011, https://www.theatlantic.com/technology/archive/2011/12/truth-lies-and-the-internet/250569/.

16. The proliferation of claims makes it difficult for the uninformed to maneuver through conflicting claims to evaluate their accuracy. At the same time, it allows a user seeking confirmation bias to find at least one source that will confirm what she wants to believe as true.

17. This is not to suggest that politicians are not above distorting reality and inventing facts associated with their policies in their 'speechifying.' The narrative that

motivates or justifies the foreign policies pursued by one nation toward another does not inevitably result from events as they unfold in the real world. Thus, the public narrative justifying a policy may be separate from the calculations underlying an action decision. When committing to actions, however, the strategy is based upon calculations of power required for achieving the nation's objectives. Basing actions on inaccurate or delusional narratives may lead to disastrous consequences.

18. Marc Lynch, 'International Relations', in *The Middle East*, ed. Ellen Lust (Washington, DC: CQ Press, 2016), 373.

19. The qualitative military edge (QME) was enshrined into US law in 2008, when Congress enacted legislation in which 'Any certification relating to a proposed sale or export of defense articles or defense services under this section to any country in the Middle East other than Israel shall include a determination that the sale or export of the defense articles or defense services will not adversely affect Israel's qualitative military edge over military threats to Israel.' The law defines QME as 'the ability to counter and defeat any credible conventional military threat from any individual state or possible coalition of states or from non-state actors, while sustaining minimal damages and casualties, through the use of superior military means, possessed in sufficient quantity, including weapons, command, control, communication, intelligence, surveillance, and reconnaissance capabilities that in their technical characteristics are superior in capability to those of such other individual or possible coalition of states or non-state actors.'

20. Although, as Legro and Moravcsik have noted, some modern realists have been forced to incorporate these factors, but without attempting to reconcile the contradictions they create in traditional realist theory. Jeffrey W. Legro and Andrew Moravcsik, 'Is Anybody Still a Realist?', *International Security* 24, no. 2 (October 1999): 7, https://doi.org/10.1162/016228899560130.

21. Writing at the end of the Cold War, theorists Joseph Nye and Sean Lynn-Jones described security studies as a product of the 1980s and the natural conclusion of neorealism's hegemonic status within the field of international relations. As Weldes notes, the field received unprecedented levels of funding at academic institutions during this time, driving its development as a discipline and guiding philosophy both in and outside of academia. Joseph S. Nye and Sean M. Lynn-Jones, 'International Security Studies: A Report of a Conference on the State of the Field', *International Security* 12, no. 4 (1988): 5–27, https://doi.org/10.2307/2538992; Jutta Weldes, ed., *Cultures of Insecurity: States, Communities, and the Production of Danger*, Borderlines, v. 14 (Minneapolis, MN: University of Minnesota Press, 1999), 3.

22. Stephen M. Walt, 'The Renaissance of Security Studies', *International Studies Quarterly* 35, no. 2 (1 June 1991): 212; Barry Buzan, Ole Wæver, and Jaap de Wilde, *Security: A New Framework for Analysis* (Boulder, CO: Lynne Rienner Publishers, 1998), 3.

23. Buzan, Wæver, and Wilde, *Security*, 11.

24. Ibid., 26.

25. Leslie E. Gerwin, 'Planning for Pandemic: A New Model for Governing Public Health Emergencies', *American Journal of Law & Medicine* 37, no. 1 (1 January 2011): 154–56.

26. Ibid.

27. Klaus Fiedler and Herbert Bless, 'The Formation of Beliefs in the Interface of Affective and Cognitive Processes', in *The Influence of Emotions on Beliefs*, ed. N.H. Frijda, A.S.R. Manstead, and S. Bem (Cambridge, UK: Cambridge UP, 1 January 2000), 144–70.

28. Jonathan Mercer, 'Emotional Beliefs', *International Organization* 64, no. 1 (2010): 1.

29. Netanyahu's rhetoric was reminiscent of George W. Bush's declaration made nine days after the 11 September attacks in which he declared, 'Every nation, in every region, now has a decision to make. Either you are with us, or you are with the terrorists.' George W. Bush, 'Transcript of President Bush's Address to a Joint Session of Congress', 20 September 2001, http://edition.cnn.com/2001/US/09/20/gen.bush.transcript/.

30. While a few scholars of foreign policy formation acknowledge the role of ethics and morality in drafting foreign policy, it is only a partial role they play. Christopher Hill, for example, notes how the positivist roots of many foreign policymakers and analysts tend to obscure the normative issues that influence the process. Hill observes that the question of morality usually only enters into policymakers' considerations when citizens are asked to die in the name of a foreign policy. Christopher Hill, *The Changing Politics of Foreign Policy* (Houndmills, Basingstoke, Hampshire; New York: Palgrave Macmillan, 2003), 17.

31. Mercer, 'Emotional Beliefs', 2.

32. Booth and Wheeler referred to this inquiry as 'the security dilemma,' by which they meant that 'those weapons that states can use for their own self-protection, potentially or actually threaten harm to others.' This enlarged the debate over the line between 'legitimate self-defense' and 'predatory behavior.' Ken Booth and Nicholas Wheeler, *The Security Dilemma: Fear, Cooperation and Trust in World Politics* (Basingstoke, UK; New York: Palgrave Macmillan, 2007), 1.

33. The resonance of a threat narrative can lead both leaders and followers to invest in an overestimation of the danger as well as the implementation of domestic security measures and, perhaps, the pursuit of an international response. Daniel Bar-Tal, 'Why Does Fear Override Hope in Societies Engulfed by Intractable Conflict, as It Does in the Israeli Society?', *Political Psychology* 22, no. 3 (September 2001): 603.

34. A prominent example of this can be found in the right-wing information ecosystem that took root during the Trump administration, where rumors that began on social media or on fringe websites were amplified and repeated in escalating fashion through major media outlets. Yochai Benkler et al., 'Study: Breitbart-Led Right-Wing Media Ecosystem Altered Broader Media Agenda', *Columbia Journalism Review*, 3 March 2017, https://www.cjr.org/analysis/breitbart-media-trump-harvard-study.php.

35. To a populist, anyone qualified to advance knowledge of the accurate facts, who contradicts his message, qualifies as an elite. In denouncing elites, a populist

negotiates a delicate balance, since they require opinion influencers to validate their message. Still, the 'us' against 'them' posturing is a useful tool for unifying a base as well as discrediting outsiders.

36. Jan-Werner Müller, *What Is Populism?* (Philadelphia: University of Pennsylvania Press, 2016), 12. This definition borrows heavily from the writings of the German political theorist Carl Schmitt, who defined the 'friend-enemy' distinction as the guiding force of political relationships. Müller adopts this distinction, but he also modifies it with the introduction of additional elements. Like Schmitt, Müller understands that the 'will of the people' is not necessarily the byproduct of an organic grassroots process. A clever leader can construct the people's will through specific actions and by tailoring their messaging to meet certain criteria. As Schmitt writes (and Müller quotes): 'The unanimous opinion of one hundred million private persons is neither the will of the people nor public opinion. The will of the people can be expressed just as well and perhaps better through acclamation, through something taken for granted, an obvious unchallenged presence, than through the statistical apparatus.' Schmitt continues, '[P]arliament appears an artificial machinery, produced by liberal reasoning, while dictatorial and Caesaristic methods not only can produce the acclamation of the people but can also be a direct expression of democratic substance and power.' Carl Schmitt, *The Crisis of Parliamentary Democracy*, trans. Ellen Kennedy, New Edition (Cambridge, MA: MIT Press, 1988), 16–17.

37. The JCPOA signatories included the permanent five members of the UN Security council along with Germany, often abbreviated as the 'P5+1.'

38. These agreements were both formal and informal. Formally, the Abraham Accords established ties between Israel and the United Arab Emirates, Sudan, Morocco, Oman, and Bahrain. Informally, it is widely believed that Israel and Saudi Arabia have been cooperating closely on anti-Iran initiatives, including intelligence sharing. Omar Rahman, 'The Emergence of GCC-Israel Relations in a Changing Middle East', *Brookings* (blog), 28 July 2021, https://www.brookings.edu/research/the-emergence-of-gcc-israel-relations-in-a-changing-middle-east/.

39. The term is adapted from Bennett and Edelman, 'Toward a New Political Narrative'.

40. Ronald R. Krebs, *Narrative and the Making of US National Security* (Cambridge, UK: Cambridge University Press, 2015), 3.

41. Ole R. Holsti, 'Cognitive Dynamics and Images of the Enemy', *Journal of International Affairs* 21, no. 1 (1 January 1967): 39.

2.   HISTORY

1.   Mehrdad Amanat, *Jewish Identities in Iran: Resistance and Conversion to Islam and the Baha'i Faith*, Reprint edition (London; New York: I.B. Tauris, 2013), 18.

2.   Temple construction would not actually begin until after Cyrus's death under the reign of his successor Darius I, but Cyrus is still widely credited with having set the precedent for religious tolerance under the Achaemenid Empire. Ibid., 18.

3. This passage appears in the latter half of the book of Isaiah, known as 'Deutero-Isiah.' Scholars attribute it to an author who lived after Cyrus the Great. Deutero-Isaiah (45:1); Moshe Reiss, 'Cyrus as Messiah', *Jewish Bible Quarterly* 40, no. 3 (1 July 2012): 160.

4. See, for example, Diana Edelman, who argues that the historic chronology does not fit the account of Jews returning under the reign of Cyrus. Lester Grabbe questions the historicity of a decree that enabled the Jews to return to their homelands. He admits that they could do so but suggests that the return was a 'trickle' over an extensive period of time. By contrast, the first-century CE historian Flavius Josephus provides the text of a letter written by Cyrus to the Jews of his kingdom. Diana Vikander Edelman, *The Origins of the Second Temple: Persian Imperial Policy and the Rebuilding of Jerusalem*, 1st edition (Milton Park: Routledge, 2014); Lester L. Grabbe, *The History of the Jews and Judaism in the Second Temple Period, Volume 1: Yehud, the Persian Province of Judah* (NY: Bloomsbury Academic, 2004), 355; Flavius Josephus, *The Complete Works of Flavius Josephus*, trans. William Whiston, 1st Edition (Cheltenham, UK: Attic Books, 2008).

5. There is no historical evidence independent of the Bible that any of the events depicted in the Book of Esther took place, nor is there any evidence of a Persian plot to murder Jews en masse. Daniel Estrin, 'Iranians and Israelis Are in a Battle Over History — and the Holiday of Purim', *The World* (Public Radio International, 25 March 2016), https://www.pri.org/stories/2016-03-25/iranians-and-israelis-are-battle-over-history-and-holiday-purim.

6. Esther 8:10–11

7. Esther 8:17–9:1.

8. Esther 9:2.

9. According to the story, the Jews killed 500 men and the 10 sons of Haman in the fortress of Shushan, the capital, and in the king's provinces 'they disposed of their enemies, killing seventy-five thousand of their foes' (Esther 9:6, 16). They reportedly did not take any spoils.

10. R.K. Ramazani, 'Iran and the Arab-Israeli Conflict', *Middle East Journal* 32, no. 4 (1 October 1978): 413–14.

11. Sohrab Sobhani, *The Pragmatic Entente: Israeli-Iranian Relations, 1948–1988* (New York: Praeger Publishers, 1989), 35.

12. Benjamin Netanyahu, 'The Complete Transcript of Netanyahu's Address to Congress', http://www.washingtonpost.com/blogs/post-politics/wp/2015/03/03/full-text-netanyahus-address-to-congress/.

13. This incident is described in further detail in Chapter five.

14. Kim Zetter, *Countdown to Zero Day: Stuxnet and the Launch of the World's First Digital Weapon* (New York: Crown, 2014).

15. The researcher found the word 'Myrtus' in the coding, a possible translation of Esther's original Hebrew name, although some dispute this interpretation. Ibid.

16. ‘پوریم» تراژدی غمبار ایرانیان', «جشن, *Farda News*, 1 April 2008, http://www.fardanews.com/fa/news/48142; ‘انتقاد عجیب از مشایی و احمدی نژاد: با انداختن چفیه', بر گردن کوروش به بسیج توهین شد!', عصر ایران 13 September 2010, http://www.asriran.com/fa/news/135963.

234

17. Judah was the southern kingdom of Israel, containing the site of Jerusalem and the Second Temple, whose construction had been authorized by Cyrus. Bruce M. Metzger and Michael David Coogan, *The Oxford Companion to the Bible* (Oxford: Oxford University Press, 1993), 220.

18. Amanat, *Jewish Identities in Iran*, 19.

19. Ibid., 37.

20. Cecolin cites the 100,000 figure. The 1956 and 1966 official censuses place the number more precisely at approximately 60,000–65,000. Alessandra Cecolin, *Iranian Jews in Israel: Between Persian Cultural Identity and Israeli Nationalism*, New edition (London: I.B. Tauris, 2015), 1; Ferydoon Firoozi, 'Iranian Censuses 1956 and 1966: A Comparative Analysis', *Middle East Journal* 24, no. 2 (1970): 226.

21. Prof. Gawdat G. Bahgat, *Israel and the Persian Gulf: Retrospect and Prospect*, 1st edition (Gainesville, FL: University Press of Florida, 2005), 28.

22. According to Ghazvinian, Iranians had harbored a soft spot for Germany dating back to World War I, due to Germany's willingness to go to war against the much-hated British and Russians. The Nazis, looking to capitalize on this predilection, sought an alliance with Reza Shah in the lead-up to World War II. Iran, however, was generally more concerned with maintaining its tradition of neutrality—Iran had, at that point, not participated in a foreign war since the 1850s—and was not interested in trading one set of foreign domination for another. John Ghazvinian, *America and Iran: A History, 1720 to the Present* (New York: Knopf, 2021), 166.

23. Bahgat, *Israel and the Persian Gulf*, 28.

24. Uzi Rabi and Ronen A. Cohen, *Iran, Israel & the 'Shi'ite Crescent'* (Daniel Abraham Center for Strategic Dialogue: Netanya Academic College, 2008), 31.

25. 'The Covenant of the League of Nations', December 1924, Article 22, http://avalon.law.yale.edu/20th_century/leagcov.asp#art22.

26. Shimoni referred to the Arab view of the Israelis shortly after Israel's founding as a 'foreign enclave in their midst.' Yaacov Shimoni, 'Israel in the Pattern of Middle East Politics', *Middle East Journal* 4, no. 3 (1950): 286.

27. See, for example, the Hussein-McMahon Correspondence, in which the British, in exchange for Arab military cooperation against the Ottoman Empire in World War I, had promised Arab independence following the war. Subsequent British actions, such as the 1916 Sykes-Picot Agreement, which divided up the region under British and French spheres of influence, and the 1917 Balfour Declaration, which pledged British support for a Jewish homeland in Palestine, contradicted that promise.

28. Firoozi, 'Iranian Censuses 1956 and 1966', 226.

29. Ramazani, 'Iran and the Arab-Israeli Conflict', 414.

30. Ibid., 415.

31. By the mid-1940s, the AIOC had established near-total dominance over the Iranian oil industry. It was the country's largest employer and a source of significant wealth both to the Shah and to Great Britain. John P. Miglietta, *American Alliance Policy in the Middle East, 1945–1992: Iran, Israel, and Saudi Arabia* (Lanham, MD: Lexington Books, 2002), 39.

32. Stephen Kinzer, *All the Shah's Men: An American Coup and the Roots of Middle East Terror* (Hoboken, NJ: John Wiley & Sons, 2003), 61.

33. During his brief administration, Mossadegh closed the Iranian consulate in Israel, although this was allegedly due to budgetary rather than political reasons and ultimately had little effect on the course of Israeli-Iranian relations. Response to Mossadegh's removal in Israel was muted; it did not significantly influence Israel's subsequent pursuit of relations with Iran. Ramazani, 'Iran and the Arab-Israeli Conflict', 415.

34. American Presidents Truman and Eisenhower expressed their support for Israel in its early years, but both were reluctant to provide extensive political or military aid. While the 'special' nature of the relationship between the United States and Israel has become conventional wisdom, Cold War strategic concerns dominated the initial period of Israel's history.

35. Avi Shlaim, 'Israel between East and West, 1948–56', *International Journal of Middle Eastern Studies* 36, no. 4 (November 2004): 657–73.

36. Alexander J. Bennett, 'Arms Transfer as an Instrument of Soviet Policy in the Middle East', *Middle East Journal* 39, no. 4 (1985): 756.

37. Ibid.

38. Yossi Alpher, *Periphery: Israel's Search for Middle East Allies* (Lanham, MD: Rowman & Littlefield Publishers, 2015).

39. Many involved in the strategy are deceased. It is possible that documentation relating to military and intelligence operations remains classified. The absence of primary sources challenges efforts to accurately understand the strategy's place in the history of Iran-Israeli relations.

40. Shimon Peres, *David's Sling* (Weidenfeld & Nicolson, 1970), 153.

41. Reuven Shiloah, founder of the Mossad, and Iser Harel, head of the Shin Bet.

42. Alpher, *Periphery*; Sobhani, *The Pragmatic Entente*, 34.

43. There are differing versions of the Periphery participants. According to Alpher, proposed redefinitions primarily occurred post-1977 in response to changing regional circumstances and threat perceptions; they were often used to reverse-engineer justification for specific Israeli strategic action rather than as a motivating factor for it. Therefore, for the purposes of this study, I will adhere only to the narrow definition of Periphery as a state-level relationship between the four main partners of Israel, Iran, Turkey, and Ethiopia. Alpher, *Periphery*.

44. Sobhani, *The Pragmatic Entente*, 23.

45. In his biography of Mohammad Reza Shah, Abbas Milani describes an incident following the Shah's attempts to play the two Cold War powers off against one another in order to obtain military and financial support. Milani suggests that when the United States caught wind of this arrangement, the Shah, seeking to repair the relationship, sought out closer relations with Israel as a means of repairing the diplomatic damage done with the United States. Abbas Milani, *The Shah* (New York: St. Martin's Press, 2011), 230.

46. Ramazani, 'Iran and the Arab-Israeli Conflict', 413.

47. There is plenty of precedent for this in Israeli history. Most successful efforts at coordination with Muslim countries had to occur under strict secrecy, lest public pressure force parties to withdraw their efforts.

48. Sobhani, *The Pragmatic Entente*, 12.

49. Behrouz Souresrafil, *Khomeini and Israel* (I Researchers Incorporated, 1988), 19.

50. This quote is taken from an interview of Trita Parsi conducted by Yossi Alpher in Oslo on 9 March 2011, cited in Alpher, *Periphery*, Chap. 2.

51. Parsi via Alpher, *Periphery*, Chap. 2.

52. Milani, *The Shah*, 205.

53. Originally, this began as a joint training operation with both the Israeli Mossad and the CIA, but, according to Sobhani, SAVAK officers grew disappointed with the quality of training from the CIA and requested that the Shah allow them to increase training with the Mossad instead. Sobhani, *The Pragmatic Entente, 1948-1988*, 28.

54. Mansour Farhang, 'The Iran-Israel Connection', *Arab Studies Quarterly* 11, no. 1 (1 January 1989): 87.

55. Ironically, these exchanges also aided the Islamic Revolutionary government by facilitating their purging of the armed forces following the Shah's abdication. Many Iranian military officials who had participated in these programs were assumed to sympathize with Israeli causes, which provided the Islamic Republic with justification for these officers' dismissal, and possibly their imprisonment or execution.

56. Documents retrieved from the United States embassy following the 1979 revolution show that Israel and Iran cooperated on Project Flower, a joint missile development program. Steven R. Ward, *Immortal: A Military History of Iran and Its Armed Forces* (Washington, DC: Georgetown University Press, 2014).

57. Alpher, *Periphery*, Chap. 1.

58. Ali M. Ansari, 'The Myth of the White Revolution: Mohammad Reza Shah, 'Modernization' and the Consolidation of Power', *Middle Eastern Studies* 37, no. 3 (2001): 4.

59. James A. Bill, 'Modernization and Reform From Above: The Case of Iran', *The Journal of Politics* 32, no. 1 (1970): 31–2, https://doi.org/10.2307/2128863.

60. Neta Feniger and Rachel Kallus, 'Israeli Planning in the Shah's Iran: A Forgotten Episode', *Planning Perspectives* 30, no. 2 (April 2015): 231, 245, https://doi.org/10.1080/02665433.2014.933677.

61. Sobhani, *The Pragmatic Entente*, 115.

62. Howard A. Patten, *Israel and the Cold War: Diplomacy, Strategy and the Policy of the Periphery at the United Nations* (New York, London: I.B. Tauris, 2013), 52.

63. Sobhani, *The Pragmatic Entente*, 42.

64. Following the 1979 Islamic Revolution, the street on which the mission was located was renamed Palestine Street and the keys to the building handed over in a public ceremony to the PLO. Representatives of the Iranian Jewish community were allegedly present at the ceremony. Robin B. Wright, *The Iran Primer: Power, Politics, and U.S. Policy* (Washington, DC: US Institute of Peace Press, 2010), 171; Lior B. Sternfeld, *Between Iran and Zion: Jewish Histories of Twentieth-Century Iran* (Stanford, CA: Stanford University Press, 2019), 111.

65. Neta Feniger and Rachel Kallus, 'Expertise in the Name of Diplomacy: The Israeli Plan for Rebuilding the Qazvin Region, Iran', *International Journal of Islamic Architecture* 5, no. 1 (1 March 2016): 103–34.

66. Alpher, *Periphery*, Chap. 10.

67. The origins of the 1967 Arab-Israeli War remain debatable, but it is uncontested that Nasser publicly promised to eliminate Israel over the decade preceding the war. He also alluded to the need for war to prevent Israel's nuclear weapons program. Howard M. Sachar, *A History of Israel: From the Rise of Zionism to Our Time* (New York: Knopf Doubleday Publishing Group, 2013), 615; Isabella Ginor and Gideon Remez, 'The Spymaster, the Communist, and Foxbats Over Dimona: The USSR's Motive for Instigating the Six-Day War', *Israel Studies* 11, no. 2 (2006): 88–130.

68. It is difficult to overstate the extent to which Cold War concerns motivated American officials. President Richard Nixon, uncertain of whether to authorize a massive military resupply to the Israelis in the early stages of the conflict, was ultimately convinced of the need to do so under the premise that a US-armed force in Israel could not be seen to lose to a Soviet-supplied Arab force. Zach Levey, 'Anatomy of an Airlift: United States Military Assistance to Israel During the 1973 War', *Cold War History* 8, no. 4 (2008): 481.

69. The Kennedy administration had restricted the Shah's weapons purchases under the 'Twitchell Doctrine,' which limited Iran's weapons purchases based on a survey of its needs and capabilities. These restrictions were loosened under Kennedy's successor, Lyndon Johnson, before being removed altogether during the Nixon administration. Gholam Reza Afkhami, *The Life and Times of the Shah* (Oakland, CA: University of California Press, 2009), 295–305.

70. To Israel's consternation, the Shah refused to risk exposing the relationship. Thus, he refused to allow Iran to be a transfer point in ferrying Jewish volunteers from Australia to join the Israeli military. However, he permitted the Soviets to use Iranian territory for resupply. Ramazani, 'Iran and the Arab-Israeli Conflict', 418–19.

71. Trita Parsi, *Treacherous Alliance: The Secret Dealings of Israel, Iran, and the United States* (New Haven, CT: Yale University Press, 2007), 48.

72. Ramazani, 'Iran and the Arab-Israeli Conflict', 419.

73. Quote cited but source not named in Parsi, *Treacherous Alliance*, 48.

74. Ibid., 54.

75. As noted later in this chapter, Saddam subsequently maintained the agreement terms were unfair and invoked it as justification for his 1980 invasion of Iran.

76. Sobhani, *The Pragmatic Entente*, 108.

77. Parsi, *Treacherous Alliance*, 57.

78. This is a disputed point. The Shah allegedly asserted in a 1974 interview with the French magazine *Les Informations* that Iran would develop nuclear weapons 'without a doubt … sooner than one would think,' if conditions in the Middle East made it necessary. The quote was republished in an article in the *Christian Science Monitor*, which ran with a disclaimer issued by the Iranian Embassy in Paris saying that this was 'information invented out of whole cloth without any foundation' and that the Shah had 'never made any statement that could be interpreted in this way.' Interestingly, the Shah was in France to visit the French National Nuclear Research Center at Sarclay, which had also been involved in

helping establish Israel's secret nuclear program in Dimona in 1955. Other sources suggest that the Shah had nuclear ambitions. A 2003 article in *Dawn* alleged that Iran discussed plans with Israel to adapt surface-to-surface missiles with nuclear warheads. In a 2003 interview in *Le Figaro*, Akbar Etemad, the head of Iran's Atomic Energy Organization under the Shah, claimed that the Shah had tasked him with creating a special team to track the latest nuclear research so that Iran would be ready to build a bomb when needed. As a signatory to the Treaty on the Nonproliferation of Nuclear Weapons, Iran had pledged not to use its nuclear capacity for military purposes, although by the mid-1970s it had not concluded a safeguards agreement with the IAEA to verify this. John K. Cooley, 'More Fingers on Nuclear Trigger?', *Christian Science Monitor*, 25 June 1974; Zetter, *Countdown to Zero Day*.

79.   The article is cited in several sources, including Parsi, Alpher, and a scholarly article on India-Iran relations by Mehrunnisa Ali. Alpher cites *Kayhan International*, 16 September 1975, as the source of this information. Ali's citation lists the publication from a newspaper or periodical called *The Sun* (most likely the Pakistani paper). Parsi, *Treacherous Alliance*; Alpher, *Periphery*; Mehrunnisa Ali, 'The Changing Pattern of India-Iran Relations', *Pakistan Horizon* 28, no. 4 (1975): 53–66; 'Iran's Strategic Intentions and Capabilities' (Institute for National Strategic Studies—National Defense University: DIANE Publishing, April 1994).

80.   A declassified 1975 CIA report cites an Iranian alliance with the more 'moderate' Arab regimes as a possible outcome of Iraq continuing its anti-Iranian foreign policy following their agreement. 'The Implications of the Iran-Iraq Agreement' (Central Intelligence Agency, 1 May 1975), https://www.cia.gov/library/ readingroom/docs/CIA-RDP79R01142A000500050002-7.pdf.

81.   Among his spiritual mentors was Ayatollah Kashani, mentioned earlier, who in 1948 had been among the leading clerical figures opposing the creation of Israel.

82.   Souresrafil, *Khomeini and Israel*, 17.

83.   Ruhollah Khomeini, '1342, 3 خرداد 13 سخنرانی حضرت امام(ره) در عصر عاشورای', June 1963, http://www.imam-khomeini.ir/fa/c75_20702/گاهنامه/عطف_نقطه 1342._خرداد_13_سخنرانی_حضرت_امام_ره_در_عصر_عاشورای/.

84.   Shiite leaders cited the location of Baha'i centers and the founder's burial site in Israel as evidence of collusion between the two religions, which merited Muslim hatred. In 1962, prominent Tehran cleric Falsafi claimed that the basis of clerical opposition to the Shah was due to 'the real threat' that Jews intended to 'make another Palestine in Iran and suffocate all the Moslems in this country and bring all the dirty elements of Bahaiism to power.' Souresrafil, *Khomeini and Israel*, 23–4.

85.   Ibid., 24.

86.   Israeli participation in training the SAVAK helped add legitimacy to the conspiracy theory pushed by Khomeini. Ronen A. Cohen, 'Iran, Israel, and Zionism Since the Islamic Revolution—From Rational Relations to Threat and Disaster' (Netanya, Israel: Netanya Academic College, 2008), http://www.academia.edu/659583/ Iran_Israel_and_Zionism_since_the_Islamic_Revolution_-_From_Rational_ Relations_to_Threat_and_Disaster.

87. Cohen, 39–40.

88. 'נציגות ישראל בטהרן', 22 November 1962, Israel State Archives.

89. Netaniel Lorch, 'תזכיר מנתנאל לורך, המנהל בפועל של מחלקת מזרח תיכון במשרד החוץ בירושלים', 9 June 1963, Israel State Archives.

90. The Shah had been diagnosed with a terminal form of cancer. This had not been widely publicized. It is unlikely that the Israelis were aware of the severity of his medical condition.

91. Uri Lubrani, 'מברק משגריר ישראל בטהראן, אורי לוברני אל שר החוץ, משה דיין', 28 September 1978, Israel State Archives.

92. Ezrael Karni, 'מברק מהיועץ עזריאל קרני בטהראן אל המחלקה למזרח התיכון ואגן הים התיכון המזרחי במשרד החוץ', 14 December 1978, Israel State Archives.

93. Arafat was the first major foreign dignitary to visit Iran in the aftermath of the revolution. Khomeini said in a speech, 'Iran's revolution would be incomplete until the Palestinians won theirs.' Farhad Kazemi, 'Iran, Israel and the Arab Israeli Balance', in *Iran Since the Revolution*, ed. Barry Rosen, 1st ed. (New York: Columbia University Press, 1985), 90.

94. It would take at least a decade for most Israeli leaders to decide—and state publicly—that Iran was an irredeemable foe.

95. This opinion was expressed to the author several times during fieldwork conversations with experts and former officials in Israel; in print, it is expressed most clearly in the introduction to Katz and Hendel's 2012 analysis of the Iranian-Israeli conflict. Yaakov Katz and Yoaz Hendel, *Israel vs. Iran: The Shadow War*, First edition (Washington, DC: Potomac Books Inc., 2012), 9.

96. The debates are described in several chapters of Arshin Adib-Moghaddam, *A Critical Introduction to Khomeini* (Cambridge; New York: Cambridge University Press, 2014).

97. Sadegh Zibakalam, 'To Rule, or Not to Rule? An Alternative Look at the Political Life of Ayatollah Khomeini Between 1960 and 1980', in *A Critical Introduction to Khomeini*, ed. Arshin Adib-Moghaddam (Cambridge; New York: Cambridge University Press, 2014).

98. As noted at the beginning of this chapter, precise statistics on the number of Jews in Iran, both pre- and postrevolution, are difficult to find. Most estimates put the prerevolution number close to 100,000, while the postrevolution number is frequently listed as somewhere between 10,000–25,000, although occasionally with larger or smaller estimates.

99. *Israel's Foreign Relations: 1979–1980* (Ministry of Foreign Affairs, 1976), 19, available online at http://mfa.gov.il/MFA/ForeignPolicy/MFADocuments/Yearbook4/Pages/INTRODUCTION.aspx.

100. *Israel's Foreign Relations*, 19.

101. Roya Hakakian, 'How Iran Kept Its Jews', *Tablet*, 30 December 2014, http://www.tabletmag.com/jewish-news-and-politics/187519/how-iran-kept-its-jews.

102. It is ironic that Begin was the first Israeli prime minister to win the Nobel Peace Prize for reaching a comprehensive peace agreement with Egypt's Anwar Sadat at Camp David, given that he was a reluctant and often intransigent negotiator.

He received the prize together with Sadat and US President Jimmy Carter. Lawrence Wright, *Thirteen Days in September: The Dramatic Story of the Struggle for Peace* (New York: Vintage, 2015).

103. 'Statement in the Knesset by Prime Minister Begin on His Talks with President Sadat', 16 January 1980, Israel Ministry of Foreign Affairs Documents.

104. This statement came at an especially tense moment for the Carter administration: the Iranians were holding American hostages having stormed the American Embassy in Tehran in November 1979. 'Exchange of Toasts by President Carter and Prime Minister Begin at the White House', 15 April 1980, Israel Ministry of Foreign Affairs Documents.

105. 'Exchange of Toasts by President Carter and Prime Minister Begin at the White House'.

106. 'Interview with Prime Minister Begin on ABC Television', 20 April 1980, Israel Ministry of Foreign Affairs Documents.

107. 'Interview with Defense Minister Sharon in the Wall Street Journal', 28 May 1982, Israel Ministry of Foreign Affairs Documents.

108. 'Statement in Knesset by Defense Minister Moshe Arens', 14 November 1984, Volume 8, Israel Ministry of Foreign Affairs Documents.

109. 'Address by Foreign Minister Shamir to the World Jewish Congress', 21 January 1981, Israel Ministry of Foreign Affairs Documents.

110. Ra'ad al-Hamdani, one of Saddam's generals during the war, cites two political motives for war. Iraq sought to redraw the Iran-Iraq border more favorably than the one drawn by the 1975 Algiers Accord. Second, Saddam wanted a decisive victory over the Iranians to solidify his claim to leadership of the Pan-Arab movement, a position unoccupied since Nasser's death and Sadat's peace treaty with the Israelis. Cited in Kevin M. Woods et al., *Saddam's War: An Iraqi Military Perspective of the Iran-Iraq War* (Washington, DC: Government Printing Office, 2009), 5.

111. Israel has a multi-party system in which political alliances are continually shifting, frequently based upon disagreements over foreign policy strategies.

112. 'Interview with Defense Minister Rabin in Yediot Achronot', 26 September 1986, Israel Ministry of Foreign Affairs Documents.

113. 'Interview with Defense Minister Sharon in the Wall Street Journal'.

114. Rabi and Cohen, *Iran, Israel & the 'Shi'ite Crescent'*, 49.

115. Alpher, *Periphery*, Introduction.

116. Haggay Ram, *Iranophobia: The Logic of an Israeli Obsession* (Stanford, CA: Stanford University Press, 2009).

117. This was not totally fanciful; Iran had tried constitutional government at various points in its past, first following the Constitutional Revolution at the beginning of the twentieth century and later, most famously, when Mohammad Mosaddegh became prime minister for a brief period before being forced out by a United States-orchestrated coup d'état.

118. By contrast, Israel's liberal elite had cause for moral panic when it realized that Iran's clerics were rejecting secularism and modernism. They feared that the rabbinical establishment might bring about a similar fate in Israel. Ram, *Iranophobia*.

119. Alpher, *Periphery*, Chap. 10.

120. Parsi, *Treacherous Alliance*, 91.

121. 'Israeli Defence Minister Says Iran Is "Israel's Best Friend"' (BBC, 30 October 1987).

122. Ronen Bergman, *The Secret War With Iran: The 30-Year Clandestine Struggle Against the World's Most Dangerous Terrorist Power*, 1st edition (New York: Free Press, 2008).

123. Walter Pincus, 'Reagan Calls Israel Prime Mover in Iran-Contra', *Washington Post*, 5 November 1990, https://www.washingtonpost.com/archive/politics/1990/11/05/reagan-calls-israel-prime-mover-in-iran-contra/71b08cdd-eaa8-43aa-a744-e5949f93764e/.

124. Lee H. Hamilton, *Report of the Congressional Committees Investigating the Iran-Contra Affair, with Supplemental, Minority, and Additional Views*, 1st Edition (Washington, DC: Government Printing Office, 1987), 6.

125. Part of the problem stemmed from an absence of trust between the two sides. The United States and Israel, knowing that Iran was desperate for military supplies in its war against Saddam, both overcharged and under-delivered. When the CIA subsequently attempted to present Iran with a forged list to justify the prices, the Iranians saw through the attempt. Ibid., 248.

126. Ibid., 279.

127. Samuel Segev, *The Iranian Triangle: The Untold Story of Israel's Role in the Iran-Contra Affair*, 29th edition (New York: Macmillan USA, 1988), 249.

128. Early in the conflict, the Israeli Air Force carried out a bombing raid against the Osirak Reactor in Iraq as part of Operation OPERA. The surprise attack successfully destroyed the reactor and was credited with halting the Iraqi nuclear development program.

129. For both Israel and Iran, the war demonstrated the Iraqi dictator's affinity for and willingness to use weapons of mass destruction. Israel's bombing of the Osirak nuclear reactor had not prevented Saddam from launching devastating chemical weapons attacks. While the protracted war with Iran reduced the threat of an Iraqi conventional war against Israel, when the war ended Iraq was free to invest in further developing chemical and biological weapons as well as to rebuild its nuclear facilities and conventional military.

130. Israeli forces remained in Lebanon until May 2000. Nicholas Blanford, *Warriors of God: Inside Hezbollah's Thirty-Year Struggle Against Israel*, 1st Edition (New York: Random House, 2011).

131. According to Blanford, the Israelis were initially welcomed as liberators by the predominantly Shiite population in southern Lebanon, but quickly lost favor due to their alliance with brutal Christian militias and lack of respect for Shiite culture and customs. In October 1983, Israeli forces intruded during an Ashura ceremony commemorating the death of Husayn ibn Ali, the Prophet Mohammad's grandson. Blanford cites this event as having 'let the Shia genie out of the bottle.' Blanford, *Warriors of God*.

3.   POLITICS

1.   Iranians accused Israelis of engaging in 'warlike' acts such as deploying a cyber-attack and assassinating Iranian nuclear scientists. Israel did not claim credit for these acts. See Appendix II.

2.   Israel is concerned about Iran extending its sphere of influence to other countries in the region, and it maintains that Iran has hegemonic ambitions that threaten Israel. Unlike the superpowers, the two nations are not openly engaged in a zero-sum competition for power, influence, or territory.

3.   Commentators on both sides have made this argument at various times with some even stressing that Israel and Iran share important interests. Bahgat examined the shared interests in his book on Israeli-Persian Gulf relations. Israeli Prof. Efraim Inbar, head of Israel's BESA Center, pointed out in 1998 that all Iran's strategic interests lie in its immediate vicinity and do not extend to Israel. Bahgat, *Israel and the Persian Gulf*; Efraim Inbar, 'The Iranian Threat Reconsidered', *Jerusalem Post*, 10 August 1998.

4.   The concept of the elimination of the 'Zionist regime' in the region typically lacks explanation. A treatise from Supreme Leader Ayatollah Ali Khamenei on Palestine suggests a possible referendum in which the original pre-1948 inhabitants of the region would vote on whether they were in favor of the existence of a Jewish State, which would inevitably result in the negative. At the same time, Iranian leaders have consistently said that they would honor any agreement the Palestinians reached with the Israelis, and at times have even been willing to consider recognizing Israel. Ali Khamenei, *Palestine* (London: Opars Books, 2012).

5.   In formal and informal discussions over the course of this project, answers varied. Many cited the 1979 Revolution, while others listed the resurgence of the nuclear program in the 1990s. Others declined to give dates, noting instead that Iran's 'ideology' made conflict with Israel inevitable.

6.   See discussion of Iran-Iraq War in Chapter 2, Part IV, Sections C–D.

7.   As former chess champion and political activist Garry Kasparov notes, 'There is an irresistible tendency to look only for big moments in history. While such moments do exist, long-term trends and patterns usually matter more than any one decision or event.' Garry Kasparov, *Winter Is Coming: Why Vladimir Putin and the Enemies of the Free World Must Be Stopped* (New York: PublicAffairs, 2015).

8.   Interview with Soli Shahvar, interview by Jonathan Leslie, Haifa, Israel, 4 November 2015.

9.   This was the explanation given by former Labor Knesset Member Ephraim Sneh, whose role in defining the Iranian threat is discussed in detail *infra*. Interview with Ephraim Sneh, interview by Jonathan Leslie, Tel Aviv, Israel, 26 November 2015.

10.   Several experts expressed this view, among them Emily Landau, a proliferation analyst at the Institute for National Security Studies (INSS) and Raz Zimmt, an Iran analyst at Tel Aviv University. Interview with Emily Landau, interview by Jonathan Leslie, Tel Aviv, Israel, 7 January 2016; Interview with Raz Zimmt, interview by Jonathan Leslie, Tel Aviv, Israel, 24 November 2015.

11. This is essentially Ronen Bergman's claim in his widely read *The Secret War With Iran* (the lessons from this book will be discussed in further detail later), but was also expressed by other authors of more recent books on the subject. Bergman, *The Secret War With Iran*; Interview with Yaakov Katz, interview by Jonathan Leslie, Jerusalem, Israel, 27 October 2015.

12. Parsi, *Treacherous Alliance*.

13. Ram, *Iranophobia*.

14. Sobhani, *The Pragmatic Entente*, 149.

15. This occupation served two purposes: to root out Palestinian resistance that might threaten Israel and to provide a buffer zone between Israel and the continuing civil war in northern Lebanon.

16. Gal Luft, 'Israel's Security Zone in Lebanon—a Tragedy?', *Middle East Quarterly*, 1 September 2000, http://www.meforum.org/70/israels-security-zone-in-lebanon-a-tragedy.

17. Blanford, *Warriors of God*.

18. The elections followed the outbreak of the Palestinian Intifada in 1987 and the reduction of Israeli occupation of South Lebanon. It pitted the hawkish Likud party, led by Shamir, against the more dovish Alignment, led by Shimon Peres. The big change was the emergence of the religious parties as a political force. Peres chose to continue the unity government in the wake of the election but the prime minister position remained in Likud's hands. Robert O. Freedman, 'Religion, Politics, and the Israeli Elections of 1988', *Middle East Journal* 43, no. 3 (1989): 406–22.

19. The Supreme Leader of Iran is selected by the Assembly of Experts (مجلس خبرگان). Its members are directly elected once every eight years, with all candidates first vetted by the Guardian Council. The first term of the Assembly of Experts, which served 1982–91, is the only group that has conducted a selection process for Supreme Leader.

20. Like the Assembly of Experts, all presidential candidates are first vetted by the Guardian Council. In 1989, it allowed only two candidates on the ballot, Ali Akbar Hashemi Rafsanjani and Abbas Sheibani. This flawed scheme produced a predictable result—Rafsanjani won the presidency with 96.1% of the vote.

21. More recent Israeli reports cite Khomeini's statement on Al Quds Day 2000 as the earliest indication of his anti-Semitic/anti-Zionist rhetoric. Joshua Teitelbaum, 'What Iranian Leaders Really Say About Doing Away With Israel: A Refutation of the Campaign to Excuse Ahmadinejad's Incitement to Genocide' (Jerusalem: Jerusalem Center for Public Affairs, 2008), 15, https://www.scribd.com/document/7632012/What-Iranian-Leaders-Really-Say-About-Doing-Away-With-Israel.

22. High-ranking Israeli officials previously expressed fear of a 'terror wave' by Iranian-backed groups. In a 1987 interview, Defense Minister Rabin claimed that a 'wave of terror' was being carried out by the 'Iranian-backed Hizbollah group.' David Horovitz, 'Middle East Terror Wave Predicted', *Jerusalem Post*, 17 July 1989; 'Interview with Defense Minister Rabin on Israel Television and on Israel Radio', 6 January 1987, Israel Ministry of Foreign Affairs Documents.

23. Editorial Board, 'U.S., Iran and the Hostages', *Jerusalem Post*, 8 May 1990.

24. *Tehran Times*, 21 December 1989. Via Wolf Blitzer, 'Gov't and Intelligence Sources Leaked Oil Story', *Jerusalem Post*, 22 December 1989.

25. David Makovsky, 'Rabin: Arms Sales Hurt by Global Peace', *Jerusalem Post*, 27 December 1989.

26. Sneh reports in his book that this event took place on 26 January 1993, but Knesset transcripts and news reports verify that it occurred six days earlier. Also on 20 January Bill Clinton's began his first term as US President. Ephraim Sneh, *Navigating Perilous Waters: An Israeli Strategy for Peace and Security* (Milton Park: Routledge, 2004).

27. Dr. Sneh was a Labor Party ally of Prime Minister Rabin. He had been a medical doctor and served in the IDF for over twenty years, retiring as a Brigadier General before entering politics.

28. '54th Meeting of the 13th Knesset', 20 January 1993, Knesset Transcripts.

29. Ibid.

30. Sobhani, *The Pragmatic Entente*; Victor Ostrovsky, *By Way of Deception: The Making of a Mossad Officer* (Scottsdale, AZ: Wilshire Press Inc., 2002); Segev, *The Iranian Triangle*; Trita Parsi, 'Israel-Iranian Relations Assessed: Strategic Competition from the Power Cycle Perspective', *Iranian Studies* 38, no. 2 (1 June 2005): 247–69.

31. Not only did Rabin confirm the sale of oil to Iran, he went further by suggesting that the only thing preventing further sales to the Iranians, including weaponry, was Iran's ideological opposition to using Israeli materials unless absolutely necessary. Makovsky, 'Rabin: Arms Sales Hurt by Global Peace'.

32. Notably, there was not much press follow-up to this Knesset event. The *Jerusalem Post* carried a short item on 21 January recapping the previous day's events, offering no further analysis or commentary on the assessments made by either Sneh or Rabin. Dan Izenberg, 'Rabin: Iran Potentially Greater Threat Than Iraq', *Jerusalem Post*, 21 January 1993.

33. See Chapter 2 for more on 'Periphery nostalgia.' Shortly after Labor's 1992 election victory, Alpher—then a top Mossad official—called Iran Israel's 'number one threat,' claiming that it had become evident that Iran, like Iraq, was capable of destroying Israel. Therefore, there was no point in playing them off against one another. Clyde Haberman, 'THE WORLD; Israel Focuses on the Threat Beyond the Arabs—in Iran', *New York Times*, 8 November 1992, sec. Week in Review, http://www.nytimes.com/1992/11/08/weekinreview/the-world-israel-focuses-on-the-threat-beyond-the-arabs-in-iran.html.

34. Parsi, 'Israel-Iranian Relations Assessed', 256.

35. Batsheva Tsur, 'PM: Without Peace, War With Syria Likely', *Jerusalem Post*, 23 June 1994. Sneh later confirmed that this was his view in a 2004 interview reflecting on this period. He said, 'In this region, we have to consider every weapon as if it is directed toward Israel.' Sneh interview with Trita Parsi. 31 October 2004. Cited in Parsi, 'Israel-Iranian Relations Assessed'.

36. Sneh, *Navigating Perilous Waters*, 55.

37. Sneh had been instrumental in laying the groundwork for the Israeli Security

245

Zone in South Lebanon and was, according to Avraham Sela, one of the Israeli commanders who had been 'personally committed to the South Lebanese Army.' Avraham Sela, 'Civil Society, the Military, and National Security: The Case of Israel's Security Zone in South Lebanon', *Israel Studies* 12, no. 1 (19 February 2007): 53–78; Oren Barak and Gabriel Sheffer, 'Israel's "Security Network" and Its Impact: An Exploration of a New Approach', *International Journal of Middle East Studies* 38, no. 2 (May 2006): 235–61.

38. Interview with Ephraim Sneh.

39. Sneh was particularly pleased that Rabin had chosen to attend the Knesset plenary himself rather than send a cabinet minister or lower-level official. The Prime Minister's presence added gravitas to an issue that had previously been treated more as an afterthought than a priority. According to Sneh, Rabin had insisted that he provide the response to Sneh's statement on Iran. Interview with Ephraim Sneh.

40. Asher Wallfish, '"Iran Greater Threat Than Iraq"', *Jerusalem Post*, 29 June 1993.

41. Ibid.

42. Ibid.

43. Alon Pinkas and David Makovsky, 'Rabin: Killing Civilians Won't Kill the Negotiations', *Jerusalem Post*, 13 April 1994.

44. A statement by a foreign ministry official at the time reflects the degree to which the Sneh-Rabin view of Iran had taken root within the foreign policy machinery of the government: 'I think that following several years of dwelling on the issue, the facts finally had their say. Iran is supporting fundamentalist movements all over the Arab world, constantly subverting moderate regimes with which we have or aspire to have a dialogue.' Alon Pinkas, 'A Watchful Eye Widens on a Menacing Neighbor', *Jerusalem Post*, 2 December 1994.

45. Itim, 'We Don't Have to Worry About Nuclear Attack, Says Bin-Nun', *Jerusalem Post*, 18 May 1993.

46. Scant information exists concerning the origins or operations of this department. It first appeared in an investigative piece by the Israeli journalist Aluf Benn in *Haaretz* on 28 September 1994, emerging during interviews with contacts within the Israeli foreign ministry. It is unclear whether it was ever announced publicly or when it disappeared. It does not reappear in subsequent publicly available foreign ministry documents or statements. Aluf Benn, 'בלימה כפולה ועסקים מהצד', *Haaretz*, 28 September 1994.

47. Peres assigned one of his deputies, Yo'av Biran, to run the new operation.

48. Benn, 'בלימה כפולה ועסקים מהצד'.

49. Iran's few mentions in Israeli strategic assessments before 1992 relate to its conflicts with Iraq. Prior to Rabin taking office, Iran is not discussed as an independent threat.

50. Barak took over from Lieutenant General Dan Shomron. Upon his departure from the post, Shomron stated that he viewed the growing threat from Iran as possibly one of the major security challenges that Israel would have to face in the years to come. Jerusalem Post Staff, 'Barak at the Helm', *Jerusalem Post*, 1 April 1991.

51. Pinkas, 'A Watchful Eye Widens on a Menacing Neighbor'.

52. Kam is currently a Senior Research Fellow at the Institute for National Security Studies. He was interviewed by the author on 2 November 2015.

53. The 1993–4 report represented a change from Kam's initial analysis. His report of a year earlier echoed Sneh and Rabin's claims that Iran was a 'growing threat to Israel.' He pointed to its military buildup, its attempts to influence Islamic movements abroad, and its efforts to obstruct the Arab-Israeli peace process. To Kam, investment of strained economic resources in military applications implied that Iran's leaders sought regional hegemony by sacrificing domestic development. He noted, however, that Iran's leaders emphasized neither their nuclear prowess nor ambitions. One year later, Kam noted that Iran's efforts to build its economy and cultivate international acceptance had become more compelling than its nuclear ambitions. Shlomo Gazit, *The Middle East Military Balance 1992–1993*, First edition (Jerusalem: Routledge, 1994), 33.

54. 'The Middle East Military Balance 1993–1994' (Tel Aviv University: Jaffee Center for Strategic Studies, 1994).

55. Gazit, *The Middle East Military Balance 1992–1993*.

56. At the time, Gold was serving as director of the US Foreign and Defense Policy Project at the Jaffee Center at Tel Aviv University.

57. Dore Gold, 'Putting the Iranian Threat in Perspective', *Jerusalem Post*, 19 February 1993.

58. Ibid.

59. Herb Keinon, 'Barak: Released Prisoners May Return to Terrorism', *Jerusalem Post*, 31 August 1994.

60. Interview with Aluf Benn, Email, 6 July 2017.

61. Steve Rodan, 'Dynamic Duo—Part I', *Jerusalem Post*, 14 October 1994.

62. In spring and summer 1995, Rabin was engaged in an intense political battle for the survival of the Oslo Peace Accords, which Israeli and Palestinian hardliners sought to discredit and dismantle.

63. According to IMF data, US trade with Iran had been growing steadily since the end of the Iran-Iraq War, leading some to suggest a possible improvement in relations between the two nations; but trade dwindled quickly to near zero following the embargo. IMF Direction of Trade Statistics available at IMF Database: 'IMF Data', IMF, n.d., http://www.imf.org/en/Data; Bill Clinton, 'Executive Order 12959: Prohibiting Certain Transactions with Respect to Iran' (1995), https://www.treasury.gov/resource-center/sanctions/Documents/12959.pdf.

64. Benjamin Gilman, 'Iran and Libya Sanctions Act of 1996', HR3107 § (1996), https://www.congress.gov/bill/104th-congress/house-bill/3107.

65. Parsi, *Treacherous Alliance*.

66. Iranians generally perceive Israel as controlling American foreign policy toward Iran, as the two were frequently in lockstep beginning in the 1990s through recent years.

67. Predicting that neighboring states would achieve nuclear capabilities was an Israeli habit. In August 1990, Science and Technology Minister Yuval Ne'eman predicted that Iraq would have a nuclear bomb within three years. In April 1991,

the *Jerusalem Post* editorialized that 'only a few years' separated Algeria from a nuclear weapon. In May 1992, Aharon Levran, a defense analyst and former senior intelligence officer, wrote that 'Iran might present the severest nuclear danger in the coming years.' In December 1992, Rabin said that Israel could face a ground-to-ground missile threat equipped with nonconventional warheads within two to seven years. Matthew Seriphs, 'Ne'eman: "Saddam Could Build N-Bombs in 3 Years"', *Jerusalem Post*, 28 August 1990; Editorial Board, 'The Real Middle East Problem', *Jerusalem Post*, 29 April 1991; Aharon Levran, 'How to Tame the Nuclear Beast', *Jerusalem Post*, 1 May 1992; Douglas Davis, 'Major: Rabin Brings New Source of Hope', *Jerusalem Post*, 10 December 1992.

68. Chris Hedges, 'Iran May Be Able to Build an Atomic Bomb in 5 Years, U.S. and Israeli Officials Fear', *New York Times*, 5 January 1995, http://www.nytimes.com/1995/01/05/world/iran-may-be-able-build-atomic-bomb-5-years-us-israeli-officials-fear.html.

69. See, for example, *Jerusalem Post* editorials 'The Iranian Threat' and 'Containing Iran' published 24 March and 2 May 1995, respectively. In these two editorials, the authors interpreted Iran's recent actions as a prelude to war with Israel. The editorial board wrote that once Iran acquires its bomb, 'it may be tempted to precipitate an all-out war' against Israel. It also dismissed as 'disingenuous' Iran's claim that it was pursuing 'peaceful nuclear energy.' Editorial Board, 'The Iranian Threat', *Jerusalem Post*, 24 March 1995; Editorial Board, 'Containing Iran', *Jerusalem Post*, 2 May 1995.

70. Daniel Kurtzer, 'The Iran Project' (Panel Presentation, Princeton University, 14 November 2013).

71. Iran had learned from Iraq's mistakes and had spread the various parts of its nuclear program around the country at different locations, locating some in deep underground bunkers to protect against the possibility of air attack from Israel or the United States. Advocates for attack saw this as proof that Iran's program had a secret weapons component.

72. Dan Ephron, *Killing a King: The Assassination of Yitzhak Rabin and the Remaking of Israel* (New York; London: W.W. Norton & Company, 2015), 143, 163.

73. Alon Pinkas, 'Peres: Iran Thinks of Us as a Collective Salman Rushdie', *Jerusalem Post*, 1 September 1994.

74. Interview with France 2 television. At the Summit, Peres claimed that Iran was the world's 'capital of terror.' Government Press Office, 'Peres: We Shall Do All It Takes to Defeat Terrorism', *Jerusalem Post*, 14 March 1996.

75. David Makovsky and Hillel Kuttler, 'Clinton to Head Anti-Terror Summit Next Week', *Jerusalem Post*, 8 March 1996.

76. Benjamin Netanyahu, *A Place Among the Nations: Israel and the World* (New York: Bantam Dell Pub Group, 1993), 126.

77. In his speech, Netanyahu chided journalists for their skepticism of Rabin's Iran warnings. He indicated that he unequivocally agreed with the prime minister and that he would not dare to 'mock such a significant existential threat' as this. '98th Meeting of the 13th Knesset', 11 January 1995, Knesset Transcripts.

78. Ibid.

79. Binyamin Netanyahu, *Fighting Terrorism: How Democracies Can Defeat Domestic and International Terrorists* (New York: Macmillan, 1995), 121–9.

80. Ibid., 123.

81. Ibid., 123.

82. Peres accorded Iran a cameo appearance during a debate, which was otherwise dominated by discussion of the Oslo Accords. In claiming that Israel was locked 'in a race with fundamentalists,' he cautioned that 'It will be a disaster if they get the nuclear weapon before we make peace.' Netanyahu, who vehemently opposed continuing the peace process and the establishment of a Palestinian State, did not mention Iran. Sarah Honig, 'Netanyahu, Peres Sharpen Debating Skills on "Popolitka"', *Jerusalem Post*, 7 May 1996.

83. In a poll conducted shortly before the election, the vast majority of Israelis said that the issues of 'Peace and the Territories' and 'Terrorism' would affect their vote 'to a great extent.' Concerns about Iran were not offered as options. Alan Arian and Michal Shamir, eds., *The Elections in Israel, 1996*, SUNY Series in Israeli Studies (Albany, NY: State University of New York Press, 1999), 8.

84. Netanyahu's margin over Peres in the 29 May 1996 election was 50.5% to 49.5%.

85. 'Iranian Media: No Big Change Whoever Wins Election', *Reuters*, 30 May 1996.

86. Benjamin Netanyahu, 'PM Netanyahu Speech to US Congress' (Joint Session of United States Congress, Washington, DC, 10 July 1996).

87. Netanyahu could not completely abandon the peace process, but he did not pursue it with the same seriousness that the previous Labor government had. His campaign had promoted skepticism, if not outright hostility, to the peace process, so this was to be expected.

88. Steve Rodan, 'PM in DC to Stress Diplomacy, Not Defense Issues', *Jerusalem Post*, 5 July 1996.

89. Ephraim Sneh's displeasure illustrated the complexity of the issues on Israel's agenda. For Sneh, Iran remained the primary threat, but he also believed that an alliance with Israel's neighbors was critical for effectively reducing the risk. One of Sneh's more radical proposals called for the formation of an Israeli-Jordanian-Palestinian axis to counterbalance the Syrian-Iranian front. Much later, Sneh recalled Netanyahu's failure to take Iran seriously as a period of immense frustration. Michal Yudelman, 'Sneh: Confrontation With Iran Inevitable', *Jerusalem Post*, 17 February 1997, Daily edition; Interview with Ephraim Sneh.

90. The Israeli Ministry of Foreign Affairs (MFA) reiterated this statement following the swearing in of Khatami several months later on 4 August 1997. In a communique, the MFA stated that 'Israel viewed the electoral victory of President Mohammed Khatami as a sign of moderation.' It continued, 'The swearing in of President Mohammad Khatami has given Iran an opportunity to open a new page in its relations with all of its neighbors to prove that its new government is inclined toward peace and not confrontation.' Israel Ministry of Foreign Affairs, 'Ministry of Foreign Affairs Communique on Iran's New President', 4 August 1997, Israel Ministry of Foreign Affairs Documents.

91. This initiative reportedly commenced prior to Khatami's election as part of an economic policy shift. According to the *Jerusalem Post*, in 1996, shortly

after Netanyahu took office, Kazakh oil minister Nurlen Balgimbaev contacted the Iranians on behalf of the Israeli government. Israel owed Iran close to $1 billion from past business dealings and was interested in settling the debt as a means toward resolving military tensions. As a gesture of goodwill, Israel halted broadcasts by opponents of the Iranian regime, which it had been channeling through its Amos satellite. Steve Rodan, 'Iran, Israel Reportedly Forging Contacts', *Jerusalem Post*, 9 September 1997.

92. The election results did not weaken Sneh's criticism of Iran. He still insisted that 'The country is based on a fascist, extremist, and racist ideology.' Thomas O'Dwyer, 'New Voice From Teheran', *Jerusalem Post*, 9 January 1998.

93. Jay Bushinsky, 'Israel Unimpressed by Khatami's CNN Interview', *Jerusalem Post*, 9 January 1998.

94. Netanyahu spoke at a Knesset State Control Meeting called by Sneh. Abandoning diplomacy, he declared 'We are talking about our lives, about our very existence.' Batsheva Tsur, 'PM: Iran Poses Most Serious Threat Since 1948', *Jerusalem Post*, 27 January 1998.

95. A *Jerusalem Post* editorial captured the Israeli mindset when it asked why Iran would continue to build long-range missiles if not to attack Israel. Editorial Board, 'In the Shadow of the Mullahs', *Jerusalem Post*, 11 January 1998.

96. The documents were given to the paper by Labor MK Rafi Elul, who claimed to have received them from an exiled Iranian nuclear scientist. He said that both Israel and the United States have 'known about this for several years.' Steve Rodan, 'MK Elul Says Israel, US Have Known of Iranian Nukes for Years', *Jerusalem Post*, 12 April 1998.

97. The story of the weapons-smuggling operation included references to Russian organized crime and Argentinian technicians. Steve Rodan, 'Documents Obtained by "Jerusalem Post" Show: Iran Has Four Nuclear Bombs', *Jerusalem Post*, 9 April 1998; Steve Rodan and Hillel Kuttler, 'Iran Paid $25m. for Nuclear Weapons, Documents Show', *Jerusalem Post*, 10 April 1998.

98. See discussion of Republican House Research Committee Report, *infra*, Chapter 4.

99. In a report to the Knesset Foreign Affairs and Defense Committee, Netanyahu claimed that Israel was doing everything it could to stop Iran without specifying what this meant. Jay Bushinsky and Liat Collins, 'PM: It May Be Too Late to Stop Iran, Iraq Nuclear Plans', *Jerusalem Post*, 9 June 1998.

100. There was some uncertainty at the time about whether the test of the Shahab-3 missile, which was based on the North Korean Nodong missile, was a success or failure. US government officials were unsure if the missile had exploded on its own—an indication of failure—or whether the Iranians had deliberately detonated the missile during its flight. Later assessments pointed toward the former. Iran attempted another test two years later, which again ended in failure. It took nearly five years for Iran to conduct a successful test of the Shahab-3 in June 2003. Gary Samore, *Iran's Strategic Weapons Programmes: A Net Assessment* (Milton Park: Routledge, 2013); Steven Erlanger, 'Washington Casts Wary Eye at Missile Test', *New York Times*, 24 July 1998, sec. World, https://www.nytimes.com/1998/07/24/world/washington-casts-wary-eye-at-missile-test.html.

101. Barry Rubin, 'Iran's Threat', *Jerusalem Post*, 30 July 1998.

102. Douglas Davis, 'Iran: Military Buildup Is Needed to Counter Israel', *Jerusalem Post*, 2 August 1998.

103. *Jerusalem Post* Staff and AP, 'Iran Unveils Shihab-3 Missile. Has Plans for Longer-Range Model', *Jerusalem Post*, 27 September 1998.

104. Recalling this period, Sneh explained that his frustration at Israel's failure to counter Iranian activities prompted his provocation. Interview with Ephraim Sneh.

105. Liat Collins and Steve Rodan, 'Mordechai: We Can Protect Our Citizens From Iran Threat', *Jerusalem Post*, 28 September 1998.

106. Ibid.

107. See discussion of Ephraim Kam's previous analysis *infra*.

108. Ephraim Kam, 'The Iranian Threat Cause for Concern, Not Alarm', Strategic Assessment (Tel Aviv: Institute for National Security Studies, October 1998).

109. Opponents disparaged his handling of the economy and the budget. Both proponents and opponents of Palestinian peace talks objected to his handling of negotiations. Many criticized the mounting death toll and Israel's failure to achieve victory in southern Lebanon.

110. One such mention concerned Iran's sponsorship of terrorism, particularly its support of Hezbollah in Southern Lebanon. The cost and consequences of Israel's continued occupation was a campaign issue.

111. One of Barak's major foreign policy initiatives involved overseeing Israel's hasty withdrawal from Lebanon in May 2000, ending eighteen years of Israeli presence in the country.

112. As IDF Chief of Staff, Ehud Barak had converted to the hawkish perception of Iran, but he was not an outspoken advocate of greater confrontation. See discussion of Barak's evolving views of Iran *infra*.

113. 'Selected Press Statements by PM Barak during His Visit to London', 23 November 1999, Israel Ministry of Foreign Affairs Documents.

114. David Rudge, 'Officials: Israel Not Iran's Immediate Target', *Jerusalem Post*, 17 July 2000.

115. Public dissatisfaction focused on immediate security concerns associated with Israel's hasty retreat from Lebanon and the outbreak of the Second Intifada. Suzanne Goldenberg, 'Barak Calls Early Election', *The Guardian*, 29 November 2000, sec. World news, http://www.theguardian.com/world/2000/nov/29/israel.

116. Sharon, a former military commander and Minister of Defense, had stirred controversy on numerous occasions. His provocative visit to the Temple Mount in Jerusalem reportedly provoked the second Palestinian Intifada. World leaders and Arab neighbors suspected his strategic judgment. As defense minister from 1981–3 under Prime Minister Menachem Begin, Sharon directed Israel's military operations in Lebanon, which included the massacres at Sabra and Shatila refugee camps. A commission convened to investigate the causes forced Sharon's resignation by holding him responsible for not taking appropriate measures to prevent violence.

117. 'Iran Data Portal', Iran Data Portal—Syracuse University, n.d., http://irandataportal.syr.edu/.

118. Editorial Board, 'No Win for Democracy in Iran', *Jerusalem Post*, 10 June 2001.

119. The United States used questionable intelligence to charge that Saddam Hussein's program for developing weapons of mass destruction justified an invasion of the country. Evidence suggesting that Iraq was developing or acquiring nuclear material subsequently proved false.

120. Later evidence would show Iraq had nothing to do with the 11 September attacks.

121. Iran funded the opposition of the Northern Alliance in Afghanistan to the Taliban government.

122. Some Israeli officials worried that the attacks would distract the United States from more meaningful fights in the region. Defense Minister Binyamin Ben-Eliezer criticized the United States for ignoring threats from Iran and Syria to build a wide coalition against Bin Laden. Gil Hoffman and AP, 'Ben-Eliezer: United States Too Soft on Iran, Syria', *Jerusalem Post*, 16 October 2001.

123. Politicians from all parties participated in the threat intensification. For example, a leader of Shinui, a centrist liberal Zionist party, penned an opinion piece warning of the start of a new world war, noting that 'history is repeating itself.' Yosef (Tommy) Lapid, 'The Warning', *Jerusalem Post*, 14 September 2001.

124. Gil Hoffman, 'Netanyahu: World Must Join to Crush Terror', *Jerusalem Post*, 12 September 2001.

125. Benjamin Netanyahu, 'Dismantle Terror-Supporting Regimes', *Jerusalem Post*, 14 September 2001.

126. Ibid.

127. Benjamin Netanyahu, 'Address to US House Government Reform Committee', Washington, DC, 24 September 2001.

128. In a speech to the Labor Knesset faction, Ben-Eliezer declared that the 'message from the Americans isn't aggressive enough,' since it failed to target Iran, 'the greatest threat to the free world today' due to 'their potential for obtaining nuclear capability by 2005.' Hoffman and AP, 'Ben-Eliezer'.

129. Al Quds (Jerusalem) Day is held annually on the last Friday of the month of Ramadan to express Iranian solidarity with the Palestinian people. It features public events and speeches by prominent political and religious leaders, who denounce the 'Zionist Regime' and call for the liberation of Palestine.

130. Akbar Hashemi Rafsanjani, 'Rafsanjani Qods Day Speech', 14 December 2001, http://www.globalsecurity.org/wmd/library/news/iran/2001/011214-text.html.

131. Foreign Minister Peres' response was typical. Calling the remarks 'bone-chilling,' he claimed that 'they leave no room for doubt as to Iran's inherent hatred for Israel and its declared goal to destroy her.' Jack Katzenell, 'Peres Protests Iranian Threat to Destroy Israel', *Jerusalem Post*, 26 December 2001.

132. Rafsanjani's clashes with the religious conservative establishment dated back to the formation of the Islamic Republic. He had advocated for a system of direct popular voting to ratify the decisions made by the Constituent Assembly,

fearing that the cleric-dominated assembly would be too reactionary. Similarly, as President of Iran, Rafsanjani pursued policies of economic liberalization that were opposed by radical religious elements. Likewise, his cabinet with only four of twenty-two positions filled by clerics, was, according to Daniel Brumberg, 'hardly revolutionary.' Ali Rahnema, 'Ayatollah Khomeini's Rule of the Guardian Jurist: From Theory to Practice', in *A Critical Introduction to Khomeini*, ed. Arshin Adib-Moghaddam (Cambridge, UK; New Yor: Cambridge University Press, 2014); Daniel Brumberg, *Reinventing Khomeini: The Struggle for Reform in Iran* (Chicago, IL: University of Chicago Press, 2001), 155.

133. Arieh O'Sullivan, 'Sharon: Arafat Is Our "Bitter Enemy." Calls Iran "Spearhead of International Terror"', *Jerusalem Post*, 7 January 2002.

134. George W. Bush, 'State of the Union', Washington, DC, 29 January 2002, http://www.washingtonpost.com/wp-srv/onpolitics/transcripts/sou012902.htm.

135. Peter Baker, *Days of Fire: Bush and Cheney in the White House* (New York: Anchor, 2014), 186.

136. Shortly after the Axis of Evil speech, Israeli officials, citing reports that Jordan's King Abdullah had uncovered a secret Iranian plot to attack Israel using its proxies Hamas and Islamic Jihad, called upon all 'reasonable' Western countries to sever ties with the Iranian regime. Iranian officials denied the reports. Arieh O'Sullivan, 'Jordan's Abdullah Exposes Iranian Plot to Attack Israel', *Jerusalem Post*, 6 February 2002.

137. This was Israel's implicit objective in seeking securitization. To take such extraordinary action required acceptance of the Iran threat by both Israel's polity and the global powers.

4.   ACTIONS

1.   The Permanent Five members of the United Nations Security Council are the United States, Russia, China, France, and Great Britain.

2.   'Full Text of the Iran Nuclear Deal', 14 July 2015, https://apps.washingtonpost.com/g/documents/world/full-text-of-the-iran-nuclear-deal/1651/.

3.   Sanctions relief covered only nuclear-related sanctions; it excluded those relating to human rights or terrorism-related conduct.

4.   Ben Brumfield and Oren Liebermann, 'Israeli Leaders Planned Attack on Iran Military', CNN, 22 August 2015, http://www.cnn.com/2015/08/22/middleeast/israel-plan-iran-military-target-strike/index.html.

5.   Benjamin Netanyahu, 'PM Netanyahu's Speech at the United Nations General Assembly', United Nations General Assembly, New York, October 2015, http://www.pmo.gov.il/English/MediaCenter/Speeches/Pages/speechUN011015.aspx.

6.   Ibid.

7.   Ibid.

8.   Ibid.

9.   42.5% said they 'strongly agreed' with the prime minister. Ephraim Yaar and Tamar Hermann, 'The Peace Index' (Jerusalem: The Israel Democracy Institute, August

2015), http://www.peaceindex.org/files/Peace_Index_Data_August_2015-Eng.pdf.

10. Additionally, experts agreed the agreement extended Iran's 'break-out time,' the minimum amount of time needed to gather the materials necessary to build one nuclear weapon, from several months to at least a year. Richard Stone, 'Technical Elements of Iran Deal Put the Brakes on Nuclear Breakout', *Science*, 3 April 2015, http://www.sciencemag.org/news/2015/04/technical-elements-iran-deal-put-brakes-nuclear-breakout.

11. The impact of economic sanctions on Iran's willingness to negotiate is unclear. Skeptics note that Iran began negotiating about the fate of its nuclear program before imposition of additional harsh sanctions. Others argue that the sanctions merely exacerbated Iran's structural economic problems due to mismanagement, corruption, and lack of transparency. Proponents of sanctions, including the Israelis, believed that sanctions had effectively crippled the Iranian economy and forced nuclear concessions. They maintain that removing sanctions prematurely reduced pressure on a regime that might have been nearing collapse. Academic and policy centers continue to debate the efficacy of sanctions. See, for example, Hossein Mousavian, 'It Was Not Sanctions That Brought Iran to the Table', *Financial Times*, 19 November 2013, https://www.ft.com/content/8d9631f4-510c-11e3-b499-00144feabdc0; Mark Dubowitz and Reuel Marc Gerecht, 'Economic Regime-Change Can Stop Iran Bomb', *Bloomberg*, 17 January 2012, https://www.bloomberg.com/view/articles/2012-01-17/economic-regime-change-can-stop-iran-commentary-by-gerecht-and-dubowitz.

12. Israel has never acknowledged the production of nuclear weapons, although it is widely assumed to possess several hundred such weapons. The US Secretary of State put the number at 200 in a 2015 leaked email, adding they were 'all targeted on Tehran.' Colin Powell, 'Re: Re:', 3 March 2015, https://www.scribd.com/document/324033115/00002715-002.

13. In particular, the Quds Force—a special division of the Iranian Revolutionary Guards Corps (IRGC)—operated abroad in conjunction with terrorist organizations. The combat exploits attributed to its commander, Major General Qasem Soleimani, symbolized both the competence and mysteriousness of Iranian military operations in the region.

14. In 2015, Iran's military spending was less than Israel's, both in terms of dollar value and in percentage of GDP. Iran spent approximately $10.6bn (2.98% of GDP) while Israel spent $16.9bn (5.66% of GDP). Compared to Saudi Arabia, the difference was even larger. The Saudis spent $87.2bn (9.85% of GDP). 'SIPRI Military Expenditure Database', Stockholm International Peace Research Institute, 2015, https://www.sipri.org/databases/milex.

15. For example, in 2016 Iran reportedly tested a missile with 'Israel must be destroyed' written on it in Hebrew. This test itself can be interpreted in a variety of ways, including as a hardliner attempt to undermine Rouhani's implementation of the nuclear deal, or to deter Israel from attacking Iran's military installations.

16. The following chapter continues the discussion by examining how Netanyahu's election as prime minister concurrent with Ahmadinejad's reelection enhanced the resonance of Netanyahu's populist messaging.

17. Concerns over the destructive force of nuclear weapons eventually led to the creation of various agencies and treaties designed to limit the proliferation of such weapons, including the International Atomic Energy Agency (1957) and the Nuclear Non-Proliferation Treaty (1968).

18. Over 100 million people and President Ronald Reagan reportedly watched *The Day After*, which portrayed a fictional nuclear war between NATO and the Soviet Union. Simon Braund, 'How Ronald Reagan Learned to Start Worrying and Stop Loving the Bomb', *Empire*, 1 November 2010, https://www.highbeam.com/doc/1P3-2307407461.html.

19. Andrew Rosenthal, 'SOVIET DISARRAY; U.S. Fears Spread of Soviet Nuclear Weapons', *New York Times*, 16 December 1991, sec. World, https://www.nytimes.com/1991/12/16/world/soviet-disarray-us-fears-spread-of-soviet-nuclear-weapons.html.

20. See, for example, North Korea state propaganda in which the development of nuclear weapons is portrayed as a source of national pride and strength.

21. Subsequent studies question the accuracy of Israel's assessment of the Iraq danger as well as its claim of success. See Dan Reiter, 'Preventive Attacks Against Nuclear Programs and the "Success" at Osiraq', *The Nonproliferation Review* 12, no. 2 (1 July 2005): 355–71; Colin H. Kahl, 'An Israeli Attack Against Iran Would Backfire—Just Like Israel's 1981 Strike on Iraq', *Washington Post*, 2 March 2012, sec. Opinions, http://www.washingtonpost.com/opinions/an-israeli-attack-against-iran-would-backfire--just-like-israels-1981-strike-on-iraq/2012/02/28/gIQATOMFnR_story.html.

22. Israel disguised its weapons development. According to Walter Pincus, Israeli officials told US Embassy personnel in June 1960 that the nuclear reactor it was building with French help was a 'textile plant,' later revising that to a 'metallurgical research installation.' Israel's accusations of Iranian activity reflect Israel's prevarications about its weapons program. Walter Pincus, 'Another Nation Blazed the Trail for Iran in Developing a Nuclear Program', *Washington Post*, 9 March 2015, sec. National Security, https://www.washingtonpost.com/world/national-security/another-nation-blazed-the-trail-for-iran-in-developing-a-nuclear-program/2015/03/09/0222ec28-c41c-11e4-ad5c-3b8ce89f1b89_story.html.

23. Non-nuclear armed signatories to the NPT commit to refraining from acquiring nuclear weapons while nations possessing weapons agree to move toward disarmament. It allows signatory nations to develop and operate a peaceful nuclear program within guidelines for nonproliferation. Along with Israel, other non-signatories to the NPT include nuclear-armed India, Pakistan, and North Korea.

24. Steve Inskeep, 'Born in the USA: How America Created Iran's Nuclear Program', *Parallels*, NPR, 18 September 2005, https://www.npr.org/sections/parallels/2015/09/18/440567960/born-in-the-u-s-a-how-america-created-irans-nuclear-program.

25. Construction of the Bushehr reactor began in 1975 but halted shortly after the 1979 Islamic Revolution. The vacant site was bombed by Iraq during the Iran-Iraq War. Reconstruction of the plant began in 1995 with help from Russia. The plant went online in September 2011. Ali Vaez, 'Waiting for Bushehr', *Foreign Policy*, 12 September 2011, https://foreignpolicy.com/2011/09/12/waiting-for-bushehr/.

26. The Shah's proclivity for military might was well-known among American and Israeli officials. He spent considerable sums on arms purchases and military training from the United States and Israel, much of it unnecessary from a strategic point of view. According to rumor, he built the largest fleet of hovercrafts in the world. Andrew Scott Cooper, *The Oil Kings: How the U.S., Iran, and Saudi Arabia Changed the Balance of Power in the Middle East* (New York: Simon and Schuster, 2011), 141.

27. 'The Nuclear Vault: The Iranian Nuclear Program, 1974–1978', National Security Archive Electronic Briefing Book (Washington, DC: George Washington University, 12 January 2009), https://nsarchive2.gwu.edu/nukevault/ebb268/.

28. According to Mohsen Rafighdoost, a close confidant of Khomeini during the early years of the Islamic Republic, the Supreme Leader explicitly rejected his advisors' recommendations to develop chemical and nuclear weapons. Gareth Porter, *Manufactured Crisis: The Untold Story of the Iran Nuclear Scare* (Charlottesville, VA: Just World Books, 2014); Gareth Porter, 'When the Ayatollah Said No to Nukes', *Foreign Policy* (blog), 16 October 2014, https://foreignpolicy.com/2014/10/16/when-the-ayatollah-said-no-to-nukes/.

29. Khomeini's successor as Supreme Leader, Ali Khamenei, reportedly issued a more explicit fatwa in the 1990s, continuing the ban on weapons of mass destruction. Since Iran did not disclose the existence of the ban until 2004, it could not influence international perceptions of Iran's intentions toward developing nuclear weapons. Even after its disclosure, which did not include producing the document, critics remained skeptical about its legitimacy. They were unsure whether Iran's Islamic principles were sincere enough to keep it from acquiring nuclear weapons, or whether the announcement was a tactical ploy designed to deceive Western negotiators. Porter, 'When the Ayatollah Said No to Nukes'.

30. This is not to say that the Israeli media did not discuss the issue, or that Iran was never mentioned by Israeli officials, only that Iran's nuclear policy was not discussed publicly in an official government capacity in the Israeli Knesset during this period.

31. A 24 December 1986 Knesset transcript mentioned the sale of French materials to Iran, but discussion quickly turned to concern about French arms sales to Saudi Arabia. '272nd Meeting of the 11th Knesset', 24 December 1986, Knesset Transcripts.

32 'Israel's Foreign Policy—Historical Documents', Israel Ministry of Foreign Affairs, n.d.

33. Israel had been asked by the United States to stay out of the conflict in order to maximize Arab participation in coalition forces. Saddam sought to provoke

Israel's entry to create a broader Arab-Israeli conflict that would reduce Arab support for the war effort against Iraq. Avi Shlaim, 'Israel and the Conflict', in *International Perspectives on the Gulf Conflict, 1990–91*, ed. Alex Danchev and Dan Keohane (London: Palgrave Macmillan, 1994), 59.

34. It produced fear that had tangible consequences. The government issued gas masks to all Israelis to carry with them at all times given the unpredictability of a chemical-carrying missile attack. The anxiety produced a significant increase in cardiac arrests and hundreds of emergency room visits for acute anxiety and panic attacks. E. Karsenty et al., 'Medical Aspects of the Iraqi Missile Attacks on Israel', *Israel Journal of Medical Sciences* 27, no. 11–12 (December 1991): 603–7.

35. See discussion *supra* at beginning of chapter. Rosenthal, 'SOVIET DISARRAY; U.S. Fears Spread of Soviet Nuclear Weapons'.

36. 'The Nuclear Vault: The Algerian Nuclear Problem', National Security Archive Electronic Briefing Book (Washington, DC: George Washington University, 10 September 2007), https://nsarchive2.gwu.edu/nukevault/ebb228/index. htm.

37. The article also cited developments in other Arab weapons programs in Syria, Libya, Saudi Arabia, and Egypt. Editorial Board, 'The Real Middle East Problem'.

38. Saddam also increasingly focused on internal security and his personal protection. During the First Gulf War, President George H.W. Bush had implied that the United States would assist Iraqi Shiites in overthrowing Saddam. When the war ended without regime change, the Iraqi military violently suppressed the revolt. Kevin M. Woods et al., *The Iraqi Perspectives Report: Saddam's Senior Leadership on Operation Iraqi Freedom From the Official U.S. Joint Forces Command Report* (Annapolis, MD: Naval Institute Press, 2006), 31–2, 51–2.

39. This was not the only false premise of the 2003 US invasion. The Bush administration maintained that Iraq had supported the 11 September terrorist attacks, which was categorically untrue.

40. Alon Pinkas, 'Thinking the Unthinkable About Iran', *Jerusalem Post*, 23 April 1992.

41. Ghazvinian, *America and Iran*, 488.

42. The page one headline of the first story claimed that 'Cheap Soviet Arms Make Iranians a Major Threat.' Alon Pinkas, 'Cheap Soviet Arms Make Iranians a Major Threat', *Jerusalem Post*, 9 January 1992.

43. Ibid.

44. Yedidya Atlas, 'Iranian Threat Never Went Away', *Jerusalem Post*, 16 February 1992.

45. Haberman, 'THE WORLD; Israel Focuses on the Threat Beyond the Arabs—in Iran'.

46. Hedges, 'Iran May Be Able to Build an Atomic Bomb in 5 Years, U.S. and Israeli Officials Fear'.

47. Pinkas, 'Thinking the Unthinkable About Iran'.

48. The sources of the claims reportedly were the US Central Intelligence Agency and other intelligence sources. Inspectors from the IAEA were never able to verify them during inspection trips to Iran. Hedges, 'Iran May Be Able to Build an Atomic Bomb in 5 Years, U.S. and Israeli Officials Fear'.

49. The Kazakhstan missile purchase was dismissed by Uri Saguy, head of Israeli military intelligence, as having 'no factual basis.' Yossi Melman, 'IRAN'S LETHAL SECRET', *Washington Post*, 18 October 1992, https://www.washingtonpost. com/archive/opinions/1992/10/18/irans-lethal-secret/2994e63c-b341-41ae-b87b-0141a68f9a27/.

50. Originally designed as a loose coalition of exiled Iranian dissident groups, two leaders of the Mujahedin-e Khalq (MEK) organization founded the NCRI in Paris in 1981. The NCRI served as the public-facing political wing controlled by the MEK. As it did with the MEK, the US Treasury Department designated the NCRI as a terrorist organization, calling it an 'alias of the MEK.' United States Treasury Department Office of Public Affairs, 'Designation of National Council of Resistance in Iran, National Council of Resistance and Peoples Mujahedin of Iran under Executive Order 13224', 15 August 2003, https://www.treasury. gov/press-center/press-releases/Pages/js664.aspx.

51. Jeffrey Lewis, 'NCRI Did Not Discover Natanz', *Arms Control Wonk* (blog), 28 October 2006, https://www.armscontrolwonk.com/archive/201274/ncri-did-not-discover-natanz/.

52. The *Jerusalem Post* made no mention of the NCRI disclosure in either its reporting or editorials.

53. Jack Caravelli, *Nuclear Insecurity: Understanding the Threat from Rogue Nations and Terrorists* (Santa Barbara, CA: Greenwood Publishing Group, 2008), 108.

54. In its December 2015 report, the IAEA noted that the 'activities to be undertaken in support of a possible military dimension to [Iran's] nuclear program' began in the late 1980s and continued into the early 2000s. These activities were 'brought to a halt in late 2003 and the work was fully recorded, equipment and work places were either cleaned or disposed of.' This was the same information that Prime Minister Benjamin Netanyahu dramatically 'disclosed' in a highly publicized speech on 30 April 2018. Board of Directors, 'Final Assessment on Past and Present Outstanding Issues Regarding Iran's Nuclear Programme' (Vienna, Austria: International Atomic Energy Agency, December 2015); Benjamin Netanyahu, 'PM Netanyahu Reveals the Iranian Secret Nuclear Program', http://www.pmo.gov.il/English/MediaCenter/Events/Pages/event_iran300418.aspx.

55. Neither the 9/11 Commission Report nor the Senate Intelligence Committee's investigation found evidence of Saddam's responsibility for the attacks. *The 9/11 Commission Report: Final Report of the National Commission on Terrorist Attacks Upon the United States* (New York: W.W. Norton & Company, 2004), 11; Senate Committee on Intelligence, 'Report on the U.S. Intelligence Community's Prewar Intelligence Assessments on Iraq' (Washington, DC: United States Senate, 7 July 2004).

56. A *Haaretz* journalist subsequently noted the similarities between Netanyahu's case for war with Iraq in 2002 and his calls for military action against Iran a decade later. Barak Ravid, 'Iraq 2002, Iran 2012: Compare and Contrast Netanyahu's Speeches', *Haaretz*, 4 October 2012, https://www.haaretz.com/blogs/diplomania/iraq-2002-iran-2012-compare-and-contrast-netanyahu-s-speeches-1.468213.

57.	Herb Keinon, 'Saddam's Fall Alters Israel's Strategic Situation—Experts', *Jerusalem Post*, 11 April 2003.

58.	Israeli officials reiterated earlier claims that Iran, if given the chance, would not hesitate to use a nuclear device against Israel and might even consider using it to support Hezbollah forces in a war against Israel. Matthew Gutman, 'US Confirms Israeli Suspicions About Iranian Nuclear Program', *Jerusalem Post*, 12 June 2003.

59.	This sense that Israelis knew what the Iranian people wanted for themselves and their future was a common theme of Israeli media coverage during this period. Many commentators predicted that the lack of popular support for the Iranian regime would make its overthrow a relatively simple task. Steyn estimated that 90% of Iranians desired regime change, while Rosenblum cited a 'secret poll by the mullahs' that allegedly found that only 4% of the populace believed the government was legitimate. In June 2003, the *Jerusalem Post* editorialized that Israel should declare itself the 'advocate for the [Iranian] people—what they truly want is to be rid of the regime.' Mark Steyn, 'It's Mullah Time!', *Jerusalem Post*, 24 June 2003; Editorial Board, 'Iran's People Power', *Jerusalem Post*, 17 June 2003; Jonathan Rosenblum, 'A Silver Lining for Dark Clouds', *Jerusalem Post*, 13 December 2002.

60.	Steyn, 'It's Mullah Time!'

61.	See *supra*, Chapter 3, Part IV, Section C.

62.	See *infra*, Chapter 5, Part II, Section D.

63.	Gideon Alon, 'Concerned About Syria and Iran', *Haaretz*, 4 August 2003, http://www.haaretz.com/concerned-about-syria-and-iran-1.96152.

64.	Ibid.

65.	A month later, Iran agreed to enter negotiations over suspending its nuclear enrichment and processing. It also considered opening its nuclear sites to unannounced inspections and signing the Additional Protocol of the NPT. 'Timeline of Iran's Controversial Nuclear Program', CNN, 19 March 2012, http://www.cnn.com/2012/03/06/world/meast/iran-timeline/index.html.

66.	Iran's nuclear program had become a battleground between the elected reformist and the conservative hardline factions. Supreme Leader Ayatollah Khamenei fought back against Khatami's popularity by marginalizing him and working to block his reformist initiatives. Thus, while Khatami sought a nuclear accord with the West, Khamenei and the IRGC made belligerent statements punctuated by the occasional missile test. The disagreement provided ammunition to both skeptics and optimists evaluating Iran's future intentions. Israeli hawks referred to Iran's hardliners to challenge those willing to pursue diplomatic solutions.

67.	'Implementation of the NPT Safeguards Agreement in the Islamic Republic of Iran' (Vienna, Austria: International Atomic Energy Agency, 10 November 2003), https://www.iaea.org/sites/default/files/gov2003-75.pdf.

68.	The Israeli military could not ignore the growing sense of urgency and uncertainty among the politicians. A brigadier general speaking anonymously to the Israeli press claimed, 'It would not be an exaggeration to say that the [Israeli Air Force] has devoted the bulk of its procurement funds in the past decade to strike at Iran's nuclear and ballistic missile facilities.' By contrast, on the record comments were more measured. Ze'evi said that it would be inappropriate to discuss details in public, but notably did not deny that the military was considering preemptive attack. Arieh O'Sullivan et al., 'Ya'alon: Terror Not Sole Threat', *Jerusalem Post*, 24 October 2003.

69. Ibid.

70. Janine Zacharia, 'Iran Will Have Nukes in a Year—Mofaz', *Jerusalem Post*, 13 November 2003.

71. By trying to clarify Iran's progress toward bomb production, Israeli officials likely muddied the analysis. Their constantly shifting assessments, often appearing in reaction to events, created more uncertainty about Iran's nuclear activities. This may have been the intended purpose since by frequently accelerating their estimates they engendered a sense of urgency among those who might otherwise be apathetic to the Iran threat. In an interview, one proliferation analyst expressed displeasure with longer timelines because they offered too much comfort to those who believed that Iran did not require urgent action. Interview with Emily Landau.

72. Herb Keinon, 'Shalom Toughens Stance on Iran', *Jerusalem Post*, 24 September 2004.

73. Silvan Shalom, 'United Nations General Assembly Presentation', https://www.c-span.org/video/?183637-2/united-nations-general-assembly-meeting.

74. See Note 461 *supra*.

75. Associated Press, 'Iran Warns Israel Against Attacking Nuke Facilities', *Jerusalem Post*, 12 May 2004.

76. In a Knesset debate on the Iran issue a week after the incident, Foreign Minister Silvan Shalom called Iran 'the most dangerous country in the world' before offering yet another accelerated timetable for Iran's completion of a nuclear bomb. He said that Iran might achieve nuclear weapons in the coming months. This contradicted the longer assessments of Defense Minister Mofaz and Major General Ze'evi from late 2003 and represented the shortest prediction by any government official. A month later, in another Knesset session, MKs from right-wing parties, including Nissan Slomianksy of NRP and Shmuel Halpert of Agudat Israel, wondered aloud what could be done in response to this threat since Iran was a country that was not 'normal' in the traditional sense. Slomiansky even questioned whether there would be any centralized command and control of future nuclear weapons systems in Iran, implying that the decision to launch a nuclear strike could be left to a motivated ideologue. The 'easiest' solution to this problem, he said, was regime change. '236th Meeting of the 16th Knesset', 21 March 2005, Knesset Transcripts.

77. There are several reasons why the Israeli public may not have shared the fears voiced by the political establishment. Evidence of Iran's weapons program was highly technical, and speculation about Iran's intentions was largely hypothetical. If Iran was directing terrorism against Israel, it was doing so through proxies without conclusive evidence of a direct linkage to the Iranian regime. Even if Israelis were not aware of the power struggle in Iran, they were hearing conflicting reports about Iran's intentions.

78. The most consistent resource for national security polling in Israel is the Peace Index produced by the Israel Democracy Institute. The survey began regularly tracking public opinion on 'the Israeli-Palestinian conflict, relations between Jews and Arabs in Israel, and current events of a political or diplomatic nature' in 1994. It asked its first question on Iran in 2006.

79. The Second Intifada began in 2000 following a controversial visit by Ariel Sharon to the Temple Mount/Al Aqsa Mosque facility in Jerusalem. It lasted roughly through early 2005, but there is no agreed upon date for its end.

80. '"Quagmire" Analogy Gets Much Use', Fox News, 28 June 2005, http://www.foxnews.com/story/2005/06/28/quagmire-analogy-gets-much-use.html.

81. In alliance with Amal, another Shiite resistance organization turned political party, Hezbollah secured thirty-five seats in the Lebanese parliament. With their election results, the Hezbollah/Amal alliance became the largest Shiite party in Lebanon. Esther Pan, 'LEBANON: Election Results', *Council on Foreign Relations* (blog), 21 June 2005, https://www.cfr.org/backgrounder/lebanon-election-results.

82. Iranian elections are, at best, partially democratic. While candidates are directly elected by popular vote, they are first vetted by the Guardian Council to ensure their commitment to the Islamic Republic and revolutionary ideals. The criteria for approval are vague and the nonpublic process is opaque. Presidential voting takes place in two rounds. All candidates compete in a first-round general election. If no candidate receives a majority of the votes cast, the two top vote-getters compete in a runoff election.

83. Ahmadinejad narrowly made the runoff in a crowded first round field. In the first round, Ahmadinejad had placed a narrow second, winning 20% of the vote to Rafsanjani's 21%. Given Rafsanjani's prominence and power in Iranian politics relative to Ahmadinejad, most outside observers assumed that the former president would easily defeat the political newcomer in the second round. '2005 Presidential Election', Iran Data Portal—Syracuse University, http://irandataportal.syr.edu/2005-presidential-election, accessed 17 July 2018.

84. The presidential victory was his first electoral victory, since the Tehran mayor is appointed by a committee.

85. 'Profile: Mahmoud Ahmadinejad', BBC News, 4 August 2010, sec. Middle East, http://www.bbc.com/news/world-middle-east-10866448.

86. 'Cabinet Meeting Minutes', 26 June 2005, Israeli Prime Minister's Office.

87. Upon his return from a trip to the United Nations in New York, Prime Minister Ariel Sharon stressed the need to prevent any agreement or compromise with Iran, especially over the issue of its nuclear program. He advocated transferring the handling of the issue from the International Atomic Energy Agency to the United Nations Security Council. 'Cabinet Meeting Minutes', 2 October 2005, Israeli Prime Minister's Office.

88. In addition to claiming the elections were rigged, Timmerman wrote in the *Jerusalem Post* that his interviews with defectors from the Islamic Republic over the past two years revealed that the 'Islamic Republic has assembled 15 nuclear

warheads.' Kenneth Timmerman, 'The Coming Nuclear Showdown with Iran', *Jerusalem Post*, 1 July 2005.

89. Caroline Glick, 'The Mask Is Off and No One Cares', *Jerusalem Post*, 5 July 2005.

90. Nissem Zeev of the Shas Party, from Knesset Transcripts, '264th Meeting of the 16th Knesset', 29 June 2005, Knesset Transcripts.

91. In one example, at a conference on Iran, Amos Gilad claimed that the dire estimations of Israel's military establishment in the late 1990s were 'repeatedly dismissed by government officials.' Gilad appeared to be engaging in revisionist history, as the majority of the 1990s' military assessments about Iran were less alarmist than those voiced by many government officials. It is possible that he was referring to the Netanyahu-led Likud government of 1996–9, which initially indicated a willingness to engage with Iran. Yaakov Katz, 'Ex-MI Chief: Jihad Tsunami on the Way. Three Gaza Terrorists Wounded in IAF Missile Strike', *Jerusalem Post*, 16 May 2006.

92. Some openly admitted pessimism, predicting that Ahmadinejad would, like his predecessors, continue to enjoy international legitimacy, however undeserving.

93. Sharon noted the threats of both nuclear weapons acquisition and support for terrorism, given Iran's 'murky fundamentalism.' Ariel Sharon, 'PM Sharon Addresses the United Nations General Assembly' (15 September 2005).

94. Notably, Israel eschewed diplomacy for engagement with Ahmadinejad's reformist predecessor, but it now embraced it as a means of internationally isolating Iran. Ze'evi, Head of Israeli Military Intelligence, lauded these efforts, claiming that their success proved the utility of international diplomacy. Other Israeli officials, however, pushed for unilateral action against Iran. Herb Keinon, 'Key Israeli Officials Declare Support for More Unilateral Steps', *Jerusalem Post*, 29 September 2005.

95. 'Cabinet Meeting Minutes', 2 October 2005.

96. There is some controversy surrounding the exact translation of Ahmadinejad's words. Most English translations of the Persian transcript posted on the Interior Ministry's website use the phrase 'wipe off the map' for the relevant section of the speech. Some, however, claim that Ahmadinejad's actual words were closer to 'must vanish from the arena of time,' implying that Israel would instead collapse. *The New York Times* posted a full English translation on its website three days after the speech. It included the 'wiped off the map' translation. 'Text of Mahmoud Ahmadinejad's Speech', *New York Times*, 30 October 2005, sec. Week in Review, https://www.nytimes.com/2005/10/30/weekinreview/text-of-mahmoud-ahmadinejads-speech.html; Glenn Kessler, 'Did Ahmadinejad Really Say Israel Should Be "Wiped Off the Map"?', *Washington Post*, 5 October 2011, https://www.washingtonpost.com/blogs/fact-checker/post/did-ahmadinejad-really-say-israel-should-be-wiped-off-the-map/2011/10/04/gIQABJIKML_blog.html.

97. Orly Halpern and Herb Keinon, 'Iranian President: "Wipe Israel off Map"', *Jerusalem Post*, 27 October 2005.

98. In an open letter to foreign ministers around the world, Shalom called on them to 'act, both bilaterally and within the framework of the United Nations to bring such Iranian behaviour to an end.' Michel Zlotowski, 'Shalom Urges Annan to

Condemn Iran. Foreign Minister Enjoys a Well-Timed Visit to France', *Jerusalem Post*, 28 October 2005; Silvan Shalom, 'FM Shalom Appeals to Fellow Foreign Ministers on Iranian Threat', 30 October 2005, Israel Ministry of Foreign Affairs Documents.

99. He referred to Rafsanjani's 2001 Al Quds day speech that he had delivered as former president. Halpern and Keinon, 'Iranian President'. See discussion *supra*. Chapter 3, Sec. V.

100. This study utilized the online Newsbank archives for the *Jerusalem Post* to carry out this analysis. The *Jerusalem Post* possesses both the most complete online archive and is written in English, which made it the best choice for corpus analysis as conducted in this project.

101. Text analysis is a useful tool but comes with some limitations. This average was determined from a simple word search of the *Jerusalem Post* on the archive site Newsbank. As Jockers notes, raw numbers in corpus analysis can be misleading and require contextual examination to certify findings as meaningful. This was done using the Jockers-developed KWIC analysis, which enables the researcher to search large text databases to identify key words within their linguistic context. This was used as a general check to ensure that the majority of references were valid. Matthew L. Jockers, *Text Analysis with R for Students of Literature*, 2014 edition (New York: Springer, 2014).

102. Explanatory note on methodology: The corpus analysis I employed in this book offers a visual representation of Iran messaging employed by a newspaper, as representative of the conservative-leaning media, and conservative Israeli political leader Benjamin Netanyahu (see Chapter 5). It uses both Microsoft Excel and the R Programming software program to present graphically the messaging analyzed in this project.

103. A Knesset session following the conference revealed the anxiety it provoked. Many MKs took to the floor to decry Ahmadinejad's speech and compare him to past enemies of the Jewish people. '284th Meeting of the 16th Knesset', 2 November 2005, Knesset Transcripts.

104. It is worth noting that the first major spike in this language took place in 2006 rather than 2005, despite the fact that Ahmadinejad was first elected in the middle of 2005. This is likely because Ahmadinejad's infamous Holocaust denial press conference did not take place until December 2005. This event reinforced Ahmadinejad's international image as a Holocaust denier and anti-Semite in the eyes of many observers.

105. Prior to 2005, articles with both of these words had not exceeded fifty in any single year since 1989.

106. Dichter had recently left Israeli public service to become a research fellow at the Brookings Institution. He analyzed the situation in a speech to a US pro-Israel organization.

107. Dichter reentered politics not long after this appearance, first in 2006 as Minister of Internal Security for Kadima, and then in 2009 as part of Netanyahu's Likud government. *Jerusalem Post* correspondent, 'Dichter: US May Have to Bomb Iran', *Jerusalem Post*, 31 October 2005.

108. Arieh O'Sullivan, 'Halutz: Sanctions Won't Deter Iran', *Jerusalem Post*, 21 November 2005.

109. Gil Hoffman and Sheera Claire Frenkel, '"I Prefer Fewer Declarations and More Deeds"', *Jerusalem Post*, 10 November 2006.

110. Interview with Yaakov Katz, 27 October 2015.

111. It is likely that Israelis understood that Iran would not fail to respond to Israeli action, as Iraq had in 1980. Iranian leaders had consistently matched Israeli threats with their own promises of retaliation, and Iran's military was far more capable than Iraq's at the time of the Osirak strike.

112. The *Jerusalem Post* described it as 'a book filled with photographs of mushroom clouds, bio-chemical treatment exercises, the bubonic plague and unguarded Soviet-era military bases.' Erik Schechter, 'Our Own 9/11?', *Jerusalem Post*, 3 March 2006.

113. Ibid.

114. Numbers of sales and readership of Azran's book are unknown. It nonetheless received media attention. Ibid.

115. The newly formed Kadima Party, led by Ehud Olmert, won a plurality in the March 2006 elections. It received 22% of the vote and secured twenty-nine seats. Amir Peretz's Labor party came in second with 15% of the vote and nineteen seats, followed by the ultra-orthodox Shas party and Likud—now led by Netanyahu—each with twelve seats. Kadima joined with Labor, Shas, and Yisrael Beiteinu to form a government with Olmert as Prime Minister. Netanyahu, as the head of the largest party not in the government, became leader of the opposition. Although Iran was increasingly recognized as a security threat, issues related to Iran did not play a large role in the election that year. Shmuel Sandler, Manfred Gerstenfeld, and Jonathan Rynhold, *Israel at the Polls 2006*, Israeli History, Politics and Society (London: Routledge, 2008).

116. Only 16% disagreed. Ephraim Yaar and Tamar Hermann, 'The Peace Index', April 2006, http://www.peaceindex.org/indexMonthEng.aspx?mark1=&mark2=&num=30.

117. Ibid.

118. Caroline Glick, 'Hitler Is Still Dead', *Jerusalem Post*, 26 May 2006.

119. Amir Taheri, 'Religious Fanatic at a Persian Bazaar', *Jerusalem Post*, 28 May 2006.

120. Shlomo Cesana, 'אני נאבק באחמדינג'אד', *Israel Hayom*, 18 May 2008.

121. Jerusalem Post Staff, 'Rabbi at Vatican Meeting Condemns Iranian President', *Jerusalem Post*, 6 October 2008, https://www.jpost.com/iranian-threat/news/rabbi-at-vatican-meeting-condemns-iranian-president.

122. Several soldiers present during the operation gave similar accounts to the author. While they asked not to be quoted, media and other reports echoed their assessment.

123. Israel had to know Hezbollah's strategy, since its leader Hassan Nasrallah had effectively announced it before the war. '[Hezbollah fighters] live in their houses, in their schools, in their churches, in their fields, in their farms, and in their factories.' Marvin Kalb and Carol Saivetz, 'The Israeli-Hezbollah War of 2006: The Media as a Weapon in Asymmetrical Conflict' (Washington, DC: Brookings Institution, 18 February 2007), 8.

124. Blanford, *Warriors of God*.

125. Steven Erlanger, 'Israeli Inquiry Finds "Grave Failings" in '06 War', *New York Times*, 31 January 2008, sec. Middle East, https://www.nytimes.com/2008/01/31/world/middleeast/31mideast.html.

126. Blanford, *Warriors of God*.

127. Gil Hoffman, 'Netanyahu: Don't Boycott the BBC', *Jerusalem Post*, 11 August 2006.

128. Editorial Board, 'A Wake-up Call', *Jerusalem Post*, 13 August 2006.

129. '، رييس جمهوري: تجاوز رژيم صهيونيستي به لبنان تعدي به ملت هاي منطقه است', *Jamejam Online*, 14 July 2006.

130. Israeli commentators bemoaned the bias against the Jewish State, particularly among international institutions like the UN. A common refrain was that anti-Israel bias prevented the world from seeing Iran's support of its proxy Hezbollah. See for example Robert Rozett, 'Recognizing Evil', *Jerusalem Post*, 22 August 2006.

131. Qom is the most religious city in Iran and an important center of Shiite religious scholarship and clerical training.

132. Shabtai Shoval, *The Chosen One—The Mossad in Iran*, ed. Phil Weinstock, trans. Asaf Epstien, Second edition (Scientific Driven Systems LTD, 2003).

133. Sam Ser, 'Tangling With Teheran', *Jerusalem Post*, 29 September 2006.

134. Interview with Ronen Bergman, interview by Jonathan Leslie, Tel Aviv, Israel, 25 January 2016.

135. Bergman, *The Secret War With Iran*.

136. Ibid.

137. Ibid.

138. Israelis consider Bergman to be the reporter best connected to the Israeli intelligence community. As one seasoned political analyst put it in an off-the-record interview: 'He is the Mossad's leak guy.' His work can therefore read in part as a public version of the Mossad's state of knowledge about Iran and the Iranian threat. The lack of knowledge about Iran within the Israeli intelligence community also squares with the general description about Iran strategic planning given by Yossi Alpher in an interview with the author. Interview with Yossi Alpher, interview by Jonathan Leslie, Tel Aviv, Israel, 9 December 2015.

139. Interview with Ronen Bergman.

140. Yossi Klein Halevi and Michael B. Oren, 'Israel's Worst Nightmare', *The New Republic*, 5 February 2007.

141. A year earlier, a study conducted by the Jerusalem Center for Public Affairs highlighted the new linkage of Iran and Ahmadinejad to the threat of genocide. The published report, picturing a mushroom cloud on the cover, compared modern Iran to the Rwandan genocide of 1994. The authors, who included prominent public intellectuals and moral leaders such as Dr. Dore Gold and Elie Wiesel, wrote, 'The critical difference is that while the huts in Rwanda were equipped with the most basic of weapons, such as machetes, Iran, should the international community do nothing to prevent it, will soon acquire nuclear weapons. This would increase the risk of instant genocide, allowing no time or

possibility for defensive efforts.' They authors recommended that, in addition to sanctions and international monitoring by the IAEA, Ahmadinejad should face charges for incitement to genocide before the International Criminal Court. Justus Reid Weiner et al., 'Referral of Iranian President Ahmadinejad on the Charge of Incitement to Commit Genocide', Jerusalem Center for Public Affairs, 2006.

142. They did not cite the source of the poll, but the figure has been repeated when speaking of Iran's threat to Zionism.

143. Not surprisingly, Ephraim Sneh used such rhetoric with increasing candidness. In his penultimate month as a Knesset Minister, he told the *Jerusalem Post* that Iran 'can't be allowed to repeat Auschwitz.' Gil Hoffman, 'Sneh: Iran Can't Be Allowed to Repeat Auschwitz', *Jerusalem Post*, 30 April 2008. Jonathan Tobin then penned an impassioned rebuttal to those criticizing Sneh's embracing of Holocaust rhetoric, writing: 'Just as today many laugh at Iranian President Mahmoud Ahmadinejad, they dismissed the murderous threats of Adolf Hitler as clownish bombast, and considered the brainwashing of a generation of German children by the Nazis unimportant. They denounced those who refused to be silent as prejudiced warmongers. Those truth-tellers were proved right, but too late to avert a world war, as well as a genocide.' Jonathan S. Tobin, 'Who's Obsessed About Obsession', *Jerusalem Post*, 22 October 2008.

144. It achieved this through the use of extremely aggressive marketing tactics. The paper was offered en masse by an army of distributers across Israel each morning, given out at bus stops and various points of transit during busy commute times. Within three years, it would have the highest circulation of any paper in Israel. *Hayom*'s popularity was credited with diminishing readership of some of Israel's other newspapers, leading to the bankruptcy and closing of several of them, including *Ma'ariv*. Noam Sheizaf, 'Wither the Israeli Press?', *The Daily Beast*, 3 October 2012, https://www.thedailybeast.com/articles/2012/10/03/wither-the-israeli-press.

145. Lieberman was, at the time, the newly commissioned Minister of Strategic Threats, a government portfolio specifically created to deal with Iran. Yaakov Katz, 'Security and Defense: Who's in Charge of Whom and Over What?', *Jerusalem Post*, 2 April 2009, https://www.jpost.com/features/front-lines/security-and-defense-whos-in-charge-of-whom-and-over-what.

146. Adelson's goals in launching the paper were so blatant that they spawned an opposition movement in the Knesset in which members proposed a bill prohibiting the distribution of a free, full-sized newspaper. They feared that the paper would skew the media landscape in favor of Netanyahu and the Israeli right. The bill passed a first reading but later failed. Anshel Pfeffer, 'Everything You Need to Know About the Israel Hayom (or Anti-Sheldon Adelson) Law', *Haaretz*, 12 November 2014, https://www.haaretz.com/.premium-a-primer-on-the-israel-hayom-law-1.5327699.

147. The statement was notable both because it was a public prediction by a serving military and because it appeared in a new newspaper impacting the Israeli media landscape. Gideon Allon, 'איראן עם יכולת גרעינית 2009', *Israel Hayom*, 7

November 2007, http://digital-edition.israelhayom.co.il/Olive/ODE/Israel/Default.aspx?href=ITD%2F2007%2F11%2F07.

148. United Nations Security Council (UNSC) Resolution 1747 imposed a ban on arms sales and expanded freezes on Iranian assets. Iran rejected the sanctions as illegitimate and restated its claim that its nuclear program was solely for peaceful purposes. 'Security Council Tightens Sanctions Against Iran over Uranium Enrichment', UN News, 24 March 2007, https://news.un.org/en/story/2007/03/213372-security-council-tightens-sanctions-against-iran-over-uranium-enrichment.

149. 'Cabinet Meeting Minutes', 25 March 2007, Israeli Prime Minister's Office.

150. Ibid.

151. Allon, 'איראן עם יכולת גרעינית 2009'.

152. The report stated, 'We judge with high confidence that in fall 2003, Tehran halted its nuclear weapons program.' This halt had 'lasted at least several years,' according to the report. The report concluded that the decision to suspend the program 'suggests [Iran] is less determined to develop nuclear weapons than we have been judging since 2005.' 'Iran: Nuclear Intentions and Capabilities', National Intelligence Estimate, Office of the Director of National Intelligence, November 2007, https://www.dni.gov/files/documents/Newsroom/Press%20Releases/2007%20Press%20Releases/20071203_release.pdf.

153. An unclassified version is available to the public; a classified version is reserved for members of the intelligence and political communities.

154. Shlomo Cesana and Eitan Livne, 'בטהראן מתו מצחוק', Israel Hayom, 5 December 2007.

155. Eitan Livne, '"אחמדינג'אד על הסוס נשיא איראן הגדיר את דו"ח המודיעין האמריקני כ"ניצחון האומה"', Israel Hayom, 6 December 2007.

156. Yaakov Amidror, 'ובכל זאת, הביווו האיראני ברור', Israel Hayom, 5 December 2007.

157. There appeared a hint of doubt when Amidror wrote that, if the United States is right about Iran's abandonment of its nuclear military program, then Israel is the 'Ze'ev Ze'ev' or 'The Boy Who Cried Wolf.' Ibid.

158. Few Israeli leaders mentioned that they had supported the Iraq invasion, relying upon intelligence reports of WMD despite reasons to question their accuracy. They overlooked the irony of equating a false claim of a weapons program in one country with a finding that no program existed in another.

159. Amos Regev, 'המודיעין האמריקני – מסורת של טעויות', Israel Hayom, 5 December 2007.

160. Prime Minister Olmert was more diplomatic in his response, stopping short of directly questioning the intelligence findings of an important strategic ally. He nevertheless reaffirmed his commitment to 'prevent Iran from attaining [nuclear] capability.' Gil Hoffman, Yaakov Katz, and Herb Keinon, 'Lieberman: No One Knows When Iran Will Have the Bomb. "We Cannot Allow Ourselves to Rest Just Because of an Intel Report From the Other Side of the Earth," Barak Says', Jerusalem Post, 5 December 2007.

161. Numbers rose steadily in the following years: first to thirty-six in 2009, then forty in 2012, eventually peaking at fifty-four in 2015. The only year with a decrease during this period was 2011. 'Publications Archive', Institute for

National Security Studies, http://www.inss.org.il/publication/, accessed 18 July 2018.

162. In a Knesset session in July, Labor MK Danny Yatom and Strategic Affairs Minister Avigdor Lieberman of Yisrael Beiteinu exchanged ideas about the dangers posed by Iran; both agreed that Iran was a menace to Israel and the entire world. '44th Meeting of the 17th Knesset', 11 July 2007, Knesset Transcripts.

163. '77th Meeting of the 17th Knesset', 25 July 2007, Knesset Transcripts.

164. Ibid.

165. Ibid.

166. Though Livni did not specify which countries she meant, she was likely referring to Saudi Arabia and other Sunni Gulf Cooperation Council (GCC) nations. The idea of 'moderate' Arab countries opposing Iran eventually became a common theme of Israeli discourse. 'Cabinet Meeting Minutes', 14 January 2007, Israeli Prime Minister's Office.

167. Demographically, threat perception of Iran was higher among older respondents as well as among the less religious. Men tended to view Iran as a greater threat to Israel's security than women. Ephraim Yaar and Tamar Hermann, 'The Peace Index', The Israel Democracy Institute, August 2008.

168. The second biggest threat—the unpreparedness of the IDF for war—was also notable in that it reflected a growing unease, especially among younger respondents, about the IDF's military capabilities. The authors of the report attributed this trend to the military's struggles in the 2006 Lebanon campaign. Ibid.

169. US President George W. Bush called the report 'eye popping,' and said that the report 'had a big impact—and not a good one.' Gregory Treverton, 'Support to Policymakers: The 2007 NIE on Iran's Nuclear Intentions and Capabilities', Central Intelligence Agency Center for the Study of Intelligence, May 2013, https://www.cia.gov/library/center-for-the-study-of-intelligence/csi-publications/books-and-monographs/csi-intelligence-and-policy-monographs/pdfs/support-to-policymakers-2007-nie.pdf.

170. 'Cabinet Meeting Minutes', 13 January 2008, Israeli Prime Minister's Office.

171. As Israeli forces bombarded Gaza City during Operation Cast Lead, Netanyahu stressed that Hamas must be removed from the Gaza Strip. 'Israel cannot tolerate an Iranian base next to its cities,' he said. Damien McElroy, 'Fighting Rages as Gaza Strip Death Toll Nears 1000', 14 January 2009, sec. World, https://www.telegraph.co.uk/news/worldnews/middleeast/israel/4236793/Benjamin-Netanyahu-says-Hamas-must-be-removed-from-Gaza.html.

172. Prime Minister Olmert told his cabinet that Hamas was 'acting as the arm of Iran' in Gaza. Cabinet Meeting Notes, 11 May 2008. Israeli media followed Olmert's lead and assigned Iran the blame for the violence. Columnist Caroline Glick wrote, 'Here it is important to note that the war today, like the war in 2006, is a war between Israel and Iran.' 'Cabinet Meeting Minutes', 11 May 2008, Israeli Prime Minister's Office; Caroline Glick, 'Iran's Gazan Diversion?', Jerusalem Post, 6 January 2009.

173. Years later, a RAND Corporation study on the Israeli-Iranian conflict observed 'Israelis have developed a siege mentality in the wake of the rocket attacks

following the Lebanon and then Gaza withdrawals.' It predicted, 'Because Israelis believed that they will be blamed no matter what they do, more defiant positions are likely, even toward the United States.' Dalia Dassa Kaye, *Israel and Iran: A Dangerous Rivalry*, Rand Corporation Monograph Series (Santa Monica, CA: RAND National Defense Research Institute, 2011).

5. MESSAGING

1. Though Likud won one fewer seat than Kadima in the election, the right-wing parties that were more likely to form a governing coalition had won more seats overall. Hence, Netanyahu was given the first opportunity to form a government.

2. This was not for lack of trying. The Khatami government made several overtures to the United States following the 'Axis of Evil' speech, including offering a 'grand bargain' in which Iran offered to address American concerns about its nuclear program, support for terrorist groups, and operations in Iraq. It also offered to accept a two-state solution in the Israel-Palestine resolution. In exchange, Iran wanted the United States to repeal sanctions, drop its 'Axis of Evil' rhetoric, and recognize Iran's regional security interests. The letter was delivered to the Bush administration via the Swiss Embassy in Washington, DC. No answer was ever sent. The Ahmadinejad government, perhaps learning from the futility of Khatami's efforts to reach out to the West to get them to drop their demonizing rhetoric, seemed to embrace the 'Axis of Evil' label and took a more antagonistic approach toward the United States and the West. Ghazvinian, *America and Iran*, 536–8.

3. The vetting process, conducted by the Guardian Council, has been used at times to conduct mass disqualification of candidates, usually reformists, in elections in which the regime wants increased control over the results. The low turnout that typically follows in elections with large numbers of disqualified candidates reflects their decreased legitimacy in the eyes of voters. While this system is highly undemocratic, it is a mistake and reductive to trivialize it as rigged. Surprises can, and often do, happen in Iran's elections.

4. Yaakov Katz, editor-in-chief of *The Jerusalem Post,* former top advisor to Jewish Home party head Naftali Bennett, and author of a book on Israel's conflict with Iran, said in an interview that Ahmadinejad was one of Israel's great public relations victories. Interview with Yaakov Katz; Katz and Hendel, *Israel vs. Iran.*

5. See *ante*, Chapter 4, Part IV, Section A for an analysis of how Ahmadinejad increased the interest of Israeli media in Iran.

6. Daniel Schorr, 'Iran Further Isolates Itself With "Holocaust Denial"', *Weekend Edition*, NPR, 17 December 2006, https://www.npr.org/templates/story/story.php?storyId=6637685.

7. Nader Habibi, 'The Economic Legacy of Mahmoud Ahmadinejad', *Middle East Brief*, no. 74 (June 2013), https://www.brandeis.edu/crown/publications/meb/MEB74.pdf.

8. For example, in 2007 a surprise announcement by the government that it would begin gasoline rationing led to the burning of twelve gas stations in Tehran. 'Iran

Fuel Rations Spark Violence', 27 June 2007, http://news.bbc.co.uk/1/hi/world/middle_east/6243644.stm.

9. Thomas Erdbrink, 'Iran's President Ties Recent Drop in Currency to U.S.-Led Sanctions', *New York Times*, 2 October 2012, sec. Middle East, https://www.nytimes.com/2012/10/03/world/middleeast/iran-president-mahmoud-ahmadinejad-ties-currency-drop-to-sanctions.html.

10. In one highly publicized incident, Ahmadinejad blamed the United States for orchestrating the 11 September attacks as part of an effort to aid Israel. His 2012 Al Quds Day speech, in which he said that the Palestinian problem could be solved by the elimination of the Zionist regime, is covered later in this chapter. Ed Pilkington, 'Ahmadinejad Accuses US of "Orchestrating" 9/11 Attacks to Aid Israel', *The Guardian*, 23 September 2010, https://www.theguardian.com/world/2010/sep/23/iran-unitednations.

11. Green was the campaign color of the opposition candidates, Mir Hussein Mousavi and Mehdi Karroubi.

12. Neil MacFarquhar, 'A Divine Wind Blows Against Iran's President', *New York Times*, 22 June 2011, sec. Middle East, https://www.nytimes.com/2011/06/23/world/middleeast/23iran.html.

13. Jamsheed K. Choksy, 'Tehran Politics: Are the Mullahs Losing Their Grip?', *World Affairs Journal*, June 2012, http://www.worldaffairsjournal.org/article/tehran-politics-are-mullahs-losing-their-grip.

14. Saeed Kamali Dehghan, 'Iran's President Mahmoud Ahmadinejad Summoned to Parliament', *The Guardian*, 14 March 2012, http://www.theguardian.com/world/iran-blog/2012/mar/14/iran-ahmadinejad-appears-parliament; 'Ahmadinejad Critic Named Speaker', *BBC News*, 5 June 2012, sec. Middle East, http://www.bbc.com/news/world-middle-east-18328882.

15. Netanyahu insisted, 'It's a totalitarian state that perhaps has elections on occasion.' Benjamin Netanyahu, Benjamin Netanyahu Interview: Full Text, interview by Jeff Glor, 15 June 2009, https://www.cbsnews.com/news/benjamin-netanyahu-interview-full-text/.

16. Israel Ministry of Foreign Affairs, 'Iran: Statements by Israeli Leaders—June 2009', 22 June 2009, Israel Ministry of Foreign Affairs Documents, http://mfa.gov.il/MFA/ForeignPolicy/Iran/Pages/Iran-Statements_Israeli_leaders-June_2009.aspx.

17. Jennifer Epstein, 'Bibi: Israel Can't Wait Long on Iran', POLITICO, 5 March 2012, https://www.politico.com/story/2012/03/netanyahu-israel-cant-wait-long-on-iran-073648.

18. Context matters. For example, in Germany, Holocaust denialism is a public offense, which protects against certain factions' disavowing the country's Nazi past. In America, the speech of pseudo-academics, publicity seekers, and aspiring leaders of far-right political organizations is protected from prosecution if it is not intended to incite violence. When an avowed white supremacist ran for political office in the US state of Louisiana, the condemnation by the Jewish community of his anti-Semitic remarks often brought him the media attention he craved. In many instances, leaders of the African American community refused

to respond to his racist remarks, arguing that the publicity would enhance the candidate's profile. John Maginnis, *Cross to Bear* (New Orleans, LA: Pelican Publishing Company, Inc., 2011), 28.

19. The most prominent example of this occurred shortly after Netanyahu took office in 2009 during his address to the United Nations General Assembly. In that speech, Netanyahu drew a direct comparison to the Nazis, saying, 'And like the belated victory over the Nazis, the forces of progress and freedom will prevail only after an [*sic*] horrific toll of blood and fortune has been extracted from mankind. That is why the greatest threat facing the world today is the marriage between religious fanaticism and the weapons of mass destruction. The most urgent challenge facing this body is to prevent the tyrants of Tehran from acquiring nuclear weapons.' Benjamin Netanyahu, 'Prime Minister Benjamin Netanyahu's Speech to the UN General Assembly', http://www.haaretz.com/news/prime-minister-benjamin-netanyahu-s-speech-to-the-un-general-assembly-1.7254.

20. Some argued that Ahmadinejad's behavior belied his dangerousness because it promoted his image as a buffoon.

21. Philip Blenkensop and Rachelle Younglai, 'Banking's SWIFT Says Ready to Block Iran Transactions', Reuters, 17 February 2012, https://www.reuters.com/article/us-iran-sanctions-swift/bankings-swift-says-ready-to-block-iran-transactions-idUSTRE81G26820120217.

22. Adiv Sterman and Mitch Ginsburg, '"US Pressure Nixed Israeli Strike on Iran Last Year"', *The Times of Israel*, 3 September 2013, http://www.timesofisrael.com/us-pressure-nixed-israeli-strike-on-iran-in-2012/.

23. Rouhani displayed the change in Iran's direction during his 2013 trip to New York. Ahead of his appearance at the United Nations, he published an op-ed in the *Washington Post* and sat for an interview with NBC news. He struck a notably moderate tone and vowed to 'engage in constructive interaction with the world.' Hassan Rouhani, 'President of Iran Hassan Rouhani: Time to Engage', *Washington Post*, 19 September 2013, sec. Opinions, https://www.washingtonpost.com/opinions/president-of-iran-hassan-rouhani-time-to-engage/2013/09/19/4d2da564-213e-11e3-966c-9c4293c47ebe_story.html.

24. Hassan Rouhani, 'President's Speech Addressing the 44th World Economic Forum', Davos, Switzerland, 23 January 2014, http://www.president.ir/en/74125.

25. '43rd Meeting of the 19th Knesset', 19 June 2013, Knesset Transcripts.

26. Lior Akerman, 'Rouhani and His Shy, Sweet Smile', *Jerusalem Post*, 22 November 2013; Emily B. Landau, 'After Round One With Rouhani: Staying Focused on the Dynamics of Nuclear Bargaining', INSS Insight, Institute for National Security Studies, 17 October 2013, http://www.inss.org.il/uploadImages/systemFiles/No.%20477%20-%20Emily%20for%20web.pdf.

27. These oversimplified narratives of Iranian governance belie the complicated truth of the Iranian political system. In a comprehensive social survey of Iranian society, one of the few conducted through extensive fieldwork inside of Iran, Kevan Harris documents the social changes in Iran in the decades since the Islamic Revolution. He explains how societal pressure was put on the government to

provide opportunities for upward mobility through the state's welfare and social policy institutions, the mechanisms through which most Iranians relate to the state. Consequently, Iran's success in implementing social welfare programs for its citizens in the postrevolutionary era has expanded the middle class and provided citizens with opportunities for social advancement, altering Iranians' view of the Islamic Republic. Similarly, the fractious nature of the ruling elite, divided along a spectrum running from reformers to hardliners, underlined the importance of mass politics. At the very least, the book dismisses the notion of Iran as a fervently religious society dominated by clerics and devoted to Islamic law. Kevan Harris, *A Social Revolution: Politics and the Welfare State in Iran*, 1st edition (Oakland, CA: University of California Press, 2017).

28. Netanyahu, who was raised in the United States, speaks English fluently with very little trace of an Israeli accent. He reportedly frequently uses English in conducting official government business, including cabinet meetings, since most of his advisors are also fluent English speakers. Anshel Pfeffer, *Bibi: The Turbulent Life and Times of Benjamin Netanyahu*, 1st edition (New York: Basic Books, 2018).

29. A notable practice among Israeli academics is that they often choose to publish their work examining political issues in English before they do so in Hebrew. Interview with Yael Berda, interview by Jonathan Leslie, Email, 13 July 2018.

30. The English language media coverage of Netanyahu's messages—both the interviews and speeches he gave to English language audiences and the reports in the English press about his statements and activities—is particularly instructive. Comparison of the English reports to those in the Hebrew press for Israeli audiences, however, are not materially different, although sometimes less extensive. The Hebrew press generally reported on significant English language speeches by the Prime Minister.

31. Significantly, the interview occurred just months before the United States and Israel reportedly launched a cyberattack on Iran's nuclear facility, which may have been planned during Netanyahu's first term. One could speculate that an additional aim of Netanyahu's messaging to American audiences was to shore up approval for such an action should it come to public attention. It set a precedent for further joint aggressive operations against Iran.

32. In his youth, Goldberg had volunteered to serve in the Israeli Defense Forces, working as a prison guard during the first Intifada. MJ Rosenberg, 'The Evolution of Jeff Goldberg: From Prison Guard in the West Bank to Lobby Poster Boy', *HuffPost*, 4 July 2010, https://www.huffpost.com/entry/the-evolution-of-jeff-gol_b_562212.

33. See discussion on Populist Securitization in Chapter 1.

34. In the following years, Netanyahu would frequently call diplomacy with Iran a 'mistake,' and warn world leaders not to be taken in by Iran's 'deception.' He repeatedly stressed that Iran was only using negotiations as a cover for its bomb-building intentions. An example of such claims is Netanyahu's response following Rouhani's address at Davos: 'Rouhani has admitted that a decade ago, he deceived the West in order to advance the Iranian nuclear program. He is doing this today as well. The goal of the Iranian ayatollahs' regime, which is hiding behind

Rouhani's smiles, is to ease sanctions without conceding on their program to produce nuclear weapons. Therefore, the international community must not go astray after this deception.' Benjamin Netanyahu, 'Prime Minister Netanyahu's Remarks on Iranian President Rouhani's Davos Speech', 23 January 2014, Israeli Prime Minister's Office.

35. Jeffrey Goldberg, 'Netanyahu to Obama: Stop Iran—Or I Will', *The Atlantic*, March 2009, http://www.theatlantic.com/magazine/archive/2009/03/netanyahu-to-obama-stop-iran-or-i-will/307390/.

36. Anyone who visits Iran knows this to be false. Memorials to individuals killed in the conflict are ubiquitous throughout the country, and Iranian leaders frequently reference the suffering of their citizens—as well as the world's refusal to recognize their victimhood—following Iraq's use of chemical weapons. Netanyahu simply asserted that Iran, unlike Britain after World War I, had not lapsed into pacifism because of the great tragedy of a loss of a generation. Ibid.

37. JPost.com Staff, 'PM: Iran's Leaders Guided by Unbelievable Fanaticism', *Jerusalem Post*, 16 September 2012, https://www.jpost.com/diplomacy-and-politics/pm-irans-leaders-guided-by-unbelievable-fanaticism.

38. 'Remarks During Meeting with U.S. President Barack Obama', 18 May 2009, Israeli Prime Minister's Office.

39. Goldberg, 'Netanyahu to Obama'.

40. Ibid. In his address to the United Nations General Assembly in fall 2009, Netanyahu used similar characterizations of Iranian leaders, who he said were 'fueled by an extreme fundamentalism.' He then warned that if this 'most primitive fanaticism can acquire the most deadly weapons, the march of history could be reversed.' Netanyahu, 'Prime Minister Benjamin Netanyahu's Speech to the UN General Assembly'.

41. Netanyahu, 'Prime Minister Benjamin Netanyahu's Speech to the UN General Assembly'.

42. Ibid.

43. Pluralizing the religious honorific as stand-ins for Iran's political leadership became a common rhetorical flourish among Iran's opponents. Portraying Iran's political leaders as a collective of religious fanatics implies that their murderous intent is motivated by Islam. Rather than acknowledging 'Ayatollah' and 'Mullah' as honorifics accorded by Islam, Israeli leaders, led by Netanyahu and facilitated by supportive media, employed these terms pejoratively.

44. According to *The Oxford Dictionary of Islam*, *taqiya* is defined as the 'Precautionary denial of religious belief in the face of potential persecution. Stressed by Shiite Muslims, who have been subject to periodic persecution by the Sunni majority.' John L. Esposito, 'Taqiyah', in *The Oxford Dictionary of Islam*, ed. John L. Esposito (Oxford: Oxford University Press, 2003), http://www.oxfordreference.com/view/10.1093/acref/9780195125580.001.0001/acref-9780195125580-e-2338.

45. Harold Rhode, an American Middle East scholar, has claimed that *taqiya* is an important part of Iranian strategy. In an introduction to a strategic assessment of Iranian negotiating behavior, which he wrote for an Israeli Center, he argued

that 'The Western concept of demanding that a leader subscribe to a moral and ethical code does not resonate with Iranians.' Harold Rhode, 'The Sources of Iranian Negotiating Behavior' (Jerusalem Center for Public Affairs), http://www.jcpa.org/text/iranian_behavior.pdf, accessed 17 December 2015.

46. Gold, a longtime friend and confidant of Netanyahu, served as an Israeli diplomat and think-tank director before being appointed Director General of Israel's Foreign Ministry.

47. Dore Gold, *The Rise of Nuclear Iran: How Tehran Defies the West*, 1st edition (Washington, DC: Regnery Publishing, 2009), 293.

48. Bergman, *The Secret War With Iran*, 13.

49. The assumption was that Iran's nuclear program was being developed in conjunction with its ballistic missile program, such that when the country developed the bomb it would also possess the capacity to deliver it. Iran had been periodically testing missiles since the mid-1990s, although they achieved only limited success. Testing increased after Mahmoud Ahmadinejad's election in 2005, including the first successful test of the Shahab-3 missile, the first medium-range missile capable of reaching Israel. The medium-range missiles were the first class of weapons that US intelligence assessments believed were 'inherently capable' of carrying a nuclear payload, although there was no evidence to suggest that Iran was attempting to pair its missile development with its nuclear technology. UN Security Council Resolution 2231 in 2010 forbade Iran from developing and testing missiles that were 'inherently capable of delivering nuclear weapons.' It did not prevent them from developing missiles as part of a conventional weapons program. Steven A. Hildreth, 'Iran's Ballistic Missile and Space Launch Programs', Congressional Research Service, 6 December 2012, 3.

50. Itamar Eichner, 'PM: Israel Won't Be Spared Even If US Attacks Iran', *Ynet News*, 8 May 2012, http://www.ynetnews.com/articles/0,7340,L-4264459,00.html.

51. Netanyahu frequently suggested that an Iranian bomb would embolden terrorists by providing them with nuclear protection against Israeli retaliation, or, worse, might enable Iran directly to supply terrorist groups with nuclear weapons they could use against Israel. He suggested both possibilities in his May 2009 joint statement with President Barack Obama, explaining, 'In this context, the worst danger we face is that Iran would develop nuclear military capabilities … if Iran were to acquire nuclear weapons, it could give a nuclear umbrella to terrorists, or worse, it could actually give terrorists nuclear weapons.' Benjamin Netanyahu and Barack Obama, 'Meeting Between PM Netanyahu and U.S. President Barack Obama', 18 May 2009, Israeli Prime Minister's Office, http://www.pmo.gov.il/english/mediacenter/speeches/pages/speechobama.aspx.

52. Ned Potter, 'Israel's Netanyahu: Let's Talk With Palestinians—and Stop Iran's Threat', ABC News, 22 September 2009, https://abcnews.go.com/Politics/netanyahu-israels-prime-minister-worries-palestinians-iran/story?id=8644832.

53. Benjamin Netanyahu, 'Prime Minister Netanyahu's Speech at the Jewish Federations of North America General Assembly', 9 November 2009, Israeli Prime Minister's Office.

54. This quote, speculating about what a nuclear bomb might do to Israel, is detailed in Chapter 3.

55. Benjamin Netanyahu, 'Prime Minister Netanyahu's Speech at the AIPAC Conference', 22 March 2010, Israeli Prime Minister's Office.

56. Asher Zeiger, 'Ahmadinejad's New Call for Israel's Annihilation Is His Most Anti-Semitic Assault to Date, Says ADL', *The Times of Israel*, 2 August 2012, http://www.timesofisrael.com/adl-blasts-ahmadinejads-latest-call-for-israels-annihilation-as-ominous/.

57. Since 2006, the Israeli Foreign Ministry has published monthly reports of statements made by Israeli leaders on Iran. In August 2012, it published its first roundup of Iranian officials' statements containing threats of destruction or delegitimization of the State of Israel and anti-Semitic remarks. Ahmadinejad was the source of most quotes, but other hardline political figures, such as Ayatollah Khamenei and IRGC Brigadier Gen. Ali Hajizadeh also made contributions. The quotes were mostly sourced from English language outlets of Iran state media. Israel Ministry of Foreign Affairs, 'Recent Iranian Statements: Threats, Delegitimization of Israel and Antisemitism', 19 August 2012, Israel Ministry of Foreign Affairs Documents.

58. Ron Prosor, 'Israeli Letter to UN on Iranian Incitement', 27 August 2012, Israel Ministry of Foreign Affairs Documents.

59. Interestingly, Netanyahu chose to use Iran's enemy Al Qaeda rather than the terrorist organizations Hamas and Hezbollah to which the Islamic Republic had known ties, perhaps believing that the global terrorist network would resonate more with his audience than more regionally focused organizations. Netanyahu pressed his case for crisis by enlarging the sources of danger to include Muslims with nuclear weapons in the hands of the 'world's most dangerous terrorist regime or the world's most dangerous terrorist organization.' Benjamin Netanyahu, 'Speech to UNGA' (United Nations General Assembly, New York, 27 September 2012).

60. Ephraim Yaar and Tamar Hermann, 'The Peace Index' (The Israel Democracy Institute, August 2012), https://web.archive.org/web/20160324083815/http://peaceindex.org/files/The%20Peace%20Index%20Data%20-%20August%202012(1).pdf.

61. Evidence of Netanyahu's fixation on the Iran threat lies in a comparison of the number of separate statements on Iran made during his administration with those of previous administrations. From 2006–9, Netanyahu's predecessor, Ehud Olmert, mentioned Iran in public statements on seventeen different occasions. Netanyahu, by contrast, did so 127 times between 2009 and 2015.

62. Sarah Moughty, 'Eyal Arad: A "Messianic" Netanyahu', 6 January 2016, http://www.pbs.org/wgbh/frontline/article/eyal-arad-a-messianic-netanyahu/.

63. Arad went on to say that Netanyahu believed that Jews can 'never trust the outside world to protect them, because it won't.' Ibid.

64. In Netanyahu's version of events, world history is comprised of a long list of nations that have sought to persecute the Jewish people, ranging from the 'bloodletting of the Middle Ages,' to 'the expulsion of the Jews from England,

and then from Spain and then from Portugal,' to 'the wholesale slaughter of Jews in the Ukraine,' and 'the pogroms in Russia.' Netanyahu, 'Prime Minister Netanyahu's Speech at the AIPAC Conference'.

65. Netanyahu also omitted mention of the final chapter, in which the Jews, having been authorized by the king to kill those who might seek to harm them, slaughter thousands of people. The text does not specify whether the killing is conducted in self-defense or revenge. The story of Purim has always played an important role in Jewish history and provides a poignant example of the way in which collective memory can be manipulated for political purposes. (See discussion in Chapter 2 for more on the Purim story.) Peter Novick points out that during the medieval period, 'these "memories" provided gratifying revenge fantasies' to the Jews, but they have been excluded from more recent celebratory traditions. Some factions in Iran have sought to exploit this detail to cast the story as a tale of Jewish savagery; some even referring to it as an 'Iranian holocaust.' Peter Novick, *The Holocaust in American Life* (Boston, MA: Houghton Mifflin Harcourt, 2000); Estrin, 'Iranians and Israelis Are in a Battle Over History—and the Holiday of Purim'; 'جشن «پوریم» تراژدی غمبار ایرانیان'.

66. The speech represented a violation of international protocol and the prime minister's insertion of himself into American politics. He had accepted the invitation of the Republican Speaker of the House without the consent of President Obama. Moreover, his remarks implicitly, but unmistakably, criticized the president's policy. The speech also came at a precarious moment: US negotiators were nearing a deal with Iran on the fate of Iran's nuclear program, while Israel's elections, in which Netanyahu was seeking reelection, were less than two weeks away. That Netanyahu was campaigning by addressing the American Congress is further evidence that Israeli politicians and intellectuals often seek to influence opinion in Israel by promoting themselves and their ideas abroad.

67. Nicky Woolf and Amanda Holpuch, 'John Boehner Invites Netanyahu to Address Congress on Iran Next Month', *The Guardian*, 21 January 2015, sec. US news, http://www.theguardian.com/us-news/2015/jan/21/boehner-netanyahu-invite-congress-iran-obama.

68. In subsequent references, Netanyahu was even bolder in co-opting the story to further his policy agenda. For example, in 2017 he told a group of Israeli schoolchildren who were celebrating the Purim festival that the holiday symbolized the efforts of modern Iran to destroy the Israeli state. Benjamin Netanyahu, !פורים שמח, 2017, https://www.facebook.com/Netanyahu/videos/10154454625947076/; Netanyahu, 'The Complete Transcript of Netanyahu's Address to Congress'.

69. Putin publicly scolded the Israeli prime minister telling him to stop dwelling on the past and that 'We now live in a different world. Let us talk about that now.' Years later, Putin would engage in a similar historical rewrite to justify his invasion of Ukraine in February 2022. *Times of Israel Staff* and AFP, 'Rejecting Purim Spiel, Putin Tells Netanyahu to Stop Dwelling on Past', *The Times of Israel*, 10 March 2017, http://www.timesofisrael.com/rejecting-purim-spiel-putin-

tells-netanyahu-to-stop-dwelling-on-past/; Isaac Chotiner, 'Vladimir Putin's Revisionist History of Russia and Ukraine', *The New Yorker*, 23 February 2022, https://www.newyorker.com/news/q-and-a/vladimir-putins-revisionist-history-of-russia-and-ukraine.

70. Arash Karami, 'Zarif Gives Netanyahu Lesson in Jewish Scripture', *Al-Monitor*, 13 March 2017, http://www.al-monitor.com/pulse/originals/2017/03/iran-purim-netanyahu-zarif-larijani-esther-persia-history.html.

71. Benjamin Netanyahu, 'PM Netanyahu's Speech at AIPAC Policy Conference 2012', AIPAC Policy Conference, Washington, DC, 5 March 2012, http://www.pmo.gov.il/English/MediaCenter/Speeches/Pages/speechAIPAC060312.aspx.

72. At the time of its publication, the book exemplified the national zeitgeist. While not fiction, the work echoes Netanyahu's warnings of the dangers posed by Iran. Katz and Hendel, *Israel vs. Iran*.

73. Interview with Yaakov Katz, interview by Jonathan Leslie, Jerusalem, Israel, 27 October 2015.

74. Yaar and Hermann, 'The Peace Index', August 2012.

75. Ephraim Yaar and Tamar Hermann, 'The Peace Index', The Israel Democracy Institute, February 2012, https://web.archive.org/web/20210309100632/http://www.peaceindex.org/files/The%20Peace%20Index%20Data%20-%20February%202012.pdf.

76. Citing disagreements with his coalition partner Yisrael Beiteinu, Netanyahu called for early elections to be held in January 2015. Netanyahu's Likud won with a plurality of the vote (23.4%), picking up thirty seats. He defeated the combined Labor/Hatunah 'Zionist Union' party, which came in second. Netanyahu joined with Naftali Bennett's Jewish Home, United Torah Judaism, Kulanu, and Hatunah to form a governing coalition with the bare minimum of sixty-one seats.

77. Mairav Zonszein, 'Benjamin Netanyahu Just Formed the Most Right-Wing Government in Israeli History', *The Nation*, 25 May 2016, https://www.thenation.com/article/benjamin-netanyahu-just-formed-the-most-right-wing-government-in-israeli-history/.

78. 'The Spy Cables: A Glimpse Into the World of Espionage', Al Jazeera, 23 February 2015, https://www.aljazeera.com/news/2015/02/spy-cables-world-espionage-snowden-guardian-mi6-cia-ssa-mossad-iran-southafrica-leak-150218100147229.html.

79. Lucas reports that Defense Minister Barak and several top military officials told Netanyahu that they believed a military engagement would result in an unsatisfactory outcome similar to the 2006 war with Hezbollah in Lebanon. Scott Lucas, 'How Israel's Military Stopped Netanyahu Attacking Iran', *The Conversation*, 26 February 2015, http://theconversation.com/how-israels-military-stopped-netanyahu-attacking-iran-38009.

80. 'Cabinet Meeting Minutes', 18 February 2015, Israeli Prime Minister's Office.

81. The 'fundamentalist mind,' according to Hofstadter, is 'essentially Manichean; it looks upon the world as an arena for conflict between absolute good and absolute evil, and accordingly it scorns compromises (who would compromise with Satan?) and can tolerate no ambiguities. It cannot find serious importance in what

it believes to be trifling degrees of difference … the secularized fundamentalist mind begins with a definition of what is right, and looks upon politics as an arena in which that right must be realized.' Richard Hofstadter, *Anti-Intellectualism in American Life* (New York: Vintage, 2012), 135.

82. 'Cabinet Meeting Minutes', 25 January 2015, Israeli Prime Minister's Office.

83. In what was perhaps the biggest defection from Netanyahu's position on Israel, former Mossad Chief Meir Dagan said publicly in 2011 that an Israeli attack on Iran's nuclear facilities would be a 'stupid idea.' Isabel Kershner, 'Ex-Mossad Chief Warns Against Strike on Iran', *New York Times*, 8 May 2011, sec. Middle East, https://www.nytimes.com/2011/05/09/world/middleeast/09israel.html.

84. Michael Walzer, *The Paradox of Liberation: Secular Revolutions and Religious Counterrevolutions* (New Haven, CT: Yale University Press, 2015).

85. Ironically, developments in Iran followed a somewhat similar historic arc. The Shah's attempt to modernize his country discounted the political power of Islam. This enabled a fundamentalist cleric to mobilize popular support and succeed in overthrowing the Shah's regime. Not all supporters of the Islamic Revolution wanted a return to a theocratic society as much as they wanted an end to the increasingly dictatorial and terrorizing government of the Shah. Unlike Israel, the backlash in Iran occasioned a revolution, while in Israel the return of orthodoxy was evolutionary.

86. Adopting modern political strategies, they made it increasingly difficult for the political elites to oppose their demands for a greater role in government. Walzer notes that a commonality among states emerging from religious-based societies and embracing a secularized national liberation is that they are, like Israel, unable to sustain their secular vision for more than a couple of generations. Walzer, *The Paradox of Liberation*, 29. His observations are applicable to Iran both as a basis for understanding the secular support for the 1979 Revolution and as a warning for regime change that would seek to establish a secular government and deny a role to religious parties.

6.   IRAN AND ISRAEL IN THE AGE OF POPULISM

1.   In the United States, the Obama administration was contending with Republican opposition to passing comprehensive healthcare reform, and thus did not feel that it possessed the necessary political capital to take on an additional sensitive foreign policy challenge. This fact was further complicated by political turmoil in Iran, where in mid-2009 Ahmadinejad secured a second term of office in an election marred by accusations of fraud. Anger over the results triggered widespread protests that eventually became known as the Green Movement. The Iranian government violently suppressed these uprisings and placed its leaders, Mir Hussein Mousavi and Mehdi Karroubi, under house arrest. The controversy significantly weakened the Ahmadinejad administration and destroyed its credibility internationally as Western leaders condemned the election and its aftermath. Ghazvinian, *America and Iran*, 612–14.

2.   Anne Gearan, 'Kerry, Iran's Zarif Hold Unusual Private Meeting on Sidelines of Nuclear Talks', *Washington Post*, 26 September 2013, sec. National Security, https://www.washingtonpost.com/world/national-security/kerry-irans-zarif-hold-unusual-private-meeting-on-sidelines-of-nuclear-talks/2013/09/26/d2fddfac-2700-11e3-9372-92606241ae9c_story.html.

3.   The deal covered only economic sanctions specifically related to nuclear activities. Some economic sanctions related to Iran's human rights abuses, missile production activities, and support for terrorist organizations remained in place and were not affected by the deal.

4.   Both during the JCPOA negotiations and in the years since its signing, Iranian leaders have steadfastly insisted that missile production and the 'defense capabilities of the Islamic Republic of Iran are not negotiable.' Michelle Moghtader and Mehrdad Balali, 'Iran Leader Slams West's 'Stupid' Missile Stance Before Talks', *Reuters*, 11 May 2014, sec. World News, https://www.reuters.com/article/uk-iran-nuclear-idUKKBN0DR0IH20140511; Associated Press, 'Iran Will Not Negotiate With US Over Missile Program, Says Foreign Minister', *The Guardian*, 10 April 2016, sec. World news, https://www.theguardian.com/world/2016/apr/10/iran-missile-program-foreign-minister-john-kerry.

5.   The reduction in the number of operating centrifuges, for example, would expire in ten years, while limits on uranium enrichment and stockpiling were due to last fifteen years. There were also several restrictions on weapons programs, such as a heavy arms embargo and ballistic missile restrictions, that would last five and eight years respectively. While not addressing Iran's ballistic missile capabilities in a broad sense, the agreement also banned Iran from undertaking 'any activity related to ballistic missiles designed to be capable of delivering nuclear weapons.'

6.   The additional protocol grants the IAEA 'expanded rights of access to information and locations' in signatory states. States that decide to bring the additional protocols into force implement a series of comprehensive safeguard agreements (CSAs) that grant the IAEA broader access to information, increased physical access, and improved administrative agreements. 'Additional Protocol', International Atomic Energy Agency (IAEA), n.d., https://www.iaea.org/topics/additional-protocol.

7.   Speaking in New York in April 2015, Foreign Minister Javad Zarif called it 'laughable' that Benjamin Netanyahu has become 'everybody's nonproliferation guru.' Citing Israel's undeclared nuclear warhead stockpile, Zarif noted, 'Israel is not a member of the NPT, but those who provided them with the technology were members of the NPT and violated the NPT to provide them with the technology, and we know who they were. And now they are the proponents of nonproliferation.' Mohamad Javad Zarif, 'Zarif in New York: Nuke Deal, ISIS, Syria', (transcript) interview by David Ignatius, 29 April 2015, https://iranprimer.usip.org/blog/2015/apr/29/zarif-new-york-nuke-deal-isis-syria.

8.   Seyyed Hossein Mousavian, *The Iranian Nuclear Crisis: A Memoir* (Washington, DC: Carnegie Endowment for International Peace, 2012), 4.

9.   Graham Allison, 'Iran Already Has Nuclear Weapons Capability', Belfer Center for Science and International Affairs, 3 March 2015, https://www.belfercenter.org/publication/iran-already-has-nuclear-weapons-capability.

10. Niall McCarthy, 'Nuclear Deal: Iran's Opportunity to Replace Its Rusty Old Airliners?', *Forbes*, 17 July 2015, sec. Business, https://www.forbes.com/sites/niallmccarthy/2015/07/17/nuclear-deal-irans-opportunity-to-replace-its-rusty-old-airliners-infographic/.

11. Scott Lucas, 'How Iran's Hardliners Still Threaten the Nuclear Deal', *The Conversation*, 18 January 2016, http://theconversation.com/how-irans-hardliners-still-threaten-the-nuclear-deal-53236.

12. For more on how conservative forces took control of the Iranian economy, see Steve Stecklow, Babak Dehghanpisheh, and Yeganeh Torbati, 'Assets of the Ayatollah', Reuters, 11 November 2013, http://www.reuters.com/investigates/iran/.

13. Saeed Kamali Dehghan, 'Europe's Big Banks Remain Wary of Doing Business With Iran', *The Guardian*, 24 January 2016, sec. World news, https://www.theguardian.com/world/2016/jan/24/europes-big-banks-remain-wary-doing-business-with-iran.

14. In September 2015, the Republican-controlled Congress initiated efforts to reject the agreement. Following debate, the Senate voted on a resolution disapproving the deal, but fell two votes short of the necessary sixty-vote threshold to pass the measure. The House passed the resolution, but this was mostly a symbolic measure. 'The Final Tally: How Congress Voted on Iran', United States Institute of Peace, 17 September 2015, https://iranprimer.usip.org/blog/2015/sep/11/congress-votes-deal.

15. The JCPOA had lifted most nuclear-related sanctions against Iran, but sanctions relating to terrorism, human rights, and missile activities remained in place. The United States also retained the right to impose additional sanctions related to non-nuclear issues after implementation of the JCPOA.

16. Donald Trump, 'Donald Trump AIPAC Speech Transcript' AIPAC, Washington, DC, 21 March 2016, https://time.com/4267058/donald-trump-aipac-speech-transcript/.

17. These donors included casino magnate Sheldon Adelson and Home Depot founder Bernard Marcus. Adelson, in particular, had become a kingmaker in both GOP and Israeli political circles. His support of the pro-Netanyahu free newspaper *Yisrael Hayom*, discussed in Chapter 4, had distorted the Israeli media landscape and granted Netanyahu a significant political advantage.

18. In a 2015 policy speech at the Brookings Institution, Clinton called her approach to Iran 'distrust and verify.' She made clear, however, that she did not believe that the JCPOA was the start of a larger diplomatic opening, and that she still expected Iran and the United States to remain adversaries. William A. Galston, 'Hillary Clinton on the Iran Nuclear Deal: "Distrust and Verify"', Brookings, 9 September 2015, https://www.brookings.edu/blog/markaz/2015/09/09/hillary-clinton-on-the-iran-nuclear-deal-distrust-and-verify/.

19. Trump, who had never shown much interest in the wider world beyond his business interests, largely avoided discussion of complicated foreign policies. Thus, his rhetoric on the JCPOA was strategic. His emphasis on its flaws, as he saw them, allowed him to attack Obama as weak and gullible while touting his

stature as a dealmaker. At the same time, the United States was still party to the deal, and the consequences of abandoning it remained uncertain at best. Thus, Trump sent mixed messages while doubling down on racist rhetoric as he echoed Netanyahu's claim that Iranians could not be trusted.

20. Married to Trump's daughter Ivanka, who had converted to Judaism, the religiously observant Kushner served as a high-ranking campaign advisor before transitioning to the White House. He came from a wealthy New Jersey family of real estate developers who had hosted Netanyahu at their family home on several of Netanyahu's visits to America prior to becoming prime minister. Reportedly, Netanyahu had slept in Kushner's childhood bed during some of these trips.

21. Yeganeh Torbati, 'Trump Election Puts Iran Nuclear Deal on Shaky Ground', *Reuters*, 9 November 2016, https://www.reuters.com/article/us-usa-election-trump-iran-idUSKBN13427E.

22. Adam Entous, 'Donald Trump's New World Order', *The New Yorker*, 11 June 2018, https://www.newyorker.com/magazine/2018/06/18/donald-trumps-new-world-order.

23. Esfandyar Batmanghelidj, 'The Brexit Risk to the Iran Deal', *LobeLog* (blog), 24 June 2016, https://lobelog.com/the-brexit-risk-to-the-iran-deal/.

24. Alireza Ramezani, 'Why Iran Shouldn't Get Too Excited about Brexit', *Al-Monitor* (blog), 15 July 2016, https://www.al-monitor.com/pulse/originals/2016/07/iran-reactions-brexit-uk-exit-european-union.html.

25. Batmanghelidj, 'The Brexit Risk to the Iran Deal'.

26. Netanyahu also had a short meeting with Clinton during this trip, but for that meeting he was speaking to a candidate and campaign that kept informed about the Middle East and Iran issues.

27. Entous, 'Donald Trump's New World Order'.

28. Ishaan Tharoor, 'Israel's Netanyahu Isn't Worried About Steve Bannon and Anti-Semitism in Trump's Camp', *Washington Post*, 12 December 2016, https://www.washingtonpost.com/news/worldviews/wp/2016/12/12/israels-netanyahu-isnt-worried-about-steve-bannon-and-anti-semitism-in-trumps-camp/.

29. Benjamin Netanyahu, 'Stopping the Iranian Threat, and the Threat Reflected in the Bad Nuclear Agreement With Iran, Continues to Be a Supreme Goal of Israel,' Tweet, *@IsraeliPM*, 22 January 2017, https://twitter.com/IsraeliPM/status/823199619073142784.

30. Karen DeYoung, 'Trump Administration Says It's Putting Iran "on Notice" Following Missile Test', *Washington Post*, 1 February 2017, sec. National Security, https://www.washingtonpost.com/world/national-security/2017/02/01/fc5ce3d2-e8b0-11e6-80c2-30e57e57e05d_story.html.

31. IAEA Director General, 'Verification and Monitoring of the Islamic Republic of Iran in Light of United Nations Security Council Resolution 2231 (2015)', International Atomic Energy Agency, 24 February 2017, https://isis-online.org/uploads/iaea-reports/documents/IAEA_JCPOA_Report_24Feb2017.pdf.

32. Donald Trump and Benjamin Netanyahu, 'Transcript And Analysis: Trump and Netanyahu Hold Joint Press Conference', NPR, 15 February 2017, sec.

Politics, https://www.npr.org/2017/02/15/514986341/watch-live-trump-netanyahu-hold-joint-press-conference-at-white-house.

33. Ibid.

34. Ashley Parker and Josh Dawsey, 'Trump's Cable Cabinet: New Texts Reveal the Influence of Fox Hosts on Previous White House', *Washington Post*, 9 January 2022, https://www.washingtonpost.com/politics/trump-cable-cabinet/2022/01/09/96fac488-6fe6-11ec-b9fc-b394d592a7a6_story.html.

35. It would later be revealed that Hannity and Trump spoke on the phone 'most weeknights,' typically before going to bed. Olivia Nuzzi, 'Donald Trump and Sean Hannity Like to Talk Before Bedtime', *New York Magazine*, 14 May 2018, https://nymag.com/intelligencer/2018/05/sean-hannity-donald-trump-late-night-calls.html.

36. 'Paul Ryan: Plan for Implementing Trump's Agenda Is on Track; Netanyahu on US-Israel Relationship Under Trump' (transcript), Fox News, 15 March 2017, https://www.foxnews.com/transcript/paul-ryan-plan-for-implementing-trumps-agenda-is-on-track-netanyahu-on-us-israel-relationship-under-trump.

37. 'Benjamin Netanyahu's Interview With Sean Hannity on Fox News' (transcript), Fox News, 21 April 2017, https://www.foxnews.com/transcript/netanyahu-calls-on-palestinian-leaders-to-confront-terrorism.

38. 'Netanyahu Calls on Palestinian Leaders to Confront Terrorism' (transcript), Fox News, 22 April 2017, https://www.foxnews.com/transcript/netanyahu-calls-on-palestinian-leaders-to-confront-terrorism.

39. Michael Holden and James Williams, 'Israel's Netanyahu Urges Britain to Join Iran Sanctions', *Reuters*, 6 February 2017, sec. Top News, https://www.reuters.com/article/cnews-us-britain-israel-iran-idCAKBN15L1TX.

40. Although Israel withdrew from the Gaza Strip in 2005, it still maintained effective control over the movement of people and goods from the area.

41. Netanyahu expected that Trump would protect his position on negotiations. The new president gave the Middle East portfolio to his son-in-law Jared Kushner, who was most unlikely to produce a proposal objectionable to Israel. Kushner would then find it difficult to satisfy the Palestinians.

42. Benjamin Netanyahu, 'I'm Determined to Speak Before Congress to Stop Iran. RETWEET if I Have Your Support. http://T.Co/5qTb89xf2i', @netanyahu (Twitter), 10 February 2015, https://twitter.com/netanyahu/status/565148423507042305.

43. A characteristic Netanyahu tweet in praise of Trump appeared following Trump's decision to refuse to certify Iran's compliance with the JCPOA in October 2017: 'I congratulate @realDonaldTrump on his courageous decision. He boldly confronted Iran's terrorist regime.' Benjamin Netanyahu, 'I Congratulate @realDonaldTrump for His Courageous Decision. He Boldly Confronted Iran's Terrorist Regime. https://T.Co/1KaHM6jdFc', @netanyahu (Twitter), 14 October 2017, https://twitter.com/netanyahu/status/919255273524490241.

44. Seventeen months elapsed between the inauguration and Trump's announcement of America's withdrawal from the JCPOA.

45. Executive Order 13769 was issued on 27 January 2017 and was immediately subjected to a variety of court challenges. It was eventually superseded in March 2017 by Executive Order 13780, which imposed a variety of immigration and visa restrictions. NPR reported that the State Department claimed that roughly 60,000 individuals' visas were provisionally revoked.

46. Trump's action became known as the 'Muslim ban.' Several federal courts issued injunctions blocking enforcement of what they determined was an unconstitutional action. After losing several cases and an appeal, Trump signed a new Executive Order E.O. No. 13,780 (6 March 2017) with a narrower ban on entry from six predominantly Muslim countries. After additional court rulings, Trump issued a third version, which minimally enlarged the excluded class to include North Koreans and certain government officials in Venezuela. Although several lower courts again ruled the ban unconstitutional, the Supreme Court in a 5-4 decision upheld the order on 26 June 2018. *Trump v. Hawaii* 585 US (2018).

47. Mark Landler, 'Trump Recognizes Jerusalem as Israel's Capital and Orders U.S. Embassy to Move', *New York Times*, 6 December 2017, sec. World, https://www.nytimes.com/2017/12/06/world/middleeast/trump-jerusalem-israel-capital.html.

48. The initial meeting with Abbas occurred in May 2017. Ironically, while Abbas decried Trump's December announcement as an insult to the Palestinians, the president was reportedly insulted when he called Abbas to inform him of the pending announcement, and the Palestinian president hung up on him. The following year Trump cut aid to the Palestinians and to the United Nations Relief and Works Agency for Palestine Refugees. He also closed the American consulate in East Jerusalem, which had served as a quasi-embassy for the Palestinians in the West Bank and Gaza. This action limited American ties to the Palestinians and facilitated Israel's consolidation of power over the city. David M. Halbfinger, 'U.S. Folding Jerusalem Consulate Into Embassy, a Blow to Palestinians', *New York Times*, 18 October 2018, sec. World, https://www.nytimes.com/2018/10/18/world/middleeast/us-palestinians-consulate-jerusalem.html.

49. Zvi Bar'el, 'Netanyahu Using Iran as Another Excuse to Put Off Peace With Palestinians', *Haaretz*, 10 December 2013, https://www.haaretz.com/.premium-the-new-patron-in-the-conflict-1.5298358. Trump did not unveil the Kushner plan until 2020, at which time Netanyahu claimed that it authorized Israel to annex large swaths of the West Bank. *Times of Israel* Staff, '"What the Hell Was That?": Netanyahu Annexation Announcement Caught Trump off Guard', *The Times of Israel*, 14 December 2021, https://www.timesofisrael.com/what-the-hell-was-that-netanyahu-annexation-announcement-caught-trump-off-guard/.

50. US law required the administration to recertify Iran's compliance with the deal every ninety days. Certification was a largely symbolic measure, particular to the United States, and had no immediate impact on the deal's terms as negotiated by the P5+1. Withholding certification opened a sixty-day window during which the United States Congress had the opportunity to reintroduce legislation reimposing nuclear sanctions on Iran under an expedited process.

Kelsey Davenport, 'Understanding the U.S. Compliance Certification and Why It Matters to the Iran Nuclear Deal', Arms Control Association, 29 August 2017, https://www.armscontrol.org/blog/2017-08-29/understanding-us-compliance-certification-why-matters-iran-nuclear-deal.

51. Anne Gearan, '"He Threw a Fit": Trump's Anger Over Iran Deal Forced Aides to Scramble for a Compromise,' *Washington Post*, 11 October 2017, sec. Politics, https://www.washingtonpost.com/politics/he-threw-a-fit-trumps-anger-over-iran-deal-forced-aides-to-scramble-for-a-compromise/2017/10/11/6218174c-ae94-11e7-9e58-e6288544af98_story.html.

52. Donald Trump, 'Remarks by President Trump on Iran Strategy' Official Remarks, Washington, DC, 13 October 2017, accessed via https://web.archive.org/web/20180130154140/https://www.whitehouse.gov/briefings-statements/remarks-president-trump-iran-strategy/.

53. Steve Holland, 'Trump Issues Ultimatum to "Fix" Iran Nuclear Deal', *Reuters*, 12 January 2018, https://www.reuters.com/article/us-iran-nuclear-decision-idUSKBN1F108F.

54. United States Treasury Department, 'Treasury Sanctions Individuals and Entities for Human Rights Abuses and Censorship in Iran, and Support to Sanctioned Weapons Proliferators', 12 January 2018, https://home.treasury.gov/news/press-releases/sm0250.

55. See for example Mark Landler and David E. Sanger, 'Trump Disavows Nuclear Deal, but Doesn't Scrap It', *New York Times*, 13 October 2017, sec. U.S., https://www.nytimes.com/2017/10/13/us/politics/trump-iran-nuclear-deal.html. The *Times* described the debate as 'fierce.'

56. Eli Clifton, 'Follow the Money: Three Billionaires Paved Way for Trump's Iran deal Withdrawal,' *LobeLog* (blog), 8 May 2018, https://lobelog.com/three-billionaires-paved-way-for-trumps-iran-deal-withdrawal/.

57. Saudi Arabia, too, understood this point. During Trump's first foreign trip as president, which included stops in Riyadh followed by Israel in May 2017, the Saudis showered Trump with affection. Gestures included projecting his image on the façade of a Riyadh hotel, lavish official ceremonies, and numerous gifts. Annie Karni, 'Saudis Give Trump a Reception Fit for a King', POLITICO, 20 May 2017, https://www.politico.com/story/2017/05/20/donald-trump-saudi-arabia-visit-238638.

58. Trump's personal animosity toward Obama will likely be the subject of psychological studies in years to come. We know that the thin-skinned Trump was particularly angered by Obama publicly ridiculing him at a White House Correspondents Dinner in 2011, in which the former US president poked fun at Trump's obsession with the authenticity of Obama's birth certificate. As president, Trump's efforts to undo Obama's achievements were motivated at least in part by his jealousy of Obama's popularity.

59. After ending the Iran deal, Trump courted relations with North Korean dictator Kim Jong-un in 2018–19. It was never entirely clear what strategic benefits Trump sought for the United States in doing so. Based upon the historic nature of the three meetings with Kim, Trump pressured Japanese Prime Minister

Shinzo Abe to nominate him for the Nobel Peace Prize, claiming himself to be deserving of such a prize. Trump also courted Saudi Arabia's Crown Prince Mohammad Bin-Salman and excused his role in ordering the brutal murder and dismemberment of Saudi dissident journalist Jamal Khashoggi in October 2018.

60. Netanyahu's expressed position that Iran could not be trusted excluded his support for an improved deal. Since he likely realized Iran would not accept Trump's terms, he could feign agreement even if dissatisfied with the lack of action.

61. Ben Smith, 'The Iran Nuclear Deal and "Decertification"', Briefing Paper, House of Commons, 25 October 2017, 9.

62. Even the threat of secondary sanctions had the potential for quelling interest in investment in Iran. For many investors, the fear of getting frozen out of American markets and banking systems—and, by extension, most of the world—was too great a risk to take.

63. French President Emmanuel Macron made several efforts to present a plan for an enhanced JCPOA, which included extended deadlines for several measures as well as plans to address Iran's ballistic missile program. Iran categorically rejected these proposals, and Trump seemingly never gave them serious thought before withdrawing. Ahmad Majidyar, 'Iranian Leaders Reject Macron's Proposal to Supplement Nuclear Deal', Middle East Institute, 19 September 2017, https://www.mei.edu/publications/iranian-leaders-reject-macrons-proposal-supplement-nuclear-deal.

64. Beginning in the last week of December 2017, Iran was rocked by widespread protests that began in Mashhad and quickly spread across the country. Among the many frustrations expressed by protestors was that the JCPOA had failed to deliver its promised benefits.

65. Yaniv Kubovich et al., 'Israel Downs Iranian Drone, Strikes Syria; Israeli F-16 Shot Down,' *Haaretz*, 10 February 2018, https://www.haaretz.com/israel-news/red-alert-sirens-sound-heavy-aerial-activity-in-northern-israel-1.5806508.

66. Reuters Staff, 'Iran Rejects Reports of Israel Downing Iranian Drone as 'ridiculous' – State TV', *Reuters*, 10 February 2018, sec. World News, https://www.reuters.com/article/uk-mideast-crisis-iran-idUKKBN1FU0I4.

67. Anshel Pfeffer, 'Two Days On, Israel Still Puzzled Why Iran Sent Drone Into Its Airspace', *Haaretz*, 12 February 2018, https://www.haaretz.com/israel-news/.premium-israel-still-puzzled-why-iran-sent-drone-into-israeli-airspace-1.5809571.

68. Benjamin Netanyahu, 'PM Netanyahu Addresses Munich Security Conference 18 February 2018' Munich Security Conference, Munich, Germany, 18 February 2018.

69. Ibid.

70. Carl Schreck, 'Israel, Iran Trade Barbs at Munich Security Conference', *Radio Free Europe/Radio Liberty*, 18 February 2018, sec. Iran, https://www.rferl.org/a/munich-netanyahu-iran-greatest-threat/29046395.html.

71. Pompeo traveled to Saudi Arabia prior to arriving in Israel. In a meeting with King Salman and other officials, he made similar promises that the United States

would abandon the nuclear deal unless the Europeans agreed to try to improve it. Noa Landau and Jack Khoury, 'Pompeo After Meeting Netanyahu: If Iran Nuclear Deal Can't Be Fixed, It Will Be Nixed', *Haaretz*, 29 April 2018, https://www.haaretz.com/israel-news/netanyahu-and-pompeo-to-talk-iran-in-sunday-meeting-1.6034929.

72. 'FULL TEXT: Netanyahu Claims Iran Nuclear Deal Based on Lies', *Haaretz*, 30 April 2018, https://www.haaretz.com/israel-news/full-text-netanyahu-s-reveals-iran-s-atomic-archive-in-speech-1.6045556.

73. Ibid.

74. 'Israel's Netanyahu Can Now Declare War With Single Vote', Al Jazeera, 1 May 2018, https://www.aljazeera.com/news/2018/5/1/knesset-gives-power-to-pm-to-declare-war-with-single-vote-backing.

75. Andrew Marantz, 'How "Fox & Friends" Rewrites Trump's Reality', *The New Yorker*, 8 January 2018, https://www.newyorker.com/magazine/2018/01/15/how-fox-and-friends-rewrites-trumps-reality.

76. Zack Beauchamp, 'Netanyahu Went on Fox & Friends to Lobby Trump on the Iran Deal', *Vox*, 1 May 2018, https://www.vox.com/world/2018/5/1/17306726/netanyahu-fox-and-friends-trump-iran-deal.

77. Ibid.

78. Peter Beinart, 'Benjamin Netanyahu: TV Star', *The Atlantic*, 1 May 2018, https://www.theatlantic.com/international/archive/2018/05/netanyahu-trump-iran-nuclear-deal/559376/.

79. Barak Ravid, 'Netanyahu Briefed Trump on Iran's "Nuclear Archive" Two Months Ago', *Axios*, 1 May 2018, https://www.axios.com/netanyahu-briefed-trump-on-irans-nuclear-archive-f5717785-fbf0-4f62-9244-77afbe19e03b.html.

80. Roy Rubinstein and Itamar Eichner, 'Experts Say No New Information in Netanyahu's Iran Presentation', *Ynetnews*, 1 May 2018, https://www.ynetnews.com/articles/0,7340,L-5247532,00.html.

81. 'America's Mired Diplomacy', *Jamhuri-Ye Eslami* (via BBC Monitoring, London), 29 April 2018, http://search.proquest.com/docview/2032751218/citation/820464E3CF6141D1PQ/8.

82. 'آمریکا، اسرائیل و عربستان محور شرارت جدید هستند', IRNA, 25 May 2018, https://www.irna.ir/news/82925673/آمریکا-اسرائیل-و-عربستان-محور-شرارت-جدید-هستند.

83. TOI Staff, 'Netanyahu Hails Iranian People's "Courage" in Anti-Regime Protests', *The Times of Israel*, 27 June 2018, https://www.timesofisrael.com/netanyahu-hails-iranian-peoples-courage-in-anti-regime-protests/.

84. John Irish and Arshad Mohammed, 'Netanyahu, in U.N. Speech, Claims Secret Iranian Nuclear Site', *Reuters*, 27 September 2018, sec. Emerging Markets, https://www.reuters.com/article/us-un-assembly-israel-iran-idUSKCN1M72FZ.

85. Parsi's title referred to the United States and Barack Obama, but 'losing an enemy' was a risk to Netanyahu. Trita Parsi, *Losing an Enemy: Obama, Iran, and the Triumph of Diplomacy*, 1st edition (New Haven, CT: Yale University Press, 2017).

86. John R. Bolton, 'To Stop Iran's Bomb, Bomb Iran', *New York Times*, 26 March 2015, sec. Opinion, https://www.nytimes.com/2015/03/26/opinion/to-stop-irans-bomb-bomb-iran.html.

87. Bolton had become a regular featured speaker at events held by MEK, which was frequently described as a cult-like Marxist-Islamist group. Despite their unpopularity inside Iran, due partially to their support for Saddam Hussein's Iraq during the Iran-Iraq War, the MEK was frequently presented by Iran's Western opponents as a possible government-in-waiting following regime change. Until 2012, it had been listed on the State Department's Foreign Terrorist Organizations list due to its alleged role in killing American personnel in Iran in the 1970s. Developing close relationships with high-profile American politicians, including Bolton, had been a key part of the MEK's lobbying campaign to get itself removed from that list. During the annual 'Free Iran' gathering in Paris in July 2017, Bolton declared, 'I have said for over ten years since coming to these events, that the declared policy of the United States of America should be the overthrow of the mullahs' regime in Tehran.' He concluded his speech by promising the crowd that 'before 2019, we here will celebrate in Tehran.' Iran Freedom, *Excerpts from Amb. John Bolton's Speech at the Free Iran Gathering Paris 1 July 2017*, 2017, https://www.youtube.com/watch?v=hTMh24qlyQA; Jonathan Masters, 'Mujahadeen-e-Khalq (MEK)', Council on Foreign Relations, 28 July 2014, https://www.cfr.org/backgrounder/mujahadeen-e-khalq-mek.

88. Iran's electoral system requires a candidate to win a majority of the votes in order to become president. If a candidate fails to reach this threshold in the first round of balloting, a runoff vote is held between the two candidates with the highest vote share. In the 2017 election, Rouhani received a majority in the first round, defeating Raisi 57% to 38%. Thomas Erdbrink, 'Rouhani Wins Re-Election in Iran by a Wide Margin', *New York Times*, 20 May 2017, sec. World, https://www.nytimes.com/2017/05/20/world/middleeast/iran-election-hassan-rouhani.html.

89. INSTEX stood for 'Instrument in Support of Trade Exchanges.' Jean-Yves Le Drian, Heiko Maas, and Jeremy Hunt, 'Joint Statement on the Creation of INSTEX, the Special Purpose Vehicle Aimed at Facilitating Legitimate Trade With Iran in the Framework of the Efforts to Preserve the Joint Comprehensive Plan of Action (JCPOA)', 31 January 2019, https://www.diplomatie.gouv.fr/en/country-files/iran/news/article/joint-statement-on-the-creation-of-instex-the-special-purpose-vehicle-aimed-at.

90. In October 2019, Iran's central bank governor, Abdulnaser Hemmati, summed up the failure of the INSTEX initiative, saying, 'I have come to the conclusion that the issue is not with INSTEX and its mechanism. The issue is that the Europeans seem to need US approval for their plans.' Ruhollah Faghihi, 'Iran's Central Bank Chief Speaks Out on Currency Plunge, $15 Billion French Credit Line', Al-Monitor, 16 October 2019, https://www.al-monitor.com/originals/2019/10/iran-central-bank-governor-hemmati-rial-economy.html.

91. Secretary of State Mike Pompeo first announced the 'maximum pressure' strategy in a speech at the Reagan Library in California on 22 July 2018: 'We have an obligation to put maximum pressure on the regime's ability to generate and move money, and we will do so.' The campaign included the reimposition of sanctions on Iran's banking and energy sectors, and included an effort to reduce

Iranian crude exports to zero by 4 November 2018. Mike Pompeo, 'Secretary Pompeo's Remarks on "Supporting Iranian Voices"', Ronald Reagan Presidential Library, Simi Valley, CA, 22 July 2018, https://tr.usembassy.gov/secretary-pompeos-remarks-on-supporting-iranian-voices/.

92.   'Six Charts That Show How Hard US Sanctions Have Hit Iran', BBC News, 9 December 2019, sec. Middle East, https://www.bbc.com/news/world-middle-east-48119109.

93.   Steven Mufson and Damian Paletta, 'Boeing, Airbus to Lose $39 Billion in Contracts Because of Trump Sanctions on Iran', *Washington Post*, 9 May 2018, https://www.washingtonpost.com/business/economy/boeing-airbus-to-lose-39-billion-in-contracts-because-of-trump-sanctions-on-iran/2018/05/08/820a8f08-5308-11e8-a551-5b648abe29ef_story.html.

94.   Ariane M. Tabatabai and Colin P. Clarke, 'Iran's Proxies Are More Powerful Than Ever', RAND Corporation, 16 October 2019, https://www.rand.org/blog/2019/10/irans-proxies-are-more-powerful-than-ever.html.

95.   Associated Press, 'A Look at John Bolton's Tenure in Trump Administration', 10 September 2019, https://apnews.com/article/donald-trump-afghanistan-iran-john-bolton-north-korea-0d619b651c44470e975a1431e27fd57e.

96.   The story noted that Secretary of State Mike Pompeo confirmed the report and said that the meeting could take place during the upcoming United Nations General Assembly the following month. Peter Baker, 'Trump Ousts John Bolton as National Security Adviser', *New York Times*, 10 September 2019, sec. U.S., https://www.nytimes.com/2019/09/10/us/politics/john-bolton-national-security-adviser-trump.html.

97.   Aaron Heller, 'Israel Leader Scorned for Wooing Holocaust-Distorting Allies', AP NEWS, 30 January 2019, https://apnews.com/article/eastern-europe-ap-top-news-world-war-ii-lithuania-international-news-2b1eb6dbe0f44763b515fb b4c6398f2b.

98.   For example, in February 2018 the ruling Law and Justice Party in Poland had enacted a law which effectively banned anyone from accusing the Polish state of complicity in the Holocaust by threatening violators with imprisonment. The law sparked such widespread global criticism, even attracting pressure from the United States, that it was amended months later to remove the criminal penalty. Netanyahu's courting of Poland and Hungary may also have initially been part of an initiative involving sale of sophisticated Israeli cybersecurity software. According to a *New York Times* investigation, right-wing leaders who secured the coveted software that enabled the hacking of encrypted mobile phones often befriended Israel by siding with it on United Nations votes. In November 2016, Netanyahu and his wife entertained Polish Prime Minister Beata Szydlo and her foreign minister, Witold Waszczyknowski, at a dinner in their home. Soon thereafter, Poland purchased the Pegasus software system. Israel did not suspend the order even after Poland enacted its Holocaust denial legislation. Sasha Ingber, 'Poland Backtracks on a Controversial Holocaust Speech Law,' NPR, 27 June 2018, sec. Europe, https://www.npr.org/2018/06/27/623865367/poland-backtracks-on-a-controversial-holocaust-speech-law; Ronen Bergman and Mark Mazzetti,

'The Battle for the World's Most Powerful Cyberweapon,' *New York Times*, 28 January 2022, sec. Magazine, https://www.nytimes.com/2022/01/28/magazine/nso-group-israel-spyware.html.

99. Lahav Harkov, 'Israel Asks IAEA Member Hungary to Act on Iran Nuclear Violations', *Jerusalem Post*, 20 July 2018, https://www.jpost.com/arab-israeli-conflict/israel-asks-iaea-member-hungary-to-act-on-iran-nuclear-violations-635698.

100. Also known as the European Quartet, the alliance of the four central European countries promotes military, cultural, and economic cooperation as well as integration into the European Union.

101. The meeting was canceled after Morawiecki refused to attend because Netanyahu reportedly said that the 'Poles cooperated with the Germans' during the Holocaust. Netanyahu's office insisted that he was 'misquoted.' Noa Landau, 'Israel to Host Summit for Europe's Emerging Nationalist Bloc', *Haaretz*, 28 January 2019, https://www.haaretz.com/israel-news/.premium-israel-to-host-summit-of-visegrad-group-of-central-european-governments-in-february-1.6878150; Oliver Holmes, 'Summit Cancelled as Israel and Poland Row over Holocaust', *The Guardian*, 18 February 2019, sec. World news, https://www.theguardian.com/world/2019/feb/18/polish-israel-visit-holocaust.

102. David E. Sanger and Marc Santora, 'Anti-Iran Message Seeps Into Trump Forum Billed as Focusing on Mideast Security', *New York Times*, 13 February 2019, sec. World, https://www.nytimes.com/2019/02/13/world/middleeast/warsaw-summit-pompeo.html.

103. British Foreign Minister Jeremy Hunt attended but reportedly refused to talk about Iran. Poland's Foreign Minister, Jacek Czaputowicz, said that Iran's presence at the conference would hamper discussion and that the language Tehran uses is 'hard to accept.' Jo Harper, 'Poland Excludes Tehran From Warsaw's Iran Conference', *Forbes*, 22 January 2019, sec. Small Business, https://www.forbes.com/sites/joharper/2019/01/22/poland-excludes-tehran-from-warsaws-iran-conference/.

104. Sanger and Santora, 'Anti-Iran Message Seeps Into Trump Forum Billed as Focusing on Mideast Security'.

105. *Times of Israel* Staff, 'Netanyahu Appears to Call for War With Iran', *The Times of Israel*, 13 February 2019, https://www.timesofisrael.com/liveblog_entry/netanyahu-appears-to-call-for-war-with-iran/.

106. Netanyahu, speaking in Hebrew, used the word '*milchama,*' which can also mean combatting. A similar Tweet from the official prime minister's account in English had used the word 'war,' until it was deleted and replaced with 'combating.' Sanger and Santora, 'Anti-Iran Message Seeps Into Trump Forum Billed as Focusing on Mideast Security'.

107. '"Poland's Hosting Anti-Iran Conference an Insult to Europe"', *Tehran Times*, 15 January 2019, sec. Politics, https://www.tehrantimes.com/news/431904/Poland-s-hosting-anti-Iran-conference-an-insult-to-Europe.

108. The trigger for the new elections nominally came from disagreements within the governing coalition over a law that would extend the military draft to the

Jewish ultra-orthodox population, who since the founding of the state had been exempt from service. For Netanyahu, there were additional considerations surrounding official investigations into corruption during his time as prime minister. Remaining in his post thus took on an added element of importance for Netanyahu as he sought to retain some authority over the investigation and possible looming indictments. He would eventually be charged with breach of trust, accepting bribes, and fraud in November 2019. Josef Federman, 'Scandals Brewing, Netanyahu Calls Early Election for April', AP NEWS, 24 December 2018, https://apnews.com/article/ap-top-news-elections-international-news-jerusalem-middle-east-6db1e4d5ecc04c78ac5dca34a2407ed9.

109. Zipi Israeli, 'National Security Index Public Opinion Survey 2018–2019' (Tel Aviv, Israel: Institute for National Strategic Studies, 2019, 2018), https://www.inss.org.il/wp-content/uploads/2019/01/%D7%9E%D7%93%D7%93-%D7%94%D7%91%D7%99%D7%98%D7%97%D7%95%D7%9F-%D7%94%D7%9C%D7%90%D7%95%D7%9E%D7%99-%D7%91%D7%90%D7%A0%D7%92%D7%9C%D7%99%D7%AA-2019.pdf.

110. *Reuters* Staff, 'Netanyahu's Likud Uses Trump Photo in Israeli Election Billboard', *Reuters*, 3 February 2019, https://www.reuters.com/article/us-israel-election-trump-idUSKCN1PS07A.

111. David M. Halbfinger and Ronen Bergman, 'Gantz, Netanyahu's Challenger, Faces Lurid Questions After Iran Hacked His Phone', *New York Times*, 15 March 2019, sec. World, https://www.nytimes.com/2019/03/15/world/middleeast/gantz-netanyahus-challenger-faces-lurid-questions-after-iran-hacked-his-phone.html.

112. Benjamin Netanyahu, 'גנץ, איזה חומר איראן מחזיקה עליך? מדינת ישראל צריכה ראש ממשלה חזק ולא סחיט שיעמוד איתן מול האויבים שלנו https://t.co/lmAeuGg8yY', @netanyahu (Twitter), 20 March 2019, https://twitter.com/netanyahu/status/1108387654477991936.

113. Technically, the Blue and White Party was a 'centrist alliance' of three parties—including Israel Resilience Party, Yesh Atid, and Telem—which formed to defeat Netanyahu. Gantz did not lead all parties but was the designated candidate for prime minister.

114. Israelis cast votes for parties, and seats are allotted to each party in proportion to its share of the total vote received. Israel has many political parties and an electorate divided over religious issues that inhibit compromise. Recently, governments have been coalitions of several parties confected in complex negotiations following general elections. The parties designate the leader who will serve as prime minister if it secures a majority of the seats. If no party wins sixty-one seats, the president directs the leader of the party receiving the most votes to try to form a government by negotiating with other parties to secure their willingness to join a coalition government. If this cannot be accomplished within twenty-eight days, the president may designate another candidate to try or may allow any member elected to the Knesset to do so. Other than performing this function, the president serves a largely ceremonial function.

115. 'Netanyahu Hails Israel Strikes Against Syria to Foil Iran "Killer Drone Attack"', *The Guardian*, 24 August 2019, sec. World news, http://www.theguardian.com/world/2019/aug/25/netanyahu-hails-israel-strikes-against-syria-to-foil-iran-killer-drone-attack.

116. Benjamin Netanyahu, 'PM Netanyahu: 'If Someone Rises Up to Kill You, Kill Him First.' In a Complicated Operation by the Security Establishment, We Revealed That Iran's Quds Force Dispatched a Special Unit of Shi'ite Militants to Syria to Kill Israelis on the Golan Heights With Explosives-Laden UAVs. https://T.Co/D2vIZwTc8S', @IsraeliPM (Twitter), 25 August 2019, https://twitter.com/IsraeliPM/status/1165645141849382913.

117. Raphael Ahren, 'Netanyahu Reveals Site Where Iran "Experimented on Nuclear Weapons Development"', *The Times of Israel*, 9 September 2019, https://www.timesofisrael.com/pm-reveals-secret-site-where-iran-experimented-on-nuclear-weapons-development/.

118. Blue and White received one more seat than Likud, although Netanyahu was granted the first opportunity to form a government. When he failed to do so, Blue and White was also given an opportunity, but they, too, failed. Unable to arrive at any compromise, the Knesset voted to dissolve and schedule a new election for March 2020.

119. Traditionally, comparatively few Arab Israelis voted in the general elections.

120. Isabel Kershner, 'Facebook Suspends Netanyahu Campaign Bot for Hate Speech', *The New York Times*, 12 September 2019, sec. World, https://www.nytimes.com/2019/09/12/world/middleeast/facebook-netanyahu-bot.html.

121. Benjamin Netanyahu, 'בני גנץ משתמש בכל תירוץ כדי שלא להקים את הממשלה שאזרחי ישראל רוצים: ממשלת אחדות לאומית. בעוד הליכוד הסכים לויתורים רבים כדי להקים ממשלה, גנץ עוד לא מוכן לדון במתווה הנשיא. גנץ גורר את ישראל לבחירות מיותרות בזמן שישראל זקוקה לממשלת אחדות חזקה מול איראן שמסכנת את קיומנו.', @netanyahu (Twitter), 8 November 2019, https://twitter.com/netanyahu/status/1192788803930480641.

122. *Times of Israel* Staff, 'Knesset Dissolves, Sets Unprecedented Third Election in Under a Year', *The Times of Israel*, 12 December 2019, https://www.timesofisrael.com/israel-calls-another-election-for-march-the-third-in-a-year/.

123. On 1 January 2020, Netanyahu asked parliament to pass legislation that would grant him immunity from prosecution. Israeli law allows members of the Knesset to seek immunity from prosecution via authorization of a special panel followed by a majority vote in parliament. The measure ultimately failed. Isabel Kershner, 'Netanyahu Seeks Immunity From Israeli Corruption Charges', *New York Times*, 1 January 2020, sec. World, https://www.nytimes.com/2020/01/01/world/middleeast/israel-netanyahu-immunity.html.

124. For example, a report of a probe into Russian interference in the 2016 presidential election concluded it could not recommend that Trump be indicted for obstruction of justice because he was the sitting president. Questions remained about his vulnerability after leaving office. Trump knew that New York officials were scrutinizing his business practices for corrupt activity. He had also been sued by a woman accusing him of sexual misconduct and defamation.

Trump could only guess at whether the many investigations of his conduct and finances would reveal additional evidence of potential wrongdoing.

125. A discussion of Soleimani's portrayal in Western media appears in Dexter Filkins, 'The Shadow Commander', *The New Yorker*, 23 September 2013, http://www.newyorker.com/magazine/2013/09/30/the-shadow-commander.

126. ISNA, 11 ,'ترور سردار سلیمانی مصداق بارز تروریسم دولتی و نقض حقوق بین‌الملل است', July 2020, https://www.isna.ir/news/99042114934/نقض-حقوق-بین-الملل-ترور-سردار-سلیمانی-مصداق-بارز-تروریسم-دولتی-و.

127. 'Iran's Parliament Designates All US Forces as "Terrorists"', Al Jazeera, 7 January 2020, https://www.aljazeera.com/news/2020/1/7/irans-parliament-designates-all-us-forces-as-terrorists.

128. Initially, Secretary of State Mike Pompeo claimed that the assassination prevented an imminent attack Soleimani was planning against American targets. Veronica Stracqualursi and Jennifer Hansler, 'Pompeo: Strike on Soleimani Disrupted an "Imminent Attack"', CNN, 3 January 2020, https://www.cnn.com/2020/01/03/politics/mike-pompeo-iran-soleimani-strike-cnntv/index.html; Caitlin Oprysko, 'Trump Claims Soleimani Was Planning To Blow up U.S. Embassy', POLITICO, 9 January 2020, https://www.politico.com/news/2020/01/09/trump-soleimani-embassy-plot-096717.

129. *Times of Israel* Staff, 'Israeli Lawmakers Praise US for Killing Iranian "Arch-Terrorist" Soleimani', *The Times of Israel*, 3 January 2020, https://www.timesofisrael.com/israeli-lawmakers-praise-us-for-killing-iranian-arch-terrorist-soleimani/.

130. Netanyahu spoke of Trump 'acting with determination, strongly and swiftly.' Gantz called the decision 'brave.' *Times of Israel* Staff, 'Netanyahu Lauds Trump for Killing of Iran's Soleimani, Says Israel Stands by US', *The Times of Israel*, 3 January 2020, https://www.timesofisrael.com/netanyahu-lauds-trump-for-killing-of-irans-soleimani-says-israel-stands-by-us/.

131. Barak Ravid, 'Netanyahu Tells Security Cabinet Israel Must Not Be Dragged Into Soleimani Killing', Axios, 6 January 2020, https://www.axios.com/netanyahu-israel-iran-soleimani-killing-b846c02b-f592-4b56-9827-9310cac092b8.html.

132. *Times of Israel* Staff, 'TV: Israel Was Likely Warned of US Plans to Kill Soleimani', *The Times of Israel*, 3 January 2020, https://www.timesofisrael.com/tv-israel-likely-warned-of-us-plans-to-kill-soleimani/.

133. Peter Baker et al., 'Seven Days in January: How Trump Pushed U.S. and Iran to the Brink of War', *New York Times*, 11 January 2020, sec. US, https://www.nytimes.com/2020/01/11/us/politics/iran-trump.html.

134. Israel confirmed its role in the attack in December 2021, when ex-military intelligence chief Major General Tamir Hayman told *Malam* magazine that the killing was one of 'two significant and important assassinations' during his tenure. According to Hayman, 'Assassinating Soleimani was an achievement, since our main enemy, in my eyes, are the Iranians.' i24NEWS, 'Ex-Military Intel Chief: Israel Was Involved In Soleimani Assassination', i24news, 20 December 2021, https://www.i24news.tv/en/news/israel/diplomacy-defense/1640017040-ex-military-intel-chief-israel-was-involved-in-soleimani-assassination; Jack Murphy and Zach Dorfman, '"Conspiracy Is Hard": Inside

the Trump Administration's Secret Plan to Kill Qassem Soleimani', *Yahoo! News*, 8 May 2021, https://news.yahoo.com/conspiracy-is-hard-inside-the-trump-administrations-secret-plan-to-kill-qassem-soleimani-090058817.html.

135. Reuters Staff, 'Iran's Zarif Says Soleimani Killing Will Boost Resistance in Region', *Reuters*, 3 January 2020, sec. World News, https://www.reuters.com/article/uk-iraq-security-blast-iranforeignminist-idUKKBN1Z209H.

136. 'Iran's Parliament Designates All US Forces as "Terrorists"'.

137. Barak Ravid, 'Trump Felt Used on Soleimani Strike: "Israel Did Not Do the Right Thing"', Axios, 15 December 2021, https://www.axios.com/trump-soleimani-strike-netanyahu-israel-8f1abba2-5c05-4909-adee-ef872e9becb4.html.

138. In a characteristically Trump move, the president bragged that no one had been seriously injured. When it emerged that those in the area of the attack had suffered debilitating concussive trauma, Trump refused to acknowledge their injuries or award those injured the Purple Heart medal, calling their injuries 'headaches' and saying that he '[did not] consider them very serious.' President Biden, who succeeded Trump, corrected the record and awarded the medals. 'Army to Award Purple Hearts to Troops Injured in Iran Missile Attack Downplayed by Trump', Axios, 9 December 2021, https://www.axios.com/army-purple-hearts-iran-missile-attack-troops-iraq-8bedfc6b-cb99-4099-a55b-c3e1142122f0.html.

139. Notably, even as Iran announced its intention to abandon its commitments to the deal, it declared it would continue cooperation with the IAEA and would return to the deal if sanctions were removed. Alissa J. Rubin et al., 'Iran Ends Nuclear Limits as Killing of Iranian General Upends Mideast', *New York Times*, 5 January 2020, sec. World, https://www.nytimes.com/2020/01/05/world/middleeast/iran-general-soleimani-iraq.html.

140. The increased tension produced a particularly tragic incident. Iranian forces accidentally shot down a Ukrainian civilian airliner shortly after takeoff from Tehran's Imam Khomeini airport. After initial denials, Iranian officials eventually admitted under pressure that the IRGC had mistaken the departing plane for an incoming cruise missile. 'Iran Plane Crash: Demands for Justice After Admission Jet Was Shot Down', BBC News, 11 January 2020, sec. Middle East, https://www.bbc.com/news/world-middle-east-51077788.

141. Independent candidates, including several seats reserved for religious minorities, accounted for the remaining eighty-three seats. Turnout was 62% for the first round and 59% for the second round. Farzan Sabet, 'Iran's 2016 Elections: Change or Continuity?', Carnegie Endowment for International Peace, 9 June 2016, https://carnegieendowment.org/2016/06/09/iran-s-2016-elections-change-or-continuity-pub-63782.

142. Parisa Hafezi, 'Iran Announces Low Poll Turnout, Blames Coronavirus "Propaganda"', *Reuters*, 23 February 2020, sec. Emerging Markets, https://www.reuters.com/article/us-iran-election-khamenei-idUSKCN20H09Z.

143. Reuters, 'Market in China's Wuhan Likely Origin of COVID-19 Outbreak—Scientist', *Reuters*, 19 November 2021, sec. World, https://www.reuters.com/world/market-chinas-wuhan-likely-origin-covid-19-outbreak-study-2021-11-19/.

144. Erin Cunningham, 'As Coronavirus Cases Explode in Iran, U.S. Sanctions Hinder Its Access to Drugs and Medical Equipment', *Washington Post*, 29 March 2020, https://www.washingtonpost.com/world/middle_east/as-coronavirus-cases-explode-in-iran-us-sanctions-hinder-its-access-to-drugs-and-medical-equipment/2020/03/28/0656a196-6aba-11ea-b199-3a9799c54512_story.html.

145. Javad Zarif, '@realDonaldTrump Is Maliciously Tightening US' Illegal Sanctions With Aim of Draining Iran's Resources Needed in the Fight Against #COVID19—While Our Citizens Are Dying From It. The World Can No Longer Be Silent as US #EconomicTerrorism Is Supplanted by Its #MedicalTerrorism', @JZarif (Twitter), 7 March 2020, https://twitter.com/JZarif/status/1236278774750158849.

146. 'This Week in Iran Policy', Fact Sheet, US Department of State, 20 March 2020, https://2017-2021.state.gov/this-week-in-iran-policy-6/.

147. Joe Biden, 'Opinion: Joe Biden: There's a Smarter Way To Be Tough on Iran', CNN, 13 September 2020, https://www.cnn.com/2020/09/13/opinions/smarter-way-to-be-tough-on-iran-joe-biden/index.html.

148. Carol Morello, 'Pompeo Calls It "Just Nuts" To Allow Iran To Trade in Arms as U.N. Rejects Embargo Extension', *Washington Post*, 14 August 2020, https://www.washingtonpost.com/national-security/pompeo-calls-it-just-nuts-to-allow-iran-to-trade-in-arms-as-critical-un-vote-nears/2020/08/14/68e2ee84-de2b-11ea-b4af-72895e22941d_story.html.

149. Steve Hendrix, Ruth Eglash, and Anne Gearan, 'Jared Kushner Put a Knife "in Netanyahu's Back" over Annexation Delay, Says Israeli Settler Leader', *Washington Post*, 4 February 2020, https://www.washingtonpost.com/world/middle_east/reports-jared-kushner-angers-netanyahu-camp-by-slowing-annexation-moves/2020/02/04/82376ac6-4719-11ea-91ab-ce439aa5c7c1_story.html.

150. The UAE made abandonment a condition of joining the Abraham Accords. According to reporting by Israeli journalist Barak Ravid, Netanyahu nearly withdrew from the accords the day before signing due to concerns that scrapping the annexation plan could cost him votes in the next election. Barak Ravid, 'Netanyahu's Cold Feet Almost Killed the Abraham Accords', Axios, 13 December 2021, https://www.axios.com/abraham-accords-negotiations-netanyahu-trump-29d48b00-6407-4d47-b576-cdf4155aa71e.html.

151. The September ceremony for the Abraham Accords included The United Arab Emirates and Bahrain. The UAE and Israel had signed a normalization agreement in August 2020. Morocco and Israel signed a normalization agreement in December 2020 following the United States' agreement to recognize Morocco's claim over the Western Sahara region.

152. Michael Crowley and David M. Halbfinger, 'A White House Ceremony Will Celebrate a Diplomatic Win and Campaign Gift', *New York Times*, 14 September 2020, sec. US, https://www.nytimes.com/2020/09/14/us/politics/trump-middle-east-accords.html.

153. In a strategy document issued half a year after the end of the Trump administration, the Abraham Accord Peace Institute—the organization created

by Jared Kushner—wrote, 'Importantly, the Accords serve to constrain shared threats from the Islamic Republic of Iran *while simultaneously* constraining the malign influence and practices of China and Russia.' Trita Parsi, 'A Better Way in the Middle East', *The American Prospect*, 15 December 2021, https://prospect.org/api/content/0150218e-5d45-11ec-b3df-12f1225286c6/; 'Abraham Accords Peace Institute Annual Strategy', Abraham Accords Peace Institute, 27 August 2021, https://www.politico.com/f/?id=0000017d-0fdf-d3c9-a77d-0fdf36d30000.

154. Donald Trump and Benjamin Netanyahu, 'Remarks Prior to a Meeting With Prime Minister Benjamin Netanyahu of Israel and an Exchange With Reporters' (transcript), Washington, DC, 15 September 2020, https://www.presidency.ucsb.edu/documents/remarks-prior-meeting-with-prime-minister-benjamin-netanyahu-israel-and-exchange-with-5.

CONCLUSION

1. Yair Lapid, a former TV anchor, founded the Yesh Atid party in 2012. After allying with Netanyahu's Likud following the 2013 general elections, in which Yesh Atid placed second, it moved to the opposition following the 2015 snap elections. Lapid joined forces with Benny Gantz in 2019 to form the Blue and White Party. Although Gantz was put forth as the possible prime minister, Lapid and Gantz co-led the party for the next three elections. Lapid split with Gantz ahead of the 2021 elections, placing Yesh Atid back on the ballot for the first time since 2015. Gantz remained the leader of Blue and White. Yesh Atid garnered seventeen seats to Blue and White's eight. Together the two parties' twenty-five seats were fewer than the thirty seats won by Likud.

2. The final coalition consisted of Yesh Atid, Blue and White, Yamina, Labor, Yisrael Beiteinu, New Hope, Meretz, and the United Arab List.

3. 'Iran's Ebrahim Raisi: The Hardline Cleric Who Became President', BBC News, 5 August 2021, sec. Middle East, https://www.bbc.com/news/world-middle-east-57421235.

4. 'Iran's Ebrahim Raisi'.

5. Earlier in his career, he had served as a judge and a state prosecutor and was accused of responsibility for thousands of death sentences handed down by revolutionary courts. He was appointed Iran's chief justice in 2019.

6. Tamar Hermann and Or Anabi, 'Does Iran Pose an Existential Threat? Israeli Voice Index November 2021', Israeli Voice Index, Israel Democracy Institute, 8 December 2021, https://en.idi.org.il/articles/36760.

7. Bennett's party, Yamina, contributed only seven seats to the necessary sixty-one needed to form the coalition, meaning if the government collapsed Bennett was in a relatively weak position to try to regain his standing in another general election. There was also tension within his own Yamina party over its participation in a coalition with parties from the left and the Arab Joint List. Netanyahu had tried to convince disgruntled Yamina MKs to defect to his coalition during government formation talks. One Yamina MK, Amichai Chikli, voted against the

coalition during the investiture vote to authorize the new government. *Times of Israel* Staff, 'Yamina MK Doubles Down on Opposing Coalition With the Left', *The Times of Israel*, 6 May 2021, https://www.timesofisrael.com/yamina-mk-doubles-down-on-opposing-coalition-with-the-left/.

8. Lahav Harkov, 'Bennett: We Want Partners Against Iran but Will Act Either Way', *Jerusalem Post*, 15 September 2021, https://www.jpost.com/israel-news/bennett-we-want-partners-against-iran-but-will-act-either-way-679508.

9. Bennett also echoed Netanyahu's other hardline positions, indicating that he planned to expand Israeli settlements in the West Bank and opposed US plans to reopen its consulate for Palestinian affairs in Jerusalem. He also rejected the idea of pursuing a peace agreement with the Palestinians during his tenure as prime minister. Patrick Kingsley and Isabel Kershner, 'New Israeli Leader Backs Hard Line on Iran but Softer Tone With U.S.', *New York Times*, 24 August 2021, sec. World, https://www.nytimes.com/2021/08/24/world/middleeast/israel-bennett-biden-iran.html.

10. Ibid.

11. Jonathan Lis, 'FULL TEXT: Bennett's UN Speech—Iran, COVID, and Not One Mention of Palestinians', *Haaretz*, 27 September 2021, https://www.haaretz.com/israel-news/full-text-bennett-s-un-speech-iran-covid-and-not-one-mention-of-palestinians-1.10246065.

12. Lazar Berman, 'PMO: Bennett's UN Speech Will Be Unlike Netanyahu's; Ex-PM: He Can Learn from Me', *The Times of Israel*, 23 September 2021, https://www.timesofisrael.com/pmo-bennetts-un-speech-will-be-unlike-netanyahus-ex-pm-he-can-learn-from-me/.

13. Lahav Harkov and Yonah Jeremy Bob, 'Bennett: Israel Won't Be Obligated to Iran Deal If US Returns', *Jerusalem Post*, 23 November 2021, https://www.jpost.com/breaking-news/iran-has-surrounded-israel-with-its-proxies-bennett-685750.

14. Ibid.

15. Jonathan Lis, 'Gantz Says He Instructed Israeli Army to Prepare Military Option Against Iran', *Haaretz*, 11 December 2021, https://www.haaretz.com/israel-news/.premium-israeli-army-has-been-instructed-to-prepare-military-option-against-iran-gantz-says-1.10457857.

16. 'Former Mossad Chief: Netanyahu's Iran Policy Was a "Dismal Failure"', *Haaretz*, 12 October 2021, https://www.haaretz.com/israel-news/former-mossad-chief-netanyahu-s-iran-policy-may-be-a-historic-failure-1.10287997.

17. Shira Rubin, 'Israel Opposed the Iran Nuclear Deal, but Former Israeli Officials Increasingly Say U.S. Pullout Was a Mistake', *Washington Post*, 9 December 2021, https://www.washingtonpost.com/world/middle_east/israel-iran-nuclear-deal-sanctions/2021/12/08/ece28168-56c0-11ec-8396-5552bef55c3c_story.html.

18. Harriet Sherwood, 'Ehud Barak Restates Case for Military Strike on Iran's Nuclear Programme', *The Guardian*, 30 April 2012, sec. World news, https://www.theguardian.com/world/2012/apr/30/ehud-barak-iran-nuclear-programme.

19.   Ehud Barak, 'What Israel Must Do to Stop Iran's Nuclear Program', *Ynetnews*, 5 December 2021, https://www.ynetnews.com/article/h1wuk11qfk.

20.   Ibid.

21.   Snyder, *On Tyranny*, 123.

22.   Ibid., 123–4.

BIBLIOGRAPHY

عصر ایران. 'انتقاد عجیب از مشایی و احمدی نژاد: با انداختن چفیه بر گردن کوروش به بسیج توهین اشد!', 13 September 2010. http://www.asriran.com/fa/news/135963.

'נציגות ישראל בטהרן', 22 November 1962. Israel State Archives.

'43rd Meeting of the 19th Knesset', 19 June 2013. Knesset Transcripts.

'44th Meeting of the 17th Knesset', 11 July 2007. Knesset Transcripts.

'54th Meeting of the 13th Knesset', 20 January 1993. Knesset Transcripts.

'77th Meeting of the 17th Knesset', 25 July 2007. Knesset Transcripts.

'98th Meeting of the 13th Knesset', 11 January 1995. Knesset Transcripts.

'236th Meeting of the 16th Knesset', 21 March 2005. Knesset Transcripts.

'264th Meeting of the 16th Knesset', 29 June 2005. Knesset Transcripts.

'272nd Meeting of the 11th Knesset', 24 December 1986. Knesset Transcripts.

'284th Meeting of the 16th Knesset', 2 November 2005. Knesset Transcripts.

'Abraham Accords Peace Institute Annual Strategy'. Abraham Accords Peace Institute, 27 August 2021. https://www.politico.com/f/?id=0000017d-0fdf-d3c9-a77d-0fdf36d30000.

'Address by Foreign Minister Shamir to the World Jewish Congress', 21 January 1981. Israel Ministry of Foreign Affairs Documents.

Adib-Moghaddam, Arshin. *A Critical Introduction to Khomeini*. Cambridge; New York, NY: Cambridge University Press, 2014.

Afkhami, Gholam Reza. *The Life and Times of the Shah*. Oakfield, CA: University of California Press, 2009.

Ahren, Raphael. 'Netanyahu Reveals Site Where Iran "Experimented on Nuclear Weapons Development"'. *The Times of Israel*, 9 September 2019. https://www.timesofisrael.com/pm-reveals-secret-site-where-iran-experimented-on-nuclear-weapons-development/.

Akerman, Lior. 'Rouhani and His Shy, Sweet Smile'. *Jerusalem Post*, 22 November 2013.

Al Jazeera. 'Israel's Netanyahu Can Now Declare War with Single Vote', 1 May 2018. https://www.aljazeera.com/news/2018/5/1/knesset-gives-power-to-pm-to-declare-war-with-single-vote-backing.

Al Jazeera. 'The Spy Cables: A Glimpse into the World of Espionage', 23 February 2015. https://www.aljazeera.com/news/2015/02/spy-cables-world-espionage-snowden-guardian-mi6-cia-ssa-mossad-iran-southafrica-leak-150218100147229.html.

Al-e Ahmad, Jalal. *The Israeli Republic: An Iranian Revolutionary's Journey to the Jewish State*. Translated by Samuel Thrope. Translation edition. Brooklyn: Restless Books, 2017.

Ali, Mehrunnisa. 'The Changing Pattern of India-Iran Relations'. *Pakistan Horizon* 28, no. 4 (1975): 53–66.

Allison, Graham. 'Iran Already Has Nuclear Weapons Capability'. Belfer Center for Science and International Affairs, 3 March 2015. https://www.belfercenter.org/publication/iran-already-has-nuclear-weapons-capability.

Allon, Gideon. '2009 גרעינית יכולת עם איראן'. *Israel Hayom*, 7 November 2007. http://digital-edition.israelhayom.co.il/Olive/ODE/Israel/Default.aspx?href=ITD%2F2007%2F11%2F07.

Alon, Gideon. 'Concerned About Syria and Iran'. *Haaretz*, 4 August 2003. http://www.haaretz.com/concerned-about-syria-and-iran-1.96152.

Alpher, Yossi. *Periphery: Israel's Search for Middle East Allies*. Lanham, MD: Rowman & Littlefield Publishers, 2015.

Amanat, Mehrdad. *Jewish Identities in Iran: Resistance and Conversion to Islam and the Baha'i Faith*. Reprint edition. London; New York: I.B. Tauris, 2013.

Amidror, Yaakov. 'ברור האיראני הכיוון זאת, ובכל'. *Israel Hayom*, 5 December 2007.

Ansari, Ali M. 'The Myth of the White Revolution: Mohammad Reza Shah, "Modernization" and the Consolidation of Power'. *Middle Eastern Studies* 37, no. 3 (2001): 1–24.

Arendt, Hannah. 'Truth and Politics'. *The New Yorker*, 18 February 1967. https://www.newyorker.com/magazine/1967/02/25/truth-and-politics.

Arian, Alan, and Michal Shamir, eds. *The Elections in Israel, 1996*. SUNY Series in Israeli Studies. Albany, NY: State University of New York Press, 1999.

'Army to Award Purple Hearts to Troops Injured in Iran Missile Attack Downplayed by Trump'. Axios. 9 December 2021. https://www.axios.com/army-purple-hearts-iran-missile-attack-troops-iraq-8bedfc6b-cb99-4099-a55b-c3e1142122f0.html.

Associated Press. 'Iran Warns Israel Against Attacking Nuke Facilities'. *Jerusalem Post*, 12 May 2004.

———. 'Iran Will Not Negotiate With US over Missile Program, Says Foreign Minister'. *The Guardian*, 10 April 2016, sec. World news. https://www.theguardian.com/world/2016/apr/10/iran-missile-program-foreign-minister-john-kerry.

———. 'A Look at John Bolton's Tenure in Trump Administration'. AP NEWS, 10 September 2019. https://apnews.com/article/donald-trump-afghanistan-iran-john-bolton-north-korea-0d619b651c44470e975a1431e27fd57e.

Atlas, Yedidya. 'Iranian Threat Never Went Away'. *Jerusalem Post*, 16 February 1992.

Bahgat, Prof. Gawdat G. *Israel and the Persian Gulf: Retrospect and Prospect*. 1st edition. Gainesville, FL University Press of Florida, 2005.

Baker, Peter. *Days of Fire: Bush and Cheney in the White House*. New York: Anchor, 2014.

———. 'Trump Ousts John Bolton as National Security Adviser'. *New York Times*, 10 September 2019, sec. US https://www.nytimes.com/2019/09/10/us/politics/john-bolton-national-security-adviser-trump.html.

Baker, Peter, Ronen Bergman, David D. Kirkpatrick, Julian E. Barnes, and Alissa J. Rubin. 'Seven Days in January: How Trump Pushed U.S. and Iran to the Brink of War'. *New York Times*, 11 January 2020, sec. US https://www.nytimes.com/2020/01/11/us/politics/iran-trump.html.

Barak, Ehud. 'What Israel Must Do to Stop Iran's Nuclear Program'. *Ynetnews*, 5 December 2021. https://www.ynetnews.com/article/h1wuk11qfk.

Barak, Oren, and Gabriel Sheffer. 'Israel's "Security Network" and Its Impact: An Exploration of a New Approach'. *International Journal of Middle East Studies* 38, no. 2 (May 2006): 235–61.

Bar'el, Zvi. 'Netanyahu Using Iran as Another Excuse to Put Off Peace With Palestinians'. *Haaretz*, 10 December 2013. https://www.haaretz.com/.premium-the-new-patron-in-the-conflict-1.5298358.

Bar-Tal, Daniel. 'Why Does Fear Override Hope in Societies Engulfed by Intractable Conflict, as It Does in the Israeli Society?' *Political Psychology* 22, no. 3 (1 September 2001): 601–27.

Batmanghelidj, Esfandyar. 'The Brexit Risk to the Iran Deal'. *LobeLog* (blog), 24 June 2016. https://lobelog.com/the-brexit-risk-to-the-iran-deal/.

BBC News. 'Ahmadinejad Critic Named Speaker', 5 June 2012, sec. Middle East. http://www.bbc.com/news/world-middle-east-18328882.

Beauchamp, Zack. 'Netanyahu Went on Fox & Friends to Lobby Trump on the Iran Deal'. *Vox*, 1 May 2018. https://www.vox.com/world/2018/5/1/17306726/netanyahu-fox-and-friends-trump-iran-deal.

Beinart, Peter. 'Benjamin Netanyahu: TV Star'. *The Atlantic*, 1 May 2018. https://www.theatlantic.com/international/archive/2018/05/netanyahu-trump-iran-nuclear-deal/559376/.

Benjamin Netanyahu. 'Benjamin Netanyahu Interview: Full Text'. Interview by Jeff Glor, 15 June 2009. https://www.cbsnews.com/news/benjamin-netanyahu-interview-full-text/.

———. 'בני גנץ משתמש בכל תירוץ כדי שלא להקים את הממשלה שאזרחי ישראל רוצים: ממשלת אחדות לאומית. בעוד הליכוד הסכים לויתורים רבים כדי להקים ממשלה, גנץ עוד לא מוכן לדון במתווה הנשיא. גנץ גורר את ישראל לבחירות מיותרות @ .בזמן שישראל זקוקה לממשלת אחדות חזקה מול איראן שמסכנת את קיומנו' netanyahu (Twitter), 8 November 2019. https://twitter.com/netanyahu/status/1192788803930480641.

'Benjamin Netanyahu's Interview with Sean Hannity on Fox News'. *Hannity*. Fox News, 21 April 2017. https://www.foxnews.com/transcript/netanyahu-calls-on-palestinian-leaders-to-confront-terrorism.

Benkler, Yochai, Robert Faris, Hal Robert, and Ethan Zuckerman. 'Study: Breitbart-Led Right-Wing Media Ecosystem Altered Broader Media Agenda'. *Columbia Journalism Review*, 3 March 2017. https://www.cjr.org/analysis/breitbart-media-trump-harvard-study.php.

Benn, Aluf. 'בלימה כפולה ועסקים מהצד'. *Haaretz*, 28 September 1994.

Bennett, Alexander J. 'Arms Transfer as an Instrument of Soviet Policy in the Middle East'. *Middle East Journal* 39, no. 4 (1985): 745–74.

Bennett, W. Lance, and Murray Edelman. 'Toward a New Political Narrative'. *Journal of Communication* 35, no. 4 (December 1985): 156–71.

Bergman, Ronen. *The Secret War With Iran: The 30-Year Clandestine Struggle Against the World's Most Dangerous Terrorist Power*. 1st edition. New York: Free Press, 2008.

Berman, Lazar. 'PMO: Bennett's UN Speech Will Be Unlike Netanyahu's; Ex-PM: He Can Learn from Me'. *The Times of Israel*, 23 September 2021. https://www.timesofisrael.com/pmo-bennetts-un-speech-will-be-unlike-netanyahus-ex-pm-he-can-learn-from-me/.

Biden, Joe. 'Opinion: Joe Biden: There's a Smarter Way To Be Tough on Iran'. CNN, 13 September 2020. https://www.cnn.com/2020/09/13/opinions/smarter-way-to-be-tough-on-iran-joe-biden/index.html.

Bill, James A. 'Modernization and Reform From Above: The Case of Iran'. *The Journal of Politics* 32, no. 1 (1970): 19–40. https://doi.org/10.2307/2128863.

Blanford, Nicholas. *Warriors of God: Inside Hezbollah's Thirty-Year Struggle Against Israel*. 1st edition. New York: Random House, 2011.

Blenkensop, Philip, and Rachelle Younglai. 'Banking's SWIFT Says Ready to Block Iran Transactions'. Reuters, 17 February 2012. https://www.reuters.com/article/us-iran-sanctions-swift/bankings-swift-says-ready-to-block-iran-transactions-idUSTRE81G26820120217.

Blitzer, Wolf. 'Gov't and Intelligence Sources Leaked Oil Story'. *Jerusalem Post*, 22 December 1989.

Board of Directors. 'Final Assessment on Past and Present Outstanding Issues Regarding Iran's Nuclear Programme'. International Atomic Energy Agency, December 2015.

Bolton, John R. 'To Stop Iran's Bomb, Bomb Iran'. *New York Times*, 26 March 2015, sec. Opinion. https://www.nytimes.com/2015/03/26/opinion/to-stop-irans-bomb-bomb-iran.html.

Booth, Ken and Nicholas Wheeler. *The Security Dilemma: Fear, Cooperation and Trust in World Politics*. Basingstoke, UK; New York: Palgrave Macmillan, 2007.

Braund, Simon. 'How Ronald Reagan Learned to Start Worrying and Stop Loving the Bomb'. *Empire*, 1 November 2010. https://www.highbeam.com/doc/1P3-2307407461.html.

Brooks, Peter. *Reading for the Plot: Design and Intention in Narrative*. Revised edition. Cambridge, MA: Harvard University Press, 1992.

Brumberg, Daniel. *Reinventing Khomeini: The Struggle for Reform in Iran*. Chicago, IL: University of Chicago Press, 2001.

Brumfield, Ben, and Oren Liebermann. 'Israeli Leaders Planned Attack on Iran Military'. CNN, 22 August 2015. http://www.cnn.com/2015/08/22/middleeast/israel-plan-iran-military-target-strike/index.html.

Bush, George W. 'State of the Union'. Washington, DC, 29 January 2002. http://www.washingtonpost.com/wp-srv/onpolitics/transcripts/sou012902.htm.

————. 'Transcript of President Bush's Address to a Joint Session of Congress', 20 September 2001. http://edition.cnn.com/2001/US/09/20/gen.bush. transcript/.

Bushinsky, Jay. 'Israel Unimpressed by Khatami's CNN Interview'. *Jerusalem Post*, 9 January 1998.

Bushinsky, Jay, and Liat Collins. 'PM: It May Be Too Late to Stop Iran, Iraq Nuclear Plans'. *Jerusalem Post*, 9 June 1998.

Buzan, Barry, Ole Wæver, and Jaap de Wilde. *Security: A New Framework for Analysis*. Boulder, CO: Lynne Rienner Publishers, 1998.

'Cabinet Meeting Minutes', 26 June 2005. Israeli Prime Minister's Office.

'Cabinet Meeting Minutes', 2 October 2005. Israeli Prime Minister's Office.

'Cabinet Meeting Minutes', 14 January 2007. Israeli Prime Minister's Office.

'Cabinet Meeting Minutes', 25 March 2007. Israeli Prime Minister's Office.

'Cabinet Meeting Minutes', 13 January 2008. Israeli Prime Minister's Office.

'Cabinet Meeting Minutes', 11 May 2008. Israeli Prime Minister's Office.

'Cabinet Meeting Minutes', 25 January 2015. Israeli Prime Minister's Office.

'Cabinet Meeting Minutes', 18 February 2015. Israeli Prime Minister's Office.

Caravelli, Jack. *Nuclear Insecurity: Understanding the Threat from Rogue Nations and Terrorists*. Santa Barbara, CA: Greenwood Publishing Group, 2008.

Cecolin, Alessandra. *Iranian Jews in Israel: Between Persian Cultural Identity and Israeli Nationalism*. New edition. London: I.B. Tauris, 2015.

Cesana, Shlomo. 'אני נאבק באחמדינג'אד'. Israel Hayom, 18 May 2008.

Cesana, Shlomo, and Eitan Livne. 'בטהראן מתו מצחוק'. *Israel Hayom*, 5 December 2007.

Choksy, Jamsheed K. 'Tehran Politics: Are the Mullahs Losing Their Grip?' *World Affairs Journal*, June 2012. http://www.worldaffairsjournal.org/article/tehran-politics-are-mullahs-losing-their-grip.

Chotiner, Isaac. 'Vladimir Putin's Revisionist History of Russia and Ukraine'. *The New Yorker*, 23 February 2022. https://www.newyorker.com/news/q-and-a/vladimir-putins-revisionist-history-of-russia-and-ukraine.

Clifton, Eli. 'Follow the Money: Three Billionaires Paved Way for Trump's Iran Deal Withdrawal'. *LobeLog* (blog), 8 May 2018. https://lobelog.com/three-billionaires-paved-way-for-trumps-iran-deal-withdrawal/.

Clinton, Bill. 'Executive Order 12959: Prohibiting Certain Transactions with Respect to Iran (1995)'. https://www.treasury.gov/resource-center/sanctions/Documents/12959.pdf.

Cohen, Ronen A. 'Iran, Israel, and Zionism Since the Islamic Revolution – From Rational Relations to Threat and Disaster'. Netanya, Israel: Netanya Academic College, 2008. http://www.academia.edu/659583/Iran_Israel_and_Zionism_since_the_Islamic_Revolution_-_From_Rational_Relations_to_Threat_and_Disaster.

Collins, Liat, and Steve Rodan. 'Mordechai: We Can Protect Our Citizens From Iran Threat'. *Jerusalem Post*, 28 September 1998.

Cooley, John K. 'More Fingers on Nuclear Trigger?' *Christian Science Monitor*, 25 June 1974.

BIBLIOGRAPHY

Cooper, Andrew Scott. *The Oil Kings: How the U.S., Iran, and Saudi Arabia Changed the Balance of Power in the Middle East*. New York: Simon and Schuster, 2011.

'The Covenant of the League of Nations', December 1924. http://avalon.law.yale.edu/20th_century/leagcov.asp#art22.

Crowley, Michael, and David M. Halbfinger. 'A White House Ceremony Will Celebrate a Diplomatic Win and Campaign Gift'. *New York Times*, 14 September 2020, sec. U.S. https://www.nytimes.com/2020/09/14/us/politics/trump-middle-east-accords.html.

Cunningham, Erin. 'As Coronavirus Cases Explode in Iran, U.S. Sanctions Hinder Its Access to Drugs and Medical Equipment'. *Washington Post*, 29 March 2020. https://www.washingtonpost.com/world/middle_east/as-coronavirus-cases-explode-in-iran-us-sanctions-hinder-its-access-to-drugs-and-medical-equipment/2020/03/28/0656a196-6aba-11ea-b199-3a9799c54512_story.html.

Dabashi, Hamid. *The Last Muslim Intellectual: The Life and Legacy of Jalal Al-e Ahmad*. 1st edition. Edinburgh: Edinburgh University Press, 2021.

Davenport, Kelsey. 'Understanding the U.S. Compliance Certification and Why It Matters to the Iran Nuclear Deal | Arms Control Association'. Arms Control Association, 29 August 2017. https://www.armscontrol.org/blog/2017-08-29/understanding-us-compliance-certification-why-matters-iran-nuclear-deal.

Davis, Douglas. 'Major: Rabin Brings New Source of Hope'. *Jerusalem Post*, 10 December 1992.

———. 'Iran: Military Buildup Is Needed To Counter Israel'. *Jerusalem Post*, 2 August 1998.

Dehghan, Saeed Kamali. 'Iran's President Mahmoud Ahmadinejad Summoned to Parliament'. *The Guardian*, 14 March 2012. http://www.theguardian.com/world/iran-blog/2012/mar/14/iran-ahmadinejad-appears-parliament.

———. 'Europe's Big Banks Remain Wary of Doing Business with Iran'. *The Guardian*, 24 January 2016, sec. World news. https://www.theguardian.com/world/2016/jan/24/europes-big-banks-remain-wary-doing-business-with-iran.

DeYoung, Karen. 'Trump Administration Says It's Putting Iran "on Notice" Following Missile Test'. *Washington Post*, 1 February 2017, sec. National Security. https://www.washingtonpost.com/world/national-security/2017/02/01/fc5ce3d2-e8b0-11e6-80c2-30e57e57e05d_story.html.

Dubowitz, Mark, and Reuel Marc Gerecht. 'Economic Regime-Change Can Stop Iran Bomb'. *Bloomberg*, 17 January 2012. https://www.bloomberg.com/view/articles/2012-01-17/economic-regime-change-can-stop-iran-commentary-by-gerecht-and-dubowitz.

Edelman, Diana Vikander. *The Origins of the Second Temple: Persion Imperial Policy and the Rebuilding of Jerusalem*. 1st edition. Milton Park: Routledge, 2014.

Editorial Board. 'U.S., Iran and the Hostages'. *Jerusalem Post*, 8 May 1990.

———. 'The Real Middle East Problem'. *Jerusalem Post*, 29 April 1991.

———. 'The Iranian Threat'. *Jerusalem Post*, 24 March 1995.

———. 'Containing Iran'. *Jerusalem Post*, 2 May 1995.

———. 'In the Shadow of the Mullahs'. *Jerusalem Post*, 11 January 1998.

————. 'No Win for Democracy in Iran'. *Jerusalem Post*, 10 June 2001.

————. 'Iran's People Power'. *Jerusalem Post*, 17 June 2003.

————. 'A Wake-up Call'. *Jerusalem Post*, 13 August 2006.

Eichner, Itamar. 'PM: Israel Won't Be Spared Even if US Attacks Iran'. *Ynetnews*, 8 May 2012. http://www.ynetnews.com/articles/0,7340,L-4264459,00.html.

Entous, Adam. 'Donald Trump's New World Order'. *The New Yorker*, 11 June 2018. https://www.newyorker.com/magazine/2018/06/18/donald-trumps-new-world-order.

Ephron, Dan. *Killing a King: The Assassination of Yitzhak Rabin and the Remaking of Israel.* New York; London: W.W. Norton & Company, 2015.

Epstein, Jennifer. 'Bibi: Israel Can't Wait Long on Iran'. POLITICO, 5 March 2012. https://www.politico.com/story/2012/03/netanyahu-israel-cant-wait-long-on-iran-073648.

Erdbrink, Thomas. 'Iran's President Ties Recent Drop in Currency to U.S.-Led Sanctions'. *New York Times*, 2 October 2012, sec. Middle East. https://www.nytimes.com/2012/10/03/world/middleeast/iran-president-mahmoud-ahmadinejad-ties-currency-drop-to-sanctions.html.

————. 'Rouhani Wins Re-Election in Iran by a Wide Margin'. *New York Times*, 20 May 2017, sec. World. https://www.nytimes.com/2017/05/20/world/middleeast/iran-election-hassan-rouhani.html.

Erlanger, Steven. 'Washington Casts Wary Eye at Missile Test'. *New York Times*, 24 July 1998, sec. World. https://www.nytimes.com/1998/07/24/world/washington-casts-wary-eye-at-missile-test.html.

————. 'Israeli Inquiry Finds "Grave Failings" in '06 War'. *New York Times*, 31 January 2008, sec. Middle East. https://www.nytimes.com/2008/01/31/world/middleeast/31mideast.html.

Esposito, John L. 'Taqiyah'. In *The Oxford Dictionary of Islam*, ed. John L. Esposito. Oxford: Oxford University Press, 2003. http://www.oxfordreference.com/view/10.1093/acref/9780195125580.001.0001/acref-9780195125580-e-2338.

Estrin, Daniel. 'Iranians and Israelis Are in a Battle over History – and the Holiday of Purim'. *The World*. Public Radio International, 25 March 2016. https://www.pri.org/stories/2016-03-25/iranians-and-israelis-are-battle-over-history-and-holiday-purim.

'Exchange of Toasts by President Carter and Prime Minister Begin at the White House', 15 April 1980. Israel Ministry of Foreign Affairs Documents.

Faghihi, Ruhollah. 'Iran's Central Bank Chief Speaks Out on Currency Plunge, $15 Billion French Credit Line'. Al-Monitor, 16 October 2019. https://www.al-monitor.com/originals/2019/10/iran-central-bank-governor-hemmati-rial-economy.html.

Farda News. 'جشن «پوریم» تراژدی غمبار ایرانیان', 1 April 2008. http://www.fardanews.com/fa/news/48142.

Farhang, Mansour. 'The Iran-Israel Connection'. *Arab Studies Quarterly* 11, no. 1 (1 January 1989): 85–98.

Federman, Josef. 'Scandals Brewing, Netanyahu Calls Early Election for April'. AP NEWS, 24 December 2018. https://apnews.com/article/ap-top-news-

elections-international-news-jerusalem-middle-east-6db1e4d5ecc04c78ac5dca34
a2407ed9.

Feniger, Neta, and Rachel Kallus. 'Israeli Planning in the Shah's Iran: A Forgotten
Episode'. *Planning Perspectives* 30, no. 2 (April 2015): 231–51. https://doi.org/10
.1080/02665433.2014.933677.

———. 'Expertise in the Name of Diplomacy: The Israeli Plan for Rebuilding the
Qazvin Region, Iran'. *International Journal of Islamic Architecture* 5, no. 1 (1 March
2016): 103–34.

Fiedler, K, and H Bless. 'The Formation of Beliefs in the Interface of Affective and
Cognitive Processes'. *The Influence of Emotions on Beliefs*, 1 January 2000, 144–70.

Filkins, Dexter. 'The Shadow Commander'. *The New Yorker*, 23 September 2013.
http://www.newyorker.com/magazine/2013/09/30/the-shadow-commander.

Firoozi, Ferydoon. 'Iranian Censuses 1956 and 1966: A Comparative Analysis'. *Middle
East Journal* 24, no. 2 (1970): 220–8.

Freedman, Robert O. 'Religion, Politics, and the Israeli Elections of 1988'. *Middle East
Journal* 43, no. 3 (1989): 406–22.

'Full Text of the Iran Nuclear Deal', 14 July 2015. https://apps.washingtonpost.
com/g/documents/world/full-text-of-the-iran-nuclear-deal/1651/.

Galston, William A. 'Hillary Clinton on the Iran Nuclear Deal: "Distrust and
Verify"'. Brookings, 9 September 2015. https://www.brookings.edu/blog/
markaz/2015/09/09/hillary-clinton-on-the-iran-nuclear-deal-distrust-and-
verify/.

Gazit, Shlomo. *The Middle East Military Balance 1992–1993*. 1st edition. Jerusalem:
Routledge, 1994.

Gearan, Anne. 'Kerry, Iran's Zarif Hold Unusual Private Meeting on Sidelines of
Nuclear Talks'. *Washington Post*, 26 September 2013, sec. National Security.
https://www.washingtonpost.com/world/national-security/kerry-irans-zarif-
hold-unusual-private-meeting-on-sidelines-of-nuclear-talks/2013/09/26/
d2fddfac-2700-11e3-9372-92606241ae9c_story.html.

———. '"He Threw a Fit": Trump's Anger Over Iran Deal Forced Aides to Scramble
for a Compromise'. *Washington Post*, 11 October 2017, sec. Politics. https://
www.washingtonpost.com/politics/he-threw-a-fit-trumps-anger-over-iran-
deal-forced-aides-to-scramble-for-a-compromise/2017/10/11/6218174c-ae94-
11e7-9e58-e6288544af98_story.html.

Gerwin, Leslie E. 'Planning for Pandemic: A New Model for Governing Public Health
Emergencies'. *American Journal of Law & Medicine* 37, no. 1 (1 January 2011): 154–6.

———. 'The Challenge of Providing the Public With Actionable Information During
a Pandemic'. *Journal of Law, Medicine & Ethics* 40, no. 3 (1 October 2012): 630–54.

Ghazvinian, John. *America and Iran: A History, 1720 to the Present*. New York: Knopf,
2021.

Gilman, Benjamin. Iran and Libya Sanctions Act of 1996, HR3107 § (1996). https://
www.congress.gov/bill/104th-congress/house-bill/3107.

Ginor, Isabella, and Gideon Remez. 'The Spymaster, the Communist, and Foxbats over
Dimona: The USSR's Motive for Instigating the Six-Day War'. *Israel Studies* 11, no.
2 (2006): 88–130.

Glick, Caroline. 'The Mask Is off and No One Cares'. *Jerusalem Post*, 5 July 2005.

———. 'Hitler Is Still Dead'. *Jerusalem Post*, 26 May 2006.

———. 'Iran's Gazan Diversion?' *Jerusalem Post*, 6 January 2009.

Gold, Dore. 'Putting the Iranian Threat in Perspective'. *Jerusalem Post*, 19 February 1993.

———. *The Rise of Nuclear Iran: How Tehran Defies the West*. 1st edition. Washington, DC: Regnery Publishing, 2009.

Goldberg, Jeffrey. 'Netanyahu to Obama: Stop Iran – Or I Will'. *The Atlantic*, March 2009. http://www.theatlantic.com/magazine/archive/2009/03/netanyahu-to-obama-stop-iran-or-i-will/307390/.

Goldenberg, Suzanne. 'Barak Calls Early Election'. *The Guardian*, 29 November 2000, sec. World news. http://www.theguardian.com/world/2000/nov/29/israel.

Gordon-Reed, Annette. *On Juneteenth*. New York: Liveright, 2021.

Government Press Office. 'Peres: We Shall Do All It Takes to Defeat Terrorism'. *Jerusalem Post*, 14 March 1996.

Grabbe, Lester L. *The History of the Jews and Judaism in the Second Temple Period, Volume 1: Yehud, the Persian Province of Judah*. London: Bloomsbury Academic, 2004.

Gutman, Matthew. 'US Confirms Israeli Suspicions About Iranian Nuclear Program'. *Jerusalem Post*, 12 June 2003.

Haaretz. 'Ex-Mossad Chief Admits: Iran Enriching More Than Under Nuke Agreement', 21 November 2021. https://www.haaretz.com/israel-news/watch-one-on-one-with-the-man-who-led-israel-s-covert-iran-war-1.10403338.

Haaretz. 'Former Mossad Chief: Netanyahu's Iran Policy Was a "Dismal Failure"', 12 October 2021. https://www.haaretz.com/israel-news/former-mossad-chief-netanyahu-s-iran-policy-may-be-a-historic-failure-1.10287997.

Haaretz. 'FULL TEXT: Netanyahu Claims Iran Nuclear Deal Based on Lies', 30 April 2018. https://www.haaretz.com/israel-news/full-text-netanyahu-s-reveals-iran-s-atomic-archive-in-speech-1.6045556.

Haberman, Clyde. 'THE WORLD; Israel Focuses on the Threat Beyond the Arabs – in Iran'. *New York Times*, 8 November 1992, sec. Week in Review. http://www.nytimes.com/1992/11/08/weekinreview/the-world-israel-focuses-on-the-threat-beyond-the-arabs-in-iran.html.

Habibi, Nader. 'The Economic Legacy of Mahmoud Ahmadinejad'. *Middle East Brief*, no. 74 (June 2013). https://www.brandeis.edu/crown/publications/meb/MEB74.pdf.

Hafezi, Parisa. 'Iran Announces Low Poll Turnout, Blames Coronavirus "Propaganda"'. *Reuters*, 23 February 2020, sec. Emerging Markets. https://www.reuters.com/article/us-iran-election-khamenei-idUSKCN20H09Z.

Hakakian, Roya. 'How Iran Kept Its Jews'. *Tablet*, 30 December 2014. http://www.tabletmag.com/jewish-news-and-politics/187519/how-iran-kept-its-jews.

Halbfinger, David M. 'U.S. Folding Jerusalem Consulate Into Embassy, a Blow to Palestinians'. *New York Times*, 18 October 2018, sec. World. https://www.nytimes.com/2018/10/18/world/middleeast/us-palestinians-consulate-jerusalem.html.

Halbfinger, David M., and Ronen Bergman. 'Gantz, Netanyahu's Challenger, Faces Lurid Questions After Iran Hacked His Phone'. *New York Times*, 15 March 2019, sec. World. https://www.nytimes.com/2019/03/15/world/middleeast/gantz-netanyahus-challenger-faces-lurid-questions-after-iran-hacked-his-phone.html.

Halevi, Yossi Klein, and Oren, Michael B. 'Israel's Worst Nightmare'. *The New Republic*, 5 February 2007.

Halpern, Orly, and Herb Keinon. 'Iranian President: "Wipe Israel off Map"'. *Jerusalem Post*, 27 October 2005.

Hamilton, Lee H. *Report of the Congressional Committees Investigating the Iran-Contra Affair, with Supplemental, Minority, and Additional Views*. 1st edition. Washington, DC: US Government Printing Office, 1987.

Harkov, Lahav. 'Israel Asks IAEA Member Hungary to Act on Iran Nuclear Violations'. *Jerusalem Post*, 20 July 2018. https://www.jpost.com/arab-israeli-conflict/israel-asks-iaea-member-hungary-to-act-on-iran-nuclear-violations-635698.

————. 'Bennett: We Want Partners Against Iran but Will Act Either Way'. *Jerusalem Post*, 15 September 2021. https://www.jpost.com/israel-news/bennett-we-want-partners-against-iran-but-will-act-either-way-679508.

Harkov, Lahav, and Yonah Jeremy Bob. 'Bennett: Israel Won't Be Obligated to Iran Deal If US Returns'. *Jerusalem Post*, 23 November 2021. https://www.jpost.com/breaking-news/iran-has-surrounded-israel-with-its-proxies-bennett-685750.

Harper, Jo. 'Poland Excludes Tehran From Warsaw's Iran Conference'. *Forbes*, 22 January 2019, sec. Small Business. https://www.forbes.com/sites/joharper/2019/01/22/poland-excludes-tehran-from-warsaws-iran-conference/.

Harris, Kevan. *A Social Revolution: Politics and the Welfare State in Iran*. 1st edition. Oakland, CA: University of California Press, 2017.

Hedges, Chris. 'Iran May Be Able to Build an Atomic Bomb in 5 Years, U.S. and Israeli Officials Fear'. *New York Times*, 5 January 1995. http://www.nytimes.com/1995/01/05/world/iran-may-be-able-build-atomic-bomb-5-years-us-israeli-officials-fear.html.

Heller, Aaron. 'Israel Leader Scorned for Wooing Holocaust-Distorting Allies'. AP NEWS, 30 January 2019. https://apnews.com/article/eastern-europe-ap-top-news-world-war-ii-lithuania-international-news-2b1eb6dbe0f44763b515fbb4c6398f2b.

Hendrix, Steve, Ruth Eglash, and Anne Gearan. 'Jared Kushner Put a Knife "in Netanyahu's Back" over Annexation Delay, Says Israeli Settler Leader'. *Washington Post*, 4 February 2020. https://www.washingtonpost.com/world/middle_east/reports-jared-kushner-angers-netanyahu-camp-by-slowing-annexation-moves/2020/02/04/82376ac6-4719-11ea-91ab-ce439aa5c7c1_story.html.

Hermann, Tamar, and Or Anabi. 'Does Iran Pose an Existential Threat? Israeli Voice Index November 2021'. Israeli Voice Index. Israel Democracy Institute, 8 December 2021. https://en.idi.org.il/articles/36760.

Hildreth, Steven A. 'Iran's Ballistic Missile and Space Launch Programs'. Congressional Research Service, 6 December 2012.

Hill, Christopher. *The Changing Politics of Foreign Policy*. Houndmills, Basingstoke, Hampshire; New York: Palgrave Macmillan, 2003.

Hoffman, Gil. 'Netanyahu: World Must Join to Crush Terror'. *Jerusalem Post*, 12 September 2001.

————. 'Netanyahu: Don't Boycott the BBC'. *Jerusalem Post*, 11 August 2006.

————. 'Sneh: Iran Can't Be Allowed to Repeat Auschwitz'. *Jerusalem Post*, 30 April 2008.

Hoffman, Gil and AP. 'Ben-Eliezer: United States Too Soft on Iran, Syria'. *Jerusalem Post*, 16 October 2001.

Hoffman, Gil, and Sheera Claire Frenkel. '"I Prefer Fewer Declarations and More Deeds"'. *Jerusalem Post*, 10 November 2006.

Hoffman, Gil, Yaakov Katz, and Herb Keinon. 'Lieberman: No One Knows When Iran Will Have the Bomb. "We Cannot Allow Ourselves to Rest Just Because of an Intel Report from the Other Side of the Earth," Barak Says'. *Jerusalem Post*, 5 December 2007.

Hofstadter, Richard. *Anti-Intellectualism in American Life*. New York: Vintage, 2012.

Holden, Michael, and James Williams. 'Israel's Netanyahu Urges Britain to Join Iran Sanctions'. *Reuters*, 6 February 2017, sec. Top News. https://www.reuters.com/article/cnews-us-britain-israel-iran-idCAKBN15L1TX.

Holland, Steve. 'Trump Issues Ultimatum to "Fix" Iran Nuclear Deal'. *Reuters*, 12 January 2018. https://www.reuters.com/article/us-iran-nuclear-decision-idUSKBN1F108F.

Holmes, Oliver. 'Summit Cancelled as Israel and Poland Row Over Holocaust'. *The Guardian*, 18 February 2019, sec. World News. https://www.theguardian.com/world/2019/feb/18/polish-israel-visit-holocaust.

Holsti, Ole R. 'Cognitive Dynamics and Images of the Enemy'. *Journal of International Affairs* 21, no. 1 (1 January 1967).

Honig, Sarah. 'Netanyahu, Peres Sharpen Debating Skills on "Popolitka"'. *Jerusalem Post*, 7 May 1996.

Horovitz, David. 'Middle East Terror Wave Predicted'. *Jerusalem Post*, 17 July 1989.

i24NEWS. 'Ex-Military Intel Chief: Israel Was Involved In Soleimani Assassination'. *i24news*, 20 December 2021. https://www.i24news.tv/en/news/israel/diplomacy-defense/1640017040-ex-military-intel-chief-israel-was-involved-in-soleimani-assassination.

IAEA Director General. 'Verification and Monitoring of the Islamic Republic of Iran in Light of United Nations Security Council Resolution 2231 (2015)'. Vienna, Austria: International Atomic Energy Agency, 24 February 2017. https://isis-online.org/uploads/iaea-reports/documents/IAEA_JCPOA_Report_24Feb2017.pdf.

IMF. 'IMF Data', n.d. http://www.imf.org/en/Data.

'Implementation of the NPT Safeguards Agreement in the Islamic Republic of Iran'. Vienna, Austria: International Atomic Energy Agency, 10 November 2003. https://www.iaea.org/sites/default/files/gov2003-75.pdf.

'The Implications of the Iran-Iraq Agreement'. Central Intelligence Agency, 1 May 1975.

Inbar, Efraim. 'The Iranian Threat Reconsidered'. *Jerusalem Post*, 10 August 1998.

Ingber, Sasha. 'Poland Backtracks on a Controversial Holocaust Speech Law'. NPR, 27 June 2018, sec. Europe. https://www.npr.org/2018/06/27/623865367/poland-backtracks-on-a-controversial-holocaust-speech-law.

Inskeep, Steve. 'Born in the USA: How America Created Iran's Nuclear Program'. NPR, 18 September 2005. https://www.npr.org/sections/

parallels/2015/09/18/440567960/born-in-the-u-s-a-how-america-created-irans-nuclear-program.

International Atomic Energy Agency. 'Additional Protocol'. IAEA, n.d. https://www.iaea.org/topics/additional-protocol.

Interview with Aluf Benn. Email, 6 July 2017.

'Interview with Defense Minister Rabin on Israel Television and on Israel Radio', 6 January 1987. Israel Ministry of Foreign Affairs Documents.

'Interview With Defense Minister Rabin in Yediot Achronot', 26 September 1986. Israel Ministry of Foreign Affairs Documents.

'Interview with Defense Minister Sharon in the Wall Street Journal', 28 May 1982. Israel Ministry of Foreign Affairs Documents.

Interview with Emily Landau. Interview by Jonathan Leslie. Tel Aviv, Israel, 7 January 2016.

Interview with Ephraim Sneh. Interview by Jonathan Leslie. Tel Aviv, Israel, 26 November 2015.

'Interview with Prime Minister Begin on ABC Television', 20 April 1980. Israel Ministry of Foreign Affairs Documents.

Interview with Raz Zimmt. Interview by Jonathan Leslie. Tel Aviv, Israel, 24 November 2015.

Interview with Ronen Bergman. Interview by Jonathan Leslie. Tel Aviv, Israel, 25 January 2016.

Interview with Soli Shahvar. Interview by Jonathan Leslie. Haifa, Israel, 4 November 2015.

Interview with Yaakov Katz. Interview by Jonathan Leslie. Jerusalem, Israel, 27 October 2015.

Interview with Yael Berda. Interview by Jonathan Leslie. Email, 13 July 2018.

Interview with Yossi Alpher. Interview by Jonathan Leslie. Tel Aviv, Israel, 9 December 2015.

Iran Data Portal – Syracuse University. 'Iran Data Portal', n.d. http://irandataportal.syr.edu/.

Iran Data Portal – Syracuse University. '2005 Presidential Election'. Accessed 17 July 2018. http://irandataportal.syr.edu/2005-presidential-election.

'"The Iran Deal Was a Mistake. Withdrawing From It Was Even Worse"', *Haaretz*, 21 November 2021. https://www.haaretz.com/israel-news/the-iran-deal-was-a-mistake-withdrawing-from-it-was-even-worse-1.10403339.

Iran Freedom. *Excerpts from Amb. John Bolton's Speech at the Free Iran Gathering Paris 1 July 2017*, 2017. https://www.youtube.com/watch?v=hTMh24qlyQA.

'Iran Fuel Rations Spark Violence', 27 June 2007. http://news.bbc.co.uk/1/hi/world/middle_east/6243644.stm.

'Iran: Nuclear Intentions and Capabilities'. National Intelligence Estimate. Office of the Director of National Intelligence, November 2007. https://www.dni.gov/files/documents/Newsroom/Press%20Releases/2007%20Press%20Releases/20071203_release.pdf.

'Iran Plane Crash: Demands for Justice after Admission Jet Was Shot Down', BBC News, 11 January 2020, sec. Middle East. https://www.bbc.com/news/world-middle-east-51077788.

BIBLIOGRAPHY

'Iranian Media: No Big Change Whoever Wins Election', *Reuters*, 30 May 1996.

'Iran's Ebrahim Raisi: The Hardline Cleric Who Became President', BBC News, 5 August 2021, sec. Middle East. https://www.bbc.com/news/world-middle-east-57421235.

'Iran's Parliament Designates All US Forces as "Terrorists"', Al Jazeera, 7 January 2020. https://www.aljazeera.com/news/2020/1/7/irans-parliament-designates-all-us-forces-as-terrorists.

'Iran's Strategic Intentions and Capabilities'. Institute for National Strategic Studies – National Defense University: DIANE Publishing, April 1994.

Irish, John, and Arshad Mohammed. 'Netanyahu, in U.N. Speech, Claims Secret Iranian Nuclear Site'. *Reuters*, 27 September 2018, sec. Emerging Markets. https://www.reuters.com/article/us-un-assembly-israel-iran-idUSKCN1M72FZ.

IRNA. 'آمریکا، اسرائیل و عربستان محور شرارت جدید هستند', 25 May 2018. https://www.irna.ir/news/82925673/آمریکا-اسرائیل-و-عربستان-محور-شرارت-جدید-هستند.

ISNA. 'ترور سردار سلیمانی مصداق بارز تروریسم دولتی و نقض حقوق بین‌الملل است', 11 July 2020. https://www.isna.ir/news/99042114934/ترور-سردار-سلیمانی-و-دولتی-و-نقض-حقوق-بین-الملل.

Israel Ministry of Foreign Affairs. 'Israel's Foreign Policy - Historical Documents', n.d.

———. 'Ministry of Foreign Affairs Communique on Iran's New President', 4 August 1997. Israel Ministry of Foreign Affairs Documents.

———. 'Iran: Statements by Israeli Leaders – June 2009', 22 June 2009. Israel Ministry of Foreign Affairs Documents.

———. 'Recent Iranian Statements: Threats, Delegitimization of Israel and Antisemitism', 19 August 2012. Israel Ministry of Foreign Affairs Documents.

'Israeli Defence Minister Says Iran Is "Israel's Best Friend"'. BBC News, 30 October 1987.

Israeli, Zipi. 'National Security Index Public Opinion Survey 2018–2019'. Tel Aviv, Israel: Institute for National Strategic Studies, 2019, 2018. https://www.inss.org.il/wp-content/uploads/2019/01/%D7%9E%D7%93%D7%93-%D7%94%D7%91%D7%99%D7%98%D7%97%D7%95%D7%9F-%D7%94%D7%9C%D7%90%D7%95%D7%9E%D7%99-%D7%91%D7%90%D7%A0%D7%92%D7%9C-%D7%99%D7%AA-2019.pdf.

Israel's Foreign Relations: 1979–1980. Ministry of Foreign Affairs, 1976.

Itim. 'We Don't Have to Worry About Nuclear Attack, Says Bin-Nun'. *Jerusalem Post*, 18 May 1993.

Izenberg, Dan. 'Rabin: Iran Potentially Greater Threat Than Iraq'. *Jerusalem Post*, 21 January 1993.

Jamejam Online. 'رییس جمهوری: تجاوز رژیم صهیونیستی به لبنان تعدی به ملت های منطقه است', 14 July 2006.

Jamhuri-ye Eslami (Via BBC Monitoring, London). 'America's Mired Diplomacy'. 29 April 2018. http://search.proquest.com/docview/2032751218/citation/820464E3CF6141D1PQ/8.

Javad Zarif. '@realDonaldTrump Is Maliciously Tightening US' Illegal Sanctions With Aim of Draining Iran's Resources Needed in the Fight Against #COVID19—While Our Citizens Are Dying From It. The World Can No Longer Be Silent as US

#EconomicTerrorism Is Supplanted by Its #MedicalTerrorism'. @JZarif (Twitter), 7 March 2020. https://twitter.com/JZarif/status/1236278774750158849.

Jerusalem Post Correspondent. 'Dichter: US May Have to Bomb Iran'. *Jerusalem Post*, 31 October 2005.

Jerusalem Post Staff. 'Barak at the Helm'. *Jerusalem Post*, 1 April 1991.

⸻. 'Rabbi at Vatican Meeting Condemns Iranian President'. *Jerusalem Post*, 6 October 2008. https://www.jpost.com/iranian-threat/news/rabbi-at-vatican-meeting-condemns-iranian-president.

⸻. 'PM: Iran's Leaders Guided by Unbelievable Fanaticism'. *Jerusalem Post*, 16 September 2012. https://www.jpost.com/diplomacy-and-politics/pm-irans-leaders-guided-by-unbelievable-fanaticism.

Jerusalem Post Staff and AP. 'Iran Unveils Shihab-3 Missile. Has Plans for Longer-Range Model'. *Jerusalem Post*, 27 September 1998.

Jockers, Matthew L. *Text Analysis With R for Students of Literature*. 2014 edition. New York: Springer, 2014.

Josephus, Flavius. *The Complete Works of Flavius Josephus*. Translated by William Whiston. 1st edition. Cheltenham, UK: Attic Books, 2008.

Kahl, Colin H. 'An Israeli Attack Against Iran Would Backfire – Just Like Israel's 1981 Strike on Iraq'. *Washington Post*, 2 March 2012, sec. Opinions. http://www.washingtonpost.com/opinions/an-israeli-attack-against-iran-would-backfire--just-like-israels-1981-strike-on-iraq/2012/02/28/gIQATOMFnR_story.html.

Kalb, Marvin, and Carol Saivetz. 'The Israeli-Hezbollah War of 2006: The Media as a Weapon in Asymmetrical Conflict'. Washington, DC: Brookings Institution, 18 February 2007.

Kam, Ephraim. 'The Iranian Threat Cause for Concern, Not Alarm'. Strategic Assessment. Institute for National Security Studies, October 1998.

Karami, Arash. 'Zarif Gives Netanyahu Lesson in Jewish Scripture'. Al-Monitor, 13 March 2017. http://www.al-monitor.com/pulse/originals/2017/03/iran-purim-netanyahu-zarif-larijani-esther-persia-history.html.

Karni, Annie. 'Saudis Give Trump a Reception Fit for a King'. POLITICO, 20 May 2017. https://www.politico.com/story/2017/05/20/donald-trump-saudi-arabia-visit-238638.

Karni, Ezrael. מברק מהיועץ עזריאל קרני בטהראן אל המחלקה למזרח התיכון ואגן הים' 'התיכון המזרחי במשרד החוץ, 14 December 1978. Israel State Archives.

Karsenty, E., J. Shemer, I. Alshech, B. Cojocaru, M. Moscovitz, Y. Shapiro, and Y. L. Danon. 'Medical Aspects of the Iraqi Missile Attacks on Israel'. *Israel Journal of Medical Sciences* 27, no. 11–12 (December 1991): 603–7.

Kasparov, Garry. *Winter Is Coming: Why Vladimir Putin and the Enemies of the Free World Must Be Stopped*. New York: PublicAffairs, 2015.

Katz, Yaakov. 'Ex-MI Chief: Jihad Tsunami on the Way. Three Gaza Terrorists Wounded in IAF Missile Strike'. *Jerusalem Post*, 16 May 2006.

⸻. 'Security and Defense: Who's in Charge of Whom and Over What?' *Jerusalem Post*, 2 April 2009. https://www.jpost.com/features/front-lines/security-and-defense-whos-in-charge-of-whom-and-over-what.

Katz, Yaakov, and Yoaz Hendel. *Israel vs. Iran: The Shadow War*. 1st edition. Washington, DC: Potomac Books Inc., 2012.

Katzenell, Jack. 'Peres Protests Iranian Threat to Destroy Israel'. *Jerusalem Post*, 26 December 2001.

Kaye, Dalia Dassa. *Israel and Iran: A Dangerous Rivalry*. Rand Corporation Monograph Series. Santa Monica, CA: RAND National Defense Research Institute, 2011.

Kazemi, Farhad. 'Iran, Israel and the Arab Israeli Balance'. In *Iran Since the Revolution*, ed. Barry Rosen, 1st edition.. Boulder, CO; New York: Columbia University Press, 1985.

Keinon, Herb. 'Barak: Released Prisoners May Return to Terrorism'. *Jerusalem Post*, 31 August 1994.

———. 'Saddam's Fall Alters Israel's Strategic Situation – Experts'. *Jerusalem Post*, 11 April 2003.

———. 'Shalom Toughens Stance on Iran'. *Jerusalem Post*, 24 September 2004.

———. 'Key Israeli Officials Declare Support for More Unilateral Steps'. *Jerusalem Post*, 29 September 2005.

Kershner, Isabel. 'Ex-Mossad Chief Warns Against Strike on Iran'. *New York Times*, 8 May 2011, sec. Middle East. https://www.nytimes.com/2011/05/09/world/middleeast/09israel.html.

———. 'Facebook Suspends Netanyahu Campaign Bot for Hate Speech'. *New York Times*, 12 September 2019, sec. World. https://www.nytimes.com/2019/09/12/world/middleeast/facebook-netanyahu-bot.html.

———. 'Netanyahu Seeks Immunity From Israeli Corruption Charges'. *New York Times*, 1 January 2020, sec. World. https://www.nytimes.com/2020/01/01/world/middleeast/israel-netanyahu-immunity.html.

Kessler, Glenn. 'Did Ahmadinejad Really Say Israel Should Be "Wiped off the Map"?' *Washington Post*, 5 October 2011. https://www.washingtonpost.com/blogs/fact-checker/post/did-ahmadinejad-really-say-israel-should-be-wiped-off-the-map/2011/10/04/gIQABJIKML_blog.html.

Khamenei, Ali. *Palestine*. London: Opars Books, 2012.

Khomeini, Ruhollah. 'سخنرانی حضرت امام(ره) در عصر عاشورای خرداد 13 ,1342', 3 June 1963. http://www.imam-khomeini.ir/fa/c75_20702/نقطه_عطف/گاهنامه‌/سخنرانی_حضرت_امام_ره_در_عصر_عاشورای_13خرداد_1342.

———. *Islamic Government: Governance of the Jurist*, 1970.

Kingsley, Patrick, and Isabel Kershner. 'New Israeli Leader Backs Hard Line on Iran but Softer Tone With U.S.' *New York Times*, 24 August 2021, sec. World. https://www.nytimes.com/2021/08/24/world/middleeast/israel-bennett-biden-iran.html.

Kinzer, Stephen. *All the Shah's Men: An American Coup and the Roots of Middle East Terror*. John Wiley & Sons, 2003.

Krebs, Ronald R. *Narrative and the Making of US National Security*. Cambridge, UK: Cambridge University Press, 2015.

Kurtzer, Daniel. 'The Iran Project'. Panel Presentation, Princeton University, 14 November 2013.

Landau, Emily B. 'After Round One With Rouhani: Staying Focused on the Dynamics of Nuclear Bargaining'. INSS Insight. Institute for National Security Studies, 17 October 2013. http://www.inss.org.il/uploadImages/systemFiles/No.%20477%20-%20Emily%20for%20web.pdf.

Landau, Noa. 'Israel to Host Summit for Europe's Emerging Nationalist Bloc'. *Haaretz*, 28 January 2019. https://www.haaretz.com/israel-news/.premium-israel-to-host-summit-of-visegrad-group-of-central-european-governments-in-february-1.6878150.

Landau, Noa, and Jack Khoury. 'Pompeo After Meeting Netanyahu: If Iran Nuclear Deal Can't Be Fixed, It Will Be Nixed'. *Haaretz*, 29 April 2018. https://www.haaretz.com/israel-news/netanyahu-and-pompeo-to-talk-iran-in-sunday-meeting-1.6034929.

Landler, Mark. 'Trump Recognizes Jerusalem as Israel's Capital and Orders U.S. Embassy to Move'. *New York Times*, 6 December 2017, sec. World. https://www.nytimes.com/2017/12/06/world/middleeast/trump-jerusalem-israel-capital.html.

Landler, Mark, and David E. Sanger. 'Trump Disavows Nuclear Deal, but Doesn't Scrap It'. *New York Times*, 13 October 2017, sec. U.S. https://www.nytimes.com/2017/10/13/us/politics/trump-iran-nuclear-deal.html.

Lapid, Yosef (Tommy). 'The Warning'. *Jerusalem Post*, 14 September 2001.

Le Drian, Jean-Yves, Heiko Maas, and Jeremy Hunt. 'Joint Statement on the Creation of INSTEX, the Special Purpose Vehicle Aimed at Facilitating Legitimate Trade With Iran in the Framework of the Efforts to Preserve the Joint Comprehensive Plan of Action (JCPOA)', 31 January 2019. https://www.diplomatie.gouv.fr/en/country-files/iran/news/article/joint-statement-on-the-creation-of-instex-the-special-purpose-vehicle-aimed-at.

Legro, Jeffrey W., and Andrew Moravcsik. 'Is Anybody Still a Realist?' *International Security* 24, no. 2 (October 1999): 5–55. https://doi.org/10.1162/016228899560130.

Levey, Zach. 'Anatomy of an Airlift: United States Military Assistance to Israel During the 1973 War'. *Cold War History* 8, no. 4 (2008): 481–501.

Levran, Aharon. 'How to Tame the Nuclear Beast'. *Jerusalem Post*, 1 May 1992.

Lewis, Jeffrey. 'NCRI Did Not Discover Natanz'. *Arms Control Wonk* (blog), 28 October 2006. https://www.armscontrolwonk.com/archive/201274/ncri-did-not-discover-natanz/.

Lis, Jonathan. 'FULL TEXT: Bennett's UN Speech – Iran, COVID, and Not One Mention of Palestinians'. *Haaretz*, 27 September 2021. https://www.haaretz.com/israel-news/full-text-bennett-s-un-speech-iran-covid-and-not-one-mention-of-palestinians-1.10246065.

———. 'Gantz Says He Instructed Israeli Army to Prepare Military Option Against Iran'. *Haaretz*, 11 December 2021. https://www.haaretz.com/israel-news/.premium-israeli-army-has-been-instructed-to-prepare-military-option-against-iran-gantz-says-1.10457857.

Livne, Eitan. 'אחמדינג'אד על הסוס נשיא איראן הגדיר את דו"ח המודיעין האמריקני כ"ניצחון האומה"'. *Israel Hayom*, 6 December 2007.

Lorch, Netaniel. 'תזכיר מנתנאל לורך, המנהל בפועל של מחלקת מזרח תיכון במשרד החוץ בירושלים', 9 June 1963. Israel State Archives.

Lubrani, Uri. 'מברק משגריר ישראל בטהראן, אורי לוברני אל שר החוץ, משה דיין', 28 September 1978. Israel State Archives.

Lucas, Scott. 'How Israel's Military Stopped Netanyahu Attacking Iran'. *The Conversation*, 26 February 2015. http://theconversation.com/how-israels-military-stopped-netanyahu-attacking-iran-38009.

———. 'How Iran's Hardliners Still Threaten the Nuclear Deal'. *The Conversation*, 18 January 2016. http://theconversation.com/how-irans-hardliners-still-threaten-the-nuclear-deal-53236.

Luft, Gal. 'Israel's Security Zone in Lebanon – A Tragedy?' *Middle East Quarterly*, 1 September 2000. http://www.meforum.org/70/israels-security-zone-in-lebanon-a-tragedy.

Lynch, Marc. 'International Relations'. In *The Middle East*, ed. Ellen Lust, 369–402. Washington, DC: CQ Press, 2016.

MacFarquhar, Neil. 'A Divine Wind Blows Against Iran's President'. *New York Times*, 22 June 2011, sec. Middle East. https://www.nytimes.com/2011/06/23/world/middleeast/23iran.html.

Magid, Jacob. 'He Led IDF Intel Gathering on Iran, Was Ignored and Fears Israel Is Now Paying Price'. *The Times of Israel*, 30 November 2021. https://www.timesofisrael.com/he-led-idf-intel-gathering-on-iran-was-ignored-and-fears-israel-is-now-paying-price/.

Maginnis, John. *Cross to Bear*. New Orleans, LA: Pelican Publishing Company, Inc., 2011.

Majidyar, Ahmad. 'Iranian Leaders Reject Macron's Proposal to Supplement Nuclear Deal'. Middle East Institute, 19 September 2017. https://www.mei.edu/publications/iranian-leaders-reject-macrons-proposal-supplement-nuclear-deal.

Makovsky, David. 'Rabin: Arms Sales Hurt by Global Peace'. *Jerusalem Post*, 27 December 1989.

Makovsky, David, and Hillel Kuttler. 'Clinton to Head Anti-Terror Summit Next Week'. *Jerusalem Post*, 8 March 1996.

Marantz, Andrew. 'How "Fox & Friends" Rewrites Trump's Reality'. *The New Yorker*, 8 January 2018. https://www.newyorker.com/magazine/2018/01/15/how-fox-and-friends-rewrites-trumps-reality.

'Market in China's Wuhan Likely Origin of COVID-19 Outbreak – Scientist'. *Reuters*, 19 November 2021, sec. World. https://www.reuters.com/world/market-chinas-wuhan-likely-origin-covid-19-outbreak-study-2021-11-19/.

Masters, Jonathan. 'Mujahadeen-e-Khalq (MEK)'. Council on Foreign Relations, 28 July 2014. https://www.cfr.org/backgrounder/mujahadeen-e-khalq-mek.

McCarthy, Niall. 'Nuclear Deal: Iran's Opportunity To Replace Its Rusty Old Airliners?' *Forbes*, 17 July 2015, sec. Business. https://www.forbes.com/sites/niallmccarthy/2015/07/17/nuclear-deal-irans-opportunity-to-replace-its-rusty-old-airliners-infographic/.

McElroy, Damien. 'Fighting Rages as Gaza Strip Death Toll Nears 1000', 14 January 2009, sec. World. https://www.telegraph.co.uk/news/worldnews/middleeast/israel/4236793/Benjamin-Netanyahu-says-Hamas-must-be-removed-from-Gaza.html.

Melman, Yossi. 'IRAN'S LETHAL SECRET'. *Washington Post*, 18 October 1992. https://www.washingtonpost.com/archive/opinions/1992/10/18/irans-lethal-secret/2994e63c-b341-41ae-b87b-0141a68f9a27/.

Mercer, Jonathan. 'Emotional Beliefs'. *International Organization* 64, no. 1 (2010): 1–31.

Metzger, Bruce M., and Michael David Coogan. *The Oxford Companion to the Bible*. Oxford: Oxford University Press, 1993.

'The Middle East Military Balance 1993–1994'. Tel Aviv University, Jaffee Center for Strategic Studies, 1994.

Miglietta, John P. *American Alliance Policy in the Middle East, 1945–1992: Iran, Israel, and Saudi Arabia*. Lanham, MD: Lexington Books, 2002.

Milani, Abbas. *The Shah*. New York: St. Martin's Press, 2011.

Moghtader, Michelle, and Mehrdad Balali. 'Iran Leader Slams West's "Stupid" Missile Stance Before Talks'. *Reuters*, 11 May 2014, sec. World News. https://www.reuters.com/article/uk-iran-nuclear-idUKKBN0DR0IH20140511.

Morello, Carol. 'Pompeo Calls It "Just Nuts" to Allow Iran to Trade in Arms as U.N. Rejects Embargo Extension'. *Washington Post*, 14 August 2020. https://www.washingtonpost.com/national-security/pompeo-calls-it-just-nuts-to-allow-iran-to-trade-in-arms-as-critical-un-vote-nears/2020/08/14/68e2ee84-de2b-11ea-b4af-72895e22941d_story.html.

Moughty, Sarah. 'Eyal Arad: a "Messianic" Netanyahu', 6 January 2016. http://www.pbs.org/wgbh/frontline/article/eyal-arad-a-messianic-netanyahu/.

Mousavian, Hossein. 'It Was Not Sanctions That Brought Iran to the Table'. *Financial Times*, 19 November 2013. https://www.ft.com/content/8d9631f4-510c-11e3-b499-00144feabdc0.

Mousavian, Seyyed Hossein. *The Iranian Nuclear Crisis: a Memoir*. Washington, DC: Carnegie Endowment for International Peace, 2012.

Mufson, Steven, and Damian Paletta. 'Boeing, Airbus to Lose $39 Billion in Contracts Because of Trump Sanctions on Iran'. *Washington Post*, 9 May 2018. https://www.washingtonpost.com/business/economy/boeing-airbus-to-lose-39-billion-in-contracts-because-of-trump-sanctions-on-iran/2018/05/08/820a8f08-5308-11e8-a551-5b648abe29ef_story.html.

Müller, Jan-Werner. *What Is Populism?* Philadelphia, PA: University of Pennsylvania Press, 2016.

Murphy, Jack, and Zach Dorfman. '"Conspiracy Is Hard": Inside the Trump Administration's Secret Plan to Kill Qassem Soleimani'. *Yahoo! News*, 8 May 2021. https://news.yahoo.com/conspiracy-is-hard-inside-the-trump-administrations-secret-plan-to-kill-qassem-soleimani-090058817.html.

National Commission on Terrorist Attacks. *The 9/11 Commission Report: Final Report of the National Commission on Terrorist Attacks Upon the United States*. New York: W.W. Norton & Company, 2004.

Netanyahu, Benjamin. *A Place Among the Nations: Israel and the World*. New York: Bantam Dell Pub Group, 1993.

———. 'Dismantle Terror-Supporting Regimes'. *Jerusalem Post*, 14 September 2001.

———. 'PM Netanyahu Speech to US Congress'. Presented at the Joint Session of United States Congress, Washington, DC, 10 July 1996.

———. 'Address to US House Government Reform Committee'. Washington, DC, 24 September 2001.

————. 'Prime Minister Benjamin Netanyahu's Speech to the UN General Assembly'. 24 September 2009. http://www.haaretz.com/news/prime-minister-benjamin-netanyahu-s-speech-to-the-un-general-assembly-1.7254.

————. 'Prime Minister Netanyahu's Speech at the Jewish Federations of North America General Assembly', 9 November 2009. Israeli Prime Minister's Office.

————. 'Prime Minister Netanyahu's Speech at the AIPAC Conference', 22 March 2010. Israeli Prime Minister's Office.

————. 'PM Netanyahu's Speech at AIPAC Policy Conference 2012'. Presented at the AIPAC Policy Conference, Washington, DC, 5 March 2012. http://www.pmo.gov.il/English/MediaCenter/Speeches/Pages/speechAIPAC060312.aspx.

————. 'Speech to UNGA'. Presented at the United Nations General Assembly, New York, 27 September 2012.

————. 'Prime Minister Netanyahu's Remarks on Iranian President Rouhani's Davos Speech', 23 January 2014. Israeli Prime Minister's Office.

————. 'I'm Determined to Speak before Congress to Stop Iran. RETWEET if I Have Your Support. http://T.Co/5qTb89xf2i'. @netanyahu (Twitter), 10 February 2015. https://twitter.com/netanyahu/status/565148423507042305.

————. 'The Complete Transcript of Netanyahu's Address to Congress'. 3 March 2015. http://www.washingtonpost.com/blogs/post-politics/wp/2015/03/03/full-text-netanyahus-address-to-congress/.

————. 'PM Netanyahu's Speech at the United Nations General Assembly'. Presented at the United Nations General Assembly, New York, 1 October 2015. http://www.pmo.gov.il/English/MediaCenter/Speeches/Pages/speechUN011015.aspx.

————. *פורים שמח!*, 2017. https://www.facebook.com/Netanyahu/videos/10154454625947076/.

————. 'Stopping the Iranian Threat, and the Threat Reflected in the Bad Nuclear Agreement With Iran, Continues to Be a Supreme Goal of Israel'. Tweet. @IsraeliPM (blog), 22 January 2017. https://twitter.com/IsraeliPM/status/823199619073142784.

————. 'I Congratulate @realDonaldTrump for His Courageous Decision. He Boldly Confronted Iran's Terrorist Regime. https://T.Co/1KaHM6jdFc'. @netanyahu (Twitter), 14 October 2017. https://twitter.com/netanyahu/status/919255273524490241.

————. 'PM Netanyahu Addresses Munich Security Conference 18 February 2018'. Presented at the Munich Security Conference, Munich, Germany, 18 February 2018.

————. 'PM Netanyahu Reveals the Iranian Secret Nuclear Program'. 30 April 2018. http://www.pmo.gov.il/English/MediaCenter/Events/Pages/event_iran300418.aspx.

————. 'גנץ, איזה חומר איראן מחזיקה עליך? מדינת ישראל צריכה ראש ממשלה חזק ולא סחיט שיעמוד איתן מול האויבים שלנו https://t.co/lmAeuGg8yY'. @netanyahu (Twitter), 20 March 2019. https://twitter.com/netanyahu/status/1108387654477991936.

317

————. 'PM Netanyahu: "If Someone Rises up to Kill You, Kill Him First." In a Complicated Operation by the Security Establishment, We Revealed That Iran's Quds Force Dispatched a Special Unit of Shi'ite Militants to Syria to Kill Israelis on the Golan Heights with Explosives-Laden UAVs. https://T.Co/D2vIZwTc8S'. @IsraeliPM (Twitter), 25 August 2019. https://twitter.com/IsraeliPM/status/1165645141849382913.

Netanyahu, Benjamin, and Barack Obama. 'Meeting Between PM Netanyahu and U.S. President Barack Obama', 18 May 2009. Israeli Prime Minister's Office. http://www.pmo.gov.il/english/mediacenter/speeches/pages/speechobama.aspx.

Netanyahu, Binyamin. *Fighting Terrorism: How Democracies Can Defeat Domestic and International Terrorists*. New York: Macmillan, 1995.

'Netanyahu Calls on Palestinian Leaders to Confront Terrorism'. *Hannity*. Jerusalem, Israel: Fox News, 22 April 2017. https://www.foxnews.com/transcript/netanyahu-calls-on-palestinian-leaders-to-confront-terrorism.

'Netanyahu Hails Israel Strikes Against Syria to Foil Iran "Killer Drone Attack"', *The Guardian*, 24 August 2019, sec. World news. http://www.theguardian.com/world/2019/aug/25/netanyahu-hails-israel-strikes-against-syria-to-foil-iran-killer-drone-attack.

Nichols, Tom. *The Death of Expertise: The Campaign Against Established Knowledge and Why It Matters*. New York: Oxford University Press, 2017.

Novick, Peter. *The Holocaust in American Life*. Boston, MA: Houghton Mifflin Harcourt, 2000.

'The Nuclear Vault: The Algerian Nuclear Problem'. National Security Archive Electronic Briefing Book. George Washington University, 10 September 2007. https://nsarchive2.gwu.edu/nukevault/ebb228/index.htm.

'The Nuclear Vault: The Iranian Nuclear Program, 1974–1978'. National Security Archive Electronic Briefing Book. George Washington University, 12 January 2009. https://nsarchive2.gwu.edu/nukevault/ebb268/.

Nuzzi, Olivia. 'Donald Trump and Sean Hannity Like to Talk Before Bedtime'. *New York Magazine*, 14 May 2018. https://nymag.com/intelligencer/2018/05/sean-hannity-donald-trump-late-night-calls.html.

Nye, Joseph S., and Sean M. Lynn-Jones. 'International Security Studies: A Report of a Conference on the State of the Field'. *International Security* 12, no. 4 (1988): 5–27. https://doi.org/10.2307/2538992.

O'Dwyer, Thomas. 'New Voice From Teheran'. *Jerusalem Post*, 9 January 1998.

Oprysko, Caitlin. 'Trump Claims Soleimani Was Planning to Blow up U.S. Embassy'. POLITICO, 9 January 2020. https://www.politico.com/news/2020/01/09/trump-soleimani-embassy-plot-096717.

Ostrovsky, Victor. *By Way of Deception: The Making of a Mossad Officer*. Scottsdale, AZ: Wilshire Press Inc., 2002.

O'Sullivan, Arieh. 'Jordan's Abdullah Exposes Iranian Plot to Attack Israel'. *Jerusalem Post*, 6 February 2002.

————. 'Sharon: Arafat Is Our "Bitter Enemy." Calls Iran "Spearhead of International Terror"'. *Jerusalem Post*, 7 January 2002.

————. 'Halutz: Sanctions Won't Deter Iran'. *Jerusalem Post*, 21 November 2005.

O'Sullivan, Arieh, Amotz Asa-El, Margot Dudkevitch, and Erik Schechter. 'Ya'alon: Terror Not Sole Threat'. *Jerusalem Post*, 24 October 2003.

Pan, Esther. 'LEBANON: Election Results'. *Council on Foreign Relations* (blog), 21 June 2005. https://www.cfr.org/backgrounder/lebanon-election-results.

Parker, Ashley, and Josh Dawsey. 'Trump's Cable Cabinet: New Texts Reveal the Influence of Fox Hosts on Previous White House'. *Washington Post*, 9 January 2022. https://www.washingtonpost.com/politics/trump-cable-cabinet/2022/01/09/96fac488-6fe6-11ec-b9fc-b394d592a7a6_story.html.

Parsi, Trita. 'Israel-Iranian Relations Assessed: Strategic Competition from the Power Cycle Perspective'. *Iranian Studies* 38, no. 2 (1 June 2005): 247–69.

———. *Losing an Enemy: Obama, Iran, and the Triumph of Diplomacy*. 1st edition. New Haven: Yale University Press, 2017.

———. *Treacherous Alliance: The Secret Dealings of Israel, Iran, and the United States*. Yale University Press, 2007.

———. 'A Better Way in the Middle East'. *The American Prospect*, 15 December 2021. https://prospect.org/api/content/0150218e-5d45-11ec-b3df-12f1225286c6/.

Patten, Howard A. *Israel and the Cold War: Diplomacy, Strategy and the Policy of the Periphery at the United Nations*. London: I.B. Tauris, 2013.

'Paul Ryan: Plan for Implementing Trump's Agenda Is on Track; Netanyahu on US-Israel Relationship Under Trump' (transcript). *Hannity*. Fox News, 15 March 2017. https://www.foxnews.com/transcript/paul-ryan-plan-for-implementing-trumps-agenda-is-on-track-netanyahu-on-us-israel-relationship-under-trump.

Peres, Shimon. *David's Sling*. London: Weidenfeld & Nicolson, 1970.

Pfeffer, Anshel. 'Everything You Need to Know About the Israel Hayom (or Anti-Sheldon Adelson) Law'. *Haaretz*, 12 November 2014. https://www.haaretz.com/.premium-a-primer-on-the-israel-hayom-law-1.5327699.

———. *Bibi: The Turbulent Life and Times of Benjamin Netanyahu*. 1st edition. New York: Basic Books, 2018.

———. 'Two Days On, Israel Still Puzzled Why Iran Sent Drone Into Its Airspace'. *Haaretz*, 12 February 2018. https://www.haaretz.com/israel-news/.premium-israel-still-puzzled-why-iran-sent-drone-into-israeli-airspace-1.5809571.

Pilkington, Ed. 'Ahmadinejad Accuses US of "orchestrating" 9/11 Attacks to Aid Israel'. *The Guardian*, 23 September 2010. https://www.theguardian.com/world/2010/sep/23/iran-unitednations.

Pincus, Walter. 'Reagan Calls Israel Prime Mover in Iran-Contra'. *Washington Post*, 5 November 1990. https://www.washingtonpost.com/archive/politics/1990/11/05/reagan-calls-israel-prime-mover-in-iran-contra/71b08cdd-eaa8-43aa-a744-e5949f93764e/.

———. 'Another Nation Blazed the Trail for Iran in Developing a Nuclear Program'. *Washington Post*, 9 March 2015, sec. National Security. https://www.washingtonpost.com/world/national-security/another-nation-blazed-the-trail-for-iran-in-developing-a-nuclear-program/2015/03/09/0222ec28-c41c-11e4-ad5c-3b8ce89f1b89_story.html.

Pinkas, Alon. 'Thinking the Unthinkable About Iran'. *Jerusalem Post*, 23 April 1992.

———. 'Cheap Soviet Arms Make Iranians a Major Threat'. *Jerusalem Post*, 9 January 1992.

————. 'Peres: Iran Thinks of Us as a Collective Salman Rushdie'. *Jerusalem Post*, 1 September 1994.

————. 'A Watchful Eye Widens on a Menacing Neighbor'. *Jerusalem Post*, 2 December 1994.

Pinkas, Alon, and David Makovsky. 'Rabin: Killing Civilians Won't Kill the Negotiations'. *Jerusalem Post*, 13 April 1994.

'"Poland's Hosting Anti-Iran Conference an Insult to Europe"', *Tehran Times*, 15 January 2019, sec. Politics. https://www.tehrantimes.com/news/431904/Poland-s-hosting-anti-Iran-conference-an-insult-to-Europe.

Pompeo, Mike. 'Secretary Pompeo's Remarks on "Supporting Iranian Voices"'. Ronald Reagan Presidential Library, Simi Valley, CA, 22 July 2018. https://tr.usembassy.gov/secretary-pompeos-remarks-on-supporting-iranian-voices/.

Porter, Gareth. *Manufactured Crisis: The Untold Story of the Iran Nuclear Scare*. Charlottesville, VA: Just World Books, 2014.

————. 'When the Ayatollah Said No to Nukes'. *Foreign Policy* (blog), 16 October 2014. https://foreignpolicy.com/2014/10/16/when-the-ayatollah-said-no-to-nukes/.

Potter, Ned. 'Israel's Netanyahu: Let's Talk With Palestinians – and Stop Iran's Threat'. ABC News, 22 September 2009. https://abcnews.go.com/Politics/netanyahu-israels-prime-minister-worries-palestinians-iran/story?id=8644832.

Powell, Colin. 'Re: Re:', 3 March 2015. https://www.scribd.com/document/324033115/00002715-002.

'Profile: Mahmoud Ahmadinejad', BBC News, 4 August 2010, sec. Middle East. http://www.bbc.com/news/world-middle-east-10866448.

Prosor, Ron. 'Israeli Letter to UN on Iranian Incitement', 27 August 2012. Israel Ministry of Foreign Affairs Documents.

'Publications Archive'. Institute for National Security Studies. Accessed 18 July 2018. http://www.inss.org.il/publication/.

'"Quagmire" Analogy Gets Much Use'. Fox News. 28 June 2005. http://www.foxnews.com/story/2005/06/28/quagmire-analogy-gets-much-use.html.

Rabi, Uzi, and Ronen A. Cohen. *Iran, Israel & the 'Shi'ite Crescent'*. Daniel Abraham Center for Strategic Dialogue. Netanya, Israel: Netanya Academic College, 2008.

Rafsanjani, Akbar Hashemi. 'Rafsanjani Qods Day Speech', 14 December 2001. http://www.globalsecurity.org/wmd/library/news/iran/2001/011214-text.html.

Rahman, Omar. 'The Emergence of GCC-Israel Relations in a Changing Middle East'. *Brookings* (blog), 28 July 2021. https://www.brookings.edu/research/the-emergence-of-gcc-israel-relations-in-a-changing-middle-east/.

Rahnema, Ali. 'Ayatollah Khomeini's Rule of the Guardian Jurist: From Theory to Practice'. In *A Critical Introduction to Khomeini*, ed. Arshin Adib-Moghaddam. Cambridge, UK; New York: Cambridge University Press, 2014.

Ram, Haggay. *Iranophobia: The Logic of an Israeli Obsession*. Stanford, CA: Stanford University Press, 2009.

Ramazani, R.K. 'Iran and the Arab-Israeli Conflict'. *Middle East Journal* 32, no. 4 (1 October 1978): 413–28.

BIBLIOGRAPHY

Ramezani, Alireza. 'Why Iran Shouldn't Get Too Excited About Brexit'. *Al-Monitor* (blog), 15 July 2016. https://www.al-monitor.com/pulse/originals/2016/07/iran-reactions-brexit-uk-exit-european-union.html.

Ravid, Barak. 'Iraq 2002, Iran 2012: Compare and Contrast Netanyahu's Speeches'. *Haaretz*, 4 October 2012. https://www.haaretz.com/blogs/diplomania/iraq-2002-iran-2012-compare-and-contrast-netanyahu-s-speeches-1.468213.

———. 'Netanyahu Briefed Trump on Iran's "Nuclear Archive" Two Months Ago'. Axios, 1 May 2018. https://www.axios.com/netanyahu-briefed-trump-on-irans-nuclear-archive-f5717785-fbf0-4f62-9244-77afbe19e03b.html.

———. 'Netanyahu Tells Security Cabinet Israel Must Not Be Dragged Into Soleimani Killing'. Axios, 6 January 2020. https://www.axios.com/netanyahu-israel-iran-soleimani-killing-b846c02b-f592-4b56-9827-9310cac092b8.html.

———. 'Netanyahu's Cold Feet Almost Killed the Abraham Accords'. Axios, 13 December 2021. https://www.axios.com/abraham-accords-negotiations-netanyahu-trump-29d48b00-6407-4d47-b576-cdf4155aa71e.html.

———. 'Trump Felt Used on Soleimani Strike: "Israel Did Not Do the Right Thing"'. Axios, 15 December 2021. https://www.axios.com/trump-soleimani-strike-netanyahu-israel-8f1abba2-5c05-4909-adee-ef872e9becb4.html.

Regev, Amos. 'המודיעין האמריקני - מסורת של טעויות'. *Israel Hayom*, 5 December 2007.

Reiss, Moshe. 'Cyrus as Messiah'. *Jewish Bible Quarterly* 40, no. 3 (1 July 2012): 159–62.

Reiter, Dan. 'Preventive Attacks Against Nuclear Programs and the "Success" at Osiraq'. *The Nonproliferation Review* 12, no. 2 (1 July 2005): 355–71.

'Remarks During Meeting With U.S. President Barack Obama', 18 May 2009. Israeli Prime Minister's Office.

Reuters Staff. Reuters Staff, 'Iran Rejects Reports of Israel Downing Iranian Drone as "ridiculous" – State TV', *Reuters*, 10 February 2018, sec. World News, https://www.reuters.com/article/uk-mideast-crisis-iran-idUKKBN1FU0I4.

———. 'Netanyahu's Likud Uses Trump Photo in Israeli Election Billboard'. *Reuters*, 3 February 2019. https://www.reuters.com/article/us-israel-election-trump-idUSKCN1PS07A.

———. 'Iran's Zarif Says Soleimani Killing Will Boost Resistance in Region'. *Reuters*, 3 January 2020, sec. World News. https://www.reuters.com/article/uk-iraq-security-blast-iranforeignminist-idUKKBN1Z209H.

Rhode, Harold. 'The Sources of Iranian Negotiating Behavior'. Jerusalem Center for Public Affairs. Accessed 17 December 2015. http://www.jcpa.org/text/iranian_behavior.pdf.

Rodan, Steve. 'Dynamic Duo - Part I'. *Jerusalem Post*, 14 October 1994.

———. 'PM in DC to Stress Diplomacy, Not Defense Issues'. *Jerusalem Post*, 5 July 1996.

———. 'Iran, Israel Reportedly Forging Contacts'. *Jerusalem Post*, 9 September 1997.

———. 'Documents Obtained by "Jerusalem Post" Show: Iran Has Four Nuclear Bombs'. *Jerusalem Post*, 9 April 1998.

———. 'MK Elul Says Israel, US Have Known of Iranian Nukes for Years'. *Jerusalem Post*, 12 April 1998.

Rodan, Steve, and Hillel Kuttler. 'Iran Paid $25m. for Nuclear Weapons, Documents Show'. *Jerusalem Post*, 10 April 1998.

Rosen, Rebecca J. 'Truth, Lies, and the Internet'. *The Atlantic*, 29 December 2011. https://www.theatlantic.com/technology/archive/2011/12/truth-lies-and-the-internet/250569/.

Rosenberg, M.J. 'The Evolution of Jeff Goldberg: From Prison Guard in the West Bank to Lobby Poster Boy'. *HuffPost*, 4 July 2010. https://www.huffpost.com/entry/the-evolution-of-jeff-gol_b_562212.

Rosenblum, Jonathan. 'A Silver Lining for Dark Clouds'. *Jerusalem Post*, 13 December 2002.

Rosenthal, Andrew. 'SOVIET DISARRAY; U.S. Fears Spread of Soviet Nuclear Weapons'. *New York Times*, 16 December 1991, sec. World. https://www.nytimes.com/1991/12/16/world/soviet-disarray-us-fears-spread-of-soviet-nuclear-weapons.html.

Rouhani, Hassan. 'President of Iran Hassan Rouhani: Time to Engage'. *Washington Post*, 19 September 2013, sec. Opinions. https://www.washingtonpost.com/opinions/president-of-iran-hassan-rouhani-time-to-engage/2013/09/19/4d2da564-213e-11e3-966c-9c4293c47ebe_story.html.

———. 'President's Speech Addressing the 44th World Economic Forum'. Davos, Switzerland, 23 January 2014. http://www.president.ir/en/74125.

Rozett, Robert. 'Recognizing Evil'. *Jerusalem Post*, 22 August 2006.

Rubin, Alissa J., Ben Hubbard, Farnaz Fassihi, and Steven Erlanger. 'Iran Ends Nuclear Limits as Killing of Iranian General Upends Mideast'. *New York Times*, 5 January 2020, sec. World. https://www.nytimes.com/2020/01/05/world/middleeast/iran-general-soleimani-iraq.html.

Rubin, Barry. 'Iran's Threat'. *Jerusalem Post*, 30 July 1998.

Rubin, Shira. 'Israel Opposed the Iran Nuclear Deal, but Former Israeli Officials Increasingly Say U.S. Pullout Was a Mistake'. *Washington Post*, 9 December 2021. https://www.washingtonpost.com/world/middle_east/israel-iran-nuclear-deal-sanctions/2021/12/08/ece28168-56c0-11ec-8396-5552bef55c3c_story.html.

Rubinstein, Roy, and Itamar Eichner. 'Experts Say No New Information in Netanyahu's Iran Presentation'. *Ynetnews*, 1 May 2018. https://www.ynetnews.com/articles/0,7340,L-5247532,00.html.

Rudge, David. 'Officials: Israel Not Iran' Immediate Target'. *Jerusalem Post*, 17 July 2000.

Sabet, Farzan. 'Iran's 2016 Elections: Change or Continuity?' Carnegie Endowment for International Peace, 9 June 2016. https://carnegieendowment.org/2016/06/09/iran-s-2016-elections-change-or-continuity-pub-63782.

Sachar, Howard M. *A History of Israel: From the Rise of Zionism to Our Time*. New York: Knopf Doubleday Publishing Group, 2013.

Samore, Gary. *Iran's Strategic Weapons Programmes: A Net Assessment*. Milton Park: Routledge, 2013.

Sandler, Shmuel, Manfred Gerstenfeld, and Jonathan Rynhold. *Israel at the Polls 2006*. London: Routledge, 2008.

Sanger, David E., and Marc Santora. 'Anti-Iran Message Seeps Into Trump Forum Billed as Focusing on Mideast Security'. *New York Times*, 13 February 2019, sec. World. https://www.nytimes.com/2019/02/13/world/middleeast/warsaw-summit-pompeo.html.

Schechter, Erik. 'Our Own 9/11?' *Jerusalem Post*, 3 March 2006.

Schlosser, Eric. *Command and Control: Nuclear Weapons, the Damascus Accident, and the Illusion of Safety*. Reprint edition. Penguin Books, 2013.

Schmitt, Carl. *The Crisis of Parliamentary Democracy*. Translated by Ellen Kennedy. New edition. Cambridge, MA: MIT Press, 1988.

Schorr, Daniel. 'Iran Further Isolates Itself With "Holocaust Denial"'. *Weekend Edition*. NPR, 17 December 2006. https://www.npr.org/templates/story/story.php?storyId=6637685.

Schreck, Carl. 'Israel, Iran Trade Barbs at Munich Security Conference'. Radio Free Europe/Radio Liberty, 18 February 2018, sec. Iran. https://www.rferl.org/a/munich-netanyahu-iran-greatest-threat/29046395.html.

UN News. 'Security Council Tightens Sanctions Against Iran Over Uranium Enrichment', 24 March 2007. https://news.un.org/en/story/2007/03/213372-security-council-tightens-sanctions-against-iran-over-uranium-enrichment.

Segev, Samuel. *The Iranian Triangle: The Untold Story of Israel's Role in the Iran-Contra Affair*. 29th edition. New York: Macmillan USA, 1988.

Sela, Avraham. 'Civil Society, the Military, and National Security: The Case of Israel's Security Zone in South Lebanon'. *Israel Studies* 12, no. 1 (19 February 2007): 53–78.

'Selected Press Statements by PM Barak during His Visit to London', 23 November 1999. Israel Ministry of Foreign Affairs Documents.

Senate Committee on Intelligence. 'Report on the U.S. Intelligence Community's Prewar Intelligence Assessments on Iraq'. Washington, DC: United States Senate, 7 July 2004.

Ser, Sam. 'Tangling With Teheran'. *Jerusalem Post*, 29 September 2006.

Seriphs, Matthew. 'Ne'eman: "Saddam Could Build N-Bombs in 3 Years"'. *Jerusalem Post*, 28 August 1990.

Shalom, Silvan. 'FM Shalom Appeals to Fellow Foreign Ministers on Iranian Threat', 30 October 2005. Israel Ministry of Foreign Affairs Documents.

———. 'United Nations General Assembly Presentation'. Presented at the United Nations General Assembly Meeting, 23 September 2004. https://www.c-span.org/video/?183637-2/united-nations-general-assembly-meeting.

Sharon, Ariel. 'PM Sharon Addresses the United Nations General Assembly'. Presented at the United Nations General Assembly Meeting, New York, 15 September 2005.

Sheizaf, Noam. 'Wither the Israeli Press?' *The Daily Beast*, 3 October 2012. https://www.thedailybeast.com/articles/2012/10/03/wither-the-israeli-press.

Sherwood, Harriet. 'Ehud Barak Restates Case for Military Strike on Iran's Nuclear Programme'. *The Guardian*, 30 April 2012, sec. World news. https://www.theguardian.com/world/2012/apr/30/ehud-barak-iran-nuclear-programme.

Shimoni, Yaacov. 'Israel in the Pattern of Middle East Politics'. *Middle East Journal* 4, no. 3 (1950): 277–95.

Shlaim, Avi. 'Israel and the Conflict'. In *International Perspectives on the Gulf Conflict, 1990–91*, ed. Alex Danchev and Dan Keohane. London: Palgrave Macmillan, 1994.

———. 'Israel Between East and West, 1948–56'. *International Journal of Middle Eastern Studies* 36, no. 4 (November 2004): 657–73.

Shoval, Shabtai. *The Chosen One – The Mossad in Iran*. Ed. Phil Weinstock. Translated by Asaf Epstien. Second edition. Scientific Driven Systems LTD, 2003.

'Six Charts That Show How Hard US Sanctions Have Hit Iran'. BBC News. 9 December 2019, sec. Middle East. https://www.bbc.com/news/world-middle-east-48119109.

Smith, Ben. 'The Iran Nuclear Deal and "Decertification"'. Briefing Paper. House of Commons, 25 October 2017.

Sneh, Ephraim. *Navigating Perilous Waters: An Israeli Strategy for Peace and Security*. Milton Park: Routledge, 2004.

Snyder, Timothy. *On Tyranny: Twenty Lessons from the Twentieth Century*. London: Tim Duggan Books, 2017.

Sobhani, Sohrab. *The Pragmatic Entente: Israeli-Iranian Relations, 1948–1988*. New York: Praeger Publishers, 1989.

Souresrafil, Behrouz. *Khomeini and Israel*. I Researchers Incorporated, 1988.

'Statement in Knesset by Defense Minister Moshe Arens', 14 November 1984. Volume 8. Israel Ministry of Foreign Affairs Documents.

'Statement in the Knesset by Prime Minister Begin on His Talks with President Sadat', 16 January 1980. Israel Ministry of Foreign Affairs Documents.

Stecklow, Steve, Babak Dehghanpisheh, and Yeganeh Torbati. 'Assets of the Ayatollah'. *Reuters*, 11 November 2013. http://www.reuters.com/investigates/iran/.

Sterman, Adiv, and Mitch Ginsburg. '"US Pressure Nixed Israeli Strike on Iran Last Year"'. *The Times of Israel*, 3 September 2013. http://www.timesofisrael.com/us-pressure-nixed-israeli-strike-on-iran-in-2012/.

Sternfeld, Lior B. *Between Iran and Zion: Jewish Histories of Twentieth-Century Iran*. Stanford, CA: Stanford University Press, 2019.

Steyn, Mark. 'It's Mullah Time!' *Jerusalem Post*, 24 June 2003.

Stockholm International Peace Research Institute. 'SIPRI Military Expenditure Database', 2015. https://www.sipri.org/databases/milex.

Stone, Richard. 'Technical Elements of Iran Deal Put the Brakes on Nuclear Breakout'. *Science*, 3 April 2015. http://www.sciencemag.org/news/2015/04/technical-elements-iran-deal-put-brakes-nuclear-breakout.

Stracqualursi, Veronica, and Jennifer Hansler. 'Pompeo: Strike on Soleimani Disrupted an "Imminent Attack"'. CNN, 3 January 2020. https://www.cnn.com/2020/01/03/politics/mike-pompeo-iran-soleimani-strike-cnntv/index.html.

Tabatabai, Ariane M., and Colin P. Clarke. 'Iran's Proxies Are More Powerful Than Ever'. RAND Corporation, 16 October 2019. https://www.rand.org/blog/2019/10/irans-proxies-are-more-powerful-than-ever.html.

Taheri, Amir. 'Religious Fanatic at a Persian Bazaar'. *Jerusalem Post*, 28 May 2006.

Teitelbaum, Joshua. 'What Iranian Leaders Really Say About Doing Away With Israel: A Refutation of the Campaign to Excuse Ahmadinejad's Incitement to Genocide'. Jerusalem Center for Public Affairs, 2008. https://www.scribd.com/

document/7632012/What-Iranian-Leaders-Really-Say-About-Doing-Away-With-Israel.

'Text of Mahmoud Ahmadinejad's Speech', *New York Times*, 30 October 2005, sec. Week in Review. https://www.nytimes.com/2005/10/30/weekinreview/text-of-mahmoud-ahmadinejads-speech.html.

Tharoor, Ishaan. 'Israel's Netanyahu Isn't Worried About Steve Bannon and Anti-Semitism in Trump's Camp'. *Washington Post*, 12 December 2016. https://www.washingtonpost.com/news/worldviews/wp/2016/12/12/israels-netanyahu-isnt-worried-about-steve-bannon-and-anti-semitism-in-trumps-camp/.

'This Week in Iran Policy'. Fact Sheet. US Department of State, 20 March 2020. https://2017-2021.state.gov/this-week-in-iran-policy-6/.

'Timeline of Iran's Controversial Nuclear Program'. CNN, 19 March 2012. http://www.cnn.com/2012/03/06/world/meast/iran-timeline/index.html.

Times of Israel Staff. 'Netanyahu Hails Iranian People's "Courage" in Anti-Regime Protests'. *The Times of Israel*, 27 June 2018. https://www.timesofisrael.com/netanyahu-hails-iranian-peoples-courage-in-anti-regime-protests/.

———. 'Netanyahu Appears to Call for War with Iran', 13 February 2019. https://www.timesofisrael.com/liveblog_entry/netanyahu-appears-to-call-for-war-with-iran/.

———. 'Knesset Dissolves, Sets Unprecedented Third Election in Under a Year'. *The Times of Israel*, 12 December 2019. https://www.timesofisrael.com/israel-calls-another-election-for-march-the-third-in-a-year/.

———. 'Israeli Lawmakers Praise US for Killing Iranian "Arch-Terrorist" Soleimani'. *The Times of Israel*, 3 January 2020. https://www.timesofisrael.com/israeli-lawmakers-praise-us-for-killing-iranian-arch-terrorist-soleimani/.

———. 'Netanyahu Lauds Trump for Killing of Iran's Soleimani, Says Israel Stands by US'. *The Times of Israel*, 3 January 2020. https://www.timesofisrael.com/netanyahu-lauds-trump-for-killing-of-irans-soleimani-says-israel-stands-by-us/.

———. 'TV: Israel Was Likely Warned of US Plans to Kill Soleimani'. *The Times of Israel*, 3 January 2020. https://www.timesofisrael.com/tv-israel-likely-warned-of-us-plans-to-kill-soleimani/.

———. 'Yamina MK Doubles Down on Opposing Coalition With the Left'. *The Times of Israel*, 6 May 2021. https://www.timesofisrael.com/yamina-mk-doubles-down-on-opposing-coalition-with-the-left/.

———. '"What the Hell Was That?": Netanyahu Annexation Announcement Caught Trump Off Guard'. *The Times of Israel*, 14 December 2021. https://www.timesofisrael.com/what-the-hell-was-that-netanyahu-annexation-announcement-caught-trump-off-guard/.

Times of Israel Staff and AFP. 'Rejecting Purim Spiel, Putin Tells Netanyahu to Stop Dwelling on Past'. *The Times of Israel*, 10 March 2017. http://www.timesofisrael.com/rejecting-purim-spiel-putin-tells-netanyahu-to-stop-dwelling-on-past/.

Timmerman, Kenneth. 'The Coming Nuclear Showdown With Iran'. *Jerusalem Post*, 1 July 2005.

Tobin, Jonathan S. 'Who's Obsessed About Obsession'. *Jerusalem Post*, 22 October 2008.

Torbati, Yeganeh. 'Trump Election Puts Iran Nuclear Deal on Shaky Ground'. *Reuters*, 9 November 2016. https://www.reuters.com/article/us-usa-election-trump-iran-idUSKBN13427E.

Treverton, Gregory. 'Support to Policymakers: The 2007 NIE on Iran's Nuclear Intentions and Capabilities'. Central Intelligence Agency Center for the Study of Intelligence, May 2013. https://www.cia.gov/library/center-for-the-study-of-intelligence/csi-publications/books-and-monographs/csi-intelligence-and-policy-monographs/pdfs/support-to-policymakers-2007-nie.pdf.

Trump, Donald. 'Donald Trump AIPAC Speech Transcript'. Presented at the AIPAC, Washington, DC, 21 March 2016. https://time.com/4267058/donald-trump-aipac-speech-transcript/.

———. 'Remarks by President Trump on Iran Strategy'. Official Remarks, Washington, DC, 13 October 2017. Accessed via https://web.archive.org/web/20180130154140/https://www.whitehouse.gov/briefings-statements/remarks-president-trump-iran-strategy/.

Trump, Donald, and Benjamin Netanyahu. 'Transcript and Analysis: Trump And Netanyahu Hold Joint Press Conference'. *NPR*, 15 February 2017, sec. Politics. https://www.npr.org/2017/02/15/514986341/watch-live-trump-netanyahu-hold-joint-press-conference-at-white-house.

———. 'Remarks Prior to a Meeting With Prime Minister Benjamin Netanyahu of Israel and an Exchange With Reporters' (transcript). Washington, DC, 15 September 2020. https://www.presidency.ucsb.edu/documents/remarks-prior-meeting-with-prime-minister-benjamin-netanyahu-israel-and-exchange-with-5.

Tsur, Batsheva. 'PM: Without Peace, War With Syria Likely'. *Jerusalem Post*, 23 June 1994.

———. 'PM: Iran Poses Most Serious Threat Since 1948'. *Jerusalem Post*, 27 January 1998.

United States Institute of Peace. 'The Final Tally: How Congress Voted on Iran', 17 September 2015. https://iranprimer.usip.org/blog/2015/sep/11/congress-votes-deal.

United States Treasury Department. 'Treasury Sanctions Individuals and Entities for Human Rights Abuses and Censorship in Iran, and Support to Sanctioned Weapons Proliferators', 12 January 2018. https://home.treasury.gov/news/press-releases/sm0250.

United States Treasury Department Office of Public Affairs. 'Designation of National Council of Resistance in Iran, National Council of Resistance and Peoples Mujahedin of Iran under Executive Order 13224', 15 August 2003. https://www.treasury.gov/press-center/press-releases/Pages/js664.aspx.

Vaez, Ali. 'Waiting for Bushehr'. *Foreign Policy*, 12 September 2011. https://foreignpolicy.com/2011/09/12/waiting-for-bushehr/.

Wallfish, Asher. '"Iran Greater Threat Than Iraq"'. *Jerusalem Post*, 29 June 1993.

Walt, Stephen M. 'The Renaissance of Security Studies'. *International Studies Quarterly* 35, no. 2 (1 June 1991): 211–39.

Walzer, Michael. *The Paradox of Liberation: Secular Revolutions and Religious Counterrevolutions*. New Haven, CT: Yale University Press, 2015.

BIBLIOGRAPHY

Ward, Steven R. *Immortal: A Military History of Iran and Its Armed Forces*. Washington, DC: Georgetown University Press, 2014.

Weiner, Justus Reid, Meir Rosenne, Elie Wiesel, Dore Gold, Irit Kohn, Eytan Bentsur, and Dan Naveh. 'Referral of Iranian President Ahmadinejad on the Charge of Incitement to Commit Genocide'. Jerusalem Center for Public Affairs, 2006.

Weldes, Jutta, ed. *Cultures of Insecurity: States, Communities, and the Production of Danger*. Borderlines, v. 14. Minneapolis, MN: University of Minnesota Press, 1999.

Woods, Kevin M., Williamson Murray, Thomas Holaday, and Mounir Elkhamri. *Saddam's War: An Iraqi Military Perspective of the Iran-Iraq War*. Washington, DC: Government Printing Office, 2009.

Woods, Kevin M., Michael R. Pease, Mark E. Stout, Williamson Murray, and James G. Lacey. *The Iraqi Perspectives Report: Saddam's Senior Leadership on Operation Iraqi Freedom From the Official U.S. Joint Forces Command Report*. Annapolis, MD: Naval Institute Press, 2006.

Woolf, Nicky, and Amanda Holpuch. 'John Boehner Invites Netanyahu to Address Congress on Iran Next Month'. *The Guardian*, 21 January 2015, sec. US news. http://www.theguardian.com/us-news/2015/jan/21/boehner-netanyahu-invite-congress-iran-obama.

Wright, Lawrence. *Thirteen Days in September: The Dramatic Story of the Struggle for Peace*. New York: Vintage, 2015.

Wright, Robin B. *The Iran Primer: Power, Politics, and U.S. Policy*. US Institute of Peace Press, 2010.

Yaar, Ephraim, and Tamar Hermann. 'The Peace Index', April 2006. http://www.peaceindex.org/indexMonthEng.aspx?mark1=&mark2=&num=30.

———. 'The Peace Index'. The Israel Democracy Institute, August 2008. http://www.peaceindex.org/indexMonthEng.aspx?mark1=&mark2=&num=22.

———. 'The Peace Index'. The Israel Democracy Institute, February 2012. http://www.peaceindex.org/files/The%20Peace%20Index%20Data%20-%20February%202012.pdf.

———. 'The Peace Index'. The Israel Democracy Institute, August 2012. http://www.peaceindex.org/files/The%20Peace%20Index%20Data%20-%20August%202012(1).pdf.

———. 'The Peace Index'. The Israel Democracy Institute, August 2015. http://www.peaceindex.org/files/Peace_Index_Data_August_2015-Eng.pdf.

Yudelman, Michal. 'Sneh: Confrontation With Iran Inevitable'. *Jerusalem Post*, 17 February 1997, Daily edition.

Zacharia, Janine. 'Iran Will Have Nukes in a Year – Mofaz'. *Jerusalem Post*, 13 November 2003.

Zarif, Mohamad Javad. 'Zarif in New York: Nuke Deal, ISIS, Syria. Interview by David Ignatius' (transcript), 29 April 2015. https://iranprimer.usip.org/blog/2015/apr/29/zarif-new-york-nuke-deal-isis-syria.

Zeiger, Asher. 'Ahmadinejad's New Call for Israel's Annihilation Is His Most Anti-Semitic Assault to Date, Says ADL'. *The Times of Israel*, 2 August 2012. http://www.timesofisrael.com/adl-blasts-ahmadinejads-latest-call-for-israels-annihilation-as-ominous/.

Zetter, Kim. *Countdown to Zero Day: Stuxnet and the Launch of the World's First Digital Weapon*. New York: Crown, 2014.

Zibakalam, Sadegh. 'To Rule, or Not to Rule? An Alternative Look at the Political Life of Ayatollah Khomeini Between 1960 and 1980'. In *A Critical Introduction to Khomeini*, ed. Arshin Adib-Moghaddam. Cambridge; New York, NY: Cambridge University Press, 2014.

Zlotowski, Michel. 'Shalom Urges Annan to Condemn Iran. Foreign Minister Enjoys a Well-Timed Visit to France'. *Jerusalem Post*, 28 October 2005.

Zonszein, Mairav. 'Benjamin Netanyahu Just Formed the Most Right-Wing Government in Israeli History'. *The Nation*, 25 May 2016. https://www.thenation.com/article/benjamin-netanyahu-just-formed-the-most-right-wing-government-in-israeli-history/.

INDEX